D0205530

Music and Merchants

Music and Merchants

The Laudesi Companies of Republican Florence

BLAKE WILSON

CLARENDON PRESS · OXFORD
1992

Oxford University Press, Walton Street, Oxford OX2 6DP
Oxford New York Toronto
Delhi Bombay Calcutta Madras Karachi
Petaling Jaya Singapore Hong Kong Tokyo
Nairobi Dar es Salaam Cape Town
Melbourne Auckland
and associated companies in
Berlin Ibadan

Oxford is a trade mark of Oxford University Press

Published in the United States
by Oxford University Press, New York

© Blake Wilson 1992

All rights reserved. No part of this publication may be reproduced,
stored in a retrieval system, or transmitted, in any form or by any means,
electronic, mechanical, photocopying, recording, or otherwise, without
the prior permission of Oxford University Press

British Library Cataloguing in Publication Data
Data available

Library of Congress Cataloging in Publication Data
Data available
ISBN 0–19–816176–X

Set by Hope Services (Abingdon) Ltd.
Printed in Great Britain by
Biddles Ltd., Guildford and King's Lynn

ML
2933.8
.F46
W5
1992

To my parents, and to Lynn,
who have been the Alpha and the Omega
of this book

PREFACE

A MUSICAL score of the past is a highly complex document. When taken at face value, the notes on the page pose one set of questions, but to wonder about the sound world implied by those written notes profoundly alters and broadens the field of inquiry. And in the pursuit of such an ephemeral art-form as music, the older repertoires require that one cast wide the net of inquiry. When nearly a decade ago I came across Liuzzi's facsimile editions of the monophonic lauda repertory, the question of how these songs might have been and might now be performed quickly led to others: just who sang these songs, in what context, who heard them, and what meanings did they hold for their hearers? As I began to haul in my net during the course of year-long research in Florence, I found not the meagre catch that has attended similar efforts among the other late medieval song repertories, but a wealth of primary documents. These documents, primarily confraternity records in the Archivio di Stato, revealed a flourishing musical subculture embedded in, and explicable only with reference to, a rich framework of devotional, social, and artistic activity. In the end, the songs proved to be a catalyst for a different and broader study, for they turned out to be the frozen records of human activity in a city that promoted the virtues of the active life. The laudesi companies and their musicians were far more numerous, diverse, and enduring than the extant music manuscripts alone would suggest, and it is these dynamic and creative entities that captured my imagination and became the subject of this study.

In trying to fit my piece into so large a puzzle as early Renaissance Florence I have relied heavily on a vast body of excellent scholarship that my bibliography can only begin to reflect. I am especially grateful to a community of scholars who have contributed directly to this book through consultation and correspondence, among them Peter Howard, Bill Kent, Gene Brucker, Bill Connell, Elizabeth Pilliod, John Henderson, Diane Zervas, Giorgio Varanini, Iain Fenlon, and Carlo Delcorno. I owe special thanks to Nello Barbieri for his meticulous and thorough job of checking and editing my many transcriptions and translations of primary documents, and to Professors George Buelow, Frank D'Accone, Richard Westfall, and Benito Rivera, who helped see this study into the world as a doctoral dissertation at Indiana University. Only one person, the irreplaceable Dr Gino Corti, could have made sense of certain illegible documents. This book is a family project as well, for my father literally lent his hand in preparing all the figures. For his long hours of careful work I am deeply grateful to Mr William Wilson. I also wish to thank Bonnie Blackburn for her patient, thorough, and expert job of copy-editing.

This project could never have been undertaken without the opportunity, provided by a Fulbright Grant, to work in the Florentine archives during the 1985–6 academic year. Nor could it have been completed without the generous assistance of a Grant-in-Aid from the American Council of Learned Societies, and summer and direct grants provided by the University Research Council of Vanderbilt University. The staff of the Archivio di Stato (and Christina Rodolico in particular) deserve a special thanks for their expert assistance in the course of a project that has spanned the transition from the old to the new archive, and the staffs at the Biblioteca Nazionale and Kunsthistorisches Institut have been no less helpful. I am greatly indebted to Bruce Phillips and the staff of Oxford University Press for their assistance in the publication of this book.

As the last of four children to finish his apprenticeship, I thank my parents for years of complete faith and unconditional support. And finally, there is only one person who helped me see this through from beginning to end: to my wife, Lynn, I owe the most.

B.W.

CONTENTS

LIST OF PLATES

LIST OF FIGURES

LIST OF TABLES

ABBREVIATIONS

Archival References

ASF	Archivio di Stato, Florence
BNF	Biblioteca Nazionale, Florence
BR	BNF, Banco Rari
CmRS	ASF, Compagnie Religiose Soppresse da P. Leopoldi
Mgl	BNF, Fondo Magliabechiano
OSM	ASF, Archivio dei Capitani di Orsanmichele
Panc.	BNF, Fondo Panciatichiano
Ricc.	Biblioteca Riccardiana, Florence
SA	ASF, Compagnie Religiose Soppresse nel Bigallo, Archive 1, Compagnia di S. Maria delle Laude detta di S. Agnese
SF	ASF, Compagnie Religiose Soppresse nel Bigallo, Archive 5, Compagnia di S. Frediano detta la Bruciata
SMN	ASF, Conventi Soppressi dal governo francese, Archive 102 (contains the volumes pertaining to the Compagnia di S. Piero Martire, detta dei laudesi di S. Maria Novella)
SPM	Company of San Piero Martire (see SMN)
SSP	ASF, Compagnie Religiose Soppresse nel Bigallo, Archive 2, Compagnia di S. Maria delle Laude e Spirito Sancto detta del Piccione
SZ	ASF, CmRS, Z.I, San Zanobi di Firenze

Manuscripts and Early Prints

Aret	Arezzo, Biblioteca Comunale, 180 della Fraternita dei Laici
Ars	Paris, Bibliothèque de l'Arsenal, MS 8521
BL	Bologna, Civico Museo Bibliografico Musicale, MS Q 15
BU	Bologna, Biblioteca Universitaria, MS 2216
Ch 266	Rome, Biblioteca Apostolica Vaticana, MS Chigiano L. VII. 266
Cort	Cortona, Biblioteca Comunale, MS 91
Fior	Florence, Archivio della Curia Arcivescovile (without shelf-number; 'Cecconi Codex')
G 20	Perugia, Biblioteca Comunale, MS 431
Gall[1–4]	Galletti (see Bibliography)

Grey	Capetown, South African Public Library, MS Grey 3. b. 12
Luc[1]	Lucca, Archivio di Stato, MS 93
MC	Montecassino, Biblioteca dell'Abbazia, MS 871
Mgl[1]	BNF, MS Banco Rari 18 (olim Mgl. II. I. 122)
Mgl[2]	BNF, MS Banco Rari 19 (olim Mgl. II. I. 212)
Panc. 27	BNF, MS Panciatichi 27
Pav	Pavia, Biblioteca Universitaria, MS Aldini 361
Petrucci[1]	*Laude Libro Primo. In. Dammonis.* Venice: Ottaviano Petrucci, 1508
Petrucci[2]	*Laude Libro Secondo.* Venice: Ottaviano Petrucci, 1507/8
Razzi[1]	*Libro Primo delle Laudi Spirituali da diversi eccell. e divoti autori, antichi e moderni composte* . . . Venice: Rampazetto ('ad instantia de' Giunti di Firenze'), 1563
Ven	Venice, Biblioteca Nazionale Marciana, Ms. It. Cl. IX. 145 (olim 7554)
Wc	Washington, DC, Library of Congress, MS ML171 J6

Abbreviations used throughout this book to refer to Florentine monetary units of the period are Fl (gold florin), L (lira), d (denaro), and s (soldo). Abbreviations used in the tables are S (soprano), A (alto), T (tenor), B (bass), P (precentor), O (organ), R (rebec), V (vielle), and L (lute).

INTRODUCTION

IN a recent review of Reinhard Strohm's book on *Music in Late Medieval Bruges*, one musicologist spoke for many of us when she expressed surprise in learning that 'city waits routinely played mensural polyphony by the 1480s', and that 'the main incentive for polyphonic composition came from private endowments by lay members of confraternities and guilds'.[1] These revelations surprise because they cut so strongly across the grain of traditional musicological historiography on late medieval and early Renaissance Europe. In this tradition, Europe at that time was divided into two musical classes, an élite and literate one associated with ecclesiastical and aristocratic institutions, and an oral, illiterate one associated with the lower classes. The former class is distinguished from the latter primarily by its cultivation of a written tradition of polyphony. That this symbol of musical *haute culture* should be found in the hands of the lower classes reveals the inadequacy of the above, two-tiered model, which in fact takes no account of an essential late-medieval social context that is inherent in Strohm's subject—the late medieval city. This same model has led us to regard the literate polyphonic tradition of Jacopo da Bologna, Francesco Landini, and their fellow courtiers and clerics as the exclusive representative of Trecento musical culture and, with the demise of that tradition in the early fifteenth century, to view the Quattrocento as a period of musical decline. Once again, this time in Landini's native city of Florence, the inadequacy of the model in accounting for the full breadth and complexity of musical life in a mercantile city is revealed by the 'surprising' arenas in which we find the *ars mensurae*: in Trecento Italy the largest number of extant polyphonic motets may be found in music manuscripts belonging to two of the smaller Florentine laudesi companies, and the largest and most stable polyphonic chapels of Quattrocentro Florence were those maintained by these same lay confraternities. In his recent book on music in fifteenth-century Ferrara, Lewis Lockwood's timely call for a 'larger vision of the Quattrocento as a pluralistic musical culture' can be extended back to the Trecento, and there is no more likely city in which to discover this pluralism than Florence.[2] The city's dozen active laudesi companies sustained a stable

---

[1] P. Higgins, review article in Journal of the American Musicological Society, 42 (1989), 152.
[2] L. Lockwood, *Music in Renaissance Ferrara, 1400–1505: The Creation of a Musical Center in the Fifteenth Century* (Cambridge, Mass., 1984), 1–2.

and widespread musical subculture that witnessed the rise and fall of Trecento polyphony, as well as the precarious existence of a polyphonic chapel at the Florentine Cathedral and Baptistry in the next century. Throughout this period the Florentine lauda repertoire ranged freely among written and unwritten traditions of both monophony and polyphony.

In varying guises, the lauda[3] has been sung in Italy since the literary foundations of the Italian language in the thirteenth century. This enduring genre of vernacular religious lyric changed often as it drew continually upon contemporary forms and styles of secular poetry and music. And the latter have contributed to the broad dissemination of the lauda, which at various times has played a part in mass flagellant processions, the civic processions of clerics and laymen, the *sacre rappresentazioni* of fifteenth-century Florence, the secretive services of flagellant companies, the liturgies of friars and reformed Benedictine monks, mendicant sermons, and the private devotions of clerics, nuns, laymen, and laywomen. But in each of these the role of the lauda was marginal, and in only one context does the lauda appear as an undisputed centrepiece—in the liturgical services of the laudesi companies.[4]

The 'compagnie delle laude' were groups of laymen (and sometimes laywomen) organized primarily under the auspices of the Dominican, Franciscan, and other mendicant orders to receive religious instruction, provide charitable services for the poor, and above all to conduct their own liturgical services that featured the devotional activity of lauda-singing. It is here, as the lyrical core of a lay, vernacular liturgy, that the lauda arose in the thirteenth century, attained a stable musico-poetic form, and became the dominant insignia of the lay religious activism fostered by the mendicant orders.

The laudesi companies, along with their penitential counterpart, the disciplinati (or flagellant) companies, were the distinctive result of the interaction between the forces of mendicant spirituality, urban piety, and the merchant culture of the early Italian city-republics.[5] The

---

[3] From among a host of variant spellings (lauda, laude, laudi, lalda, lalde, lade, lode, etc., and, with respect to the singers, laudese, laudesi, laldese, laudiere, etc.) I have chosen to use throughout this study those versions that appear most often in contemporary Florentine documents: lauda (sing.)/laude (pl.) and laudese (sing.)/laudesi (pl.).

[4] Current usage favours the term 'laudesi confraternities', while the most common contemporary designation was 'lauda companies' ('compagnie delle laude'). The term laudese/laudesi, as opposed to lauda/laude, appears primarily in the payment records of these organizations, whose focus, however, was upon the song (lauda) and not the singers (laudesi) *per se*. The terms 'confraternitas', 'fraternitas', 'congregatione' (and their Italian forms, 'confraternita', 'fraternità', and 'congregazione') are derived from Latin documents, but I have chosen to substitute in current usage the term 'compagnia', the preferred form in documents maintained by company members.

[5] Strictly speaking, merchants in Florentine society were distinguished from artisans, feudal nobility, professional groups (lawyers, notaries, physicians, humanists, theologians), clergy, labourers, and vagabonds, and though merchants were more numerous and influential in Florence

companies flourished in the bustling mercantile centres of Tuscany and Umbria, from the late thirteenth to the late fifteenth century, and Florence in particular stands out in the history of the lauda-singing lay companies. During the period when most of the laudesi companies were founded, *c.* 1270–1340, Florence was among the largest cities in Europe. The Arno republic excelled in its mercantile activity and in the number and greatness of its mendicant houses, and it was peerless in its zeal for the principles of republican government, of which Florence was to be among the last strongholds in the early sixteenth century. These were favourable conditions for the lauda and the laudesi companies, and indeed Florence was a centre of lauda composition, and the Florentine companies were the wealthiest, most numerous, and most enduring of their kind.

This study is devoted to the history of the Florentine laudesi companies from their founding in the late thirteenth century to their decline after the expulsion of the Medici in 1494, during which time their traditional practices and institutions remained relatively stable and continuous. The confraternity documents in the Florentine Archivio di Stato contain such a wealth of information on the companies' considerable musical activities that it became both possible and necessary to distinguish their general features and practices from those particular to each company. These same documents also reveal a good deal about the conditions and patterns of activity of the numerous Florentine laudesi, who from the early fourteenth century were an active, freelancing corps of singers and instrumentalists hired by the companies to perform in their services. The core of this study is necessarily concerned with these professional laudesi, for their names and activities are revealed in conjunction with their contracts and payments recorded in the company account-books. There is little trace of the earliest phase of confraternal lauda singing (late thirteenth century), since, as the company statutes of the period imply, the singers were skilled amateurs drawn from among the ranks of company membership. With the advent of polyphonic laude in the late fourteenth and early fifteenth century, the repertoire underwent a broad diffusion and was no longer so exclusively associated with the laudesi companies. But to the extent that the musical repertoire of the lauda, both monophonic and polyphonic, can be linked to the Florentine

than in other Italian cities (except Venice), Florentine society was not exclusively mercantile in this sense; cf. P. Jones, 'Economia e società nell'Italia medievale: La leggenda della borghesia', *Storia d'Italia: Annali*, I, *Dal feudalismo al capitalismo* (Turin, 1978), 230–58. However, in the title as well as the text of this study I use the terms merchant and mercantile in the same sense as does Christian Bec in his *Les Marchands écrivains: Affaires et humanisme à Florence (1375–1434)* (Paris, 1967) to describe Florentine society of this time as pervasively influenced by mercantile values and mental habits, which transcended the stricter divisions between merchants *per se* and other classes of Florentine society.

companies, this repertoire is surveyed in conjunction with what the company documents reveal about shifting patterns of laudesi activity and, ultimately, changes in performance practices.

It is an important premiss of this study, however, that the lauda singing of the Florentine companies is poorly understood apart from serious consideration of the devotional and social context in which it functioned. In fact, the greatest significance of this repertoire may derive less from the intrinsic qualities of the music itself (often the subject of musicological inquiry), though it is not lacking in this regard, than from an appreciation of the lauda as a rich and resonant manifestation of a complex society. It is also the intention of this study, therefore, to explore the vital interaction between mercantile society and mendicant spirituality which shaped the lay companies and laudesi devotion, and to discuss the devotional and liturgical setting in which lauda singing took place. Only in this manner can one properly explain, for example, the shift from amateur to professional laudesi activity around the turn of the fourteenth century, which facilitated the adoption of polyphonic performance. The companies became the favoured recipients of bequests for lauda services at this time, which legally bound them to the satisfactory fulfilment of the terms of the bequest, and which in turn drew the attention of the business-minded *confratelli* to the increasingly competitive activity of attracting bequests. To these ends able, experienced, and dependable musicians were essential. The bequests to the laudesi companies were motivated by the popularity of the devotion which they sponsored, a popularity that was determined by the relationship between the companies and the society in which they functioned.

However, precisely because the lay companies were so deeply embedded in the guild society of early republican Florence, they were subject to the gradual transformation of that society that began in the late fourteenth century. From this time it is possible to trace the decline of the lay companies along with the conditions that had been favourable to their formation, from curtailment of their semi-autonomous corporate status (through means such as communal suppression and taxation) during the first half of the fifteenth century, to late fifteenth-century covert control through Medici patronage and infiltration by Medici partisans, to the overt decline of traditional laudesi structures after the Medici expulsion in 1494. The companies' documents thus afford us both a microcosmic view of Florentine society during the republican period, as well as a detailed record of the oldest written musical tradition in Western society to thrive outside the élite circles of aristocracy and clergy.

The Social Context

THROUGHOUT the history of republican Florence conflict has been both a debilitating and a generative force. The ceaseless clash of factions was a constant source of both private and public misery to Florentines, yet this strife could also be transformed in a society that drew vitality from the ebb and flow of a highly politicized environment.

One of the most generative conflicts of this society was, broadly speaking, that between sacred and secular forces, between a church shaped to the needs of a feudal, rural society, and a burgeoning mercantile, urban society that required a fundamental redefinition of religious practice and belief.[1] The inhabitants of Europe's young cities, and above all the most numerous and characteristic of them, the guildsmen, proposed an entirely new *ordo* to late medieval society.[2] While they were neither peasant, knight, nor monk, they nevertheless worked hard, fought a little, and wanted very much to pray. The medieval citizen thus appropriated something from each of the old *ordines*, but did so according to concepts of work, wealth, and faith which underwent profound reinterpretations in an urban context. This new *ordo* was a radical proposition for the existing ecclesiastical structures of diocese, parish, monastery, and papal court, and it prompted a rich array of new forms of religious life.

The *vita apostolica* movements of the twelfth century, the well-springs of which were urban and laic, indicated the need for an urban redefinition of religious life. Their major theme was evangelical, the exemplary lives of Jesus and the Apostles, and they found fulfilment in the new mendicant orders of the early thirteenth century—the Franciscans and Dominicans. The friars were both in and of the city, just as Francis, the prototype of a new kind of urban saint, was the son of an Assisi cloth merchant.

---

[1] R. W. Southern, *Western Society and the Church in the Middle Ages* (New York, 1970), 274–5; and P. Mandonnet, *Saint Dominique*, 2 vols. (Paris, 1938), 28. The disjunction is particularly evident in the area of preaching (discussed below); see R. and M. Rouse, *Preachers, Florilegia, and Sermons: Studies on the 'Manipulus florum' of Thomas of Ireland* (Toronto, 1979), 43.

[2] M.-D. Chenu, *Nature, Man, and Society in the 12th Century: Essays on New Theological Perspectives in the Latin West*, ed. and trans. J. Taylor and L. K. Little (Chicago, 1968), 225–7, 263–4.

Fig. 1. Florence and its laudesi companies

Santa Croce Quarter
  1. Company of Orsanmichele (Orsanmichele, lay)
  2. Company of Santa Croce (Santa Croce, Franciscan)

San Giovanni Quarter
  3. Company of San Zanobi (Santa Maria del Fiore, Cathedral)
  4. Company of San Gilio (San Gilio, Sacchite)
  5. Company of San Bastiano (Santissima Annunziata, Servite)
  6. Company of San Marco (San Marco, Dominican)

7. Company of San Lorenzo (San Lorenzo, Collegiate)

Santa Maria Novella Quarter
  8. Company of San Piero Martire (Santa Maria Novella, Dominican)
  9. Company of Ognissanti (Ognissanti, Humiliati)

Santo Spirito Quarter
  10. Company of Sant'Agnese (Santa Maria del Carmine, Carmelite)
  11. Company of San Frediano (San Frediano, Cistercian)
  12. Company of Santo Spirito (Santo Spirito, Augustinian)

The remainder of this study concerns the creative conflict between the church, interpreted through the ideals of mendicant spirituality, and the exigencies of late medieval urban life, for it was out of this encounter that the lay religious company arose. In structure and practice it was modelled on commune, guild, and church. This hybrid institution was the essential expression of the guildsman's need to define his religious aspirations in terms that derived from his side of the rood-screen and, conversely, to bring spiritual authentication out of the church and into their daily lives, and in particular to sacramentalize a secular, mercantile activity that for centuries had been regarded by the church as *ignobile*. The friars became the chief agents in the layman's need to strike this bargain.

The lay companies, like the friars and the guilds, were characteristic and pervasive features of the late medieval city. Their proliferation in central and northern Italy testifies to the urban strength of that area in the thirteenth century, and their greater number, wealth, and duration in Florence testifies to its particular urban precocity. The pious laity of Florence came to the altars of the mendicant churches to cultivate connections, not with other Florentines for wealth, public office, and family ties, but with Jesus, Mary, and the saints for the assurance of salvation. Common to both the secular and the sacred arena was the habit of negotiation and the welding of relationships, and a closer look at lay company activities reveals what they considered to be one of the most effective means of persuasion—song. The lauda of the laudesi companies was deemed strong spiritual currency, for as sung prayer it passed swiftly up the ladder of carefully cultivated sacred connections, from deceased members, through the saints small and great, to Mary and Jesus to join the eternal *canto celestiale*.

Chanto celestiale	There was a celestial song
fu et somm'allegressa	and very great joy
quando in tanta grandessa	when the supreme mother was
assunt'è in ciel la madre supernale.	received into heaven with great joy.
Non si poria contare ad compimento	One could not fully recount
lo gaudio grande che fu in paradiso	the great exultation that was in paradise
quando vi giunse l'aluminamento	when the light of Jesus
di ihesu còlla madre chiaro viso	arrived there with his mother, a shining face.
con quelle schiere assiso	He was seated among the
d'angeli gloriosi	clusters of glorious angels
et santi virtudiosi	and virtuous saints, all
tutti cantando in voce spiritale.	singing with spiritual voice.

Or vi pensate qual fue quel canto	Just imagine what a song
quando vi giunse quel choro tamanto	when that great choir gathered,
et l'allegressa in quella magna corte	and what happiness in that noble court
con quelle voce cantando si forte	when the voices sang so strongly.
entrando per le porte	As the queen entered the
delli ciel la regina	gate of Heaven,
si la turba divina	the divine crowd all together
tutta li fe canson celestiale.[3]	performed a celestial song.

MERCANTILE SOCIETY

Corporate Pluralism

The promotion and protection of mercantile activity was the single strongest impetus behind the late thirteenth-century consolidation of the Florentine republic.[4] This interest was made explicit in the prerequisite for public office-holding—matriculation in one of the merchant guilds. The strongest of the Tuscan city-republics, whether Guelph, like Florence and Lucca, or Ghibelline, like Pisa and Arezzo, were societies in which mercantile institutions and tastes prevailed, and all supported laudesi activity. Daily urban life made an inevitably strong imprint on the religious beliefs and practices of the Florentine laity. The pious guildsman was a new kind of Christian, and his novel society demanded and suggested new models for religious organization and expression.

Late medieval Florentine society developed under the assumption that 'il bene del comune' (primarily mercantile interests) was to be protected at all costs from the manipulation of special-interest groups.[5] The violence and narrow loyalty of the old noble families was met, in 1293, with the Ordinances of Justice, which barred magnates from public office-holding.[6] But the most effective constraint against the monopolization of political power was the intensely pluralistic nature of this communal society. The church, the guilds, the Guelph party, religious companies, the Merchant Court, ecclesiastical tribunals, courts of feudatories, and the councils of parishes and rural communities, all quasi-public bodies, coexisted in a 'loose, complex bundle of immunities,

[3] Assumption lauda from a 14th-c. Pisan laudario; E. Staaff (ed.) 'Le Laudario de Pise du ms. 8521 de la Bibliothèque de l'Arsenal de Paris: Étude linguistique', *Skrifter utgivna av Kungl. Humanistika Vetenstkaps-Samfundet i Uppsala*, 27 (1931–2), 1–295 at 195 (no. 70, lines 1–20). Translated by Nello Barbieri.

[4] For an excellent survey of republican Florence see G. Brucker, *Renaissance Florence* (New York, 1969).

[5] Antony Black has noted with respect to medieval European society that 'in several places merchant law (*ius mercatorum*) formed the basis for civil codes'; *Guilds and Civil Society in European Political Thought From the Twelfth Century to the Present* (Ithaca, NY, 1984). 56.

[6] Ibid. 133.

privileges, and liberties'.[7] Likewise, the city government consisted of an amalgam of governing councils. The eight priors, the highest ranking officials, were limited to two-month terms (in isolation from the citizenry), and subject to an elaborate system of scrutiny designed to prevent consolidation of private power-bases. This pluralistic order reproduced itself at the more intimate social level of neighbourhood (variously defined by parish, *gonfalone*, and quarter), where the roles of customer, partner, competitor, kinsman, neighbour, and friend inevitably overlapped.[8]

To the extent that office-holding was a measure of power, that power was diffusely distributed in Florence, allowing its citizens a high degree of mobility and visibility. Even at a time when this corporate pluralism had begun to erode, Buonaccorso Pitti could note in 1419 that he had recently served as an *ufficiale del'onestà, operaio* of the cathedral, *podestà* (captain) of Montepulciano, prior of the Guelph party, and a captain of Orsanmichele, the most prestigious of the city's laudesi companies.[9]

Patronage

Florentine society offered extensive economic opportunity and a high degree of social mobility, but with the attendant condition that the wheel of fortune turned with unprecedented speed. Contemporary chronicles suggest that the constant tensions of conflicting obligations and the chronic insecurity of wealth and social position were the most salient features of Florentine life. Leonbattista Alberti wrote in the early fifteenth century:

The world is so full of human variety, . . . differences of opinion, changes of heart, perversity of customs, ambiguity, diversity, and obscurity of values. The world is amply supplied with fraudulent, false, perfidious, bold, audacious, and rapacious men. Everything in the world is profoundly unsure. One has to be farseeing, alert, and careful in the face of frauds, traps, betrayals.[10]

To advance in such a world one had to be well connected, and Florence teemed with a ceaseless manipulation of relationships. Around 1400, the advice of the wealthy Florentine merchant Giovanni Morelli to his son was to

---

[7] M. Becker, *Florence in Transition*, 2 vols. (Baltimore, Md., 1967–8), ii. 16.

[8] For an excellent study of neighbourhood society in Quattrocento Florence, see D. V. and F. W. Kent, *Neighbours and Neighbourhood in Renaissance Florence: The District of the Red Lion in the Fifteenth Century* (New York, 1982). The lay companies in their late medieval social context are examined by R. Weissman, *Ritual Brotherhood in Renaissance Florence* (New York, 1982), ch. I. He describes a typical late medieval Florentine lay company as a 'miniature commune' (p. 59).

[9] A. Bacchi della Lega (ed.), *Cronica di Buonaccorso Pitti* (Bologna, 1903), 230.

[10] Trans. in Weissman, *Ritual Brotherhood*, 26, where this unstable aspect of Florentine society is discussed.

Connect yourself by marriage with those who are in power . . . and if you cannot arrange this, then make him [the man of influence] your friend by speaking well of him, by serving him in whatever way you can . . . Seek his advice . . . Show him your trust and friendship; invite him to your house, and act in ways that you think will please him, and will dispose him benevolently toward you. Always keep on good terms with those in power: obey and follow their will and their commands; never speak ill of them and their activities, even if they are evil. Keep silent and do not speak unless in commendation.[11]

The mediator in this dense and fluctuating web of personal relationships was the patron. A reasonably well-connected man might be variously petitioned by *raccomandati* (clients) seeking tax relief, a government post, an ecclesiastical benefice, or release from prison.[12] A well-placed friend or relative with legal training might plead (*avvocare*) a special case in the merchant court or before city officials, and in financial affairs a letter of *raccomandazione* was essential.[13] Even guild matriculation turned on personal sponsors, as well as personal and family reputation.[14]

Patronage, in turn, functioned quite naturally in this context as an expression of both private and corporate power. The most enduring testaments to the prestige of successful Florentine individuals and institutions are the great monuments of art, architecture, and literature spanning the republican period from Giotto to Michelangelo. Thereby the business of cultivating the saints as sacred patrons held for pious Florentines a ready significance, as did the prestige that derived from dispensing and displaying patronage in the decoration of confraternity altars and chapels.

The Active Life

It was a given condition of late thirteenth- and fourteenth-century Florence that a citizen participated in public life, whether in the structured proceedings of numerous and diverse corporations, or the competitive wrangling of marketplace and *bottega*. The most popular Florentine activities of the time seem to have been talking, calculating, and seeing a great deal of one another, all at once and in the public eye. When fourteenth-century conditions became early fifteenth-century ideals,

[11] Giovanni Morelli, *Ricordi*, ed. V. Branca (Florence, 1955), 81–3; trans. in Brucker, *Renaissance Florence*, 99.

[12] Ibid. 99–100; Kent, *Neighbours and Neighbourhood*, 16 ff. For a different view of these patron-client relationships in Florence as feudal ties of lord and vassal in an urban context, see R. Mackenney, *Tradesmen and Traders: The World of the Guilds in Venice and Europe, c.1250–c.1650* (Totowa, NJ, 1987), 35.

[13] Weissman, *Ritual Brotherhood*, 22–6.

[14] A. Doren, *Le arti fiorentine*, 2 vols. (Florence, 1940), i. 130–1.

one of the great advocates of civic humanism, Coluccio Salutati, proclaimed that so important was active participation in the political life of the community that even monks 'cannot live without serving society'.[15] Happiness and virtue might now be found not only in the perfect life of contemplation and inner peace, but in action and service for the community.[16] Just as the cities provided opportunity for participation and advancement, they also confronted its citizens with responsibilities to large and highly visible numbers of the sick and poor.

This intense and, in Western European civilization, unprecedented exposure of person to person in society inevitably fostered a particular mentality. The daily business of Florentine life was an experience of the concrete, the specific, and the unique. It entailed an appreciation of the possibilities and risks of human relationships, and an education in the full range of strengths, weaknesses, and needs of people in community. Preeminently in Florence, this urban experience helped foster new vernacular traditions in the arts which breathed with the spirit of a confident, familiar, and active humanity, a spirit that would contribute greatly to the transformation of lay religious practice and expression. At the heart of this lay religion was a devotional, as opposed to a contemplative or liturgical, Christianity, and devotions (like lauda singing)

were not primarily what one read or saw, but what one did. Devout Christians manifested their devotion by saying their prayers, going on pilgrimages, fasting, participating in processions, joining in the activities of confraternities, wearing hairshirts, giving alms, attending sermons, and performing other pious acts.[17]

The 'Arithmetical Mentality'

In 1303, in one of his many sermons to the Florentines, the popular Dominican preacher Fra Giordano da Pisa quipped that the Florentine merchant 'did nothing day or night but think and calculate'.[18] 'Arithmetical Florence' was the heartland of late medieval banking and commerce, and formal training in commercial arithmetic was a prerequisite

---

[15] *De Nobilitate legum et medicinae: De Verecundia*, ed. E. Garin (Florence, 1947), 162; D. Herlihy, *Medieval and Renaissance Pistoia* (New Haven, Conn., 1967), 259 n. 60. On the Florentine revival of the philosophy of the active political life, see H. Baron, *In Search of Florentine Civic Humanism*, 2 vols. (Princeton, NJ, 1988), i. 134–57.

[16] H. Baron, 'Cicero and the Roman Civic Spirit', *Bulletin of the John Rylands Library*, 22 (1938), 22–3; G. Holmes, 'The Emergence of an Urban Ideology at Florence, *c.*1250–1450', *Transactions of the Royal Historical Society*, 5th ser., 23 (1973), 111–34.

[17] R. Kieckhefer, 'Major Currents in Late Medieval Devotion', in J. Raitt (ed.), *Christian Spirituality II: High Middle Ages and Reformation* (New York, 1987), 81.

[18] A. Murray, *Reason and Society in the Middle Ages* (Oxford, 1978), 194, from ch. 7 of which I have borrowed the title of this section.

for advancement in this society.[19] Giovanni Villani, the Florentine chronicler with a Florentine penchant for numbers, estimated in 1345 that 1,000 to 1,200 Florentine children were studying *abbaco* and *algorismo*.[20] Study in the *bottega* of a *maestro dell'abbaco* began at age six or seven in the *botteghuzza* (primary school), where a boy learned reading and writing with some elementary business correspondence and notarial formulas.[21] This was followed by four years of *abbaco* (secondary school), a more intensive study of mathematics and some more advanced reading in literature. A few proceeded from here to legal studies at a university, but for most the *abbaco* was the culmination of formal studies. The written legacy of this new *arte della mercatantia* are the *trattati dell'abbaco*, *pratiche di mercatura*,[22] and the legions of carefully maintained confraternity account books housed in the Florentine state archives.

The impact of this constant arithmetic activity on how people thought and spoke must have been revolutionary, engendering new modes of perception that were increasingly empirical, inductive, and quantitative.[23] Alexander Murray suggests the occurrence of a profound change in human attitudes with the tendency to quantify the value of human beings.[24] Inevitably, the mercantile mental habits of calculating and negotiating also shaped religious outlook. A strong motivation for the pious layman to sing or to hear *laude* was the opportunity to earn spiritual credit against his long-standing penitential debt. Indulgences, in precise quantities of days, were available from the 'store of supplemental merit and good works on deposit there from the lives of Christ, Mary, and the saints'.[25] Salvation, no less than other aspects of life, was subject to a quantifying mental habit. In mercantile terms a 'compagnia' was any partnership in which 'the profit is to be shared', and 'meritto' was used with reference both to mercantile earnings and spiritual benefits.[26] The

[19] A. Murray, *Reason and Society in the Middle Ages* (Oxford, 1978), 169–72, 183–4, 198.

[20] G. Villani, *Cronica*, ed. F. Dragomanni (Florence, 1844–5), Bk. xi, ch. 94.

[21] M. Baxandall, *Painting and Experience in Fifteenth-Century Italy* (2nd edn., Oxford, 1988), 86. For more detailed information on the abacus tradition in Florence, see G. Arrighi, 'Il Codice L. IV. 21 della Biblioteca degl'Intronati di Siena e la "Bottega dell'Abaco a Santa Trinita" in Firenze', *Physis*, 7 (1965), 369 ff.; W. van Egmond, 'The Earliest Vernacular Treatment of Algebra: The *Libro di Ragioni* of Paolo Gerardi (1328)', *Physis*, 20 (1978), 155–89; and R. Franci and L. Rigatelli, *Introduzione all'aritmetica mercantile del medioevo e rinascimento* (Urbino, 1982).

[22] Ibid. 27–8, 34–5.

[23] M. Meiss, *Painting in Florence and Siena after the Black Death* (Princeton, NJ, 1951), 60; Murray, *Reason and Society*, 180–7.

[24] Ibid. 186.

[25] B. Rosenwein and L. K. Little, 'Social Meaning in the Monastic and Mendicant Spiritualities', *Past and Present*, 63 (1974), 24. For a list of indulgences granted in 1304 to confraternities in and around Pisa (including 140 days for singing and hearing *laude*), see G.-G. Meersseman, *Ordo fraternitatis* (Rome, 1977), ii. 1058–60.

[26] Franci and Rigatelli, *Introduzione*, 74: 'Delle compagnie: Le compagnie non è altro si non comunno sia el guadanio o vero in parte, et il compagno o la parte sie sicondo l'brigo del partecipare al guadanio o alla parditta overo a divisione de capitalli o utili o dani come ocore e questo el modo da

laudesi companies were, in this sense, a parody of the secular mercantile world, a sacred business run for the purpose of earning shared spiritual profits. This analogy between the sacred and secular worlds of Florence was one that the nurturers of the laudesi companies, the friars, would not have failed to make.

THE FRIARS

The eleventh- and twelfth-century apostolic religious movements, such as the hermits, itinerant preachers, Cathars, Humiliati, and Waldenses, expressed a quickening desire for a lay religious life of greater relevance and participation.[27] They drew their vision and authority directly from the New Testament, and their frequent defiance of ecclesiastical authority widened the long-standing rift in medieval culture between clergy and laity.[28] Appearing early in the thirteenth century, the Franciscans and Dominicans proclaimed a rapprochement and assured their survival by submitting their new organizations to church authority.[29] Furthermore, each stepped into the breach from opposing directions: the first Dominicans were Augustinian canons who borrowed important elements from the spiritual life of the canonical reformers, itinerant preachers, and the Cathars, while the strictly lay origins of the Franciscans were to be found among the hermits, itinerant preachers, Humiliati, and Waldenses.[30] Other orders followed in the new mendicant tradition, and of those to survive their curtailment by the Council of Lyons in 1274 were the Carmelites, the Augustinian (or Austin) friars, and the Servites.[31]

'Wherever there was a town there were friars; and without a town there were no friars.'[32] It was the dense human society of the medieval city that gave meaning to the mendicant ideal of *imitatio Christi*, the imitation of a visible example of ideal human behaviour. And what the

dividere proporzionattamente.' Ibid. 86: 'Meritto non vol dire altro si no ragionevolmente vedere quanto una quantità guadagnia in uno certo tempo e questo è detto meritto sempricie'. From Dionigi Gori, *Libro di arimetricha*, 1571.

[27] J. Trout, 'Preaching by the Laity in the 12th Century', *Studies in Medieval Culture*, 4 (1973–4), 92–108; Rosenwein and Little, 'Social Meaning', 16–18; Chenu, *Nature, Man, and Society*, 204 ff.

[28] C. Waddell, 'The Reform of the Liturgy from a Renaissance Perspective', in R. Benson and G. Constable (eds.), *Renaissance and Renewal in the Twelfth Century* (Cambridge, Mass., 1982), 95.

[29] For a useful survey of these two orders, see Southern, *Western Society and the Church*, 272–99. For more detailed studies, see J. Moorman, *A History of the Franciscan Order from its Origins to the Year 1517* (Oxford, 1969), and W. A. Hinnebusch, *The History of the Dominican Order* (New York, 1965), i.

[30] Rosenwein and Little, 'Social Meaning', 18.

[31] Southern, *Western Society and the Church*, 329; R. Emery, 'The Friars of the Sack', *Speculum*, 18 (1943), 323–34.

[32] Southern, *Western Society and the Church*, 286.

friars chose to imitate were the more social aspects of Christ's mission, his preaching and his poverty. The Franciscans, 'prompted by the violence, glitter, and instability of the emerging municipal oligarchies of Italy', followed their leader's example in selling everything and giving to the poor.[33] The Dominicans, the 'preaching friars', arose in response to the need for effective preaching in combating the Cathar heresy in Languedoc. Each would always retain something of their original character, the Franciscans their sympathetic humanity, and the Dominicans their academic discipline, but many similarities between the two orders developed as they engaged in a kind of marketplace competition for their urban clients. Preaching (and therefore learning) was equally indispensible to the Franciscans, who borrowed much of the Dominican model of organization and followed them into the universities, while the Franciscan attitude towards poverty strengthened the urban appeal of the Dominicans as well.[34] The religious companies gravitated to the mendicant churches, and display among them a similarity of structure and character that testifies to the shared features of the mendicant orders.[35] The common themes of mendicant spirituality were the promotion of a personal and affective devotion, encouraged through imitation of the most human of divine *exempla* (Mary, Jesus, and the saints), the cultivation of this devotional style through vernacular preaching and material renunciation, and the provision of an orthodox framework for the expression of lay piety through skilful adaptations of the secular, urban world. At heart was a new, evangelical spirituality, born of a 'vital interaction between traditional faith and new secular values'.[36]

The Secular Made Sacred

'The born chaplains of the guilds',[37] the friars seemed to take as their credo Paul's statement that 'I am made all things to all men, that I might by all means save some'.[38] In this spirit the friars encouraged the formation of religious corporations, the lay companies, closely modelled on guild structures. Lay brothers met regularly, elected officers, paid dues, provided burial services, sponsored charitable activities and religious

---

[33] Southern, *Western Society and the Church*, 281.   [34] Ibid. 284.

[35] J. Henderson has estimated that during the 14th and 15th cc., 41% of all the Florentine lay companies met in the five main friaries; 'Piety and Charity in the Late Medieval Florence: Religious Confraternities from the Middle of the Thirteenth to the Late Fifteenth Century', Ph.D. thesis (University of London, 1983), 24.

[36] Chenu, *Nature, Man, and Society*, 234. On late medieval affective devotion in general, see D. Gray, *Themes and Images in the Medieval English Religious Lyric* (London, 1972), 18–30, and Kieckhefer, 'Major Currents in Late Medieval Devotion', 75–108.

[37] Chenu, *Nature, Man, and Society*, 226.

[38] I Cor. 9: 22 (King James Version).

festivals, and kept meticulous account books within a format quite familiar to the merchant guildsman. It would not have escaped the friars' notice that the guild structure, as a door to a higher world of secular political and social activity, eminently suited a spiritual reinterpretation.

The friars recognized the importance of the saints in lay devotion, and especially through preaching emphasized the role of the latter as patrons.[39] Effective devotion might influence one who is spiritually well connected to intercede with the powerful on behalf of the weak, or, rather, the indebted. In popular devotion spiritual debt was strongly associated with the notion of purgatory, a kind of spiritual debtor's prison.[40] A purgatorial sentence was mitigated by acts of spiritual clientage—prayers, charitable acts, bequests for masses and vigils, processing, burning candles, lauda-singing, etc.—executed on behalf of the dead. The 1446 statutes of the Company of San Piero Martire (the laudesi company at the Dominican church of Santa Maria Novella) explain that the bequests of the deceased for such spiritual acts (frequently a vigil with lauda-singing) were to be carried out 'considering above all that these bequests were all made for the cure of souls who were obliged to [endure] some penalty of purgatory'.[41] Moreover, in hastening the release of the deceased from purgatory, these commemorative acts functioned to advance and supplicate the dead in their capacity as intercessors.[42] Thus the interests of the living and the dead alike were recommended ('raccomandati') to the divine court of justice, through intercession of divine lawyers ('avvocati'). A Florentine's concern for the dead was motivated by a vivid image of purgatory as a place of spiritual exile and isolation; geographic exile was the bitter punishment dealt to citizens from Dante to Machiavelli who fell too far into political disfavour. In his *Libro di buoni costumi*, the fourteenth-century merchant Paolo da Certaldo advised his readers to

Often say masses for the souls of your dead ones and also for the abandoned souls that have passed out of this life. Imagine that you were in prison and were abandoned by relatives and friends, and no one ever came to visit you and free you from prison—how would you feel? Thus it is for abandoned souls.[43]

[39] On the cult of the saints in the late Middle Ages, see Kieckhefer, 'Major Currents', 93–6.

[40] Southern, *Western Society and the Church*, 290; Weissman, *Ritual Brotherhood*, 48–9; N. Davis, 'The Study of Popular Religion', in C. Trinkaus and H. Oberman (eds.), *The Pursuit of Holiness in Late Medieval and Renaissance Religion* (Leiden, 1974), 328. Although formulated by Parisian theologians, the doctrine of purgatory was widely disseminated by the late 14th c.; J. Le Goff, *La Naissance du purgatoire* (Paris, 1981), 436.

[41] SMN 324, fo. 4r [1447 statutes]: '. . . considerando maximamente che detti lasci sono tuti fatti per rimedio delle anime che fossono obrigate ad alcuna pena del purgatorio'.

[42] S. Strocchia, 'Burials in Renaissance Florence: 1350–1500', Ph.D. thesis (University of California, Berkeley, 1981), 330.

[43] Paolo di Messer Pace da Certaldo, *Il libro di buoni costumi*, ed. S. Morpurgo (Florence, 1921), 101–2, trans. in Weissman, *Ritual Brotherhood*, 48. Paolo's father, a judge, was a captain of Orsanmichele in 1330; Ricc. 391, fo. 8[v].

In secular and sacred arena alike, a social network was essential. The statutes of lay companies typically open with an invocation of divine personages ranging from the universal to local and special patron saints, comprising a carefully graded and well-connected chain of sacred relationships. The 1441 statutes of the Company of San Bastiano (the laudesi company at the Servite church of Santissima Annunziata) open in the following manner:

Ever may it be to the praise, glory, and honour of the omnipotent God, Father, Son, and Holy Spirit, perfect trinity and unity, and of his most glorious Mother, Madonna Holy Mary, always our advocate, and of his glorious servant Messer Sancto Philippo, and of the glorious knight and martyr Messer Sancto Sebastiano, and of the devout Messer Sancto Gerardo, all our advocates, and of all the celestial court of paradise. Amen.[44]

The friars understood, and could reinterpret in spiritual terms, the concrete world of the mercantile city, a society in which one could quickly rise through the assiduous cultivation of carefully chosen relationships, or, through neglect of the same, just as quickly fall into debt, prison, and exile.

The Sacred Made Secular

Mendicant spirituality, however, was not merely a response to the conditions of secular urban life. Rather, the alignment of the forces of urban piety with ecclesiastical organization, achieved by the friars in the thirteenth century,[45] provided fertile ground for the growth of the new learning that had emanated from the twelfth-century cathedral schools. Scholars like Honorius of Autun, Hugh of St Victor, and Alan of Lille proposed a view of a homogeneous, non-hierarchical cosmos, in which nature, in all its earthly reality, acquired a religious significance and a capacity to lead man to God.[46] Man, as a microcosm of the divine, acquired a new validity in his natural setting, and it was in light of this humanistic perception of man's dignity that twelfth-century thinkers, both clerical (the Cistercians and Austin Canons) and lay (the apostolic movements), were struck by the central fact of the gospels— that God

---

[44] ASF, CmRS, Capitoli 6, fo. 1ʳ: 'Sempre sia a laude e gloria e honore e reverenza dell'omnipotente Iddio Padre, Figluolo, et Spirito Sancto, Trinità et unità perfecta, et della sua gloriosissima madre Madonna Sancta Maria nostra sempre avocata, et del suo glorioso servo messer Sancto Philippo, et del glorioso cavaliere et martire di Cristo messer Sancto Sebastiano, et del divoto messer Sancto Gherardo, tutti nostri avocati di tutta la celestiale corte di paradiso amen . . .'.

[45] Holmes, 'The Emergence of an Urban Ideology', 116.

[46] Chenu, *Nature, Man, and Society*, 5, 24 ff.

himself had become man.[47] Honorius of Autun described this new *imago mundi*:

The supreme artisan made the universe like a great zither (*citharam*) upon which he placed the strings to yield a variety of sounds, for he divided his work in two—into two parts antithetical to each other. Spirit and matter, antithetical in nature yet consonant in existence, resemble a choir of men and boys blending their bass and treble voices . . . Material things similarly imitate the distinction of choral parts, divided as things are into genera, species, individuals, forms, and numbers; all of these blend harmoniously as they observe with due measure the law implanted within them and so, as it were, emit their proper sound. A harmonious chord is sounded by spirit and body, angel and devil, heaven and hell, fire and water, air and earth, sweet and bitter, soft and hard, and so are all other things harmonized.[48]

The assertion of a dignity and divinity in things created, above all in man, and regardless of, but including, his station in life, had profound implications for the future of lay spirituality, and no one understood these implications better than the friars. Thirteenth-century mendicant scholars developed a theology appropriate to an active and earthly Christian society, which was transmitted to a broad social spectrum through a universal organization of convents, schools, handbooks, and well-trained preachers.[49] Honorius' twelfth-century vision of a resonant harmony between things natural and divine had travelled far by the fourteenth century, when a lay member of a Florentine laudesi confraternity would perceive his song as a direct contribution to the *canto celestiale*.[50]

At the heart of the friars' humanistic spirituality was a deepened concept of repentance and conversion. The friars exhorted their lay audiences to engage in personal prayer, examine their conduct, and practice moral criticism.[51] Confession became a more frequent and soul-searching sacrament, and conversion no longer meant joining a religious order. It was an invitation to enter into a more active role in the process of salvation, such as previously had been the domain of an ordained clergy acting for the vicarious benefit of the laity. It was a calling befitting a more literate and psychologically aware urban society that

---

[47] Waddell, 'The Reform of the Liturgy', 90–2.
[48] Honorius of Autun, Liber XII, quaest. ii (Patrologia Latina, 172, 1179); ed. and trans. in Chenu, *Nature, Man, and Society*, 8.
[49] Rosenwein and Little, 'Social Meaning', 29 ff.
[50] For example, the following lines (55–8) of a lauda from a Florentine laudario belonging to the Company of San Gilio, Mgl² (BNF, *Banco Rari* 19, olim Mgl. II. I. 212), fo. 50ᵛ, text ed. C. Del Popolo, 'Il laudario della Compagnia di Sant' Egidio', *Studi e problemi di critica testuale*, 16 (1978), 15: 'O santo Gilio, confessor beato / pe' nostri morti Gesù Christo humanato / preghianti che prieghi, dove se' collocato / che gli conduca a quella melodia.'
[51] Chenu, *Nature, Man, and Society*, 284 ff.; Rosenwein and Little, 'Social Meaning', 19.

sought, and was encouraged to seek, a religious status commensurate with the quality of life to which it aspired in secular society.

The invitation to enter was literal, as well. Commune and guild subsidized the construction of the great Florentine mendicant churches between *c.*1270 and 1320, and immediately lay burial sites and private family chapels were granted in an unprecedented fashion.[52] The members of laudesi companies passed through the choir-screens of Dominican Santa Maria Novella and Franciscan Santa Croce to bury their dead and conduct their services at the new chancel altars, which they maintained in their dual capacity as patron and chaplain. As the laudesi at Santa Croce sang their vivid and sensuous narratives of the lives of Jesus, Mary, and the saints, Giotto and his followers painted them in the neighbouring chapels, endowing their earthly and human characters with a new range of emotional awareness and moral strength.[53] The sacred indeed infused the secular as these frescos revealed sacred events unfolding in earthly settings, and liturgical practices and settings transformed an association of pious lay people into a microcosm of the church, an 'ecclesiola in ecclesia'.[54] In the apt words of Georges Duby, the friars brought to confraternity members 'the liturgy of the cloisters and cathedral chapter houses but by transporting it into their daily life and the intimacy of their hearts'.[55]

In Florence, the appeal of the mendicants was strengthened by their initial lack of involvement in traditional social structures. Many of the urban parishes were enmeshed in a web of coveted clerical benefices and the ancient patronage rights of prominent parish families.[56] Moreover, fourteenth-century Florentine chroniclers expressed the prevailing sentiment that the ecclesiastical courts and clerical hierarchy were staffed and exploited by the scions of the magnate families.[57] The mendicant orders cut across these narrower loyalties of Florentine society, attracting a city-

[52] E. Borsook, *The Mural Painters of Tuscany* (2nd edn.; Oxford, 1980), xviii; M. Becker, 'Aspects of Lay Piety in Early Renaissance Florence', in Trinkaus and Oberman (eds.), *The Pursuit of Holiness*, 184. According to H. Saalman, 'the whole idea of enlarging the old Romanesque church had, presumably, been initiated because of strong demand by the parish patricians for suitable family chapels'; 'San Lorenzo: The 1434 Chapel Project', *Burlington Magazine*, 120 (1978), 363. R. Gaston has noted with respect to San Lorenzo that during 1297–1356, eleven choral chapels were endowed by laymen; 'Liturgy and Patronage in San Lorenzo, Florence, 1350–1650', in F. W. Kent and P. Simons (eds), *Patronage, Art, and Society in Renaissance Italy* (Oxford, 1987), 120.
[53] Meiss, *Painting in Florence and Siena*, 60.
[54] O. Clemen, *Die Volksfrömmigkeit des ausgehenden Mittelalters* (Dresden and Leipzig, 1937), 7.
[55] *The Age of the Cathedrals: Art and Society, 980–1420*, trans. E. Levieux and B. Thompson (Chicago, 1981), 223.
[56] G. Brucker, 'Urban Parishes and their Clergy in Quattrocento Florence: A Preliminary Sondage', in A. Morrogh (ed.), *Renaissance Studies in Honor of Craig Hugh Smyth* (Florence, 1985), 17–28.
[57] M. Becker, 'Church and State on the Eve of the Renaissance', *Speculum*, 37 (1962), 511–12.

wide following.[58] The confraternities, especially the laudesi companies, tended to be widespread and socially heterogeneous in their membership, and further strengthened the relationship between the friars and the larger framework of Florentine civic life.

The Active Life

While cloistered monks and nuns embodied the ideal of contemplative life, the friars presented the greatest clerical examples of civic participation. Through preaching, mendicancy, and charitable activity, the lives of Francis and Dominic proclaimed from the outset the mendicant ideal of a religious life of activity in the world, and they were quick to tap the active disposition of secular urban life. In a sermon of November 1305, Fra Giordano da Pisa exhorted Florentines to

Make use of confession, make use of communion, make use of the church, make use of Masses, keep good company, make use of prayers, make use of the sermons . . . and especially read good little books, and other such things.[59]

In the early fifteenth century, the Franciscan preacher St Bernardino reminded Florentines of the citizens' responsibility to care for the poor, the sick, and the aged:

While in his true fatherland in heaven, man may be destined to lead a contemplative life, it is his calling in this world to act and to love.[60]

This disposition was nowhere more strongly evident than among the members of the laudesi companies, who made relatively frequent 'use' of the sacraments and sermons, who managed numerous charitable enterprises, and who came every evening of the week to conduct their own liturgical services and to sing that liturgy in their own language.

Preaching

No activity was more characteristic of the friars' evangelical ideals and practices than vernacular preaching to the laity; it was the ultimate *imitatio Christi* for a religious sensibility oriented to a loquacious urban society. The widespread and often heretical lay preaching of the twelfth century, coupled with a 'most dreadful silence' of the clergy with respect

[58] Weissman, *Ritual Brotherhood*, 44–6; Strocchia, 'Burials in Renaissance Florence', 114–15, 161.
[59] C. Delcorno, *Giordano da Pisa e l'antica predicazione volgare* (Florence, 1975), 67: 'Usare la confessione, usare di comunicante, usare la chiesa, usare la messe, usare colle buone persone, usare l'orazione, usare la predicha . . . e spezialmente di leggere buoni libricciuoli, e l'altre cose.'
[60] Becker, 'Aspects of Lay Piety', 187.

to the laity,[61] pointed to the desperate need for an organized and well-trained corps of preachers.[62] This challenge the friars took upon themselves with spectacular success. By the late thirteenth century in many Italian cities, a different mendicant order commonly preached every evening of the week, and in the early fourteenth century an anonymous observer reported that the friars' sermons could be heard 'daily, in great numbers'.[63] Throughout the towns and cities of Europe, moreover, the friars often delivered their sermons to large gatherings, either in the large piazzas adjoining their churches, or in their great church halls built for that purpose.[64] Here a primarily lay audience would receive what was for many the 'richest and most familiar literary experience of their lives', as preachers sought to capture the ears of their audience through recourse to jokes, riddles, mime, image, popular science and pseudo-science, history, practical technology, and exotic narrative.[65] With or without such extra-spiritual references, however, the heart of mendicant preaching was vivid and direct biblical exegesis, from which an attendant laity received an unprecedented and widespread familiarity with the basics of church doctrine.[66] During the intense and popular preaching activity of Lent, certain sermon cycles, such as that preached in 1306 by Fra Giordano to Florentines on the third chapter of Genesis, constituted 'a kind of school of theology for the laity'.[67]

Franciscan and Dominican preaching in Trecento Florence each tended to manifest distinctive characteristics which probably exemplified the range of mendicant preaching in general. The more professorial Dominicans appear as mediators of a Latin, clerical theology, drawing more heavily on classical monastic literature, especially the *Lives of the Holy Fathers* and the *Dialogues* of St Gregory. Influenced by their lay origins,

[61] Peter the Chanter, *Verbum abbreviatum*, 62 (Patrologia Latina, 205, 189), quoted in Chenu, *Nature, Man, and Society*, 244.

[62] On heretical and unauthorized preaching, as well as the church's response, see Trout, 'Preaching by the Laity', *passim*, and Rouse, *Preachers, Florilegia, and Sermons*, 43–64, where it is pointed out that the initial response to the need for qualified preachers predates the friars, and occurs in the schools of Paris, among the Cistercians, and in the early years of Innocent III's papacy.

[63] Meersseman, *Ordo fraternitatis*, ii. 937–42.

[64] Meersseman, 'L'Architecture domincaine au XIIIᵉ siècle: Législation et pratique' *Archivum Fratrum Praedicatorum*, 16 (1946), 189. See the appendix of Delcorno, *Giordano da Pisa*, which contains an index of Fra Giordano's Florentine sermons, with rubrics indicating the piazzas and churches where the sermons were delivered.

[65] J. Fleming, *An Introduction to Franciscan Literature of the Middle Ages* (Chicago, 1977), 122–3.

[66] Often memorized in youth, these appear to have been the ten commandments, the twelve articles of faith, the seven mortal sins, the five senses of the body, the seven works of mercy, the seven sacraments of the church, the *Pater noster*, and the *Ave Maria*. See, for example, the 14th-cent. statutes of the Compagnia della Purificazione, a Florentine youth confraternity (ages 12–18), which required that these items be memorized; Biblioteca Laurenziana, Acquisti e Doni 336, fo. 6ᵛ. The same items recur in the 15th-cent. statutes of the laudesi company of San Bastiano, affiliated with the Servite church of Santissima Annunziata; ASF, CmRS, Capitoli 6, fo. 4ᵛ [1441].

[67] Delcorno, *Giordano da Pisa*, 71.

the Franciscans rejected the scholastic sermon, and drew on the lives of saints more recent and familiar, above all their charismatic founder.[68] Contemporary accounts of St Francis's preaching describe a style less like a preacher than a political orator (*contionator*).[69] Through diffusion and mutual influence among the mendicant orders, what emerged by the fourteenth century was a range of various sermon types, appropriate for different audiences: the Latin *sermo modernus*, employing scholastic formal logic and complex scriptural concordances, destined for clergy and university students; the less refined vernacular sermon, which exploited the expressive possibilities of the vernacular but retained the basic scheme of the *sermo modernus*; and the older homily, a brief moral and allegorical explication of the day's scripture readings, usually delivered at Mass.[70] These divisions correspond to those outlined in a Florentine *Ars predicandi* of 1412, which calls 'subtilis' those sermons for experts in theology, 'devotus' those easily understood, edifying, and shunning elaboration, and 'facilis' those for people newly introduced to theology.[71] The anonymous author especially recommends the 'devotus' style as 'like the sermons of the saints which are read in church . . . good for instructing the people'.[72]

The *devotus* style of preaching was probably that most familiar to Florentines, and especially to confraternity members who were neither neophytes nor experts in theology, for *devotio* was the spiritual state that mendicant vernacular sermons above all aimed to create. According to the great Dominican theologian St Thomas Aquinas, *devotio* was the conscious and willed turning of the mind to God, with the intended effect of mingled joy at God's goodness, and sadness at man's inadequacy.[73] This dichotomy runs deep in the lay spirituality of the time; the lauda stands as the consummate lay expression of the former, while the latter, the focus of disciplinati spirituality, was intended to move the hearer to contrition and penance. Confession invariably followed the friars' sermons (as it often did lauda singing), and thus 'the seed is sown in preaching, the fruit is harvested in penance'.[74]

[68] C. Delcorno, 'Predicazione volgare e volgarizzamenti', *Mélanges de l'école française de Rome: Moyen âge*, NS 89 (1977), 688.
[69] Ibid. 680–1.
[70] Ibid. 683; D. Lesnick, 'Dominican Preaching and the Creation of a Capitalist Ideology in Late-Medieval Florence', *Memorie domenicane*, NS, 8–9 (1977–8), 219, who notes that the vernacular sermon might be modified according to whether the audience was literate (*maiores*) or not (*minores*). D. D'Avray has argued that the *sermo modernus*, which developed at the University of Paris during the 13th c., was easily adapted for routine preaching to the laity; *The Preaching of the Friars: Sermons Diffused from Paris before 1300* (Oxford, 1985), 193. For a more recent and comprehensive formulation of Lesnick's arguments, see *Preaching in Medieval Florence: The Social World of Franciscan and Dominican Spirituality* (Athens, (Georgia) and London, 1989).
[71] Baxandall, *Painting and Experience*, 150. [72] Ibid. 150.
[73] Ibid 149, from the *Summa Theologica*, 2ª–2ᵃᵉ, q. 180, aa. 1 and 7.
[74] Humbert of Romans, quoted in Rosenwein and Little, 'Social Meaning', 22.

But how did one attain the state of *devotio*? For Aquinas, it was through contemplation, but for the friar-preacher's lay audience it was through a popularized form of contemplation that depended upon mental imagery, developed and expanded through simile. D'Avray has observed two related 'mental habits' of mendicant preaching—the incessant quotation of scripture (which itself relies heavily on imagery), and the use of similitude.[75] A mendicant sermon typically began with a brief scriptural reference (*thema*), usually the source of an image or key word, then proceeded to develop distinctive levels of meaning through recourse to *distinctiones* (or *divisiones*), different senses of a term contained in scripture. Preachers had recourse to *distinctio* collections, alphabetized word-lists which linked a repertory of key scriptural words to their diverse interpretations among various *auctoritates*, and made possible the ready amplification of an image or word through simile.[76] For example, the word *naviculum* from a passage in Luke, 'Ascendens Jesus in unam naviculum . . .', called up a fourfold simile, likening the ship to penance (*poenitentia*), the church (*ecclesia*), the cross (*crucis*), and the mind (*mentis*). This framework of scripture and *distinctiones* was then further amplified with vivid narrative material drawn from another genre of mendicant preaching aids, the *exemplum*. Collections of *exempla*, based primarily on saints' lives (of which Voragine's *Legenda aurea* was a primary source), provided the preacher with his most concrete pulpit material.

In the *distinctiones* cited above may be seen another important element of late medieval popular sermons, a recourse to rhyme and verse. D'Avray noted a tendency 'to formulate *distinctiones* and divisions in what is not far from being a rhymed verse meter', especially in the use of rhymed clusters (often three) such as *intellectus–affectus–effectus*.[77] Wenzel's study of a popular, early fourteenth-century Franciscan sermon collection reveals the variety of rhetorical and structural functions served by vernacular verse in popular sermons: the articulation of sermon divisions (*distinctiones*), biblical quotations, liturgical prayers, and a variety of summarizing, mnemonic, and dramatic purposes.[78]

To summarize, the literary tools used by the friars to preach and teach the faith were scripture, and, as suggested by scripture, moralized

---

[75] D'Avray, *The Preaching of the Friars*, 235. The following discussion is indebted to this excellent study, principally to pp. 225–59.

[76] Rouse, *Preachers, Florilegia, and Sermons*, is a study of one such collection, with an introduction to 13th-c. preaching aids in ch. 1.

[77] D'Avray, *The Preaching of the Friars*, 248; S. Wenzel, *Verses in Sermons: 'Fasciculus morum' and its Middle English Poems* (Cambridge, Mass., 1978), 75; and Rouse, *Preachers, Florilegia, and Sermons*, 76–7.

[78] Wenzel, *Verses in Sermons*, 82–6. Rouse observed that 'it would be difficult to name any other genre of medieval literature that consumed the "raw materials" of literary composition so rapidly as did the sermon'; *Preachers, Florilegia, and Sermons*, 64.

image, similitude, and narration (*exempla*), further amplified through a rhetorical and structural use of rhymed verse and word-play. Precisely these 'mental habits' may be detected in the laude of the lay religious companies, the members of which constituted the 'fixed nucleus' of the friar-preacher's audience, and for whom these sermons were the 'culminating moment' of their meetings.[79] The following refrain and first three strophes of a lauda to the Virgin are found in three fourteenth-century Florentine laudari:

Ave, donna sanctissima,	Hail most saintly Lady,
regina potentissima.	most powerful queen.
La virtù celestiale	The celestial virtue
co la gratia supernale	with supernal grace
in te, virgo virginale,	descended most benignly in you,
discese benignissima.	virgin of virgins.
La nostra redemptione	Our redemption
prese incarnatione	was incarnated
ch'è sanza corrutione	without corruption
in te, donna dolcissima.	in you, sweetest Lady.
Tu se' porta, tu se' domo,	You are the door, the dwelling,
di te naque Dio et homo,	from you God and man was born,
arbore con dolce pomo,	O tree bearing sweet fruits,
che sempre sta' florissima.[80]	and always in full flower.

The lauda proceeds for five more strophes in its narration of the Virgin's Assumption, the end of each strophe presenting a different quality—'purissima', 'carissima', 'gaudissima', etc. These rhymed key words, typical of the early lauda repertory, sound very much like the rhymed *distinctiones* of the friars' word-lists. Through the use of simile, the Virgin is likened to a door, a home (line 11), and a tree with a sweet apple (line 13). It may not be stretching the analogy to suggest that the various strophes of some laude may have been heard as a sermon-like expansion, through *distinctiones* and *exempla* (often drawn, like sermon *exempla*, from the *Legenda aurea*) of the short, epigrammatic refrain (the *thema*) sung at the outset and after each strophe. The strophes of the lauda quoted above each elaborate upon the subject of the refrain, the Virgin, and in particular upon the source and nature of the Virgin's power, and

---

[79] Delcorno, *Giordano da Pisa*, 71.

[80] Text from Mgl¹, ed. J. Grossi in, 'The Fourteenth Century Florentine Laudario Magliabechiano II. I. 122 (B. R. 18): A Transcription and Study', Ph.D. thesis (Catholic University of America, 1979), 149; F. Liuzzi, *La lauda e i primordi della melodia italiana*, 2 vols. (Rome, 1935), ii, no. 31; also found in Mgl² and Fior (as well as in two other Tuscan laudari, Ars and Aret), all of which date from the 14th c. The text has been emended according to Grossi's notes, p. 150, and the translation is by Nello Barbieri. The two versions of this lauda with musical settings (from Cort and Mgl¹) are transcribed in Music Example 3. A 13th-c. lauda using similar epithets is 'Rayna possentissima', ed. G. Varanini in *Laude dugentesche* (Padua, 1972), 23.

the rhyme link between the last word of each strophe and the refrain reinforces the thematic link.[81] The didactic nature of many laude texts, the emphasis on scripture and narrated saints' lives, and the analogy between lauda and sermon suggested by shared techniques and the fact that confession customarily followed either of these devotion-inspiring activities, reinforce the impression that many laude looked two ways— towards heaven as sung prayer, and to the *confratelli* as sung sermon.

The preaching of the friars was also their ambivalent response to a mercantile society. The message of apostolate poverty and a strong condemnation of usury resulted from the unprecedented social and spiritual problems of a cash economy.[82] Human suffering now seemed to stem from the greed of urban merchants, rather than from the violence of feudal nobility. The remedy proposed by the mendicant preachers was a *carità* derived from the twofold Biblical formula: to love God (through the complementary and self-denying practice of penance and praise), and to love one's neighbour. The redefinition of neighbourly love in this context of urban greed led to a notion of 'charity' familiar to moderns: feeding and clothing the poor, visiting the sick and imprisoned, caring for widows and orphans, and building and managing hospitals. Ministering to the 'poveri di Dio' through some combination of these charitable acts was *de rigueur* for the mendicant-sponsored religious companies. While condemning greed and usury as the dark side of a mercantile society, the friars were also compelled by their urban circumstances to discover the redeeming qualities of wealth. Dominican and Franciscan theologians provided new theories of social utility that legitimized private wealth and the Christian merchant, much as the Crusades had done for an equally intractable aspect of earlier medieval society, the violence of the Christian knight.[83] The friars were thus instrumental in both curbing and sanctioning mercantile activity, and thereby rendering it acceptable in the eyes of the church.[84]

In order to repudiate effectively certain aspects of the society to which they ministered, the friars engaged through their preaching in a very Pauline identification with that society. Preaching, commercial bargaining, and legal pleading alike depended upon one's ability to argue and negotiate persuasively.[85] The friars frequently enlisted commercial and political imagery. In the 'workshop of your conscience' ('nella

---

[81] The same structure may be seen in the lauda quoted at the beginning of this chapter, 'Canto celestiale', where the subject is the familiar scene of the Virgin's Assumption. The tendency of many lauda texts to 'portray' sacred persons and scenes in graphic and sensuous terms in order to excite devotion is another vital point of contact between lauda and sermon, and is discussed in Ch. 5.

[82] Rosenwein and Little, 'Social Meaning', 24–31; Lesnick, 'Dominican Preaching', 242–3.

[83] Rosenwein and Little, 'Social Meaning', 26–30.

[84] Lesnick, 'Dominican Preaching', *passim*; Chenu, *Nature, Man, and Society*, 224.

[85] Rosenwein and Little, 'Social Meaning', 23.

bottega della tua conscientia'),[86] the merchant is to regard Christ as a *bonus negotiator*, and to prefer heavenly to earthly riches.[87] Lent, like a great trade-fair, is a good time for making a profit, because spiritual money-changers (*cambitores*) are ready to hear confessions, during which the sinner may profitably exchange base money (sin) for precious money (grace).[88] There is an excellent display of the goods (the preaching is frequent), and money is available (vigils, prayers, and fasts, with which the kingdom of heaven is bought). The sinner who dies unrepentant is like the debtor who forfeits in perpetuity his security (his soul) to the usurer (the devil), if he fails to buy it back before the end of the trade-fair (death).

Christ might also be *advocatus*, God the father *iudex*, and the cross the *locus iuris*, with notarial angels keeping the Book of Life.[89] Fra Giordano told Florentines that a man who wished to rule the city well as a *signore* must first learn to rule ('signoreggiare') himself, the first of four steps to the perfect *signoria* of beatitude.[90]

This by no means exhausts the range of imagery used in mendicant sermons, but it does indicate the 'mental habit' so readily appropriated by lauda poets. In a long simile based on sea-going merchants, Mary is both 'gran mercatantrice' and 'navatrice', then she herself becomes the *navicella* who bears her precious cargo into the world 'sens' alcuno rio'.[91] In a lauda bearing the rubric 'Della ricordans della morte', the deceased recites a litany of wrongdoing, climaxing with his greed:

Ove son le perle
et li botton dell'argento,
lo vel della seta
che menav'al vento?

Where are the pearls
and silver buttons,
the silken veil
that you waved in the wind?

and usurious practices:

Non vo chiamare
  ch'io son chiamato:
tu puoi vedere
  come io sto agiato
ad cui piacesse
  questo mercato
comperi terre
  et presti ad usura.[92]

I do not need to call
  for I am called upon:
you can see
how rich I am.
If someone would like
this business,
let him buy land
and lend on usury.

---

[86] Ricc. 1301, fo. 105ʳ, discussed below.

[87] D. D'Avray, 'Sermons to the Upper Bourgeoisie by a Thirteenth-Century Franciscan', *Studies in Church History*, 16, (1979), 198.

[88] Ibid. 204–16.   [89] Ibid. 198.

[90] Lesnick, 'Dominican Preaching', 238–9. On juridical notions in 'local' religion, see R. W. Scribner, 'Interpreting Religion in Early Modern Europe', *European Studies Review*, 13 (1983), 96.

[91] Staaff, 'Le Laudario de Pise', no. 109, ll. 173–86.   [92] Ibid., no. 48, ll. 107–8, 131–4.

In the passion narrative of the lauda repertory, the betrayal by Judas for thirty silver pieces assumes a special significance:

Trenta denari fu lo merchato	Thirty coins was the deal
che fece giuda et fue pagato.[93]	that Judas made, and so he was paid.

The greatest tribute is paid to 'holy poverty', the value of which eludes and transcends the mercantile capacity to measure and count:

tal virtu de amare	That way of loving
non si può contare	cannot be measured,
tant'è 'l suo valore.[94]	such is its value.

Juridical imagery, however, occurs more frequently in the Tuscan lauda repertory. A patron saint is usually referred to as 'nostro avocato', and is perceived as giving divine 'consiglio' (one wonders how many pious Florentines perceived the 'celestial court' referred to in most company documents as a legal, rather than a princely, court). The politically charged terms *balìa* (political authority) and *signoria* are used often to represent divine power, and a saint might be a *gonfalonier* (standard-bearer, a high-ranking commune official) of God.[95]

The proximity of lauda and sermon is evident elsewhere, as well. A saint frequently appears in a lauda refrain as an 'exemplo', a concept very likely transmitted by mendicant preachers.[96]

These thematic links between lauda and sermon suggest the possibility that laude were sung or recited in conjunction with sermons, and that some laude may have been composed for that purpose. A cursory search through Florentine archives for manuscripts containing lauda texts turned up several that closely juxtapose lauda and sermon, a relationship that seems to have been particularly close during Lent.[97] Ricc. 1301 (Florence, fifteenth century) contains forty-six Lenten sermons in the vernacular attributed to Giovanni Dominici (1357–1419). Following a sermon on fasting delivered on the fourth day of Lent, there is entered a lauda 'composed for this holy gospel', which paraphrases the reading of

---

[93] Staaff, 'Le Laudario de Pise', no. 29, ll. 7–8, and Cort, ed. Liuzzi in *La lauda*, i. 356, ll. 7–8.

[94] Staaff, 'Le Laudario', no. 62, ll. 22–4.

[95] e.g. ibid., no. 9, ll. 21–2 [Nativity of Christ]: 'nato è in questo mondo, / per dar consilglio'. From Mgl², ed. in Del Popolo, 'Il laudario', 19: 'Venite a laudare la donna, e pregare / che sempremai ci tengha in sua balìa. / Que' son di croce segnati / cherici, laici, frati: / a voi, Madonna, sian racchomandati, / che sempre steano a vostra signoria.' And ibid. 22: 'Paolo infiammato, tu de' gonfalonier di Dio beato'.

[96] e.g. Staaff, 'Le Laudario', no. 79: 'San Giovanni baptista / exemplo della gente . . .'. See also P. Brown, 'The Saint as Exemplar in Late Antiquity', *Representations*, 1 (1983), 1–25.

[97] The relationship between laudesi company services (including sermons) and sung Lenten devotional texts (gospels, passions, and laments), is discussed in Ch. 2, 'Lent'.

the day upon which the sermon is based.[98] In Mgl. II. XI. 35 (Florence, fifteenth century), three sections of approximately equal length are devoted to the 'Storia di Barlaam et Iusaphat', a collection of Lenten sermons in the vernacular, and forty-six laude of a distinctly penitential cast.[99] Many of the ninety-five laude in Panciatichi 22 (fifteenth century) are attributed to the Franciscan poet Jacopone da Todi, and are rubricated in a manner that suggests they were used as sermon material.[100] Two other laude by Jacopone were the avowed source of sermon *exempla* for St Bernardino's Florentine preaching in 1425, and his recorded sermons indicate a familiarity with the repertory of Jacopone laude.[101] The association between lauda singing, Vespers, and preaching was noted on four different occasions by Luca Dominici, who chronicled the events of the penitential Bianchi processions in Pistoia during 1399–1400.[102]

According to the record of his companions, St Francis himself encouraged this combination of preaching and vernacular praise lyrics ('laudes Domini'). Having just composed his famous 'Canticle of Brother Sun' (regarded as part of the earliest lauda tradition[103]), Francis wanted brother Pacifico

... who in the world had been known as the king of verses and who had been a really courtly doctor of singers, to be sent for and given some good and holy friars that they might go through the world preaching and praising God. He said he wanted it that first one of them who knew how to preach should preach to the people and after the sermon they were to sing the praises of God as minstrels of the Lord.[104]

[98] Ricc. 1301, fo. 40r: 'Lauda fatta per questo sancto vangelio a l'amore di Dio' (based on Matt. 5, re fasting): 'Figliuoli mei diletti / quando voi digiunate / fate che voi non siate / chome y poeti tristi maladetti . . .'. The MS is catalogued in S. Morpurgo, *I manoscritti della R. Biblioteca Riccardiana di Firenze* (Rome, 1900), 367–9.

[99] Inventory in G. Mazzatinti, *Inventari dei manoscritti delle biblioteche d'Italia* (Florence, 1890–), xii. 80–1.

[100] For example, on fo. 46ᵣ is the lauda 'O amor chontrafatto', accompanied by the rubric 'In che modo l'amore sanza le tre virtù theologiche e quatro chardinali non è virtuoso amore, ma vizioso'.

[101] C. Delcorno, 'L'*Exemplum* nella predicazione di Bernardino da Siena', in *Bernardino predicatore nella società suo tempo* (Convegni del centro di studi sulla spirituale medievale, 16; Todi, 1976), 73–107.

[102] Luca Dominici, *Cronache*, ed. G. Gigliotti, 2 vols. (Pistoia, 1939), i. 158: '. . . e ivi cantorno molte laudi e un bello vespro e predicossi'; see also pp. 161, 164, 166. Cited in B. Toscani, 'Contributi alla storia musicale delle laude dei Bianchi', *Studi musicali*, 9 (1980), 165.

[103] Varanini, *Laude dugentesche*, p. ix.

[104] R. B. Brook (ed. and trans.), *Scripta Leonis, Rufini, et Angeli: sociorum S. Francisci* (Oxford, 1970), 164–7 [1246]: '. . . qui in seculo vocabatur rex versuum et fuit valde curialis doctor cantorum, et dare sibi aliquos fratres bonos et spiritales, ut irent per mundum predicando et laudando Deum. Nam volebat et dicebat, quod prius aliquis illorum predicaret populo, qui sciret predicare, et post predicationem cantarent laudes Domini tanquam ioculatores Domini'.

The thirteenth-century Franciscan chronicler Salimbene praises a number of friars for being both *boni predicatores* and *boni cantores*.[105]

Perhaps the most provocative circumstantial evidence for the relationship between lauda and sermon is the earliest recorded reference to lauda singing, which attributes the origins in Siena of this 'mira devotione' to the devotion excited by the preaching of the Dominican Ambrogio Sansedoni (d. 1267).[106] As will become evident in the course of the following chapter, there was rarely an occasion in the various laudesi services when preaching and lauda singing were not closely juxtaposed.

THE LAY COMPANIES

The lay religious companies of republican Florence represented the mendicant programme of a more deeply converted laity at its most successful, as well as the layman's aspiration to the religious validation of a life lived in the world at its most eloquent. That the lay company was a point of vital interaction between various religious and secular forces is evident in the prismatic array of views brought to the subject by historians of Florence. Martines saw in the companies a possible source of education in statecraft and fulfilment of the administrative ambitions of lower guildsmen.[107] For Weissman the lay company offered to older members a 'liminal' escape from and transformation of the conflicting relationships of Florentine society, and a means for younger men to broaden family and neighbourhood networks.[108] Trexler sees the potential for participation in the larger ritual life of the city,[109] while others, including Holmes, see a creative encounter between the forces of urban piety and ecclesiastical organization, resulting in new institutions adapted to the active life of the city, and constituting the roots of a humanistic 'urban ideology'.[110] The *confratelli* have also been viewed as recipients of the torch of religious renewal, passed from monk to canon, to friar, and then to layman by the late thirteenth century.[111] However much the layman's motives for participation in a religious company varied, clearly the previously passive role of the laity in the process of their salvation

[105] Fra Ognibene di Guido di Adamo Salimbene, *Cronica*, ed. G. Scalia (Bari, 1966), 263 ff., 803 ff.
[106] This event is discussed more fully in Ch. 2.
[107] L. Martines, *Lawyers and Statecraft in Renaissance Florence* (Princeton, NJ, 1968), 53.
[108] Weissman, *Ritual Brotherhood*, 58, 161.
[109] R. Trexler, *Public Life in Renaissance Florence* (New York, 1980).
[110] Holmes, 'The Emergence of an Urban Ideology', 111–34.
[111] Becker, 'Church and State', 511–12; R. Trexler, 'Ritual in Florence: Adolescence and Salvation in the Renaissance', in Trinkaus and Oberman (eds.), *The Pursuit of Holiness*, 232.

was no longer acceptable to the late thirteenth-century Florentine citizen.[112]

In Florence, among the other mercantile cities of central and northern Italy, two distinct types of lay religious company emerged in the second half of the thirteenth century, and remained the dominant and vital forms of organized lay devotion to the end of the fifteenth century, the laudesi and the disciplinati.[113] Their early history is linked to the simultaneous expansion of the mendicant orders and the rise of the guilds,[114] and earlier dates, especially for laudesi companies in Florence in 1183 and 1233, are untenable.[115] Lay religious groups of the eleventh and twelfth centuries, such as the *conversi*, the Cluniac *confratelli*,[116] and the early penitential orders,[117] provided early models of organized lay devotion, but tended to assume the disciplined and world-renouncing character of the monastic orders with which they were associated.[118]

In fact, the earliest datable laudesi and disciplinati companies appeared in the 1260s, and multiplied rapidly in the following decades, especially in Florence.[119] The assignment of precise dates before mid-thirteenth century to certain Florentine laudesi companies stems from the fact that the earliest mendicant-sponsored companies did not practice lauda singing (or ritual scourging), and only after mid-century adopted one of these new specialized devotions.[120] The situation in Florence requires some

---

[112] Meersseman, *Ordo fraternitatis*, ii. 949–50.

[113] The laudesi companies were most prominent during the late 13th and early 14th cc., but declined somewhat during the 15th c., when disciplinati companies were most numerous, and other types of lay company (trade, charitable, and boy companies) increased. Henderson, 'Piety and Charity', 32.

[114] Weissman, *Ritual Brotherhood*, 44; Mackenney, *Tradesmen and Traders*, pp. xii, 1–2. The general ascent of the guilds in the 13th c. and their decline by the 16th c. closely corresponds, and is linked, to the flourishing of the friars, the lay companies, and republican forms of government in Florence.

[115] The source of these frequently cited dates seems to have been L. Muratori, *Dissertazioni sopra le antichità italiane* (Milan, 1751), iii, Diss. 75 (relying in part on early Servite chroniclers who attribute the foundation of their order in 1233 to seven young noblemen who were supposedly members of a laudesi company at the Cathedral); perpetuated in E. Betazzi, *Notizia di un laudario del secolo XIII* (Arezzo, 1890), 14; A. Tenneroni, *Inizii di antichi poesie italiane religiose e morali* (Florence, 1909), p. ix; G. M. Monti, *Le confraternite medievali dell'alta e media Italia*, 2 vols. (Venice, 1927), i. 35–6; Liuzzi, *La lauda*, i. 23; and more recently by J. Stevens, 'Lauda spirituale', *New Grove Dictionary* (London, 1980), x. 539. These dates have been refuted in the more recent and authoritative studies of Meersseman, *Ordo fraternitatis*, ii. 922–3 n. 4, 954; and Varanini, *Laude dugentesche*, pp. xiv–xvi.

[116] D. Osheim, 'Conversion, "Coversi", and the Christian Life in Late Medieval Tuscany', *Speculum*, 58 (1983), 368–90; H. Cowdrey, 'Unions and Confraternity with Cluny', *Journal of Ecclesiastical History*, 16 (1965), 152–62.

[117] Meersseman, *Ordo fraternitatis*, i. 263–304; B. Bolton, 'Innocent III's Treatment of the Humiliati', *Studies in Church History*, 8 (1971), 73–82.

[118] M. Becker, *Medieval Italy: Constraints and Creativity* (Bloomington, Ind., 1981), 136–8.

[119] Meersseman, *Ordo fraternitatis*, ii. 955–6, 976–7.

[120] Ibid. 922–3. Although Weissman (*Ritual Brotherhood*, 44 n. 3) and Henderson ('Piety and Charity', 25 ff., 46) provide foundation dates in the 1240s for several lay companies that eventually

explanation, for it helps account for the strength and number of the lay companies there.

The earliest mendicant-sponsored lay companies in Florence appear to have been fostered by the order most adept at organization—the Dominicans.[121] In 1244, Pope Innocent IV sent the Dominican preacher/ inquisitor Peter of Verona (St Peter Martyr) to Florence to resolve a situation that had grown beyond the control of the Florentine bishop and local inquisitor. The Cathar heresy, which had been brutally crushed in southern France by the Albigensian crusade, was deeply entrenched in Florence, where it enjoyed the support of the local *podestà*.[122] Armed with Dominican eloquence and the authority to grant papal privileges and indulgences to the laity, Peter succeeded in Florence with the same persuasive, non-violent formula that had worked for him during previous campaigns in Lombardy. Peter's victory has been attributed primarily to 'the creation of lay confraternities to combat heresy, whose importance in this regard can hardly be overemphasized. These confraternities, which were founded as a result of the efforts of Peter the Martyr . . . organized popular religious support behind the banner of the inquisition'.[123] The founding of these lay companies in the 1240s was the culmination of a roughly twenty-five year period beginning with the establishment of the Franciscan and Dominican orders in Florence (*c.*1218–21). During this period these orders carried on a kind of political/ devotional propaganda campaign which sought to discredit the imperial Ghibelline cause by linking it to heresy.[124]

Two types of lay religious company existed in Florence prior to Peter's arrival. The Order of Penitence was founded *c.*1220 to administer bequests and donations left to the Dominicans, and distribute the proceeds to the poor.[125] The Society of Faith (*Societas Fidei*), a religious militia of laymen, was mobilized to promote the papal cause of the inquisition

---

adopted lauda singing and came to be called laudesi companies, it is not quite accurate to designate these as laudesi companies at the time of their foundation.

[121] Del Popolo, 'Il laudario', 8, notes the predominance of Dominican saints in the Tuscan lauda repertory (in contrast to the Franciscan predominance in Umbria), and attributes this to the strength of the Dominican *studio* at Santa Maria Novella and of Dominican preachers throughout Tuscany.

[122] Meersseman, *Ordo fraternitatis*, ii. 766–70.

[123] J. N. Stephens, 'Heresy in Medieval and Renaissance Florence', *Past and Present*, 54 (1972), 29. The unusually large indulgences granted to the audiences of Dominican preachers in Lombardy (Rouse, *Preachers, Florilegia, and Sermons*, 62) undoubtedly were a factor in their success, and the extension of these indulgences to other lay devotional activities such as processing, hearing Mass, and, eventually, singing laude and practicing ritual scourging, certainly contributed to the success of the lay companies, which became the exclusive devotional framework for these activities.

[124] M. Papi, 'Confraternite ed ordini mendicanti a Firenze, aspetti di una ricerca quantitativa', *Mélanges de l'école française de Rome*, NS, 89 (1977), 725.

[125] Henderson, 'Piety and Charity', 24; Meersseman, *Ordo fraternitatis*, i. 365–70, 384–6; A. Benvenuti Papi, 'I frati della penitenza nella società fiorentina del Due-Trecento', in M. D'Alatri (ed.), *I Frati penitenti di San Francesco nella società del Due e Trecento* (Rome, 1977), 191–2.

(including lobbying for communal legislation and perhaps acting as bodyguards for the Inquisitor and Bishop), and seem to have been disbanded when the Tuscan inquisition passed to the Franciscans at Santa Croce in 1254.[126] Neither of these types of lay company, however, appealed broadly to the Florentine laity. Companies devoted to the Virgin Mary, on the other hand, were established directly by Peter, and these were undoubtedly the immediate predecessors of the laudesi companies, for whom Marian devotion was central.[127] Although the Florentine laudesi companies were often distinguished in vernacular documents by the name of their special saint, in official Latin documents of the thirteenth and fourteenth centuries the companies are referred to specifically as Marian companies (*Societas Beate Marie Virginis*), and all observed her special feast-days and named her as principal patron in the dedications of their statutes.[128] In 1329, communal legislation concerning lay company elections listed the companies of the Bigallo (the 'Societas Maioris Beate Marie Virginis'), the Misericordia (originally part of a Marian company), Orsanmichele, and the nine other Florentine laudesi companies, all Marian confraternities whose grouping here suggests that they were viewed as the principal lay guardians of the Virgin's cult in Florence.[129] The Mother of God had long been the symbol of the true faith, but now she was promoted as the special patron of the new lay companies, and she remained the dominant theme of laudesi devotion.[130] The champions of Marian devotion among the laity were the Dominican and Franciscan inquisitors, who promoted her divine maternity against a Cathar heresy that denied the divinity of the incarnate Christ, and emphasized her intercessory power with God.[131]

---

[126] Meersseman, *Ordo fraternitatis*, ii. 767, 770; Henderson, 'Piety and Charity', 24–5; S. Orlandi, 'Il VII centenario della predicazione di S. Pietro Martire a Firenze (1245–1945)', *Memorie domenicane*, NS, 21 (1946), 71–7.

[127] Stephens, 'Heresy', 29; Meersseman, *Ordo fraternitatis*, ii. 922–32, where it is shown that the statutes of many laudesi companies through the 16th c. record Peter's claim, 'principalis auctor extiti et inventor'.

[128] This is true even of companies that were strongly associated with their special patron saints; the Company of San Piero Martire referred to itself in 1325 as the 'Compagnia di Sancta Maria Novella delle laude' (SMN 291, fo. 23r), and in 1345 the Company of San Zanobi referred to itself as the 'Compagnia di Madonna Sancta Maria' (SZ 2182, fasc. 36, fo. 114ᵛ). With the shift to more specialized devotions emphasizing special patron saints in the 15th c., references to Mary in company titles tended to disappear in favour of special saints.

[129] The Misericordia was originally linked with the Marian company that was to become the laudesi at Santa Maria Novella. A copy of the document is preserved in the San Piero Martire records, SMN 311, fo. 13ʳ. On the significance of this document (and other copies in the records of the Bigallo, Orsanmichele, and Santa Maria Novella), see Henderson, 'Piety and Charity', 357 n. 70, and J. Rondeau, 'Lay Piety and Spirituality in the Late Middle Ages: The Confraternities of North-Central Italy, *ca*.1250 to 1348', Ph.D. thesis (Cornell University, 1988), 153–6.

[130] Meersseman, *Ordo fraternitatis*, ii. 927–32.

[131] Ibid., and Rouse, *Preachers, Florilegia, and Sermons*, 51–7.

The early lauda repertory reveals this anti-heretical devotion to the Virgin:[132]

Madonna sancta Maria	Madonna holy Mary
che n'ai mostrata la via	You who have showed us the way
ore scacia ogne resia	now drive away all heresy (and)
receve ki vol tornare.	receive who wishes to return.

(IV, 5–8)

Stella chiarita	Bright star
col grande splendore	with great splendour,
gente smarita	a lost people
traheste d'errore	you led out of error.

(X, 3–4)

Vergene pura parturisti	Virgin pure, you gave birth
e depoi partu permansisti	and after childbirth remained
vergene, perkè credesti	a virgin, because you believed
a Gabriel senza fallanza	in Gabriel without error.

(XI, 23–6)

The strongly pedagogical nature of these early texts suggests why papal indulgences were granted both for the singing *and* the hearing of laude, and indicate that lauda singing probably arose in the educative environment bequeathed by St Peter Martyr's preaching.

Most of the other mendicant orders (the Augustinians, Carmelites, Servites, and Sacchites) had settled in Florence by c. 1260, and new lay companies soon followed.[133] By the 1270s, changes in the Florentine lay companies fell in step with social, political, and economic changes of the commune. The threat of heresy had subsided by c. 1265, and there commenced a period of fertile alliance (c. 1260–1340s) between the triumphant papal cause of Guelphism and the mercantile interests of the city. During this period of considerable growth, Florentine bankers secured papal accounts, and mercantile activity and trading privileges expanded (notably into the newly-established south Italian kingdom of Charles of Anjou).[134] The constitutionally anchored guild system was consolidated through communal legislation as 'il bene del comune' became defined in terms of this rapid economic expansion. The new wealth of Florence spawned an unprecedented public building programme: work on the new Cathedral of Santa Maria del Fiore began under the supervision of the guilds, and the Palazzo Vecchio and major mendicant

[132] Examples are from the late 13th-cent. Cortona MS. (Cort); references are to Liuzzi, *La lauda*, i.
[133] Papi, 'Confraternite ed ordini', 725; A. Benvenuti Papi, 'Ordini mendicanti e città: Appunti per un' indagine, il caso di Firenze', in D. Maselli (ed.), *Da Dante a Cosimo I* (Pistoia, 1976), 129.
[134] Brucker, *Renaissance Florence*, 52–4; Becker, *Florence in Transition*, i. 28.

churches were built.[135] At the end of this period Florence was among the largest and wealthiest cities in Europe, and at no other time would the causes of church and state identify so easily with one another.

By the 1270s the Florentine lay companies had shed their combative nature and were adopting the new and specialized devotions of lauda singing and ritual scourging, while at the same time new companies were being organized around these activities. This change has been attributed by Meersseman to the general growth of lay religious aspirations, 'the fruit of their social and political education acquired in the corporations and urban democracies', and a commensurate need to manifest their piety with 'new, more spectacular paraliturgical practices'.[136]

The majority of Florentine laudesi companies were established in the two decades after c.1270. Some were newly founded, others derived from previous Marian companies, but all were devoted to singing the praises of Mary, Christ, and the saints. The disciplinati companies arose immediately after the greatest of the late medieval flagellant processions in 1260.[137] These spontaneous and often disruptive processions were outlawed by papal and communal authorities, and lay companies were organized along the broad lines of pre-existent company structures. As with the laudesi companies, some disciplinati groups were transformations of earlier companies (sometimes of older Marian congregations, or of laudesi companies so that lauda singing was retained among the disciplinati), while others were newly founded, especially during the fourteenth century, as this devotion seems to have spread more gradually than lauda singing.[138] By the mid-fourteenth century, laudesi and disciplinati companies were situated in numerous Florentine churches, and were often affiliated with one another for the purpose of procuring ecclesiastical privileges.[139]

Both types of lay company were organized according to the older, threefold model of the Marian companies: assisting at Mass, some form of active, participatory devotion, and receiving instruction through sermons. A good deal of mendicant preaching appears to have been directed specifically to the Marian companies (and their successors). Generally they were the exclusive audience of preachers during an

---

[135] R. Goldthwaite, *The Building of Renaissance Florence: An Economic and Social History* (Baltimore, 1980), 2.

[136] Meersseman, *Ordo fraternitatis*, ii. 589.

[137] Ibid. 451 ff.; Monti, *Le confraternite*, i. 199–202.

[138] J. Henderson, 'The Flagellant Movement and Flagellant Confraternites in Central Italy, 1260–1400', *Studies in Church History*, 15 (1978), 155–6. According to Meersseman, the first disciplinati companies organized in the wake of the great penitential processions of 1260 began to adopt marginal lauda-singing around the year 1267; *Ordo fraternitatis* i. 507.

[139] Ibid. 963; M. Papi, 'Confraternite ed ordini', 728, where he provides a map of the 13th- and 14th-c. lay companies in Florence.

evening *collatio* delivered throughout Lent or the octave of an important feast.[140] At various times throughout the church year, Fra Giordano directed his preaching to the Florentine laudesi companies at Santa Maria Novella (Dominican), the Cathedral, Orsanmichele (lay), and Santissima Annunziata (Servite).[141]

The mercantile guild structure provided the model of institutional organization: monthly meetings, the payment of dues, the election of officers (captains, chamberlains, and councillors) to short terms of office, provision for the burial of deceased members, social security for members and their families, and charitable activities.[142] The guild model also prescribed that the company statutes, especially those concerned with proper behaviour, were to be read aloud at the monthly meeting, and that no member might belong to another guild. As with other Florentine institutions of this period, the sacred was inseparable from the secular affairs of the guilds; each had its patron saint, attendant rituals and festivals, and special altars in certain churches. The religious companies adapted the guild model to the spiritual programme of the mendicants, who provided a strong liturgical dimension. Members were to attend Mass (often assisting) and to hear the sermon, especially during Lent. They were obliged to process and offer candles at specified altars, recite prayers and Masses for deceased members, confess and take communion regularly, and conduct private, usually evening, services in which the special devotional activity of the company (such as lauda-singing) was embedded in a liturgical framework of readings, prayers, recited or sung Latin liturgical items, and confession. A friar or priest was chosen to serve as a spiritual adviser, and the spiritual benefits of the order (prayers, Masses, *intra muros* burial) were extended to company members.

There were significant differences between laudesi and disciplinati, however. While both were rooted in mendicant spirituality, each was an institutional distillation of two opposing but complementary currents of that spirituality—praise and penance. St Thomas had defined the effect of devotion as joy at God's goodness and sadness at man's inadequacy. The dichotomy ran deep in Florentine spirituality of the time, between the human art of Giotto and the hieratic works of Orcagna, between the heavenly assurances of Domenico Cavalca (1270–1342) and the hellfire preaching of Jacopo Passavanti (1302–57), and between the dual loyalty

---

[140] Meersseman, *Ordo fraternitatis*, ii 940; iii. 1129–30.

[141] Delcorno, *Fra Giordano*, 71–7.

[142] Becker, *Florence in Transition*, ii. 11 ff.; in general: Mackenney, *Tradesmen and Traders*; Black, *Guilds and Civil Society*, where he notes that 'parish confraternities and merchant guilds formed the first cells of many village and urban communities' (p. 11); Doren, *Le arti fiorentine*; S. Thrupp, 'Gilds', in M. Postan, E. Rich, and E. Miller (eds.), *Cambridge Economic History* (Cambridge, 1963), iii. 230–80.

of the city to the gentle Queen of Heaven and the archpenitent John the Baptist.[143] The dichotomy is rooted in the psalms: the penitential psalms were a part of disciplinati liturgy, and in the Vulgate the praise psalms resound with 'laudare', often cited as the etymological source of the word lauda.[144] To the usually joyful lauda repertory, the disciplinati contributed a penitential vision, especially in the lament and passion laude sung by laudesi and disciplinati alike during Holy Week.[145]

Whereas the gaze of the laudesi was fixed on their human and humane saints situated in a celestial court, the disciplinati outlook was Christo-centric and world-renouncing. Their purpose, as frequently set forth in their statutes, was to 'fare memoria della passione del nostro signore Yhesu Christo crocifisso'.[146] Their practices seem closer to the spirit of monasticism: their elaborate services borrowed heavily from the monastic Latin liturgy,[147] their corporate life was more strict and self-contained, and their secretive services reveal a greater concern with their own inner spiritual development than with public acts of ritual and charity. Clad in hooded garments that concealed their individual identity, members performed 'la disciplina' in a self-renouncing and isolating darkness.

The laudesi were more public in almost every respect. The core of their services was the vernacular lauda, heard and understood by all, and communally addressed to a community of saints. Though their ferial services were usually conducted in a private oratorio, their major festal services were heralded throughout the city and celebrated at the altars of the major churches, the central theatres of public devotion. Their charitable aspect was strong: they distributed alms (often bread or grain) to the poor at regular intervals, and often managed a hospital, a hospice for widows or the elderly, or dowries for poor or orphaned young women. In this respect, the laudesi companies realized most successfully the friars' urban ministry, which sought to tap the 'mental habits' of a merchant society to the broad advantage of that society.

The contrast between laudesi and disciplinati spirituality was reflected in their membership. The disciplinati tended to be more élitist and exclusively male. They drew members from throughout the city, at-tracting younger and upwardly mobile men primarily from among the patriciate.[148] The communal rites of the laudesi attracted a more local and heterogeneous segment of Florentine society, the shopkeepers and local tradesmen, as well as a small number of more prominent citizens. The

---

[143] Meiss, *Painting in Florence and Siena*, 84.   [144] Varanini, *Laude dugentesche*, ix.

[145] For a detailed and sensitive analysis of selected themes, esp. those of death and penance, among the lauda texts, see Rondeau, 'Lay Piety and Spirituality', ch. 6.

[146] Meersseman, *Ordo fraternitatis*, ii. 634.

[147] C. Barr, 'Lauda Singing and the Tradition of the Disciplinati *Mandato*: A Reconstruction of the Two Texts of the Office of Tenebrae', *L'Ars nova italiana del Trecento*, 4 (Certaldo, 1978), 21–44.

[148] Weissman, *Ritual Brotherhood*, 74–5.

male members were generally older, married heads of households, and wives were usually admitted to non-voting membership. While the artisan/shopkeeper remained the core of laudesi membership, the varying wealth and status of the companies were reflected in the shifting proportions of membership drawn from the outer extremes of the social spectrum. A small company in a working-class neighbourhood, like the Company of San Frediano, might admit certain numbers of *sottoposti* (wage-earners who subcontracted to the guilds, and were denied the right to form guilds). The membership lists of Orsanmichele or the Company of San Zanobi, on the other hand, show a significant number of prominent Florentine family names, and the high offices in the larger laudesi companies formed a part of the Florentine office-holding network. The officers of Orsanmichele included the chronicler Dino Compagni, Francesco Barberino, Franco Sacchetti, and Dante's father-in-law (a Donati), and of San Zanobi, Antonio Squarcialupi and the poets Antonio Pucci and Feo Belcari. In the politicized environment of the late fifteenth-century lay company, the greatest of Florentine citizens, Lorenzo de' Medici, held offices in the laudesi companies at the Cathedral, Santa Maria del Carmine, and Santo Spirito.

The items listed in a 1383 inventory of the Cathedral laudesi company of San Zanobi offer perhaps the most revealing testimony to the nature of the relationship between a laudesi company and the society in which it flourished. Among the company's possessions, intended to be borne forth in processions and displayed at its altar during special feast days, were a gold star with escutcheons of the twenty-one guilds, and escutcheons bearing the arms of the company, the commune, liberty crowned, the Guelph party, the king of France, the Church, Pope Urban V, and the 'Popolo'.[149] The company offered to its members a share of what the wealthiest and most powerful Florentines enjoyed—the opportunity to publicly define their worth and aspirations in terms that embraced the sacred and secular life of the city.

---

[149] SZ 2176, fasc. 12, fo. 45ʳ.

2

Lauda–Singing and the Laudesi Company in Florence

ORIGINS AND OVERVIEW

THE early history of institutional lauda-singing in Florence belongs to the second half of the thirteenth century. Most of the laudesi companies (and there were at least twelve by the fourteenth century) were founded in the two decades between 1270 and 1290, and had either developed directly from, or were modelled upon, the older Marian congregations established by St Peter Martyr in 1244–5.

The manner in which lauda-singing developed during the years between 1244 and c. 1270 is unclear. The Marian and anti-heretical nature of many early lauda texts suggests that the earliest confraternity laude were composed immediately in the wake of inquisition activity like that of St Peter Martyr,[1] and then became an expanded and specialized devotion as heresy declined in the late thirteenth century (by c. 1265 in Florence). Two early laude ('orazioni') were coupled with papal indulgences, which may well have been a factor in the spread of lauda-singing.[2] The chief agent in the confraternal adoption of this new devotion may have been St Peter Martyr himself, but the cultivation, and perhaps popularization, of the lauda as a musico-poetic form was more likely fostered by the Franciscans. They were generally more inclined than the Dominicans to borrow from the popular culture in which the lauda certainly arose, and while the Dominicans excelled at teaching and organizing, the medieval friar/lauda poets, such as Jacopone da Todi (c. 1230–1306) and Ugo Panziera (1265–1330), were Franciscans.[3]

Dramatic changes in the poetic form of the lauda also suggest the rapid development of confraternal lauda-singing during the third quarter of the thirteenth century. The poetic forms of the earliest laude, appearing throughout the thirteenth century, are extremely varied in form and

---

[1] See Varanini, *Laude dugentesche, passim*, and all 13th- and 14th-c. laudari, in which Marian laude are predominant.

[2] Ibid. 23–7 ('Rayna possentissima'), 27 ('Vergine gloriosa').

[3] See Fleming, *An Introduction to Franciscan Literature*, 107–9.

style, though related by virtue of their lyrical, devotional, and vernacular qualities. These early laude appear to have been composed either for private devotion or for peripheral, sporadic use in confraternity services.[4] During a formative period in Tuscan poetry, between the 1250s and 1270s, the ballata appeared in the Italian lyric, during which time '. . . the elementary early lauda meters . . . were being enriched by ballata forms suited to choral recitation by the new mendicant-inspired confraternities'.[5]

The oldest extant corpus of Italian texts set to music are the laude of Cortona, Biblioteca Comunale, MS 91, the first section of which was compiled sometime between 1260 and 1297 for use by the 'Fraternità di Santa Maria delle Laude', associated with the Cortonese church of San Francesco.[6] A striking feature of its forty-six laude is not so much the flexible adoption of the ballata scheme, but its pervasive adoption, here and throughout the lauda repertory of the next century. This clearly indicates a widespread, uniform, and institutional practice, the dissemination of which might easily occur through the mobile network of mendicant convents.

Dissemination of the lauda also must have occurred along mercantile channels. Florentine merchants of the upper guilds, frequently office-holders in the laudesi companies, traded and travelled widely, and of necessity communicated often with their representatives who resided in other mercantile centres.[7] The laudesi companies acted with both the independence of a mercantile *compagnia* and the motivation of a religious house in lending and borrowing service-books among themselves for copying. The Company of San Piero Martire recorded an expense in 1323 for the separation of a fascicle of motets to be sent to the laudesi company of Santa Caterina at the Dominican convent in Pisa, and another in 1337 to retrieve a laudario from Pistoia.[8] The prominence of the mendicant churches, the strength of commerce, and, related to both, the strength of confraternal life in the city destined Florence to become and remain the most favoured climate for the lauda.

Although we shall probably never know who, if any single person, was responsible for the graft of ballata onto lauda, three candidates are

---

[4] Varanini, *Laude dugentesche*, pp. xii–xv, 3–41; G. Cattin, *Music of the Middle Ages* (Cambridge, 1986), 146–7.

[5] V. Moleta, *The Early Poetry of Guittone d'Arezzo* (London, 1976), 9. Not only did the ballata admit choral participation, but in the context of the laudesi companies' liturgical services, its responsorial performance may have been perceived as imitative of the more sophisticated, soloistic liturgical chants.

[6] Varanini, *Laude dugentesche*, 54–5. See also Varanini, L. Banfi, and A. C. Burgio (eds.), *Laude cortonesi dal secolo XIII al XV* (Florence, 1981), i, pt. 1, 40–1, 64.

[7] I. Origo, *The Merchant of Prato* (New York, 1957), pp. 98 ff.

[8] SMN 292, fo. 23ᵛ: 'demo dì xxiii d'otobre [1323] per fare aseprare moteti per ma[n]dare a la cho[m]pagnia di Sancta Caterina a Pisa . . . L. 1 s. 2'; fo. 53ʳ [1337]: 'demo per richogliere uno libro di laude ch'era [im]pegnio a Pistoia il quale libro si marrì [sic] già più tempo . . . L. 1 s. 6.'

favoured, the only known names in an otherwise anonymous late thirteenth-century repertory: a certain Garzo, and the poets Jacopone da Todi and Guittone d'Arezzo (c. 1235–1294).[9] What these three names do reveal, however, is the characteristic impossibility of distinguishing between lay and clerical initiative in the development of the lauda repertoire. Garzo was a layman (possibly a notary), and both Jacopone and Guittone experienced dramatic mid-life conversions (in 1269 and c. 1265, respectively) and joined religious orders.[10] The special role of lauda-singing in confraternal devotion was prepared by a decree of the Council of Bordeaux (1255), which reveals the church's concern with the place of lay companies within the ecclesiastical organization. The Council enumerated the possible duties and functions of the confraternities, including the provision for offices of the dead and vigils. In fact, evening lauda vigils ('vigilie alle laude'), often performed in commemoration of the dead, became the primary arena of confraternal lauda-singing.[11]

The third quarter of the thirteenth century emerges in this discussion as a period of vital interaction between the expressive impulses of organized lay devotion, a nascent vernacular lyric, and the forces of ecclesiastical organization. From this encounter, the lauda-ballata quickly developed into the lyrical expression and characteristic insignia of urban confraternal devotion.

The earliest known laudesi company was founded in 1267 at the Dominican church of Camporegio in Siena.[12] The statutes of the company are preserved in a letter from Bishop Tommaso Fusconi to his diocese, in which he announces the founding of the company:

Since, in the house of Dominican brothers at Siena, at Campo Regio, by our will and with our consent a fraternity has been founded in honour of blessed Mary ever virgin and of blessed Dominic our father, because of the devotion of its members and the usefulness and many benefits which we believe may arise from it, with God's help, we decree that this fraternity shall bear the names of blessed Mary and blessed Dominic, and with our authority we confirm its existence, as also we confirm its statutes, authenticating them with our seal . . .[13]

The general format of the statutes was borrowed from the merchant guilds, and was to remain the basic model of laudesi statutes until the

[9] The question is examined in Varanani, *Laude dugentesche*, pp. xxiv– xxxiii.

[10] L. Banfi, 'Garzo laudese', *Giornale italiano di filologia*, NS, 7 (1976), 137–53; Moleta, *The Early Poetry of Guittone D'Arezzo*, 9; Jacopone da Todi, *Laude*, ed. F. Mancini (Rome, 1974), 345.

[11] Cited in V. Bartholomaies, *Le origini della poesia drammatica* (Bologna, 1924), 197; G. D. Mansi, *Sacrorum conciliorum, nova et amplissima collectio* (Florence, 1759, repr. Graz, 1961), xxiii (1225–68), col. 865: '. . . vel ad sepulturas vel vigilias, seu ad aliud officium defunctorum . . .'.

[12] Meersseman, *Ordo fraternitatis*, ii. 954–8, 1029–34; id., 'Nota sull'orgine delle Compagnie dei Laudesi (Siena, 1267)', *Rivista di storia della chiesa in Italia*, 17 (1963), 395–405. The translations used here are from Cattin, *Music in the Middle Ages*, 183–5.

[13] There follows a twenty-five-day indulgence, then the statutes. Ed. Meersseman, *Ordo fraternitatis*, ii. 1029.

sixteenth century. In order, the Sienese statutes prescribe the election of
officers (rectors, councillors, and chamberlains, to six-month terms),
the structure of the meetings, and the execution of processions (on
twelve designated feast days), prayers (especially the *Pater noster* and the
Ave Maria), and alms-giving. The principal activity of the meetings is
clear:

We ordain that every day, in the evening, at the hour of Compline or a little
before, according to the season, a meeting shall take place in the house of the
Dominicans at Campo Regio, for the singing and hearing of laude, and that
there may be a brief sermon on such occasions, if the prior of the Dominicans
thinks it appropriate, especially in Lent . . .

We further ordain that on the second Sunday of the month, early in the
morning, the members of the fraternity shall meet at Campo Regio to listen to
laude, and to hear Mass and a sermon. For the same purpose and at the same time
the members shall meet in the same place every Monday following [the second
Sunday] and shall sing a requiem for the souls of dead members of the fraternity
and their relatives . . .[14]

In a characteristic and influential document of the period, the purpose of
the confraternity was confirmed by a letter of indulgence from another
Sienese bishop, Bernardo Gallerani, in 1273:

Since, then, beloved children, you continue every day to sing laude to blessed
Mary, mother of Christ and ever virgin, and to blessed Dominic (from whom
your fraternal community takes its name), and to the whole company of heaven,
and since we too wish to share in such wonderful laude . . ., with the aim of
increasing devotion among the faithful who sing praises [*laudantes*] to the
mother of God . . ., for every day in which, according to statute and your
custom, you gather together in peace to raise up your laude to God, we allow
you one hundred days' indulgence.[15]

A remarkable contemporary account of Sienese lauda-singing was written
around 1288 by the Dominican Fra Recupero d'Arezzo, in his biography
of the famous Dominican preacher, the blessed Ambrogio Sansedoni
(d. 1268):

In his city of Siena, where he [Sansedoni] usually lived, the fruits of the action of
the Holy Spirit are particularly evident, and they have there confraternities
[*congregationes*] of outstanding men, even laymen. Some of them take as their
aim the singing of praises [laude] to God; these are sung every day with
remarkable devotion in the religious houses (especially and above all among his
fellow Dominicans), even by boys, whose keep is paid for and who are trained
to sing these laude. This custom has spread from there [Siena] to several other
cities . . . [there follows a brief account of the charitable and disciplinati

---

[14] Ed. Meersseman, *Ordo fraternitatis*, ii. 1032.   [15] Ibid. 1039.

fraternities also activated at this time] . . . All of these were begun or redoubled in the time of the aforementioned father [Sansedoni].[16]

Significant here is the maintenance of a *schola* of trained boy singers (the Florentine laudesi companies maintained a similar institution), the spread of lauda singing to other cities (with the implication that it originated as a Sienese custom), the prominent role of the Dominicans concerning the institutional aspects of lauda-singing, and the proximity of mendicant preaching and lauda-singing. Also interesting is the apparent pre-eminence, in Fra Recupero's view, of the laudesi over the other types of lay company in the city.

Fra Recupero's account also points to an essential aspect of lauda-singing, that is, its spontaneous origin and rapid dissemination as a vital form of lay devotion. The surviving documents, at least in Florence, shed only a half light on the original character and practice of this 'mira devotione', for they date primarily from a period (after the early fourteenth century) when the inclinations of friars and merchants had combined to steer the devotion into a strong institutional and professional framework. What began as the lyrical expression of amateur company members soon became the specialized activity of professional, freelancing singers, but the character and function of lauda-singing remained essentially devotional.[17] When in 1470 the Company of Santa Croce reaffirmed its commitment to the 'ancient custom' of lauda-singing on feast days, it was because 'through these devotions a great spiritual and temporal utility is generated and acquired'.[18] Like other spiritual exercises sanctioned by the Church, it was understood to strengthen relationships between human and divine personalities, to tap the divine nature to the benefit of the human soul ('per rimedio dell'anima').

Something of this early, unrehearsed spirit of the devotion infuses Giovanni Villani's early fourteenth-century account of how lauda-singing arose at Orsanmichele, the greatest of the Florentine laudesi companies:

In that year [1292], on the 3rd of July, there began to be manifested great and obvious miracles in the city of Florence by a figure [*figura*] of the Virgin Mary painted on a pilaster of the loggia of Orto San Michele, where the grain is sold . . . but the friars preachers [Dominicans] and minors [Franciscans], out of envy or another reason, did not believe them, wherefore they have fallen into great disgrace with the Florentines . . . out of custom and devotion, a number of laity sang laude before this figure, and the fame of these miracles, for the merits

[16] Meersseman has twice edited and discussed this document, first in 'Nota sull'orgine,' 395, where he gives Sansedoni's death date as 1286, and in *Ordo fraternitatis*, ii. 955–6, where it is given correctly as 1268.

[17] This transition from unpaid, in-house singers to paid, freelancing laudesi is described in more detail in Ch. 4.

[18] See App. 1, doc. 22.

of Our Lady, so increased that people came from all over Tuscany in pilgrimage, just as they come now for all the feasts of Our Lady, bringing various wax images, for great miracles accomplished, wherefore a great part of this loggia, and around this pilaster, is crowded with these wax images.

The remainder of Villani's description alludes to the subsequent prosperity and organization of the Company:

. . . and since [its membership] was the greater part of the *buona gente* of Florence, the state of this company so improved that the many benefits and alms of bequests for the poor amounted to more than 6,000 lire, and thus it [the company] continues to our day, without acquiring any possessions.[19]

In the late sixteenth century, by which time the Company of Sant' Agnese had abandoned the ancient devotion altogether, the company officers gazed over nearly three and a half centuries to recall their institution's origin as a *Societas fidei* during the era of St Peter Martyr's Florentine preaching. The following passage from the company's 1584 statutes refers to the same transition from an activity to an institution, via the receipt of alms and bequests, as that experienced by Orsanmichele:

The venerable and religious company of the standard entitled Madonna Santa Maria delle Laude et Santa Agnese di Firenze . . . had its beginning around the year of the Lord 1245, and was called 'of the standard' because the men and women who belonged to that [company], wearing the sign of a white and red cross on the right shoulder, followed the standard of the Sacred Holy Inquisition whenever there arose the need, to help the Sacred Holy Church in the eradication of heretics and heresy, which at that time had sprung up in this city of Florence. And besides this, because some of them, out of devotion, met in the said church of the Carmine to sing *laude spirituali*, they took the name 'delle laude', and because they received alms and bequests, it was decided that the captains and officials should meet on certain prescribed days to conduct works of mercy and distribute alms . . .[20]

Like an elaborate reliquary intended to preserve and celebrate its contents, the complex liturgy and administration in which lauda-singing gradually became embedded both reveals and obscures its essential nature.

The programme of the early Marian confraternities founded by St Peter Martyr was threefold: to assist at Mass, receive instruction by sermon, and honour the Virgin.[21] The Florentine laudesi companies, which were either descended from or modelled upon these earlier congregations, retained this programme and adopted lauda-singing as a special means of honouring the Virgin. In his *Decameron* (*c.* 1350–2), Boccaccio alludes to these activities in his satirical depiction of Friar Puccio, a lay member of

[19] G. Villani, *Cronica*, ed. Dragomanni, Bk. VII, ch. 154, pp. 362–3.
[20] App. 1, doc. 1.   [21] Meersseman, *Ordo fraternitatis*, ii. 929.

the Franciscan order, and a 'simple-minded man [who] always said his Our Fathers and went to Mass, attended sermons, and never failed to show up when laude were being sung by laymen'.[22]

The *Societas Sanctissime virginis Marie*, founded in 1244 by Peter Martyr at the Florentine Dominican convent, was not a laudesi company at that time.[23] According to Meersseman, by 1267 the company had split into two. The *Compagnia Maggiore della Vergine* assumed administration of the Bigallo hospital,[24] while the *Societas Sanctae Mariae virginis ecclesiae Sanctae Mariae Novellae* remained situated at the Dominican convent; by 1288 the latter had become a laudesi company.[25] The Marian congregations at Santa Maria del Carmine (Carmelite) and Santa Croce (Franciscan) underwent a similar transformation, adopting lauda-singing sometime between their foundation in 1245 and 1244 (respectively) and the earliest reference to lauda-singing in 1280 and 1282 (respectively). The earliest reference to a Florentine laudesi company is that associated with the Servite church of Santissima Annunziata. The *Societas beatae Mariae Virginis* was founded in 1264 by San Filippo Benizi, and by 1273 had adopted lauda-singing and was called the *Societas Laudum Ecclesie S. Marie*. The Florentine laudesi companies whose documents provide explicit dates of foundation appeared during this same period (*c.* 1270–90): at the Sacchite convent of San Gilio (Egidio) in 1278, the Cathedral in 1281, and at Orsanmichele in 1291. The company at the Augustinian convent of Santo Spirito, proprietors of the famous laudario B. R. 18 (Mgl[1]), is first mentioned in 1322. In 1329 there were laudesi companies at the collegiate church of San Lorenzo (where the great fourteenth-century Florentine musician Francesco Landini later served as organist) and the other major Dominican convent of San Marco. A company founded at the ancient Cistercian priory of San Frediano was not a laudesi company at its founding in 1324, but by *c.*1370 had adopted lauda-singing. A laudesi company was founded at the Humiliati church of Ognissanti in 1336, but few traces of it survive. In sum, all but one Florentine laudesi company arose during the period 1270–1340, and the majority of these were either founded as laudesi, or underwent transformation from an older type of Marian company to a laudesi company, during the first two decades of this period.

On 29 March 1329, the captains of all the laudesi companies in Florence collaborated in a petition to the city concerning the management

---

[22] Day 3, 4th story; trans. M. Musa and P. Bondanella (New York, 1982), 185.

[23] A prevalent misconception; see Monti, *Le confraternite*, i. 155, and Weissman, *Ritual Brotherhood*, 44 n. 3.

[24] Meersseman, *Ordo fraternitatis*, ii. 1034 (doc. 21), and 923. This company was later joined to another, the Misericordia, and still functions in Florence as a hospital.

[25] Ibid. 923–4, 1042–3, and 976, where Meersseman asserts that this laudesi company was the first in Florence, but offers no evidence.

of bequests.[26] The companies are all listed according to church of affiliation: Orsanmichele, Santa Maria Novella, Santa Croce, Santo Spirito, Santa Maria del Carmine, Santissima Annunziata, Santa Reparata (the old Cathedral), San Lorenzo, Sant'Egidio, and San Marco. The document testifies to the contemporary perception of these companies as a distinct and self-conscious type of lay company with shared interests, and their central devotion to the Virgin Mary suggests a collective self-image as the principal lay guardians of the Florentine cult of the Virgin.

All the known Florentine laudesi companies were founded before the fifteenth century, most during the period of rapid economic expansion (c. 1270–1340) outlined in the previous chapter. Disciplinati groups and various charitable and craft companies continued to appear in the late fourteenth and fifteenth centuries, but the majority of the laudesi companies survived into the sixteenth century to be regarded as the most ancient and venerable institutions of Florentine lay devotion. Only the company at Ognissanti appears not to have outlived the fourteenth century. There is no clear record of the Company of San Marco after c. 1430, and the San Lorenzo company was suppressed by the city in 1432. The rest of the companies maintained their lauda-singing devotions, primarily through bequests, into the early sixteenth century. Only at the two wealthiest companies, Orsanmichele and San Piero Martire, did the expensive practice of polyphonic lauda-singing survive the profound upheaval of those years to be cultivated in the changed world of the Medici principate and the Counter-Reformation.

The lay companies were designed to endure, to provide stability in a society that offered little of it to the individual. Their resilience was tried by the events of the 1340s—economic contraction brought on by the failure of major Florentine banks, and the Black Death, which struck Florence in the spring of 1348 and swiftly killed two-thirds of one of Europe's largest urban populations. It was in part her size that enabled Florence to stage a recovery that was beyond the crippled means of the other Tuscan cities; it is likely that many of the laudesi companies in a city like Siena suffered the same fate as the monumental expansion of the Sienese Cathedral, which was halted and never resumed.

The construction of the Florentine Cathedral did continue, and so did the many Florentine lay companies, but they were stretched to their

---

[26] There are several extant versions of the document, one reportedly from the Orsanmichele records, ed. in La Sorsa, *La compagnia d'Or San Michele* (Trani, 1902), 208–9 (partial transcription, and La Sorsa provides no exact source); and others in the records of the Company of San Piero Martire, SMN 311, fos. 13^r–14^v, the *diplomatico* of Santa Maria Nuova (with which the church of San Gilio was associated) in the Archivio del Bigallo, vol. 1669, fo. 6^r, under the above date, and in a 1330 addition to the statutes of the Company of San Zanobi, SZ 2170, fasc. 1, fo 12^v, ed. in L. Orioli, *Le confraternite medievali e il problema della povertà* (Rome, 1984), 35–6 (cap. XXXVI).

limits to provide relief during and after the plague. In addition to the difficult task of continuing to satisfy the obligations of bequests (including lauda-singing during vigils), the laudesi companies provided their members (and, for a modest fee, non-members) the most critical of services at this time—a dignified burial with the proper prayers, Masses, candles, and burial paraphernalia.[27]

The small Company of San Frediano, situated in a working-class neighbourhood in the *Oltrarno*, subsidized burial services by the hundreds during 1348–9, then appears to have collapsed for the next five years. Recovery was underway when debit–credit entries recommenced in 1356, and between 1367 and 1373 the company purchased the lectern, laudario, and altar paraphernalia required for laudesi devotion. The larger laudesi companies appear to have continued their musical activities without serious disruption. In fact, it was probably during the wake of the plague that the survival of the lay companies was assured by the bequests of Florentines, many of whom died in a state of extreme guilt and penance. The companies were also favoured as executors of testaments, since there was little assurance that individual relatives or friends would survive to oversee the proper execution of a will. The lay companies could always summon from their varied ranks the business and legal acumen for such a potentially complicated task, and the business-minded Florentines, no less careful with their *post-mortem* investments, had by this time lost some respect for the friars in matters of money. For the companies, bequests became the same vital source of material security that they had long been for ecclesiastical institutions, and it is very likely that the Company of San Frediano wanted to capture a small part of the bequest market when it decided to adopt lauda-singing as soon after the plague as its resources permitted.

STRUCTURE AND PRACTICE

The most comprehensive portrait of company life is provided by a company's statutes.[28] These prescribe the institution of officers, the conduct of members, and the activities and customs of the company.

The highest-ranking officers were the captains (*capitani, rettori*) who were elected by a carefully scrutinized body of voting members (usually twenty-five to thirty 'buoni huomini'). The captains in turn elected six to eight councillors (*consiglieri*) and two treasurers (*camarlinghi*) who kept the company account books and held keys to the cash boxes. In the fourteenth century it became customary to retain a special accountant

---

[27] An excellent study of the subject is Strocchia, 'Burials in Renaissance Florence, 1350–1500'.
[28] App. II contains an annotated list of the various types of books kept by the laudesi companies.

(*sindaco*) to manage the financial and legal aspects of the expanding business of bequests, and to pay a company notary (*notaio*). A sacristan (*sagrestano*) was either selected from among the membership or hired from the host church to prepare for liturgical services. In the fifteenth century, a lawyer (*avvocato*) and doctor (*medico*) were frequently added to the company payroll.

The captains also elected a priest or friar from the host church to serve as the company's spiritual adviser. This *priore* (or *corettore*), whose authority was confined to doctrinal matters, was required for the administration of the sacraments, especially communion (which members were required to take several times a year), confession (which took place every evening at the conclusion of a lauda service), and extreme unction (to sick or dying members).

The officers, together with the voting block of the membership, usually met twice each month to conduct business, either 'sotto le volte' (beneath the vaults) of the church, in the refectory, in a sacristy or oratory hall, or in a private residence owned by the company or a member. These meetings usually included prayers, readings, and sometimes a Mass conducted at an altar in the meeting-room.

Members were required, above all, to avoid the greatest social vices of the day—violence and usury. Scandalous behaviour, such as public drinking, gaming, or fighting, brought correction, and, after a third admonition, expulsion. The company reputation was to be further guarded through secrecy: members were prohibited from fraternizing with expelled members, from divulging company affairs, or from joining another lay company.[29] The officers, particularly the captains, commanded obedience and respect. Those seeking admission had to be at least fourteen to sixteen years old, to be sponsored by an active member, and to be free from scandal. Women appear to have been excluded from administrative affairs, but they were admitted (usually through kinship) to a passive role in the company's cultic life.

The *raison d'être* of the laudesi company was its active life, which embraced both ceremonial and charitable activities. Alms (*limosine*) in the form of food or money, which were often provided by bequests, were distributed on designated feast days to the poor, to widows, and to prisoners. The provision and management of dowries for poor or orphan girls became an increasingly important business during the fifteenth and sixteenth centuries. The company offered considerable material benefits: medical care, sick calls from company officers (*visitatori*) and priest, welfare for poor members and the families of deceased members, burial services for the latter, and a share in the legal and

---

[29] The latter prohibition applied also to members of mercantile *compagnie*; Origo, *The Merchant of Prato*, 104–5.

financial security of the company (for example, short-term loans). In exchange, members paid monthly dues of two or three denari, and as much for the candles they were required to offer at liturgical services.[30]

The ceremonial life of the laudesi companies provided the framework for their most characteristic activity. Throughout the republican period, company statutes describe three primary types of service: annual, to celebrate designated liturgical feasts (festal); monthly, on Sunday after Mass, primarily for processing; daily, in the evening, for singing laude (ferial). Lauda-singing, in varying degrees, was a part of all three services. Liturgical services, involving Masses, prayers, and readings, were also conducted at the bimonthly business meetings, and the semi-annual installation of new officers, and for special requiem services (*luminarie*) for deceased members. Special laude *pro defunctis* were probably performed during these requiem services, which were conducted at a company-owned sepulchre in the church. The laudesi companies also maintained a weekly *scuola* on Sunday afternoons, during which elected teachers (*insegnatori*) taught and rehearsed laude.

Annual Feasts

The laudesi companies celebrated the annual feasts of the liturgical *cursus* with a vigil service on the eve before the feast, attendance at Mass and preaching the morning of the feast, and, on the most solemn occasions, another vigil that evening.[31] The evening vigil, always called a 'lauda vigil' (*vigilia alle laude*), involved the singing of laude proper to the feast, the offering of candles, prayers, readings, and a brief sermon by the prior, all performed either at the church altar patronized by the company, or another selected as more appropriate for the feast. Special liturgical paraphernalia marked the solemnity of the occasion. In 1326, the *camarlingo* of the Company of San Zanobi was instructed to 'prepare the larger lectern, the better altar-cloth, and the candlestick with figures' for special feast-days.[32] Then on the vigils of all the prescribed feasts

[30] Florenitine money was based on both a silver and gold currency. Silver: 1 lire = 20 soldi; 1 soldo = 12 denari; the gold florin varied in value from 3.1 lire (*c.*1325), to 3.8 (*c.*1400), to 6.7 (1500). G. Brucker, *Florence: 1138–1737* (London, 1984), 71. In 1427, the annual rent on a small house was about 3 or 4 florins.

[31] *Vigilia* could refer either to a vigil in the strict sense (the evening before a feast) or generally to an evening service. A 1288 statute of the Company of Sant'Agnese required that 'in tutte le feste di nostra Donna se facesse vigilia due volte; cioè la vigilia dela festa e la sera dela festa.' Ed. A. Schiaffini, *Testi fiorentini del dugento e dei primi del trecento* (Florence, 1954), 61. In a 1304 letter of indulgence to the Company of San Piero Martire, the evening services are generally referred to as vigils ('. . . que cum de sero fit, vigilia appellatur'); the document is edited in Meersseman, *Ordo fraternitatis*, ii 1047–8.

[32] The statute is edited in Orioli, *La confraternite medievali*, 32.

. . . the laude should be sung . . . that is, everyone should be ordered *a coro* [on benches before the altar] holding lighted candles. And on these evenings the Ave Maria should first be sung.[33]

The members then came forth one by one to offer their candles at the altar as the laude were sung. A soloist (or several soloists) sang the strophes from the lectern in alternation with members, who sang the choral refrains. The officers, who were seated near the foot of the lectern, remained kneeling during the singing. All this activity was directed to a devotional image (usually a painting of the Madonna) placed upon the altar. The 1297 statutes of the Company of Orsanmichele required them to

. . . conduct the solemn vigils of lauda-singing before the figure of the Virgin, each member present [holding] a lighted candle as long as the lauda-singing lasts, each evening of the vigils of these feasts [a list follows].[34]

The most important Florentine feasts, like those of the Virgin or St John the Baptist (the city's patron saint), called forth a city-wide procession. Dressed in robes bearing the company's insignia, members processed with their standard (*gonfalone*) and holiest images, and company payments to both lauda-singers and instrumentalists on these occasions indicate that music was often an integral element of such processions.

These solemn feasts were also the occasion for special decorations in the church, such as those described in the 1485 statutes of the laudesi at Santa Croce:

We desire that on the vigil of the Assumption of Our Lady the flaming star be placed in the middle of the church, and laude are to be sung on that evening, according to a good and ancient custom.[35]

Most laudesi companies hired extra singers for feast day services, and the wealthier companies of Orsanmichele, San Zanobi, and San Piero Martire hired instrumentalists as well.

The calendar of annual feasts for a given company was determined by its community of patron saints. Common to all were the major feasts of Christ (Nativity, Epiphany, Easter, Pentecost), the Virgin (Nativity, Annunciation, Purification, and Assumption), John the Baptist, and All Saints. Various of the feasts for the twelve apostles were also celebrated, often as a name-day of an individual who left a bequest to the company. To this were added local Florentine saints (St Reparata and St Zenobius, the first bishop of Florence), saints of the religious order with which the company was affiliated (Dominic, Francis, etc.), and those unique to the

---

[33] The statute is edited in Orioli, *La confraternite medievali*, 24.
[34] Ed. in A. Castellani, *Nuovi testi fiorentini del dugento* (Florence, 1952), 669.
[35] App. I, doc. 2.

company (like St Agnes). The special company affiliation with saints like St Zenobius at the Cathedral of St Agnes at the Carmine was determined by the presence of those saints' relics within the church.

Bequests

The annual services of the laudesi companies multiplied during the fourteenth and fifteenth centuries as the lay companies became favoured recipients of bequests providing for commemorative services.[36] These services were usually celebrated on the anniversary of the benefactor's death, or on the feast of the saint for whom the benefactor was named.[37]

The terms of bequests to the laudesi companies specified three types of commemorative service: a lauda vigil, an anniversary meal (*pietanza*), and an anniversary Mass (*rinovale*).[38] In the latter two the role of the lay brothers was primarily administrative and supportive. The company arranged the meal for the *pietanza*, and the company captains joined the clerics of the church in an anniversary meal that was an invocation of the Last Supper, as well as compensation for the clerics' prayers and services on behalf of the deceased. The *pietanza* also assured the proper execution of the *rinovale*, which immediately preceded the meal. Company officers also attended the Mass, which included the singing of the penitential psalms by priests or friars, a formal procession with lighted candles through the cloister (or to the Baptistery of the Cathedral), and a Requiem or 'Gregorian' Mass.

The 1428 statutes of the Cathedral company of San Zanobi provide a detailed account of a commemorative lauda vigil. The large lectern was to be placed before the company altar (dedicated to the Virgin) where the laude were sung, and the candles on the lectern lit. Members were to gather at the sound of the company bell in the bell tower (nicknamed 'ferrantina') and say twenty-five *Pater nosters* and *Ave Marias*, and then after twelve final tolls of the bell, the candles were distributed: three to the chaplain of the company, two to the captains and relatives of the deceased, and one each to all others present. The candles were lit as the laude were begun, and the laudesi were to perform those laude 'which

---

[36] On the political consequences for the lay companies of increased benefactions and testamentary gifts in the wake of the Black Death, see Becker, 'Aspects of Lay Piety', 177 ff., and on a parallel trend in the Florentine churches see Gaston, 'Liturgy and Patronage in San Lorenzo', 132, where he observes that 'when a church's economy had become to a degree dependent on pious donations tied to the liturgy, the attraction of more patronage was an obvious direction to take'. Precisely the same may be said of the laudesi companies during the 14th and 15th cc., although the trend pre-dates the Black Death; an Orsanmichele book of *testamenti* for the years 1340–7 (OSM 470) records over 600 bequests (some of which directly benefited the company, all of which were to be managed by the company).
[37] Strocchia, 'Burials in Renaissance Florence', 349. The relationship between bequests to the laudesi companies and the rise of the professional laudese is discussed in Ch. 4 of the present study.
[38] Ibid. 330 ff.

were composed for the said devotion, and to finish [them] in the accustomed manner'. The chaplain, assisted by three priests (with two candles each), then sang the '*Dies ire*, etc.', after which they announced the individual on whose behalf the vigil was being conducted, and recommended his soul with the '*De profundis*, etc., et l'oratione'. There followed a general confession and announcement of indulgences granted for participation in the vigil, and the service concluded with the *Ave Maria* and the priest's benediction.[39] Bequests sometimes called for a 'rinovale alle laude', on which occasion an anniversary Mass, for which clerics were hired, was interpolated into the lauda vigil service.

Fourteenth- and fifteenth-century bequests to the laudesi companies reflected a 'mix of ascetic renunciation, profound social concern, and personal immortality'.[40] Typically, the annual proceeds from a house or farm were to be divided among commemorative services of clerics and laymen, alms for the poor, hospitals, and great civic projects like the Cathedral or new city wall. The desire of a testator to engage, for his/her money, the broadest, most diverse, and therefore most efficacious network of spiritual benefits involved company executors in overseeing commemorative services conducted throughout Florentine churches. The will of Orlandino Lapi (d. 1388), a wealthy silk merchant from the San Frediano neighbourhood, provides for commemorative services by the friars of Santa Croce and Santa Maria Novella, the two great city-wide churches, but also reveals his neighbourhood loyalty through generous bequests to the Carmine friars, and to the laudesi companies of the Carmine and Santo Spirito (the two major churches in the *Oltararno*).[41] Occasionally a large bequest established a prebend for a chaplaincy in addition to commemorative services, all to be managed by the company.[42]

Bequests to a company often called for a commemorative meal within the company (a *collazione*), in addition to the lauda vigil. Thus the laymen's lauda vigil and *collazione* formed a vernacular counterpart to the clerical *rinovale* and *pietanza*. A bequest to the Company of San Frediano, established in 1415 by frate Giovanni Lozzi, provided that

. . . from this time every year in perpetuity on the first Sunday after the [feast]-day of San Frediano, laude are to be sung in the church of San Frediano with a vigil for the soul of the said fra' Giovanni. Afterwards, according to custom, roast chestnuts are to be given out. And in the evening among our company there is to be a *collazione* for the priests, the lauda-singers (*laudieri*), and the men of the company, at a total cost of around L. 8.[43]

[39] App. I, doc. 3.   [40] Becker, *Medieval Italy*, 166.

[41] App. I, doc. 4.

[42] This was the case, for example, at the Company of San Frediano in 1436 when a bequest from a barrel-maker named Michele di Simone brought the church's St Michael altar under the company's governance. This and other such instances are discussed in more detail in Ch. 3.

[43] App. I, doc. 5.

On 9 August 1377, Chiaro d'Ardinghello, a wealthy 'merchatante [e] devotis[s]imo u[o]mo' of the Company of Sant'Agnese, left to the company a farm with buildings, vineyards, and olive orchards, in the region of San Piero a Montecelli, outside the gate of San Frediano. The property generated an annual income of L. 56, which the company was to spend annually in the following manner:

L. 34 to the friars of Santa Maria del Carmine:
  L. 12 for a solemn Mass and *pietanza* on 25 March, the feast of the Annunciation, to be performed at the Annunciation chapel (one of the company's chapels)

  L. 10 for a solemn Mass on 6 December, the feast day of St Nicholas, to be performed at the Nicholas chapel

  L. 12 for bread and wine, for a *pietanza* with 8 lb. of candles, on 8 December, the feast of the Immaculate Conception

L. 22 to the Company of Sant'Agnese:
  L. 12 for bread to be distributed on Christmas Day to the poor of the neighbourhood (*gonfalone* of the Green Dragon)

  L. 6 for a lauda vigil in August

  L. 4 to be given to the Company of San Frediano for a lauda vigil in August.[44]

All the services were to be performed in perpetuity. The two lauda vigils in August commemorated the deceased in the month of his death, a frequent occasion for lauda-singing which indicates the strong link between laudesi devotion and the cult of the dead. Chiaro's bequest to the Company of San Frediano (their first recorded bequest for lauda-singing just after having adopted the devotion) was a gesture of solidarity to the neighbourhood in which he had lived, since the two churches of the Carmine and San Frediano were situated across the Piazza Carmine from one another in Chiaro's neighbourhood.

One of the earliest datable lauda bequests was made in 1313 by the silk merchant Michele to the Company of San Zanobi.[45] The rent of a house was to provide for the annual distribution of bread to the poor on the morning of the feast of St Thomas (21 December) and a lauda vigil on the feast of St Michael, his namesake (29 September).[46]

Among the many bequests to the Company of San Piero Martire was one by Francesco Comucci da Castelfiorentino, who requested a *rinovale*

---

[44] The above is a paraphrase and conflation from two sources relating information about this bequest: SA 29, fos. 2ᵛ–3ʳ (transcribed in App. I as doc. 6) (Plate 9), and SA 115, fo. 3ᵛ.

[45] This company met in the Cathedral, and during the 14th c. was variously called the 'Compagnia della Vergine Maria', 'Compagnia di Santa Maria Vergine Annunziata' (1362), 'Chompagnia di Santa Liperata [Reparata]' (as late as 1398, although the old Cathedral of Santa Reparata was destroyed in 1375), and, after the new Cathedral, the 'Chompagnia di Santa Maria del Fiore' (1399). The first recorded use of the new title of San Zanobi was in 1413 (SZ 2170, fasc. 4, fo. 15ʳ). For the sake of convenience, the company is hereafter referred to as San Zanobi.

[46] SZ 2170, fasc. 4 fo. 1ᵛ [1313]: '. . . facciano con candele accese le laude e la vigilia predetta'.

by the friars, and two *rinovali alle laude* on consecutive evenings (15–16 April), followed by a *pietanza*. In 1429 the Company spent over L. 45 on altar candles (L. 2), a sacristan to furnish the company altar (L. 4), candles 'a mano' (L. 3 s. 10), and cheese, 36 lb. of meat, and 300 eggs (*c.* L. 36).[47] In 1439, Mona Pagola, wife of Baldassare di Giovanni Boni, left 250 florins of the city's funded debt (*monte comune*), the interest from which was to be spent on an annual *rinovale* and *pietanza* by the friars, and

. . . at the lauda [service] of the company every year [for] 6 lb. of candles to burn when the laude are sung for the soul of the said Mona Pagola.[48]

In 1421, the Company of San Piero Martire compiled a calendar of bequests under its management, which lists ninety-three *pietanze* and/or *rinovali* to be celebrated during the year.[49] These numerous bequests to the lay company benefited primarily the Dominican friars at Santa Maria Novella, a situation which suggests the possibility that the lay companies owned property on behalf of the friars, thereby allowing the latter to circumvent vows of poverty prohibiting ownership of goods. However, the bequests of friars to the companies (six of the ninety-three to the Company of San Piero Martire) for lauda vigils presents a striking reversal of traditional roles, with the cleric purchasing the efficacious prayer and ritual of the layman.

During the fourteenth century, the management and fulfilment of bequests gradually become the primary occupation of the laudesi companies, especially with the high death rate from plague and its periodic recurrences after mid-century. It was in the long wake of the plague that the small laudesi company of San Frediano adopted the practice of lauda singing, very likely in an effort to capture a part of the burgeoning bequest market, as well as to become involved in a strong and popular devotion. The company documents show the purchase, between 1368 and 1373, of lauda paraphernalia—the necessary lectern, candle-holders, altar adornments, and an illuminated laudario (including a detailed account of the materials and services purchased in the preparation of the manuscript).[50] The change brought success to the company, which by this time managed an altar in the small Cistercian church of San Frediano, and could offer lauda vigils and *collazioni*, as well as the management of

---

[47] SMN 290, fo. 5ʳ.

[48] SMN 306, fo. 37ᵛ [2 July 1439]: 'Alle lalde della chonpagnia ognianno libre sei di chandele per acienderce quando si canta le lalde per per l'anima della detta Mona paghola.'

[49] SMN 326, 1st folio (without pagination). Lauda vigils and clerical *rinovali* are not distinguished in the calendar, but the individual bequests are described on the folios following the calendar. The oldest dated bequest was made in 1299, over a third were made by women, and many prominent families of the quarter, such as the Bardi, Strozzi, Tornabuoni, Tornaquinci, and Altoviti, are represented.

[50] SF 30, fos. 95ᵛ ff.; SF 88, fos. 92ᵛ ff.

the more expensive commemorative services of the clergy. The aforementioned bequest of Chiaro d'Ardinghello (who had been a captain of
the company in 1350) for a lauda vigil in 1377 was followed by at least
nine others during the following century. The ritual capacity of the
company expanded in the early, and again in the late, fifteenth century
with the endowment of chaplaincies at other altars in the church.

Through their bequests to the lay companies Florentine citizens de-
monstrated their confidence in the companies' institutional stability and
ritual efficacy. These bequests, in turn, exercised a profound influence on
the institutional and ritual development of the companies, for bequests
involved the companies in a series of obligations and activities (payments
to relatives of the deceased, the buying and selling of property, collecting
of rent from tenants) beyond the vision of their founders,[51] and shaped
patterns of organization and activity that would remain intact, if not *in
perpetuo*, until at least the sixteenth century.

Funerals
A company was prepared to respond quickly when a member died. A
burial service was arranged as soon after death as possible, and shop
closure and attendance was usually mandatory. The members gathered
in the church at the company sepulchre to participate in a Mass, offer
candles, and recite 'xii Pater Nostri con Ave Maria overo co[n] Requiem
Eterna[m]',[52] while the deceased lay in state, then burial followed
immediately. According to their 1333 statutes, the Company of Orsanmichele provided two torches, a golden *drappo* (for the casket), a cushion
of vermilion silk, and candles for this service.[53] On the evening of the
burial, the company conducted a special lauda vigil, or *luminaria*, which
included a Mass and candle offering. Although company statutes do not
specifically call for laude to be sung at this time, the evening vigil was
undoubtedly the occasion for the performance of special laude *pro
defunctis*, contained in most laudarios.[54] On the morning after the burial,
the company subsidized a Requiem Mass, which involved a candle and
small cash offering.

---

[51] Henderson, 'Piety and Charity', 117.
[52] A typical formula, from the 1294 statutes of the Company of Orsanmichele; ed. Castellani,
Nuovi testi fiorentini, 655.
[53] La Sorsa, *La compagnia*, 202 (Statute XXXII); Strocchia, 'Burials in Renaissance Florence', 201.
[54] e.g. Mgl[2], no. 97; 'O fratello del nostro core / ke giace in questo munimento'; the lauda 'Chi
vuol lo mondo disprezzare' is found in the above MS (no. 99) with the rubric *Lauda di morti*, and in the
Pisan laudario Ars (Staaff, 'Le Laudario', no. 49) with the rubric 'Della memoria della morte', and in
every other extant Tuscan laudario (including Mgl[1] with music; Liuzzi, *La lauda*, ii, no. 88). See also
Ricc. 1690, fo. 48[v]: *Lauda del fratello morto*; and ASF, Capitoli 6 (the 1441 statutes of the laudesi
company of San Bastiano), where the above lauda ('O fratello nostro, che se' morto e sepolto') is
included among Latin items for the Office of the Dead.

Each laudesi company conducted a special annual commemorative service, an *ufficio generale*, or *rinovale generale*, on behalf of all deceased members. Like other commemorative services celebrated by a company, this one consisted of an evening lauda vigil and *pietanza*, followed the next morning by a Mass.[55] Most laudesi companies celebrated their *ufficio* on or near the feast of St Martin (11 November), shortly after the official liturgical commemoration of the dead on the feasts of All Saints Day (1 November) and All Souls day (2 November).[56]

The captains of the Company of Santo Spirito noted in their *ricordanze* that

On 11 November 1424, the said *rinovale* and Mass and Office were conducted in the morning above the sepulchre of the company in front of the chapter, with four captains and many guests of the company present, and then the friars, with large candles, went around the cloister and returned through the great door, and we gave frate Bernardo Giambollari, sacristan, L. 5 . . . And on the evening before we conducted a solemn lauda vigil with six friars and men [of the company] with candles in hand and 3 lb. of new candles . . . L. 1 s. 7.[57]

According to 1428 statutes, the Company of San Zanobi lit candles for their *ufficio* procession during Mass at the elevation of the host (i.e., during the communal meal that united the living and the dead), then recited the *De profundis* and the prayers *Deus veniam largitor* and *Fidelium Deus*. Company members and a large number of clerics then processed to the company sepulchre near the campanile, across to the Baptistry, then back to the high altar, where candles were offered and the morning service completed.[58]

Feasts of Patron Saints
The feast-day of a laudesi company's patron saint was usually the grandest of the year. As on other feast-days, the companies celebrated both an elaborate morning mass and a lauda vigil that evening. Following

---

[55] Lauda no. 98 in Mgl², with the rubric 'Lauda di morti de la compagnia', was certainly performed on this particular annual vigil.

[56] The All Saints lauda, 'Facciam laude a tuct'i sancti' (Plate 1), and the lauda *pro defunctis* 'Chi vuol lo mondo desprezzare' are closely juxtaposed only in the three Florentine laudarios: Mgl¹ (nos. 96 and 97), Mgl² (102 and 99), and Fior (39 and 42). This suggests a Florentine laudesi practice of performing the latter lauda during the vigils of their *ufficio generale*. In his study of the miniatures in Mgl¹, V. Moleta questioned the function of this lauda, but assumed its importance in the overall structure of the laudario since the scale of its decoration matches that of the manuscript's elaborate frontispiece; 'The Illuminated *Laudari* Mgl¹ and Mgl²', *Scriptorium*, 32 (1978), 42, plate no. 7 (Mgl¹, fo. 134ᵛ). An equally elaborate illumination of 'Facciam laude', a single folio now believed to have been part of a laudario belonging to the Company of Sant'Agnese, suggests the solemnity of this occasion; A. Ziino, 'Laudi e miniature fiorentine del primo trecento', *Studi musicali*, 7 (1978), 55, 61 ff., fig. 14b, and C. Barr, *The Monophonic Lauda* (Kalamazoo, Mich., 1988), 126–9, fig. 13.

[57] App. I, doc. 7. As was often the case in the other laudesi companies, the Santo Spirito *ufficio generale* was subsidized by a bequest.

[58] SZ 2170, fasc. 2 [1428 statutes], fos. 48ʳ–49ᵛ.

one or the other of these two services, however, the companies then sponsored a large communal meal that honoured not the dead, but the company singers. The larger companies hired instrumentalists (often municipal brass- and wind-players), to play for these special *feste*.

In the earliest laudesi statutes (*c.* 1270–1340) this feast-day is not distinguished from others, except to indicate that a lauda vigil might occur on both the evening before and of the feast.[59] Throughout the fourteenth and fifteenth centuries, however, these special company feasts, usually subsidized by bequests, grew in number and splendour.[60] In the early fourteenth century the Company of San Piero Martire added to the feast of its martyred Dominican saint two others, the feasts of St Dominic and St Thomas Aquinas.[61] The Companies of Orsanmichele and San Frediano instituted special feasts in conjunction with the consecration of a new altar; the St Anne altar was established at Orsanmichele through communal subsidy in the mid-fourteenth century, and a bequest established the altar of St Michael at San Frediano in the early fifteenth century. The Company of Sant'Agnese traditionally worshipped at the altar and celebrated the special feast of their namesake, but by the fifteenth century the company's annual Ascension feast was, like that of Pentecost at Santo Spirito, a monumental affair that had come to dwarf all other company activity.

These patron-saint feasts were a company's most public occasion, during which a laudesi company competed with other lay and ecclesiastical institutions in an outward display that testified to the efficacy of the company's most coveted saints and devotions. A *banditore,* blowing a trumpet draped with a company pennant, heralded the occasion in the public squares of Florence, and for several days before the feast company pennants were displayed outside the church. The area around the company altar was decorated with flowers, painted candles with ornate holders, oil-lamps, painted silk and linen hangings for the altar, lectern, and walls, an appropriate painting on the altar, and an array of escutcheons. The ceaseless round of these feasts must have provided the minor artists and artisans of Florence with a steady market of small commissions.

The more elaborate patron-saint feasts were celebrated by the wealthier companies of San Piero Martire and San Zanobi, beginning in the early fourteenth century. Between 1327 and 1330 the former recorded pay-

[59] As in a 1293 addition to the statutes of the Company of Sant'Agnese; ed. in Schiaffini, *Testi fiorentini*, 67.

[60] See Gaston, 'Liturgy and Patronage in San Lorenzo', *passim*, on the ecclesiastical proliferation of the festal liturgy during these centuries.

[61] Canonized in 1323. The name of the 'gloriosissimo doctore' first appears in company invocations in 1325 (SMN 291, fo. 23ʳ), and on 27 Sept. of that year the company paid s. 9 '. . . per fare scrivere lauda e 'l motetto di Sa[n] Tomaso . . . (SMN 292, fo. 27ᵛ).

ments to *trombadori* (municipal trumpeters) for the feasts of St Thomas Aquinas (28 January), St Peter Martyr (29 April), and St Dominic (5 August).[62] For the latter two feasts a special *collazione* for the laudesi followed a lauda vigil on the evening of the feast. In 1391, the Company of San Piero Martire noted a payment 'for wine to be bought [for] the evening of the feast of St Dominic to honour the singers of laude'.[63] All the laudesi companies sponsored a similar honorific meal for the singers, and by the late fourteenth century San Zanobi and San Piero Martire began hiring *trombadori* and *pifferi* (wind-players) to play at the *collazione*, as well as in conjunction with the services.[64] In the early fifteenth century, the feast of St Zenobius, sponsored by the laudesi company at the Cathedral, involved a morning Mass with a procession, a lauda vigil on the evening before and of the feast, and a *collazione* for the singers after the Mass. The company hired instrumentalists on all these occasions, and extra singers for the lauda vigils. In 1396, this company spent L. 4 on wine, bread, and other food 'to honour the singers on the vigil and the day of St Zenobius'.[65] In 1439, the company spent over L. 21 for flowers, laurels (for the bell tower), bread, fruit, and other food, and for municipal players ('sonatori di palagio') and extra lauda singers ('più laudesi').[66] For the 1442 feast, payments to musicians were for *trombetti*, 'when the laurel wreaths are hung on the bell tower', the 'pifferi di palagio', and singers from the recently formed polyphonic Cathedral choir, the 'Cantori di San Giovanni'.

The 1428 statutes of the company provide the most detailed picture of events.[67] Six to eight *festaiuoli* were elected to supervise the preparation: the various arms of the company were displayed for fifteen days before the feast; eight days prior to the feast the company banner (*gonfalone*) was hung above the altar of St Zenobius 'in the middle of the church'; and the area around the altar was decorated with festive wall hangings. The lauda were to be sung with special reverence during this period. During the feast, roses and violets adorned the escutcheons. At least two each of

---

[62] SMN 292, fos. 33ʳ, 38ʳ; F. D'Accone, 'Le compagnie dei laudesi in Firenze durante L'Ars Nova', in *L'Ars nova italiana del Trecento*, 3 (Certaldo, 1970), 255 n. 9.

[63] SMN 294, fo. 108ʳ. The singers honoured on these occasions probably included the company members who sang the refrains (see discussion of the *scuole* below); all references to the *collazione* mention a number of singers ('cantatori'), although some companies, like San Frediano, normally retained only a single singer.

[64] These municipal wind-players were also frequently hired to fulfil a similar function at weddings, to provide a musical background to a festive meal, but one of their civic duties was to play during the meals of the city priors. The tradition is an ancient one, and conceivably derives from a secular courtly milieu.

[65] SZ 2171, fasc. 6B, no. 3, fo. 223ᵛ.

[66] SZ 2170, fasc. 5K, fo. 6ᵛ.

[67] App. I, doc. 8.

trombetti, sonatori,[68] and extra laudesi were invited to both lauda vigils, and to the *collazione* following Mass on the morning of the feast. For both vigils, the large lectern, the 'libro grande' (presumably a laudario), an altar cloth, and a large candle-holder were situated before the altar of St Zenobius (not the usual company altar), and the service was to conclude with the *Te Deum* and accompanying prayers, recited by the company chaplain. At morning Mass, a procession and candle offering began in the company's sacristy (the Cathedral chapter room); the two (and later six) *trombetti* led a procession that proceeded two by two, with the company chaplain and prior, officers, and members arranged according to rank, all given various grades of candles reflecting the procession's hierarchy. The statute ends here, but presumably the occasion was similar to the company's monthly processions at Sunday Mass (the *offerta*, discussed below), when the procession took place between the Gospel reading and the elevation of the Host, probably as an Offertory procession.

Along with the fifteenth-century expansion of these patron-saint feasts, several companies initiated a tradition of including the guest singers ('laudesi invitati') in the feast-day meal. By 1429, a bequest to the Company of San Frediano provided for an annual *collazione* 'a tutti i laldieri di firenze' on the feast of St Fredianus.[69] By 1446, the Company of Sant'Agnese was also pursuing the tradition to its logical extreme by inviting 'tutti i chantori delle laude di firenze' to their *collazione* for the feast of St Agnes (21 January). Because of 'certain impediments', the event was postponed a week in 1446, but on 28 January the feast, subsidized by a bequest from Mona Filippa di Grano, included 'singing in the church at the chapel of St Agnes', followed by a *collazione* in the refectory of the Carmine church. On this occasion, the lauda-singers of Florence consumed apples, fennel, puff-pastries, and white wine.[70]

Processions

Although members were required to attend all Sunday Masses and sermons, on a designated Sunday of the month the laudesi companies held a special service in conjunction with Mass. The central activity of this service was a procession and candle-offering (the *offerta*), which

---

[68] This may refer not to specially hired *pifferi*, but to the rebec-, vielle- and lute-players that the company usually hired for its special feasts. They generally accompanied laude during the vigil services, but occasionally played in procession as well; SZ 2171, fasc. 6C, fo. 246ʳ [1 June 1395]: 'ispesi a dì primo di giugno per fare onore a' sonatori quando andonno a procisone [*sic*] in vino . . . s. 7 d. 8; Ispesi per dare a Berzola [a rebec-player] e al Puccio quando sonarono andano [*sic*] a la procisone a dì primo di giugno . . . L. 1 s. 10'; and 19 pairs of gloves for the procession '. . . quando ci vene la tavola di Santa Maria Inpianetta [Imprunetta]'.

[69] ASF, Catasto 293, fo. 31ᵛ.   [70] App. I, doc. 9.

constituted a kind of lay Offertory procession. Members generally paid several denari for a candle, then processed with lighted candles throughout the church and cloister, two by two, singing laude and offering the candles at a designated altar. The public nature of this occasion is attested to by a 1285 statute of the Company of Sant'Agnese, which provided for the hiring of a *banditore* to 'proclaim our procession on the first Sunday of each month'.[71]

Company documents frequently, but not always, indicate the performance of laude during the procession, but the monthly *offerta* with lauda singing was a type of laudesi service that was at least as old as that described in the 1267 statutes of the Sienese company at San Domenico di Campo Regio:

We ordain that on the second Sunday of the month, at the appropriate time of the morning, the people of the said fraternity should meet in Campo Regio for the hearing of laude, Mass, and preaching.[72]

These same statutes prescribe processions for twelve major feast-days of the year, though not for the monthly Sunday reunion, but the earliest Florentine laudesi statutes indicate that processions with lauda-singing had become a tradition by the early fourteenth century. In 1304, one hundred days of indulgence were granted by Cardinal Nicola da Prato to the laudesi at Santa Maria Novella for gathering every second Sunday of the month to process with lighted candles and 'offer devout laude', perhaps an indication that lauda-singing was by this time perceived as part of the offering.[73] A 1291 statute of the Company of Sant'Agnese, which outlines the duties of official lauda instructors (*insegnatori delle laude*), provides an indirect testimony to the presence of lauda-singing in the procession:

So that the office of those who are lauda instructors is properly executed, it is decided that those who are lauda instructors have the authority at the evening lauda service, and also at the morning processions, to send in front those singers whom they choose, and to have performed those laude that please them.[74]

In 1312, a laudesi company in Perugia, the Congregazione della Vergine, met every first Sunday at the Dominican church. Men and women paid

---

[71] Schiaffini, *Testi fiorentini*, 60: 'Anche fue ordinato . . . che si dovesse bandire la nostra processione la primaia [*sic*] domenica di ciascheuno mese per Angnello banditore.'

[72] Meersseman, *Ordo fraternitatis*, ii. 1032.

[73] The letter is edited in Meersseman, *Ordo fraternitatis*, ii. 1047–8, where the context of the document ('ad cantandas laudes') makes it clear that the phrase 'devotas laudes reddunt' refers specifically to lauda-singing, and not more generally to 'praises'.

[74] Ed. in Schiaffini, *Testi fiorentini*, 64.

two denari, received a candle, then heard the entire sermon. Following this,

. . . everyone is to process holding lighted candles, through the church, through the cloister, or through the town, devoutly singing a lauda, which at that time is to be started by the singers in front [*cantores precedentes*].[75]

As was often the case among laudesi companies, there were female members, who in this particular ceremony were required to participate in the procession, though during the actual *offerta* at the culmination of the procession they were to 'devoutly and quietly remain in the church with their lighted candles'.

The 1326 statutes of the Company of San Zanobi describe their meeting on the first Sunday of the month, the procession of which was to take place during Mass at the Cathedral:

The rectors should arrange with the leaders of the said church [Santa Reparata] that on this morning a solemn Mass should be celebrated in honour of the Blessed Virgin Lady Holy Mary. At this Mass the chamberlains are to burn two candles, which are to be new and 2 lb. each in weight. And after the Gospel which will be sung at this Mass, the rectors are to gather in the cloister or wherever they please those of the company who will have come that morning . . . The chamberlains [then] give a candle to each one. Having done this, the rectors then order them two by two. At the front are placed two young men of the said company who are to carry two large, lighted candles. And next after them . . . are placed several who begin to sing a lauda. And then all the rest are ordered two by two, the councillors, chamberlains, and rectors . . . they are [then] to go in procession with the above lighted candles in hand, singing and responding [to] the lauda which the foremost singers will begin. And they are to go through the said church, proceeding as far up as the choir, and here offer the above candles at the altar. When the *offerta* is finished, everyone should devoutly stand and remain here until the Mass is finished, or at least until the elevation of the body of Our Lord Jesus Christ at the altar.[76]

Certainly such a public lay procession with vernacular song enhanced the participation of the Cathedral congregation in the service, while enabling company members to more closely identify their ritual activities with official church liturgy.

On the Monday morning following the Sunday procession, all the laudesi companies sponsored a commemorative Mass for the deceased members of the company (not to be confused with the annual *ufficio generale*). The number and solemnity of these masses varied among the companies, but lauda-singing is never mentioned in connection with this Monday service.

[75] Ed. in Meersseman, *Ordo fraternitatis*, ii. 1063.
[76] Ed. in Orioli, *Le confraternite medievali*, 22–3 (cap. 3).

Lauda-singing and processing were combined not only in these monthly meetings, however, but on a number of major feast days throughout the year when these activities would have contributed to the solemnity of the occasion. A book of candle sales belonging to the Company of San Piero Martire records an expense for candles 'for the laude at the procession of Epiphany' in 1486. Candle payments recorded during the 1480s indicate lauda processions on around eighteen different feast-days, and many of these occasions involved multiple processions.[77] During Christmas of 1484 the company spent nearly L. 30 on candles for five processions, and double that was spent on candles for the vigil and feast-day of St Peter Martyr two years later.

Ferial Services

Although lauda-singing was clearly a part of a laudesi company's monthly processions, the indulgences for these services were granted principally for processing rather than singing. It is only in the regular evening services of the companies that we find a setting in which the lauda was the undisputed centrepiece. For nearly two centuries, the members of the Florentine laudesi companies met every week-night around the time of Compline to sing and hear laude. The 1326 statutes of the Company of San Zanobi required the chamberlain to come 'every evening to the said church at that time when the office of Compline is finished' to prepare for the service; the two statutes that prescribe the actual service read as follows:

We ordain and establish that the entire company is to meet every evening in the aforesaid church of Madonna Santa Reparata to sing laude with the 'Ave Maria' to the honour of God and Our Lady. But those who cannot come in the evening to the above church to sing laude . . . should say three *Paternostri cum Ave Maria* in honour of God and Our Lady . . . the chamberlains [in advance of the service] should come every evening at the time when the office of Compline is finished, and light three candles which are to remain lit until the laude are completed . . .[78]

This custom of ferial singing around the time of Compline was observed as well by other laudesi companies in central Italy.[79] It was a time (*c*.7–8 p.m.) that suited the working schedule of merchants and

---

[77] SMN Appendix 72, fos. 50ʳ–57ʳ. Since candle expenses for processions are distinguished from those for lauda vigils, it seems fairly certain that the processions were separate from, though perhaps contiguous with, the lauda services.

[78] Ed. in Orioli, *Le confraternite medievali*, 23–4 (cap. 6).

[79] Meersseman, *Ordo fraternitatis*, ii, cites documents from Siena, 1267 ('at the hour of Compline'), p. 1032; Pisa, 1312 ('following Compline'), p. 1056; and Imola, 1335 ('after Compline'), pp. 1067–8.

artisans,[80] and deepened the liturgical aspects of his devotion by providing a service parallel to the ecclesiastical office of Compline.

Like the festal services and monthly processions, the ferial services took place at an altar in the host church. The primary focus of laudesi devotion was the altar which the company managed in the dual role of patron and chaplain. Like a chaplain, the company was responsible for conducting the round of devotions associated with their particular altar. Feast days had to be properly observed and bequests faithfully executed, and both involved the company's own devotions (primarily lauda-singing), as well as the recitation of Masses and Offices (for which clergy were hired), and the offering of candles, the weight, number, and quality of which were prescribed by the liturgical solemnity of the occasion.[81] A laudesi company also often assumed many of the rights and responsibilities of a secular patron with regard to its altar. It assumed the costs of repairing and decorating the chapel, and retained the right to display there the company's insignia, the counterpart of a wealthy Florentine family's coat of arms. Thus a member might enjoy a measure of the best of two overlapping worlds: the prestige of secular wealth and position prominently displayed, and an active priestly role in the religious life of the city.[82]

The formal procession that attended other laudesi services appears not to have been a part of the ferial services. Rather their character was more contemplative and devotional, influenced, perhaps, by the more serene nature of clerical Compline. The focus of devotion was a painting, usually of the Madonna and Child, placed upon the company altar for the service.[83] These paintings were the most important possession of the company, and professional painters were contracted to execute images which the lay brothers believed their sung devotions would render spiritually efficacious. A few of these devotional images, such as the Madonna of Orsanmichele, attained a miracle-working status, and in turn contributed to the material growth of the company through an increase in bequests, candle sales, and membership. Company inventories

[80] That these services took place on the evenings of the work week is indicated by the description of a lectern in a 1383 inventory of the Company of San Zanobi: 'Uno leggio vecchio con uno ferro istà in chiesa per dire le laude la sera da [sic] lavorare'; SZ 2176, fasc. 12, fo. 45ʳ.

[81] Strocchia, 'Burials in Renaissance Florence', 80–2.

[82] Laudesi company documents are somewhat ambiguous about the exact location of the ferial services, but for most companies it seems likely that they would have gravitated to their altar in the sanctuary rather than to one in their meeting-room or another within the church but outside the sanctuary. The usual designation of a time *after* Compline would seem to indicate a desire to avoid a conflict in the sanctuary with the host clerics' service, and for many (though not all) companies their patronage rights to their sanctuary altars were clearly strong enough to allow them that choice. This complex relationship to the host church varied among the companies, and is discussed in more detail in Ch. 5.

[83] On the laudesi altars and paintings see Ch. 5.

list paintings of other patron saints, who were honoured at least on patron-saint feasts with special laude drawn from the *sanctorale* section of company laudarios. The image was sometimes locked away in a large wooden tabernacle or covered with a curtain, to be unveiled only on prescribed occasions. In 1333, the Orsanmichele Madonna was covered with a silk veil and uncovered only on 'the Sundays and feast-days deemed appropriate by the rectors and captains'.[84] Candles and lamps were carefully maintained before the image as well. The 1284 statutes of the Company of San Gilio required an officer to 'burn two candles every evening when the laude are sung, and to maintain a lamp burning continuously before the picture of the Lady'.[85] Members were to show reverence to the image, and the laude were to be devoutly sung before it.

A chamberlain or company sacristan was responsible for setting up the ferial service. He adorned the altar with the requisite items: an altar-cloth (usually bearing the company insignia), candles (often painted with company insignias and saints' images), candlesticks, and the image of the Virgin. As symbols of prayer and sources of illumination, candles were clearly an integral liturgical item. A strict liturgical protocol governed the use of candles, which were probably prepared according to a calendar like that used in 1312 by the laudesi company at the Dominican church of Santa Caterina in Pisa.[86] The calendar prescribed the size and number of candles according to the liturgical solemnity of the feasts, which were ranked 'luminare maggiore', 'meczana', or 'minore':

Maggiore: six large candles, the tabernacle (containing the image); an altar-cloth placed upon the altar; all present, men and women, are given a lighted candle (Nativity, vigils of Easter, Assumption, and St Catherine);

Meczana: three large candles, tabernacle, altar-cloth; all the lauda-singers (who remain kneeling) are given lighted candles (vigils of Epiphany, Ascension, Annunciation, nativity of the Virgin, Pentecost, All Saints, Circumcision, and numerous saints);

Minore: three large candles, tabernacle, altar-cloth; no candles among the congregation (octaves of feasts, and many saints);

Feriale: two large candles, tabernacle, altar-cloth (weekdays outside the octaves of major feasts).

These officials also arranged benches before the company altar, and a lectern (with candles and candle-holders), upon which was placed the

---

[84] Ed. in La Sorsa, *La compagnia d'Or San Michele*, 202; document translated and discussed in Ch. 5.

[85] Ed. in Schiaffini, *Testi fiorentini*, 37.

[86] Document ed. in Meersseman, *Ordo fraternitatis*, ii. 1054–6.

laudario for the singers. Thus at San Gilio (1284), the chamberlains were instructed to

. . . come every evening to the church of San Gilio and prepare the lectern and the book of laude, and other things which are used for the singing of laude, placing two lighted candles into the candle-holders before the altar, and one [lighted candle] with a candle-holder before the *gonfalone* which is unfurled on the weekdays when the laude are sung.[87]

The preparation of the laudario undoubtedly included marking the laude to be sung that evening, including those proper to the liturgical season. According to a 1291 statute of the Company of Sant'Agnese, the company was to elect an official

. . . to prepare the laude for the evening [service], and this official is to be called a sacristan. This sacristan is to retain one of the keys to the lectern, and the other key is to remain with the chamberlains. And the said sacristan is to be the chamberlain of the following things, that is: two candles with holders, the *libro minore*, the altar-cloth, the candle-holder, the lamp, an inkstand and pen [for recording candle and dues payments], and a blackboard for writing above the [names of] novices. The chamberlains are obliged to furnish the sacristan with candles at the request of the said sacristan. Also he should locate the laude in the sequence in which they are to be sung at the evening [service], and this was decided in order to ease the chamberlains' duties, and to improve the office of lauda-singing at the evening [service].[88]

Laudarios were loosely modelled on ecclesiastical service-books both in their organization and variety. The selection of laude for a given service was facilitated by the organization of laudarios into sections *de tempore* and *de sanctis*,[89] and by a functional distinction between large laudarios for festal services, and smaller books for ferial use. Most companies owned a large, usually ornate (and often noted) laudario and an equally festive lectern to match, and a small laudario and lectern for ferial use.[90] The functional difference between festal and ferial books is

---

[87] Ed. in Schiaffini, *Testi fiorentini*, 44.   [88] Ibid. 63–4.

[89] Late 13th- and 14th-c. laudarios were generally divided into three sections: laude to Mary, laude to Christ (both generally ordered *de tempore*), and laude to the saints (*de sanctis*). The contents of Mgl[1] are outlined below, and the structure of both Cort and Mgl[1] are discussed in more detail in Barr, *The Monophonic Lauda*, 68–70, 103–5; Mgl[2] is discussed below in Ch. 3 in conjunction with the Company of San Gilio.

[90] For example, the *libro grande* and *legio grande* used by the Company of San Zanobi for their patron-saint feast discussed above, and the *libro minore* just cited with respect to ferial services at Sant'Agnese in 1291. Among 14th-c. inventories of San Zanobi are references to 'due legii dove si cantano le laude, uno grande e l'altro piccolo' (SZ 2170, fasc. 4, fo. 20ᵛ [*c.*1354]; 'uno legio grande intarsiato, et due mezani da chantare le laude, uno ferro grande da pore al legio magiore, lavorato molto maestrevole' (ibid., fos. 22ʳ⁻ᵛ [1394]); 'uno leggio vecchio con uno ferro istà in chiesa per dire le laude la sera da lavorare' (SZ 2176, fasc. 12, fo. 45ʳ [1383]). The references in company documents to laudarios almost always distinguish between large and small books, and in 1452 even the modest company of San Frediano owned '3 libri di lallde, uno grande, uno mezano, uno picholo' (SF 4, fo.

revealed in a 1394 inventory of the Company of San Zanobi, which at that time owned

A book with minatures and gold storiation for nearly all the feasts of the year, provided with laude that follow the stories depicted above.

Two books of 'laude chomuni' for singing throughout the year.[91]

The ornate laudario was probably that commissioned by the company in 1339 ('iscritto di lettere grosse e notato e storiato'), and mentioned in a 1383 inventory as 'miniato e notato'.[92] An earlier inventory compiled sometime after 1354 listed 'a red leather book of laude, in which are written laude which are sung every evening'.[93] The large and illuminated festal laudarios were usually the ones to contain musical notation, helpful to the singers who on feast days were performing laude that were proper to the season, and perhaps not sung often enough to be easily memorized. Their large size, moreover, accommodated the larger number of singers that the companies hired for special feast days. The elegant and noted manuscript that belonged to the laudesi company at Santo Spirito (Mgl^1) is certainly such a festal laudario.[94]

The ferial books, on the other hand, were smaller, usually lacked notation and illumination, and contained those laude of the *ordinarium* ('laude comune'), the music of which was easily memorized through frequent repetition during the year. That none have survived may be explained by their hard use and, relative to the festal laudarios, lack of value beyond their utility.

The actual sequence of events in the evening ferial services is difficult to reconstruct. The chamberlain began setting up the service around the

70^r). In 1466, the Company of Sant'Agnese listed five laudarios in its inventory, among them one 'grande . . . richamente fatto suvi iscritto molte laude cho molti begli mini istoriato', one with 'molte laude antiche dipintovi suso un crocifiso e più altri mini. Adoperasi ogni di', one 'miniato di mini grandi a penello e a penna', and one containing 'molte laude zolfate e fighurate basso' (i.e. containing musical signs if not actual notation); the inventory lists only one lectern, but several types of candle-holder, crucifix, and dossal to be attached to the lectern, which were intended either for festal or ferial use; SA 115, fo. 164^r, and C. Barr, 'A Renaissance Artist in the Service of a Singing Confraternity', in R. Goffen, M. Tetel, and R. Witt (eds.), *Life and Death in Fifteenth-Century Florence* (Durham, NC, 1989), 105–24.

[91] SZ 2170, fasc. 4, fo. 22^v [1394 inventory]: 'Uno libro miniato e messo ad oro esstoriato quasi di tutte le feste che sono tutto l'ano scrito di laude sechondo che s'achade alle storie che vi sono. Due libri di laude chomuni da chanta' tutto l'anno'.

[92] The complete document is shown in Pl. 11 and translated in Ch. 3.

[93] SZ 2170, fasc. 4, fo. 20^v: 'uno libro di coiame rosso di laude nel quale sono scritte laude che ssi cantano ogni sera'.

[94] An index at the front of the laudario begins with the heading: 'Questa et lla tavola delle laude delle feste maddiore [maggiore] che ssono nell'anno Domini.' The ninety-seven laude are then organized in the following manner (after Barr, *The Monophonic Lauda*, 103–5): 1–5 Dedication and opening non-meditative cycle; 6–25 Temporal cycle (6–11 Nativity; 12–20 Passion; 21–3 Resurrection); 26–45 Marian cycle; 46 John the Baptist; 47–96 Sanctoral cycle (47–61 Apostles; 62–9 Martyrs; 71–89 Confessors; 90–6 Holy Women and All Saints); 97 Pro Defunctis.

time the friars (or priests) completed Compline. The lay service began with the reciting or singing of the Ave Maria, preceded by 'a small bell which sounds the Ave Maria at the evening lauda [service]'.[95] The captains or an appointed lauda instructor oversaw the execution of the laude, which throughout the fourteenth century at least involved a responsorial performance between one or a few soloists singing the strophes from a laudario at the lectern, and the congregation responding on the refrain. Present at services was either a blackboard with the 'incipits of the laude', or a wooden board listing all the laude with pegs (usually seven) that could be moved around so as to 'find the laude' for a particular service, which probably functioned also to announce the order of the service and jog the memories of the congregational singers on the refrains.[96] The officers, who sat on separate benches near the foot of the singers' lectern, kneeled throughout the lauda singing.[97] On ferial days and minor feasts, two or three large altar candles remained lit throughout the lauda singing, and candles were distributed to the congregation only on more important feast days.

The oldest laudesi statutes (Siena, 1267) allowed for a brief sermon during the evening service, especially during Lent ('et hoc maxime in quadragesima, poterit breviter predicari'). Between 1273 and 1283, the Dominican friar Nicola da Milano preached on Wednesday evenings to the Marian congregations of Lombardy, where he delivered his 'collazione'.[98] Here, as in the Sunday morning services and during Lent, lauda and sermon were closely juxtaposed.[99]

[95] SZ 2176, fasc. 12, fo. 46^r [1383 inventory]: 'una champana piccholetta che suona la sera alle laude l'Ave Maria'.

[96] SZ 2170, fasc. 4, fo. 23^r [1394 inventory]: 'Tre tavole a modo che tavole di giesso, che nell'una sono scrite prencipii di laude e nell'altra è scrito e perdoni e lle indu[l]gienze della compagnia e quello a che è obrighato ciasschuno dela compagnia . . .'; fo. 20^v [c.1354 inventory]: '. . . una tavola con sette bischeri dove sono scritte le laude che si cantano . . .'; SPM 292, fo. 3^r [Nov. 1313]: 'Spendemo nella tavola del gesso ove sono segnate le laude . . . s. 12'; ibid., fo. 60^v [1340]: 'demo a far fare vii piuoli per la tavola de le laude e per farchi [sic] dipingnere e per le chatenuze chosta in tucto . . . s. 11 d. 8'. CmRS 1340, fasc. C, fo. 2^r [San Gilio, 1420 inventory]: 'Due tavole da trovare le laude con certe bischeri'. The two references above to boards with seven pegs may indicate the maximum number of laude sung at an evening service.

[97] This was required by a 1298 statute of the Company of Sant'Agnese (Schiaffini, Testi fiorentini, 72): '. . . tutti coloro li quali vengono a dire, overo udire, le laude la sera al predicto luogho di Sancta Maria del Charmino, sì chom'è usato, debiano stare ginochioni, tanto quanto le laude si dichano, a rendere laude a Dio e a la gloriosa vergine Madonna Santa Maria'; SZ 2170, fasc. 4, fo. 22^v [1394 inventory]: 'Quatro panchete la quali si ponghono dina[n]zi al legio et a' pie' de' chapitani quando si dichono le laude per istarvi suso ginochioni'.

[98] Probably a vernacular descendant of the collatio, an evening spiritual reading preceding Compline in medieval monastic communities; Meersseman, Ordo fraternitatis, iii. 1128–30; G. Podhradsky, 'Compline', New Dictionary of the Liturgy (London, 1967).

[99] The 1312 statutes of the Pisan laudesi company of Santa Caterina required members to come to the Cathedral on Sunday evenings to hear the sermon and sing laude; Meersseman, Ordo fraternitatis, ii. 1057: 'Cap. VIII. Item che ciascuno della compagnia delle laude che iustamente più debbia venire la domenica da sera a la predica e cantare le laude a duomo.'

Common to both Compline and the lay ferial services was confession and absolution, which concluded the laudesi services. The 1451 statutes of the Company of San Bastiano (at the Servite church of Santissima Annunziata) requested their religious leader to

... come and remain at the laude every time they are said, and to give confession after the laude, and if it is necessary occasionally at the said laude to sing some hymn like *Ave Maria Stella, Salva Regina, Te Matrem laudamus, Te Deum laudamus,* or other hymns he should begin them.[100]

The *collazione*, singing, confession, and especially the concluding Marian antiphons all reflect the Compline liturgy.[101]

Lent

During Lent the evening lauda services were transformed by a penitential mood and phenomenal preaching activity. For Florentines, this was the longest and busiest of annual liturgical events; for the forty days preceding Easter, the pulpits of Florence resounded with exhortations to prayers, fasting, penance, and confession. Citizens flocked to hear the often dramatic public sermons, delivered by the most popular and charismatic preachers in the major churches and piazzas of the city. In the laudesi companies, lauda-singing took place every evening of Lent, and was combined with the Lenten preaching of a friar who was procured to preach at many, if not all, of these services. The 1294 statutes of Orsanmichele provided for the hiring of 'uno savio predicatore' to preach every Sunday morning and each day of Lent after Vespers.[102] Each year the Company of San Zanobi hired a friar to preach during the evenings of Lent.[103] These two laudesi companies were the only ones to record payments to Lenten preachers during the fourteenth and fifteenth centuries. Since they were the only two major companies not associated with a mendicant church, they apparently needed to import the preaching skills of the friars, while the other companies may have made in-house

---

[100] ASF, CmRS, Capitoli 6, fo. 12ʳ: 'Cap. X. [Il corectore] . . . debba venire e stare alle laude ogni volta se dicessono e fare la confessione dopo le laude, e bissognando per alcuna volta alle dette laude cantare alcuno ymno come Ave Maris Stella, Salve Regina, Te Matrem Laudamus, Te Deum Laudamus, o altre ymni, gli debba chominciare.'

[101] Following the San Bastiano statutes (1451) are textual incipits for the Latin liturgy of Compline, beginning with *Jube dom[i]ne benedicere*; ASF, Capitoli 6, fos. 26 ff.

[102] Castellani, *Nuovi testi fiorentini*, 653. According to Delcorno, preaching took place 'dopo mangiare'; *Giordano da Pisa*, 76–8. A fragment of Orsanmichele statutes drawn up in 1329 indicates the time as 'dopo compieta [Compline]'; Ricc. 391, fo. 4ʳ⁻ᵛ.

[103] Friars were clearly the preferred preachers during this time, and San Zanobi drew freely from among the various churches and orders in Florence. According to a slightly different version of the company's 1427 *Catasto* (tax report), it was paying L. 16 per year 'Al predicatore che predicha la quaresima'; Mgl XXXVII, 298, fos. 23ᵛ–24ʳ. On 28 June 1433, the company elected as Lenten preacher for the following year 'frate Antonio Pierozzi de l'osservanza di San Domenicho da Fiesole', who was to become Archbishop of Florence and St Antoninus; SZ 2186, fasc. 48, fo. 92ᵛ.

arrangements with a friar (perhaps their prior) of the church with which they were associated.[104]

During Lent, the musical activity of the laudesi companies intensified along with the preaching. From the early fourteenth century on, the Florentine companies had hired lauda-singers from outside the membership for contracted periods of service lasting three or four months. During Lent these singers either assumed the added duties or extra singers were hired. Fifteenth-century records indicate that pairs of singers were paid about four times their normal monthly salary, so that their Lenten duties must have been considerable.

Although company statutes say little about what these extra duties were, payments to singers consistently mention the singing of the Passion, the lament (of the Virgin), and, by the early fifteenth century, the Gospels. Passion and lament laude, of which laudarios contain a substantial number, continued to be sung every evening, even in the small *Oltrarno* company of San Frediano. On 26 March 1441, the captains elected 'two to sing laude in the said church [of San Frediano] every evening throughout Lent for the devotion of the people'.[105] A fragment of a fourteenth-century inventory of the Company of San Zanobi provides a glimpse of the scene for Lenten lauda-singing:

. . . one lectern, which is placed in the middle of the church where the laude are sung, with an iron lamp and a square [on] which are placed 4 wooden torch-holders and 4 oil-lamps, which stands inside to provide light in the evening during Lent.[106]

While the Passion and lament were popular subjects among lauda poets, Lenten singing in the laudesi companies included a broader repertoire of rhymed, vernacular settings. In the records of payments to singers, the terms *passione* and *lamento* are used consistently and in contradistinction to *lauda*. The lament was sung only on Good Friday, while the Passion was sung throughout Lent. Two lengthy settings of the Passion are well represented in Florentine manuscripts of the fourteenth and fifteenth centuries, one attributed to Niccolò Cicerchia (*c.*1364), and another by Messer Dolcibene, both in *ottave rime*.[107] The

---

[104] Beginning in 1360, the friars at Santa Maria Novella elected an annual Lenten preacher, who then may have served the laudesi company's needs as well. S. Orlandi, *Necrologio di Santa Maria Novella*, 2 vols. (Florence, 1955), ii. 533 ff.

[105] App. I, doc. 24. Tuscan laudarios contain 8–12 Lenten laude, and these laude in particular display among them a high degree of textual concordance.

[106] SZ 2182, fasc. 36, fo. 169 [loose]: 'un legio che ssi pone in mezo della chiesa là dove si chanta le laude con una lanterna de ferro e una squadra che ssi pone ongi sera quattro torchietti de lengnio e quattro lucerne che vi istanno entro per far lume la sera di quaresima'.

[107] Cicerchia's setting is dated and discussed by Meiss, *Painting in Florence and Siena*, 125; several laude are attributed to Dolcibene; see Tenneroni, *Inizii*, 47, 62. Among later rhymed, vernacular settings of the Passion are those by Leonardo Giustiniani (*c.*1387–1446), ed. F. Luisi, *Laudario*

Florentine manuscript Ricc. 1294/2760, apparently the property of a fourteenth-century Florentine Franciscan, is a large miscellany of rhymed, vernacular devotional poetry, preaching aids, and Latin, liturgical items. Among its contents is Dolcibene's Passion (fos. 57v–60v), two rhymed, vernacular laments,[108] and among a number of laude one by the Florentine poet Antonio Pucci (1309–88) 'sopra la passione'.[109]

The lay companies were as much an heir to this vivid, affective Passion literature as any Florentine, especially to the extent that it was widely propagated by the friars. The long poems on the Passion were probably either intoned (like Passion settings in the Latin liturgy), or sung to improvised melodies with instrumental accompaniment according to an established Florentine practice.[110] So familiar were some of these melodies that a number of fifteenth-century lauda texts in Florentine sources were accompanied by the rubric 'cantasi come la passione'. In 1394, the Company of San Piero Martire recorded a payment to Baccio, 'che canto il pasio chola viola,' and the Company of San Zanobi may have had the same function in mind when in 1406 and 1408 they hired Andrea di Giovanni 'to play during the preaching of Lent'.[111]

There is no mention of sung Gospels in the laudesi services until the early fifteenth century, when the practice was probably borrowed from among the friars' preaching strategies in order to augment the solemnity of the lay companies' services. The Gospels referred to here are not the strict Biblical texts sung to liturgical recitation tones, but, like the

---

giustinianeo, 2 vols. (Venice, 1983), i. 331–52 (*terza rima*, in 14 parts); Messer Castellano Castellani (1461–*c*.1519), ed. A. D'Ancona, *Origini del teatro italiano*, 2 vols. (2nd edn., Turin, 1891), i. 303–25; and Francesco Corteccia, 'Passione secondo Giovanni' (1527), reportedly composed for use in the services of a 'Compagnia di S. Maria delle Laude'; see M. Fabbri, 'Laude spirituali di travestimento nella Firenze della Rinascenza', in M. Rosito (ed.), *Arte e religione nella Firenze de' Medici* (Florence, 1980), 158.

[108] One attributed to Petrarch, 'Ave vergine, virgo glorioso' (fos. 62ʳ–64ʳ), the other to St Bernard (fos. 70ʳ–74ᵛ). In one of Boccaccio's tales in the *Decameron* (day 7, story 1), the famous lament of St Bernard was among the 'nonsense' given by the friars of Santa Maria Novella to the pious and simple Gianni Lotteringhi, who was 'often elected leader of the laudesi' and provided the friars with meals and the goods of his wool-weaving trade; trans. Musa and Bondanella, 418. Among the many versions of the lament, the *Stabat mater*, attributed to Jacopone da Todi, remained popular during and long after the 15th c., and Leonardo Giustiniani's 'Donna del paradiso' circulated widely during the 15th c. (ed. F. Luisi, *Laudario giustinianeo*, i. 324–7).

[109] 'Veggendo ben Gesù', fos. 12ʳ and 90ᵛ. The contents of the manuscript are listed in Morpurgo, *I manoscritti*, 356–63.

[110] On the liturgical musical settings of both the Passion and lament, see F. Ghisi, 'Un processionale inedito per la Settimana Santa nell'Opera del Duomo di Firenze', *Rivista musicale italiana*, 55 (1953), 362–9; other relevant studies are cited by F. D'Accone, 'Alcune note sulle compagnie fiorentine dei Laudesi durante il Quattrocento', *Rivista italiana di musicologia*, 10 (1975), 93 n. 37. On the Florentine tradition of accompanied, improvisatory singing (*canta in panca*), see B. Becherini, 'Un canta in panca fiorentino, Antonio di Guido', *Rivista musicale italiana*, 50 (1949), 241–7.

[111] SZ 2183, fasc. 39, fo. 12ʳ. The Lenten musical activity of individual companies is discussed in Ch. 3.

Passion, rhymed vernacular paraphrases which assumed a variety of popular lyrical forms, including that of the lauda. Passion and Gospels alike were sung throughout Lent, sometimes by the same singer. In 1446, the Company of Sant'Agnese paid one of their regular singers, Romolo di Niccolò di Betto, 'because he sang the Gospels and the Passion at the evening lauda service throughout all of Lent'.[112] Two years earlier, the same company heard their Lenten music performed by a polyphonic ensemble consisting of one boy who sang the lament, and another who sang the Gospels, both accompanied by a *tenore*.[113]

At least one Florentine manuscript suggests that laude composed as Gospel paraphrases were sung (or recited) in conjunction with Lenten sermons,[114] but again the sources suggest a broader literature than the laude *per se*. In 1425, the laudesi company at Santo Spirito compiled a fascicle of forty-six rhymed Gospels in the vernacular to be sung during Lent. These were auditioned in August and September by frate Lorenzo, the church sacristan, and Antonio de' Loci, the company laudese, judged to be 'beautiful and useful for the lauda service and for retention by the company', then planned to be sewn into 'nostro libro grande delle laude' in time for the following Lenten season.[115] The Franciscan friar's collection mentioned above contains, in addition to Passion, lament, and lauda literature, a collection of 'I vangelii de la quaresima in volgare e rima' attributed to Antonio Pucci (fos. 1ʳ–113ʳ). These are eighty-one Gosepl paraphrases in the form of sonnets and canzone, and each rhymed paraphrase for the day is followed by several other poems linked with the Gospel reading ('sopra el detto vangelio') which provided the subject of the day's sermon. The circumstance for the composition of one poem is related, along with its incipit, in a rubric for the 27th day of Lent: 'On the day when this Gospel was sung in Santa Croce, Antonio Pucci saw a friar girded with a cord white as milk, whereupon the [Pucci] wrote to him thus: "Dice el Vangelio, se ben mi ricorda" . . .'[116] In addition to the five parchment laudarios owned by the Company of Sant'Agnese in 1466, their inventory also lists a book of rhymed Gospels and another containing

---

[112] SA 24, fo. 281ʳ [15 Apr. 1446]: '. . . perchè chantò tutta la quaresima la sera al lauda e' vengielli e 'l passio'.

[113] See Ch. 3, 'Company of Sant'Agnese'.

[114] See discussion of preaching in Ch. 1. Also significant in this context is a 'libro di laude evangelice . . .' listed in the 14th-cent. inventory of a Perugian company at the church of San Domenico; Bartholomaeis, *Le origini della poesia drammatica*, 235.

[115] SSP, 1, fo. 58ᵛ: 'A ispese di fare scrivere e' libro di 46 vangeli in volgare e rima da cantare . . .'; ibid., fo. 42ʳ: 'I sopradetti capitani al tempo loro feciono copiare e scrivere uno libretto di 46 vangeli della quaresima disposti in volgare e pe' rima, che sono cantati del mese d'agosto e di settembre 1425 per frate Lorenzo sagrestanno e per Antonio de' Loci, belli e utoli [*sic*] alle lalde e per retenerli nella compagnia . . .' The 'libro grande' must refer to Mgl¹ since 15th- and 17th-c. inventories mention only one, large laudario, but Mgl¹ contains no such collection of Gospels.

[116] Ricc. 1294/2760, fo. 10ʳ; Morpurgo, *I manoscritti*, 358.

the Passion of Christ in rhyme (which, in light of the above payments to singers, were probably intended to be sung).[117] Given the laudesi companies use of Passion settings, laments, and Gospel paraphrases both within and without the lauda literature, their Lenten literary tradition clearly extended beyond what was contained in company laudarios.

The sources discussed above suggest a process whereby lay and clerical religious practices in Florence so nearly approached and resembled one another as to make cross-fertilization inevitable. The desire of the friar-preachers to make their message accessible through sung, vernacular poetry invited the efforts of lay versifiers like Antonio Pucci, and, conversely, rendered available to a lay company the liturgical practices of sung Passions, laments, and Gospels.[118] Pucci provides a glimpse of a type of Florentine layman who facilitated this cross-fertilization: socially active and literate, he was author of both sensuous love lyrics and Gospel paraphrases (inspired, we are told, by the Franciscan friars of his resident quarter of Santa Croce), an improvisatory singer in the Florentine *canta in panca* tradition, a member of the merchant court, and in 1377 he was a captain of the Cathedral laudesi company of San Zanobi.[119] Certainly there is in this connection between the active layman Pucci and the Franciscan friar's Lenten collection at least a hint of the context in which laude were composed and disseminated, as is suggested by the inclusion in Ricc. 1294/2760 of two laude by Pucci.

The Scuole

Until at least the early fifteenth century, weekly schools for the teaching of laude were a regular feature of Florentine laudesi organization.[120] The companies of San Piero Martire, San Zanobi, Orsanmichele, Sant'Agnese,

---

[117] SA 115, fo. 164ʳ.

[118] This intermediate position of late medieval devotions (such as sung Gospels, etc.) has been clearly discussed by Kieckhefer, 'Major Currents in Late Medieval Devotion', 101, where he notes that devotions 'represent a mixture of clerical and lay initiative', and because devotions tended to occupy a position 'between the public acts of liturgy and the private act of contemplation, [they] provided not just for flexibility but also for a sense of linkage between church and the home'. Furthermore, the sacred and secular mingled easily here, for the lay confraternity was 'a kind of miniature church . . . Devotions could thus become symbolic reinforcement for social or political boundaries within society'.

[119] Pucci was a trumpeter and bell-ringer for the city in his youth; he later joined the merchant guild, and occasionally served as an ambassador for the commune. He was famous for the agile *ottava rima* of his love lyrics. A. Sadun, 'Antonio Pucci', *Enciclopedia italiana* (Rome, 1935), xxviii. 488; Becherini, 'Un canta in panca', 241–2. He is listed among the captains of San Zanobi in 1377 as 'Antonio Pucci dalla merchatantia', SZ 2170, fasc. 4, fo. 16ᵛ. Tenneroni, *Inizii*, lists four laude attributed to Pucci (pp. 110, 176, 178, 256), as well as paraphrases of the *Pater noster* and *Ave Maria* (p. 17, contained in Mgl. VII, 373 [1407]).

[120] As in other practices, this laudesi custom is first mentioned in connection with early Sienese practices discussed earlier in this chapter.

and San Frediano certainly maintained such schools, and it is likely that the other companies did as well.[121]

The earliest extant statutes of Sant'Agnese (1291) and Orsanmichele (1294) designated the special office of lauda instructors ('insegnatori delle laude'), whose specified duties were the selection of laude and singers for the services, and the supervision of the singing during the services.[122] However, there is no explicit reference to a weekly *scuola* until the early fourteenth century. In 1326, the Company of San Zanobi drafted the following statute:

We order and establish that the rectors should see to it that on Sundays the singing of laude is taught to those who did not know them. And therefore [the rectors] have full authority to order whom and how many of the company should meet on Sunday in the said church to sing, both those who know [the laude] to teach, and those who don't know them to learn.[123]

The relationship between the *insegnatori* and the *scuola* was made explicit in the 1333 statutes of the Company of Orsanmichele:

The duty of the *governatori* of the laude is to arrange and order how the laude are to be sung every evening before the image of Our Lady on the pilaster beneath the loggia, and to conduct the school on Sundays to learn to sing the laude. And they are to sing in the establishment of the company before the image of Our Lady . . . [and] the laudesi are to obey these *governatori* according to the statutes . . .[124]

The companies of San Zanobi and San Piero Martire retained similar officials in charge of lauda-singers and singing.[125] No statutes prior to the fifteenth century survive for the Company of San Piero Martire, but their account books indicate that 'la schuola la domenicha' existed as early as 1313.[126] There are no extant fourteenth century documents for the Company of Sant'Agnese, but references after 1444, coupled with the company's 1291 provision for lauda instructors, suggests that a *scuola* existed between those dates.[127] In 1428 the Company of San Zanobi drafted the last known statute concerned with the Florentine lauda schools:

---

[121] With the exception of Orsanmichele, all these companies referred to their patron-saint feast as *la festa della scuola*, meaning that the celebration took place at the same time (Sunday, after Mass and midday meal) and in the same location as the weekly *scuola*. Most likely the liturgical portion of the feast took place at an appropriate sanctuary altar, while the commemorative meal occurred in the same location as the *scuola*, the company's private meeting-room.

[122] The Sant'Agnese document is translated above under 'Monthly Processions'.

[123] Ed. in Orioli, *Le confraternite medievali*, 29 (cap. 20).

[124] Ed. in La Sorsa, *La compagnia d'Or San Michele*, 196.

[125] SMN 295, fo. 152ᵛ [1406], indicates that the singers' salaries were determined by the 'chapitani dele lalde'.

[126] SMN 292, fos. 6ʳ, 7ᵛ, 16ᵛ, 58ʳ.   [127] SA 24, fo. 210ᵛ; fo. 225ʳ.

We wish, considering that the first devotion and reverence undertaken by our ancestors and founders . . . was the devotion of singing laude in honour of God, the ever virgin Mary, and glorious Messer Sancto Zenobio, Florentine bishop, that therefore the captains . . . are to provide that on all Sundays the laude are to be taught to those of the company or outside it who are inclined to such things . . . And this is always to be done on the said days after None [c. 3 p.m.] and after eating in our sacristy [of the Cathedral] and residence.[128]

The school, in conjunction with a meal, was conducted in the same place as the company business meetings, usually a church sacristy or chapter room equipped with an altar.[129] The question remains as to exactly who attended the laudesi *scuole*. The companies began hiring salaried singers at about the same time the schools appear to have been instituted, that is, during the first quarter of the fourteenth century. Both developments were probably linked to effective attraction and satisfactory fulfilment of the bequests which the companies were just beginning to receive at this time. But among two centuries of detailed accounts and *partiti* describing the singers' conditions of service, there is no indication that the paid singers ever had anything to do with the schools. It is apparent from the statutes quoted above that both the teachers and the audience of the *scuole* were company members, which the paid singers rarely were, since membership in one company would restrict their freedom to freelance among the other companies (a common practice). Besides, during the republican period the Florentine laudesi were a concentrated and active pool of singers whose individual periods of activity frequently exceeded fifteen years, so that knowledge of the lauda repertory must have been a condition of employment, precluding the need of a *scuola* solely for that function. The probable purpose of the *scuole*, then, was to teach the choral refrains of the laude, which in 'singing and responding' the members sang in responsorial alternation with the longer and numerous strophes sung by the soloists. The Orsanmichele statute cited above (1333) indicates that the *governatori* were to know these refrains well enough to teach them to members, and to lead in the performance of the refrains and assure a smooth alternation between choral refrains and soloistic strophes during the services as a part of their obligation to order the singing. This is very likely the meaning of the 1284 statute of the Company of San Gilio, which decreed that those who came to sing laude in the evening 'in singing and responding should obey the captains'.[130] This responsorial situation

---

[128] App. I, doc. 10.
[129] The 1394 inventory of the Company of San Zanobi lists, among the paintings and altar paraphernalia in the Company's sacristy, the following items (SZ 2170, fasc. 4, fo. 22ᵛ): 'Uno leggio sanza piedi ove si chanta le laude alla schuola . . . Una cisscᴐanna [armchair] a tre serrami dove seghono i chapitani alla schuola'.   [130] Ed. in Schiaffini, *Testi fiorentini*, 39.

corresponds with several documents that grant indulgences for the singing *and* hearing of laude, that is, for singing the refrains and hearing the more spiritually edifying strophes.[131]

The *scuole* may also have been the occasion for teaching laude to young boys. A fourteenth-century inventory of the Company of San Zanobi lists 'a very small book . . . in which are written laude to teach to boys'.[132] The practice is reminiscent of that described in the late thirteenth-century *vita* of the Sienese preacher Ambrogio Sansedoni, which relates that laude were sung 'even by boys, whose keep is paid for, and who are trained to sing these laude'.[133]

After the San Zanobi statute of 1428 cited above, references to the *scuole* disappear from the Florentine laudesi company documents. The change reflects a larger shift in company practices that took place during the first half of the fifteenth century. A decline in the traditional forms and practices of the lauda was dictated by waning zeal for the ancient devotion, and by the advent of new forms and styles in music and poetry. Monophonic practice began to yield to polyphonic lauda singing, as performing forces and references to *tenori* and *biscantatori* increased towards the middle of the century. The refrain form of the trecento ballata ceased to be an essential poetic (and performance) element of fifteenth-century lauda repertoire, which was now clothed in 'frottolesque' forms that did not exclusively employ refrains.[134] This undoubtedly undercut the *scuole*, which had functioned to teach the refrains, but their disappearance must be linked primarily to the declining interest of the congregation in learning the laude and participating in their performance, and the passing of lauda performance entirely into the hands of paid singers. The single greatest sign of the decline of traditional laudesi devotion was the abandonment of company ferial services during this time. During the second quarter of the fifteenth century, all but two companies discontinued the ancient practice. It was retained only by the two wealthiest companies: San Piero Martire, which abandoned ferial singing in 1478, and Orsanmichele, the only company to retain it into the sixteenth century. One of the most truly popular of Florentine devotions had ceased to be truly popular by mid-century. After this time, lauda singing was to be maintained less by the zeal of lay devotion than by the bequests made *in perpetuum* at a time when that zeal was greater.

[131] For example, the 1267 Sienese statutes. Meersseman, *Ordo fraternitatis*, ii. 1058 documents indulgences granted in 1304 to the Pisan Marian companies for singing and hearing laude: 'E se si cantassero le laude, chiunqua le cantasse u stesse a udire, per ciascuna volta arae di perdono die CXL'.

[132] SZ 2170, fasc. 4, fo. 20ᵛ [c.1354]: 'Uno libricciuolo piccolino coperto di cuoio vermiglio dove sono scritte laude per insegnare a' fanciulli'.

[133] See above, n. 16.

[134] N. Pirrotta, 'The Oral and Written Traditions of Music', in *Music and Culture in Italy from the Middle Ages to the Baroque* (Cambridge, Mass., 1984), 75–6.

3

The Companies of Florence

THE SANTA CROCE QUARTER

The Company of Orsanmichele[1]

STILL located midway between the Cathedral and the palace of the Signoria, the meeting place of the Compagnia della Madonna d'Or San Michele from its thirteenth-century origins was the city's greatest confluence of mercantile sensibility and lay spirituality. There is no better image of this city's passionate and worldly piety than the spontaneous veneration of an image of the Virgin that developed beneath the loggia of a bustling grain market, a veneration which in 1291 assumed the popular institutional form of a lauda-singing lay confraternity.[2] Contemporary references indicate both the fame of this devotion, as well as the envy and resentment of the ecclesiastical institutions, of which Orsanmichele was independent. In one of his sonnets, Guido Cavalcanti wrote of the image:

Una figura della Donna mia
S'adora, Guido, a San Michele in
   orto...

A figure of My Lady
Guido adores at San Michele in
   Orto...

La voce va per lontane cammina
Ma dicon che è idolotra i fra minori
Per invidia, che non è lor vicina.[3]

Its fame travels far
But out of envy the
Franciscans say this is idolatry,
   that it is not near their churches.

And having described the new devotion in some detail, the fourteenth-century Florentine chronicler Giovanni Villani added '... but the friars preachers [Dominicans] and minors, out of envy or another reason, did not believe them, wherefore they have fallen into great disgrace with the

---

[1] Short for San Michele in Orto, referring to the little church that originally occupied the site, built in 750 near a stretch of land used for market gardening.

[2] The *orto*, along with the ancient little church of San Michele, was transformed into a grain and cereal market in 1240 by order of the Commune. The company's 1294 statutes state that it was founded on the feast of St Lawrence (10 Aug.), 1291; Castellani, *Nuovi testi*, 651.

[3] G. Cavalcanti, *Rime*, ed. N. Arnone (Florence, 1881), sonnet XXXI, 89. Translated in R. Trexler, 'Florentine Religious Experience: The Sacred Image', *Studies in the Ranaissance*, 19 (1972), 22.

Florentines'.[4] The ambitious programme of building and decorating that transformed Orsanmichele during the next two centuries was a testimony to its great civic and religious importance, as the building, frescos, paintings, sculptures, stained-glass windows, tabernacles, and altars were variously financed and managed by the company, the guilds, the city, and the Parte Guelfa. Nowhere in Florence were the religious affiliations and aspirations of the guilds more publicly displayed.

In the late 1280s, a loggia of brick pillars with a wooden roof, designed by Arnolfo di Cambio, was erected to protect grain merchants during bad weather. Located on one of these pillars was the miraculous *Madonna delle grazie*, which (according to Villani) began to work miracles in 1292, and spawned such an intense devotion that the lay company was organized to venerate and care for the image as well as receive offerings and manage their distribution to the poor.[5] A temporary structure was erected following a fire in 1304, and it was probably sometime during the next three decades that the elaborate wooden tabernacle depicted in the Biadaiolo Codex (*c.*1340) was built to protect a replica of the original Madonna (Plate 4).[6] In 1337 the commune began financing construction of the current structure, a 'palace in which the veneration of the glorious Virgin Mary could be more fittingly carried out and the grain and wheat better protected, preserved, and gathered'.[7] Two upper floors were built to house grain and corn reserves and offices of the communal grain magistracy, and in the new loggia beneath, each of the twenty-one guilds was assigned a pilaster upon which its patron saint was to be painted.[8] Although the silk guild was to supervise construction of the building, the company assumed financial responsibility for religious activities in the

[4] G. Villani, *Cronica*, Bk. VII, ch. 159. Villani was a member of the company, and served as a captain in 1335 and 1342.

[5] N. R. Fabbri and N. Rutenburg, 'The Tabernacle of Orsanmichele in Context', *Art Bulletin*, 63 (1981), 386. The company's images and altars are discussed in Ch. 5. Henderson ('Piety and Charity', *passim*) and Barr (*The Monophonic Lauda*, 156 n. 23) stress the point that the Company of Orsanmichele was first and foremost a charitable society engaged in poor-relief. This is certainly true insofar as the bulk of the company's assets and activities were linked to charitable activities, but the fact that such activities were a part of all Florentine laudesi company activity, that Orsanmichele cultivated lauda-singing longer and more elaborately than any other Florentine company, and that Orsanmichele clearly aligned itself with the other laudesi companies of the city (see Ch. 2 n. 26), would seem to qualify its denomination as one of the most prominent types of lay confraternity in late medieval Florence—a laudesi company.

[6] Fabbri and Rutenburg, 'The Tabernacle of Orsanmichele in Context', 388; B. Cassidy, 'The Financing of the Tabernacle of Orsanmichele', *Source: Notes in the History of Art,* 8 (1988), 2.

[7] G. Gaye, *Carteggio inedito d'artisti dei secoli XIV–XVII*, 3 vols. (Florence, 1839–40), i, 48, citing ASF, Provvisione, filza 28.

[8] L. Artusi and S. Gabbrielli, *Orsanmichele in Firenze* (Florence, 1982), 4. A number of the frescos were executed by Jacopo Landini ('Il Casentino'), the father of the Florentine organist-composer Francesco Landini; ibid., 49. D. Zervas presents basic information on the decoration and construction of the current building in *The Parte Guelfa, Brunelleschi, and Donatello* (Locust Valley, NY, 1987), ch. 4. More detailed information will become available in her forthcoming article on the enclosure of the loggia, and a monograph on Orsanmichele between the 12th and 15th cc.

loggia, including the decoration and maintenance of the Virgin's shrine. The company acquired extraordinary wealth through bequests and candle sales, especially during and after the plague (1348–9), and around this time the company commissioned Orcagna (Andrea di Cione) to construct a huge, Gothic tabernacle, in which was placed a new image of the Orsanmichele Madonna painted by Bernardo Daddi in 1346–7 (Plate 2).[9] In the early 1350s, the commune assumed control of the company after a scandalous mismanagement of finances, and thereafter the company *borsa* (the list of members eligible to hold office) was assembled from those of the Parte Guelfa, the seven major guilds (two each), and the fourteen minor guilds (one each).[10] In 1365 (and again in 1386 and 1388) the Signoria proclaimed the Orsanmichele Madonna as the special protectress of the city, and after company complaints that the noise and dust of the grain market provided an unsuitable devotional environment for this special shrine, communal legislation removed the market from the loggia in 1367.[11] The architectural transformation from grain market to oratory was essentially complete by 1390, when at least the arches nearest the tabernacle had been filled in. Beginning in 1399, the guilds once again placed their patron saints in Orsanmichele, this time commissioning Donatello and his fellow Florentines to fill tabernacles in the exterior piers with some of the most famous sculpture of the Italian Renaissance.[12]

The company's independence of ecclesiastical models was remarkable. There was no consecrated altar until 1343, when a portable altar dedicated to St Anne was installed, and the first fixed altar to which the company had access was in the Church of St Anne, built by decree of the Signoria (and the expense of the company) in 1349 immediately opposite the east façade of Orsanmichele.[13] The tabernacle, although it was the object of lauda-singing devotions, was not an altar, but originally a kind of booth

[9] Zervas, *The Parte Guelfa*, 104–5; Cassidy, 'The Financing of the Tabernacle', 2–4.

[10] G. Brucker, *Florentine Politics and Society, 1343–1378* (Princeton, 1962), 97 n. 169; OSM 25, fos. 28ᵛ–29ʳ; Cassidy, 'The Financing of the Tabernacle', 3 n. 18. Matteo Villani estimated that the company received fl. 350,000 during the plague, much of which was required through bequests to be distributed as alms by the captains. Villani noted, however, that the very poor and needy were dead, and that scandal ensued when the captains used the money otherwise, including, presumably, for the Orcagna commission, for which (according to Ghiberti) the company spent fl. 86,000; M. Villani, *Cronaca*, ed. F. G. Dragomanni, 2 vols. Florence, 1846), Bk. I, ch. 7; Meiss, *Painting in Florence and Siena*, 78. On the disputed issue of how and when the company financed the tabernacle, see Cassidy, 'The Financing of the Tabernacle', 2–6, and Zervas' forthcoming book on Orsanmichele.

[11] Zervas, *The Parte Guelfa*, 104–5.

[12] Ibid. 107 ff. The plan was begun in 1339, but only three sculptures were completed by 1340, and none thereafter until the plan was resumed in 1399 at the company's urging.

[13] Both were to honour the expulsion of the tyrannical duke of Athens on 26 July 1343 (the feast day of St Anne, Mother of Mary), and the cult of St Anne that arose thereafter at Orsanmichele. Ibid. 104. The duke had been appointed ruler for life the previous year but had failed to manage the deepening economic crisis in Florence.

that was used day and night for the sale of candles. With the expulsion of the grain market in 1367, the captains voted to 'construct two altars, furnished as is necessary, beside the tabernacle of Our Lady'.[14] Like the other lay companies, Orsanmichele hired clergy to say Masses, preach, and administer sacraments, and even after the oratory became a collegiate church in 1415, the company remained independent and continued to administer the services and resources of the oratory.[15]

Like other late-medieval corporate entities in Florence, Orsanmichele did not thrive in the fifteenth-century conditions of increasingly centralized government and weakened popular ritual. But with assets of fl. 14,947 in 1427, the company was still the wealthiest of the city's laudesi companies (see Table 1), and its numerous bequests *in perpetuum* assured an enduring ritual life. Orsanmichele remained the epicentre of Florentine laudesi activity through the sixteenth century, and beyond the scope of this study.

TABLE 1. *The Florentine laudesi companies*

Company	Church	Order	Assets[a]
Orsanmichele	Orsanmichele	lay[b]	14,947
S. Piero Martire	Santa Maria Novella	Dominican	11,362
San Zanobi	Cathedral	Diocesan	2,146
Sant'Agnese	S. Maria del Carmine	Carmelite	593
San Gilio	San Gilio[c]	Sacchite	358
Santo Spirito	Santo Spirito	Augustinian (friars)	285
San Lorenzo	San Lorenzo	Collegiate	123
San Frediano	San Frediano[d]	Cistercian	76
San Marco	San Marco	Dominican (observant)	42
San Bastiano	Santissima Annunziata	Servite	
Santa Croce	Santa Croce	Franciscan	
Ognissanti	Ognissanti	Humiliati	

a In florins, according to the Florentine *catasto* of 1427.
b Became a collegiate church in 1415.
c Located within the hospital of Santa Maria Nuova.
d Distinct from San Frediano in Cestello, a larger church in the same quarter.

[14] OSM 56, fo. 82ᵛ [6 Dec. 1367]: 'Deliberarono i capitani detto dì che si faccia fare due altari fornite come bisongnia allato al tabernacholo di Nostra Donna . . .'
[15] Monti, *Le confraternite*, i, 172.

When the earliest extant company statutes were drafted in 1294 and 1297, Orsanmichele appointed four lauda instructors, but at this time the company sang laude 'before the oratory' (i.e. the pilaster supporting the 'figure' of the Virgin) only on feast-days. By the time new statutes were drafted in 1333, the company had begun to sing laude 'every evening before the image of Our Lady on the pilaster beneath the loggia', in spite of the latter's makeshift condition.[16] Between the fire of 1304 and the construction of the new loggia in 1337, the pilaster bearing the image of the Madonna was surrounded by a wooden structure in which the members met, and protected from rain by a tent that was raised during the singing of laude.[17]

A year after the company drafted its 1333 statutes, the captains recorded the following incident:

. . . because the *governatori* of the laude have erased [the names of] certain laudesi of the said company without the knowledge of the captains of the company, a scandal was caused among the said laudesi which proved to be embarrassing to the captains and to the entire company . . . It was therefore decided that a book shall be made in which shall be written all the laudesi of the said company . . . by name and nickname. The company notary shall keep that book, and diligently preserve and guard it . . . and give a copy to the *governatori* of the laude or to their sacristans. And none of [the names of] the laudesi recorded in the said book may be erased or cancelled by a *governatore* or other official or other person of the said company, except by the company notary, and in the presence and at the volition of the captains . . .[18]

Although the exact nature of the 'scandal' is not clear, it probably proceeded from the fact that these were paid singers, in which case the document is an early witness to the conflict of interest that arose between company and singer when the latter no longer sang for devotion alone.

The above document also suggests that more than a few laudesi were retained by the company, and indeed Orsanmichele maintained the largest and most stable professional musical establishment in Florence throughout the fourteenth and fifteenth centuries. During the late fourteenth century, the company's chapel varied between six and ten salaried musicians (probably three to five each for ferial and festal services; see Tables 2 and 3). The oldest surviving records of payments to musicians

[16] Castellani, *Nuovi testi*, 650–73 (1294/1297 statutes); the relevant documents concerning the loggia and the images are translated and discussed in Ch. 5. La Sorsa, *La compagnia*, 191–205 (1333 statutes), 196.

[17] R. Davidsohn, *Forschungen zur Geschichte von Florenz*, 4 vols. (Berlin, 1896–1908), ii, pt. 2, 292; Monti, *Le confraternite*, i, 167.

[18] Ed. in G. Biagi, 'I capitoli della Compagnia della Madonna d'Or San Michele', *Bulletino dell'associazione per la difesa di Firenze antica* (1909), 84–5, from Florence, Biblioteca Medicea Laurenziana, Ms. Antinori 29/66; these OSM statutes were compiled between 1329 and 1333, and differ somewhat from those edited by La Sorsa, whose source was OSM 474 (no longer extant), and which lacks this 1334 addition.

TABLE 2. *The Company of Orsanmichele: salaried musicians, 1361–1591*

Year	Singers			Instrumentalists		Total
	Ferial	Festal	Undesig.	Festal	Undesig.	
1361	3	2		1 V		6
1365–6	5	1	3	1 V		10
1367	4	1	3	1 V		9
1370–80			4		1 V, 1 O	6
1383			6		1 V, 1 O	8
1388			7		1 V, 1 O	9
1406–8			10		1 V, 1 R, 1 O	13
1410			8		1 V, 1 R 1 O	11
1412		3	7		1 V, 2 R, 1 L, 1 O	15
1415–16	6	4			1 R, 1 L, 1 O	13
1427	6	6			1 V, 1 L, 1 O	15
1436–7	6	7			2 R, 1 O	16
1438	5	4	3		1 O	13
1450			12		1 O	13
1508	5 S, 6 T		4 S		1 O	16
1521			5 S, 7 T		1 O	13
1522			6 S, 6 T		1 O	13
1568			6 S, 6 T		1 O	13
1570			6 S, 6 T		1 O	13
1573			6 S, 6 T		1 O	13
1574			9 S, 5 T, maestro		1 O	16
1583–90			8 S, 5 T, maestro		1 O	15
1591			8 S, 2 A, 2 T, 2 B, maestro		1 O	16

V = vielle O = organ R = rebec L = lute S = soprano T = tenor A = alto
B = bass

TABLE 3. *Company of Orsanmichele: salaried musicians in 1388*

	Years	Profession	Other tenures	Total years
Giovanni di Giuliano	1383–1416	wool-carder	SPM, SZ	41
Mazza Palmieri	1370–89		SZ	27
Niccolò di Lippo	1361–87		SZ	36
Niccolò di Lapo	1370–88	music-master	SZ	18
Antonio di Petro	1383–1415		SPM, SZ, SSP	38
Giovanni di Michele	1387–8			2
Antonio di Giovann: Biffoli	1387–1410		SZ, SPM, SF	22
Giovanni di Niccolò Mazzuoli (degli Organi)	1378–1426	organist	Cathedral, S. Felicita	48
Maestro Luigi di Matteo	1384–1413	piffero	SZ, Commune	29

begin in 1361, when the company was paying six singers, 'three singers who sing laude every Saturday and Sunday, and on other solemn days', and 'three other singers who sing laude every evening'.[19] By 1365–66, when the Orsanmichele Madonna became the city's protectress, the company's chapel had nearly doubled to ten salaried musicians. These early company payrolls also reveal a characteristic feature of laudesi activity; the names recorded indicate that two fathers and their sons provided a number of singers for the company, a reflection of a guild society in which professional skills were typically passed from father to son in a master/apprentice relationship.[20]

During the fifteenth century the chapel varied between eleven and sixteen musicians, and then as in the preceding century Orsanmichele generally paid the highest wages in the city. The long list of financial obligations recorded in the company's 1427 tax report begins with the salaried employees who attended to the company's ritual life, and indicates that in spite of the severe contraction of the Florentine economy at this time the Orsanmichele chapel was still the city's largest (fifteen

[19] OSM 1bis, fo. 11ᵛ [July 1361]: 'Tribus cantoribus qui canunt laudas quolibet die sabati et dominice et aliis diebus solempnibus per eorum salario [lacuna] ad rationem [lacuna]. Tribus aliis cantoribus qui canunt quolibet sero laudas pro eorum salario [lacuna].' For more detailed information on the companies' musicians, see B. Wilson, 'Music and Merchants: The Laudesi Companies of Republican Florence, c. 1270–1494' (Ph.D. thesis, Indiana University, 1987), ch. 4.

[20] Domenico Cecchi and his son Cristofano, and Nuto Tendi and his three sons Francesco, Juliano, and Piero served the company during the 1360s and 1370s. Family patterns in laudesi activity are discussed in more detail in Ch. 4.

musicians) and most remunerative (s. 50 per month for ferial musicians, s. 40 per month for festal musicians):

To the sacristan who manages the oratory fl. 3 per month
To 9 chaplains who officiate the oratory L. 756
To 2 clerics who serve at Mass L. 96
To 3 ministers who extinguish the tapers L. 270
To 6 laudesi who sing the laude every day L. 180
To 6 laudesi who sing the laude on feast-days L. 144
To 2 vielle- and lute-players L. 60
To Ser Piero who plays the organ L. 66[21]

This list reveals another extraordinary feature of music at Orsan-michele, the regular use of accompanying instruments in their lauda services.[22] Among Florentine laudesi companies, only San Zanobi used similar instruments, though much less frequently, and Orsanmichele was unique in employing a regular organist throughout the fourteenth and fifteenth centuries. From at least the time of its earliest 1361 records the company was served for long periods of time by a series of professional instrumentalists, beginning with Chellino della Viuola (1361–88), who is most often listed with one or two singers on feast-days.[23]

The careers of the Orsanmichele instrumentalists thereafter reveal how strong were the secular and vernacular currents in this company's practices. Instrumentally-accompanied lauda-singing was certainly modelled upon contemporary secular performance practice, and may well have originated at Orsanmichele, where the conditions were uniquely advantageous for the grafting of that practice onto laudesi devotional practices—the church's traditional censure of instrumental participation in religious services held no force here, and in turn the company's connections with secular musical practices and institutions in the city were particularly strong. One such institution was the city government, which had assumed control of the company in the mid-fourteenth century. The two players who succeeded Chellino were obliged by a single contract to play for both the company and the city. Maestro Luigi della Viuola served the company from 1384 to his death in 1413, when he was succeeded by Pagolo di Ser Ambruogio chiamato Vinci (b. 1368) in both civic and confraternal capacities.[24] As 'excellent player of vielles,

---

[21] ASF, Catasto 291, fos. 72^{r-v}. The ritual (and functional) importance of candles is indicated not only by the fourth item above, but also by the fact that in a single year the company spent more on wax (L. 208 for 520 lb.) than on the salaries of its ferial singers.

[22] Instrumental performance practice in the companies' services is discussed in Ch. 4.

[23] OSM 1bis, fo. 16^r, and D'Accone, 'Le compagnie', 271–3. Chellino is also sometimes listed as a *cantatore*, so he very likely sang and played, as did subsequent instrumentalists.

[24] Maestro Luigi is first mentioned in connection with the company when he and Chellino petitioned the Signoria for robes; ASF, Provvisione 73, fo. 4^r [30 Mar. 1384]. My thanks to Diane Zervas for bringing this document to my attention.

rebecs, lutes, and other instruments', Pagolo replaced Maestro Luigi, 'vielle-player, who in the duration of his life continuously served this company with the song of his vielle in praise and reverence of blessed Mary', as the company's higher paid stringed-instrument player; and Pagolo also replaced Luigi in the service of the Signoria, playing during their meals 'with [a] vielle or another instrument'.[25] In 1388 both Orsanmichele and the city recorded the institution of a new service in the company, the description of which relates the untroubled transformation of a secular civic ceremony into a religious devotion:

The *pifferi* and *sonatores*[26] of the said commune, with their trumpets, bells, and instruments, are obliged to come to the said oratorio on each solemn [feast]-day, the solemn vigils of the Virgin Mary, the Paschals [of Christmas and Easter], and every Sunday morning, and to play devoutly and solemnly render *mactinata* while the image of the gracious Mother of God is unveiled.[27]

[25] G. Zippel, *I suonatori della Signoria di Firenze* (Trent, 1892), 22–3 '. . . optimum sonatorem viole, ribeche, liuti et aliorum instrumentorum'; '. . . sonitor viole, qui tempore sue vite dicte societati in laudem et reverentiam beate Marie cum melodia dicte viole continue serviebat'; '. . . cum viola vel aliquo instrumento'. Pagolo served the company from 1405 to at least 1437; for a more detailed profile based on his 1427 tax report, see Appendix III. In 1404 both institutions recorded the service of the singer Bernaba di Cristofano Loci, a 47-year-old cloth-cutter who served the Company between 1403 and at least 1437, and served the city as 'cantor dominorum priorum'; for documents and profile see Appendix III.

[26] *Pifferi*: players of wind instruments in general, including shawms and bombards (*ceramelle*), pipes (*fistule*, *zuffoli*), bagpipes (*cornamuse*), but also including percussion (*tamburini*, *nacherini*, and *cembalo*, a type of frame drum). *Sonatores* (*suonatori*) usually refers to instrumentalists in general, but in this particular context probably indicates the other prevalent category of instrumentalists, *trombadori*: players of brass instruments in general (*trombetti*), including curved trumpets, cornetts, and sackbuts, as opposed to *tubatores*, players of the straight trumpet; Zippel, *I suonatori della Signoria di Firenze, passim*; L. Cellesi, 'Documenti per la storia musicale di Firenze', *Rivista musicale italiana*, 34 (1928), 579–602. Outdoor brass- and wind-players were numerous in Florence, for they were integral to the civic ceremonial life of the Italian communes; the Florentine city government, as well as the Parte Guelfa and the Merchant Court, employed their own retinues throughout most of the republican period. On the city's instrumentalists, see Zippel, *I suonatori*. The Merchant Court reported in the 1427 *catasto* a payment of L. 180 per year to six 'trombetti e pifferi'; ASF, Catasto 291, fo. 1ʳ. Each of the twenty-one guilds also sponsored a patron-saint festival for which brass- and/or wind-players were hired; in 1427, the *calimala* (merchant's) guild spent L. 26 per year on two feasts, the Beheading of John the Baptist, and St Anne, which included 'trombetti e pifferi'; ibid., fo. 4ʳ.

[27] OSM 1, fos. 62ᵛ–63ʳ; ed. in D'Accone, 'Le compagnie', 274. The Orsanmichele musicians for this year are listed in Table 3. The first recorded payments to communal musicians for this service date, however, from 1387; OSM 16, fo. 16ʳ. 'Mactinata' (*mattinate*) was a part of the duties of the city musicians in Italian communes, an early morning salutation for the priors, usually played in the piazza before the priors' *palazzo*; Zippel, *I suonatori*, 11. This seems, however, to be an anomalous use of a term that more typically denoted noisy, often lewd, parodies of serenades sung to women (often widows) from the streets in the late-medieval towns of central and northern Italy; C. Klapisch-Zuber, 'The "Mattinata" in Medieval Italy', in *Women, Family, and Ritual in Renaissance Italy*, trans. L. Cochrane (Chicago, 1985), 261–82. The term might also refer to the popular, bawdy tunes that were sung on these occasions; W. Prizer, 'Games of Venus: Secular Vocal Music in the Late Quattrocento and Early Cinquecento', *Journal of Musicology*, 9 (1991), 33–4. In 1416 the company recorded the feast-days, on the vigils and mornings of which the image of the Virgin might be unveiled: Saturday evenings, Sunday mornings, the four principal feasts of the Virgin, Christmas, Easter, the two feasts of St Michael, the Ascension of Christ, the Visitation of St Elizabeth, the feast

The Orsanmichele organists were another vital point of contact with the city's larger musical life, for organists tended to be the most well-trained Florentine musicians, and Orsanmichele's was clearly one of the more desirable posts in the city (along with those at the Cathedral and San Lorenzo). Parts of the oratory were sufficiently enclosed by 1368 for the company's organ to be tuned and installed in the oratory,[28] and thereafter the company was served by three generations of organists from a single family: Maestro Niccolò di Lapo Mazzuoli (1370–6), Maestro Giovanni di Niccolò Mazzuoli (1378–c.1426), and Ser Piero di Giovanni Mazzuoli (d. 1430). We know relatively little about Niccolò, but D'Accone's research has shown that Giovanni and Piero were leading Florentine musicians, both as organists and as composers of secular polyphony.[29] Piero (who is the Ser Piero in the 1427 *catasto* cited above) was succeeded shortly after his death in 1430 by the most famous Italian organist of his time, Antonio Squarcialupi.[30]

The tax report filed by the Company in 1438 reveals a significant economic decline during these lean years. The cash value of the company's assets had diminished from nearly fl. 15,000 in 1427 to fl. 10,570 in 1438, but the company continued to maintain its 1427 level of expense for musicians' salaries (about L. 450 per year), although significant changes in the complexion of the chapel had taken place during the intervening years. The company was now paying one organist (L. 72/year), nine

of St Anne, and for all processions; OSM 23, fo. 4ᵛ. [11 Jan. 1415/16]. Zippel records a 1452 Provvisione indicating that the Orsanmichele service was still a part of the instrumentalists' duties; *I suonatori*, 19–20 n. 4.

[28] OSM 56, fo. 91ᵛ [7 Feb. 1367/8]. In 1376 the captains elected Niccolò di Lippo to play the organ in the appointed place '. . . quod fiat expressis sotus [*sic*] locus clausus ubi possit sonari, cum non sit honestum sonari in tabernaculo' (OSM 10, fo. 15ᵛ [14 July 1376]), which implies that the organ (probably a small *portativo*) had been kept and played in the tabernacle for the previous eight years until the oratory had reached a stage of enclosure sufficient to allow its removal to a more proper and adequate location in the oratory.

[29] F. D'Accone, 'Giovanni Mazzuoli: A Late Representative of the Italian Ars Nova', *L'Ars nova italiana del Trecento*, 2 (Certaldo, 1968), 23–38; 'Una nuova fonte dell'ars nova italiana: il codice di San Lorenzo, 2211', *Studi musicali*, 13 (1984), 3–27. Niccolò also served as a singer during his tenure at Orsanmichele, and also as an officer for the Company of San Zanobi in 1397 (SZ 2171, fasc. 6C, fo. 254ʳ). Giovanni is the *Magister Johannes de Florentia* for whom 21 blank pages were allotted in the largest and most sumptuous manuscript of Trecento secular polyphony, the Squarcialupi Codex, and he seems also to have held posts as organist at the Cathedral and the smaller church of Santa Felicita. Several weeks after his election to the Orsanmichele post on 5 Jan. 1379, the company provided 40 gold florins for the purchase of a new pair of organs (OSM 11, fo. 26ᵛ), and though his long career with the company is recorded only through 1415, he probably served until his death in 1426 (documents are lacking for 1419–33). Piero was a public notary and communal judge by profession, but he served as organist at the Cathedral (temporarily assuming his father's duties) and at San Lorenzo (1403–15) where he succeeded Francesco Landini, and he has recently been discovered to have been one of the last Florentine composers of Trecento style polyphony; D'Accone, 'Una nuova fonte', 15–17.

[30] Squarcialupi (1416–80) turns up in the scant company records of this period in 1431–3, 1436 (OSM 26, fos. 16ᵛ ff.), and 1450–3, and he was also the Cathedral organist during 1432–80; F. D'Accone, 'Antonio Squarcialupi alla luce di documenti inediti', *Chigiana*, 23 (1966), 3–24.

laudesi (L. 246/year), one 'master who is appointed to sing at certain times and to teach two boys' (fl. 24/year), and 'one boy in residence, who sings' (L. 24/year).[31] This new configuration of musicians had already been established by 1436; see Table 4. In effect, the company had discontinued the regular use of all string instruments (they disappear from even the occasional use of all the laudesi companies at this time), cancelled the positions of one ferial and one festive singer, and re-channelled those salaries into the position of a singing master. The presence of a singing master and young students signifies an important musical development in which Orsanmichele was very likely the vanguard among the city's lay companies—the cultivation of polyphonic lauda-singing. There are strong signs that such performances were already underway at Orsanmichele in the late fourteenth century, and the above reference is predated by one in 1412 to the singing master Bertino di maestro Francesco and 'due fanciulli biscantatori e laudesi'.[32] In 1436 the Company hired Magister Benoctus de Francia to 'retain two

TABLE 4. *Company of Orsanmichele: salaried musicians in 1436*

	Age	Salary	Years	Profession	Other tenures	Total years
ferial singers:						
Maso di Niccolò	59	s. 50/mo.	1418–37	laudese	SPM, SZ	28
Guasparre d'Ugolino Prosperi	50	s. 50	1418–53	glove-maker	SZ	35
Piero di Niccolò Crinelli		s. 50	1403–37		SPM, SF	42
Lorenzo di Giovanni		s. 50	1432–7	furrier	SZ, SSP	7
Francesco di Niccolò degli Asini	21	s. 50	1436–7		SZ	10
Vettorio d'Agnolo Bordoni	54	s. 50	1418–36	cloth-burler, laudese	SZ, SPM	34
festal singers:						
Bartolomeo di Lodovico		s. 40	1418–37		SZ	42
Goro di Maso		s. 40	1432–7		SZ, Cathedral	11
Bernaba di Cristofano Loci		s. 40	1403–37	cloth-shearer	SZ, Commune	34
Francesco di Bartolo		s. 40	1436–7	priest	Cathedral	2
Benocto de Francia, 2 boys		fl. 2	1436–7	cantor	Cathedral	2
instrumentalists:						
Pagolo di Ser Ambruogio ('Vinci'), R, V	71	s. 50	1405–37	piffero	SZ, SA	35
Prospero di Guasparre R, V	17	s. 20	1436–7		SZ	2
Antonio Squarcialupi O	20	L. 4	1431–53	organist	Cathedral	22

[31] ASF, Catasto 602 (1438), no. 1: '1 sonattore d'orghano . . . 9 ladesi . . . 1 maestro ch'è diputtato a chantare a cierti tempi e 'nsengniare a 2 fanc[i]ulli . . . 1 fanciullo in luogo di ministro che chanta . . .' The nine laudesi were five ferial singers at s. 50/mo., and four festal singers at s. 40/mo.; the salary of the boy in residence (s. 40/mo.) indicates that he was a festal singer.

[32] OSM 20, fos. 84ᵛ, 158ʳ; OSM 21, fo. 12ʳ [Oct 1412–Oct. 1413]. The two boys were Martino di Vanni Martino and Domenico di Salvestro Tati, both of whose fathers were active Florentine laudesi (see the profile of Vanni, who was a laudese by profession according to his 1427 tax report, in Appendix III), and all four of whom sang together for the companies of Orsanmichele and San Piero Martire between 1412 and 1417, as paired boys and as father/son pairs.

boys whom he will teach to sing, and all of whom are to sing on the vigils and days of the customary feasts'.[33] This is certainly a reference to Magister Benottus de Ferraria ('Benoit'), the first master of the Florentine Cathedral's new polyphonic chapel, which was formed in 1438 shortly after the consecration of the Cathedral, and during the transfer from Ferrara to Florence of the Council for the Union between the Greek and Latin Churches.[34] Maestro Benotto was a musician of international stature, a Burgundian singer and polyphonic composer who during 1448–55 was also recorded in the service of the Este court in Ferrara and the papal court in Rome, and may well have been a key figure in the dissemination of polyphonic repertoire among these cities.[35] During 1436–7 Orsanmichele retained at least two other singers who later joined the élite polyphonic chapel at the Cathedral, and while the Cathedral *operai* (and Medici patrons) may have succeeded in their desire to musically 'excel all other churches in honour', Orsanmichele surely continued to provide the city with its most splendid vernacular liturgy.[36] Polyphonic performance, almost exclusively a clerical activity

[33] OSM 26, fo. 24ᵛ [13 Nov. 1436]: 'Item condusserunt [sic] Magistrum Benoctum franciscum magistrum musicum qui retinere debeat duos pueros quos doceat cantare et qui omnes cantent vigiliis et diebus festivis consuetis cum salario florenorum duorum pro quolibet mensis initiando die xv presentis mensis.' On fo. 29ᵛ he is referred to as 'Magister Benocto de francia cantori [sic]'. How long he served the company is unclear, since there are no extant documents for 1437–49.

[34] F. D'Accone, 'The Singers of San Giovanni in Florence during the 15th Century', *Journal of the American Musicological Society*, 14 (1961), 308–14; A. Seay, 'The 15th-Century Cappella at Santa Maria del Fiore in Florence', *Journal of the American Musicological Society*, 11 (1958), 45. Benotto served the Cathedral until 1448.

[35] P. Starr, 'The "Ferrara Connection": A Case Study of Musical Recruitment in the Renaissance', *Studi Musicali*, 18 (1989), 3–17. See esp. 8–12, where Dr Starr confirms the identity of Maestro Benotto (also referred to as Benedetto di Giovanni and 'Benoit') as the papal singer Benedictus Siredé, a cleric from the province of Sens in Haute-Bourgogne, and suggests that he may have had a hand in the compilation and copying of Modena α.X.1.11 (Mod B), a major collection of 15th-c. polyphony which contains three works attributed to 'Benoit'. On Benotto in Ferrara, see also Lockwood, *Music in Renaissance Ferrara*, 54 and 57.

[36] The company recorded a payment on 14 Feb. 1437 to Maestro Benocto, whose name was then crossed out and replaced by Francesco Bartoli, 'et 4 suis sotiis cantoribus in ecclesia . . . pro missa predicta cantanda . . . L. 2 s. 15'; OSM 26, fo. 36ʳ. Francesco was also a member of the Cathedral's original polyphonic chapel, officially established late the following year. Either he and his companions were hired by the company from among the cathedral's chant choir, or, given the apparent presence at the Cathedral of both Francesco and Benocto in Feb. 1437, the Cathedral's polyphonic chapel was being informally established by the Medici nearly two years before its first documented existence on 9 Dec. 1438. Starr suggests that both musicians were lured to Ferrara between these dates (while the Council was still in that city), where they were then engaged by the Medici; 'The "Ferrara Connection"', 8 n. 16. Company documents suggest that Francesco was an organist and a priest as well, for from Feb. to Aug. of 1436, the organist for the company was 'Ser Francesco Bartoli presbitero, sonatori orghanorem'; [sic] OSM 26, fos. 5ʳ, 16ᵛ. Goro di Maso was a festal and ferial singer for Orsanmichele in 1432 and 1437 (OSM 62, fo. 36ʳ; 26, fo. 4ᵛ), and as 'Ser Ghoro di Maso' (probably a priest), a *tenorista* among the Cathedral's six singers in 1445–6; D'Accone, 'The Singers of San Giovanni', 313. On Cosimo de' Medici's role in both the transferral of the Council to Florence, and the establishment of the Cathedral's polyphonic choir (the singers of which were also in the private employ of the Medici), see ibid. 307–13.

throughout most of Europe until this time, became increasingly frequent among the lay singers of the Florentine laudesi companies during the early fifteenth century, and might be viewed as a degree of musical literacy commensurate with the broad cultural literacy that marked Quattrocento Florence.

The validity and prestige of Orsanmichele as a devotional centre was confirmed in 1413 by a sustained visit from the papal singers (*cantori del papa*). Particularly impressive is the city-wide network of goods and services that were assembled for a series of events inspired by the St Anne feast (26 July), but which embraced also the feasts of St James (25 July) and St Lawrence (10 Aug.). The company recorded expenses for the visitors for singing on the feast of St Anne (as well as several Masses on other occasions), 'trombadori, trombetti, e pifferi' of the commune as well as the Parte Guelfa, vestments, relics, and friars from Santo Spirito, food for five commemorative meals, and pages from the Parte Guelfa 'to assemble many citizens to attend the said feast [of St Anne]'.[37] The papal entourage must have been that of John XXIII (Baldassare Cossa), who from 21 June to 6 November of that year stayed at the monastery of Sant'Antonio del Vescovo outside Florence while he sought Florentine support during his flight from the troops of King Ladislaus.[38] Apparently the pope was never admitted to the city since the Florentines wished to avoid the appearance of siding too strongly against Ladislaus, and in fact the Orsanmichele documents never mention the pope, but the participation of his singers in the popular Florentine feast of St Anne at the city's most visible lay confraternity may well have been part of John XXIII's campaign to lobby for Florentine support.

During a long lacuna in the Orsanmichele records (1454–1507), it is likely that the company continued to maintain a chapel of thirteen to sixteen singers, who by at least the 1470s were designated as *sovrani* (sopranos) and *tenoristi*, a change that is documented below with respect to the companies of San Piero Martire and San Zanobi.[39] Orsanmichele

---

[37] OSM 21, fos. 4ᵛ–5ᵛ [31 Aug. 1413]. Of the 23 patron-saint feasts recorded in the company's 1427 tax report (St Michael, St Anne, and one each for the 21 guilds), musicians were hired regularly only for the St Anne feast (L. 5 for instrumentalists and the considerable sum of L. 20 'to the friars who sing the laude on the feast of St Anne'); ASF, Catasto 291, fo. 73ᵛ. This latter is the same amount paid to the Santo Spirito friars for the 1413 feast, an indication that the papal singers shared the musical celebration of the St Anne services with the lauda-singing friars (and probably with the Orsanmichele musicians, as well), and that clerics were already becoming involved in singing laude for the companies' services (which they came to dominate in the 16th c.).

[38] G. Brucker, *The Civic World of Early Renaissance Florence* (Princeton, 1977), 370–5.

[39] Contemporary Cathedral records indicate that the term *tenorista* (*tinorista, tenore, tinore*) referred to all the lower parts in a polyphonic ensemble, whether two-, three-, or four-part; D'Accone, 'Alcune note', 109. The usage probably derives from the original designation of these lower parts as tenor, contratenor altus, and contratenor bassus. The six to seven *tenoristi* maintained by Orsanmichele during this time were therefore probably two to three each of alto, tenor, and bass. 1591 statutes specify six sopranos and two each of altos, tenors, and basses; OSM 478, fo. 4ᵛ.

continued to attract the city's leading musicians. Among the ferial *sovrani* in 1508 was Bernardo di Benedetto Pagoli, who was to become the well-known composer Bernardo Pisano.[40] In 1509, the company was served by another of the city's long line of illustrious organist/composers, Bartolomeo degli Organi. Between 1488 and 1500, he had sung and accompanied laude at the church of Santissima Annunziata, and in 1509 he was organist in three of the leading Florentine musical establishments—Orsanmichele, the Cathedral, and Santissima Annunziata.[41] Perhaps the last of the eminent Florentine musicians to begin their musical careers in the city's laudesi companies was Jacopo Peri (1561–1633), who on 11 November 1572 was listed among the Orsanmichele sopranos.[42]

Company documents regarding musical activities are lacking for the years between 1529 and 1567. Most of the other laudesi companies in the city suffered a complete disruption of cultic activities during this period of great social and political upheaval, but it is likely that Orsanmichele's substantial assets and its close association with the communal government enabled it to function in spite of these conditions.[43] From 1568 to 1593 the company recorded payments to an organist, a choirmaster, six 'cantori delle laude' (the *tenoristi*), four to five ferial sopranos, and four festive sopranos.[44] The company also continued to support a singing master and what had now become a school for all the salaried boy sopranos; a *memoriale* of 29 April 1573 outlined the duties of the choirmaster (at that time Maestro Stefano d'Antonio Gallacini), who was responsible for the instruction:

[Maestro Stefano] . . . is required to teach all the sopranos who are paid to serve in the chapel, for two hours in the morning and two in the afternoon, in the school set aside for that purpose, [which is] in the house of the [company's] priest above our meeting-room.[45]

---

[40] Id., 'Bernardo Pisano: An Introduction to his Life and Works', *Musica disciplina*, 17 (1963), 115–35.

[41] Id., 'Alessandro Coppini and Bartolomeo degli Organi: Two Florentine Composers of the Renaissance', *Analecta musicologica*, 4 (1967), 74–5.

[42] OSM 34, fo. 34ᵛ:'Jacopino di [*lacuna*] Peri . . . L. 3'. Peri's eminence as an adult singer and composer reached well beyond Florence, especially after his association with Jacopo Corsi's Florentine academy when he composed music for the earliest extant opera, *Euridice* (1600). In 1573 he was a lauda-singer (with organ accompaniment) at Santissima Annunziata, and from 1588 a court musician for the Medici; D'Accone, 'The Florentine Fra Mauros: A Dynasty of Musical Friars', *Musica disciplina*, 33 (1979), 101–2; William V. Porter, 'Peri, Jacopo', in *The New Grove Dictionary of Music and Musicians* (London, 1980).

[43] The decline and transformation of the companies during this period is discussed in Ch. 6.

[44] OSM 31bis [1568–9], fos. 51ᵛ–52ʳ; 32 [1569–70], fos. 34ʳ⁻ᵛ; 33 [1570–1], fo. 34ᵛ; 34 [1572–3], fos. 34ʳ⁻ᵛ; 35 [1574–5], fos. 34ᵛ–35ʳ; 38 [1583–4], fo. 34ʳ; 42 [1589–93], fos. 65ᵛ, 93ᵛ.

[45] OSM 34, fo. 13ʳ [29 Apr. 1573]:'[Maestro Stefano] . . . è tenuto due hore la mattina e due il giorno insegnare a tutti sovrani che sono stipendiati per servitio di essa cappella nella scuola ordinata per ciò nella casa del proposto sopra la nostra audientia.'

1591 statutes stipulate that the company was to retain at least twelve
lauda singers (six sopranos and two each of basses, tenors, and altos), a
choirmaster (who was to sing, as well as teach singing to boys so as to
provide sufficient numbers of soprano lauda-singers), and an organist
who accompanied the laude as well as the sung Masses and Vespers.[46]
The 'cantori delle laudi' and the organist were to 'serve at the church in
celebrating the Masses and Divine Offices, and in singing the laude', and
the occasions are specified in detail: Vespers on Saturdays, Mass and
Vespers on Sundays, and Mass and Vespers on the vigils of the four feasts
of the Virgin (Annunciation, Nativity, Purification, and Assumption),
Ascension, Corpus Christi, Pentecost, St John the Baptist, All Saints,
and Christmas. During Holy Week the singers were also required to
perform the Lamentations and Benedictus, and on the feast of St Anne a
polyphonic Mass and special Vespers music, all in addition to 'the
customary laude'. The ancient association between lauda-singing and
the evening liturgical services is reflected here, as well as in the 1563 lauda
publication of the Dominican friar Serafino Razzi, whose *Libro primo
delle laudi* (Razzi[1]) bears a title-page with the words 'for use in the
churches of Florence after Vespers and Compline'.

   Clearly Orsanmichele continued throughout the sixteenth century to
maintain a vital tradition of polyphonic lauda-singing; clerics gradually
displaced the companies' lay performers, but the Latin liturgy had not
displaced the lauda. In fact, Orsanmichele appears to have continued
acquiring new repertoire; in 1569 the company paid Ser Jacopo Raphaelis
de Campio 'for 230 laude copied by him in the new book of the said
oratorio at the rate of s. 13 d. 4 for each lauda'.[47]

   During this period, the laymen gradually disappeared from the ranks
of Orsanmichele's adult singers while the lay vigil gave way to the
ecclesiastical liturgy as the primary context for the performance of laude.
By 1584 the lower polyphonic parts were sung almost entirely by clergy,
and although the company was apparently training its own sopranos and
admitting lay singers like Peri, Orsanmichele was after all a collegiate
church and the school was probably an informal *schola* which served
primarily boys receiving a clerical training. Only a handful of non-
clerical singers who had acquired training in polyphonic singing continued
to maintain the ancient association between layman and lauda.[48]

   [46] OSM 478, fo. 4[v]: 'Sianci li cantori delle laude in numero xii al meno, cioè dua contrabassi, dua
tenori, dua contralti, et sei soprani, con un maestro di canto, quale soprastia a tutti et chiamisi
Maestro di Cappella, et l'organista per sonare l'organo. Et questi tutti servino all chiesa in celebrar le
messe et divini offitii, et incantare [*sic*] le laude . . .'.
   [47] OSM 31bis, fo. 58[v].
   [48] From 1515 to 1521 the company paid a 'magister capelle laudensium', Agniolo del Favilla, who
also served as choirmaster for the Companies of Santo Spirito (1518–22) and San Zanobi (1512).
Among the *tenoristi* who served the company between 1568 and 1574 was Bastiano di Tommaso

The Company of Santa Croce

One would expect the great Florentine Franciscan church and devotional centre of the quarter to shelter one of the major laudesi companies of the city, but we shall never know the real stature of this company since most of its documents were destroyed by floods in 1333 and 1557. Even its 1427 tax report is inexplicably absent from among those filed by the other lay religious companies, although it is possible that this company was unique among the Florentine laudesi companies in declining to accept bequests and acquire property.[49] What remains of its first 350 years of existence are two late thirteenth-century letters of indulgence, several sets of late fifteenth- and sixteenth-century statutes, and an early sixteenth-century inventory.

Certainly one of the oldest lay companies of Florence, the 'Compagnia di Santa Maria delle laulde' was founded during the preaching of St Peter Martyr, for its 1589 statutes recall the drafting of its first set in 1244.[50] The first reference to it as a laudesi company is a letter from the General of the Franciscan order, frater Raymundus, dated 25 May 1290, which confers upon the company a share of the spiritual benefits of the Order.[51] On 7 February 1297 the bishop of Florence, Francesco Monaldeschi, granted forty days of indulgence to the 'Sotietas Sancte Crucis de Florentia' for processing and singing laude in the church of Santa Croce (see Plate 10).[52] The company's 1470 statutes imply that ferial singing had been discontinued, but nevertheless reveal a strong spiritual and material commitment to the devotion:

. . . and for the obligatory feasts laude are to be sung in the church of Santa Croce in honour of [the Virgin Mary] our advocate, according to ancient custom . . . [Having] considered that through these great devotions a great spiritual and temporal utility is generated and acquired, as many as possible of the captains and *fratelli* of our company are to take part in these laude . . . And for the said laude may be spent as much as seems advisable to the said captains and their councillors.[53]

Arditi, the tailor who also served as choirmaster for the Company of San Piero Martire during c. 1550–80.

[49] See Henderson, 'Piety and Charity', 133 n. 35, where he notes that the company's 1470 and 1485 statutes do not mention property.

[50] ASF, CmRS, Capitoli 74, fo. 1ʳ.

[51] ASF, Diplomatico Patrimonio Ecclesiastico, 25 May 1290. The document is catalogued with the above date, but is actually signed with the date 8 June 1290. Meersseman states that the Company of Santa Croce was founded as a laudesi company before 1278 (*Ordo fraternitatis*, ii, 977), but in relying upon Davidsohn he mistakenly cited another lay company with a similar title founded on that date, the 'Societas mediocris S. Marie de Sancta Cruce ad Templum' (*Forschungen*, iv. 431).

[52] Appendix I, doc. 21, lines 9–10, 16–21.

[53] ASF, CmRS, Capitoli 53, Cap. I (incomplete and without foliation); Appendix I, doc. 22.

Company members were still receiving a forty-day indulgence 'alla nostra cappella', that is, for attending the lauda services. The men and women of the company gathered on the feast days of the Virgin, the feasts of St Lucy (for the *ufficio generale*) and Holy Cross, and every second and fourth Sunday of the month, for which occasions the sacristan was to set up the lectern for the laude, the altar, and the benches.[54] Inventories of 1521 and 1523 list 'uno libro di lalde grande . . . miniato d'oro' that was probably the festive laudario used on these occasions, while a ferial 'libro di lalde minore' listed in 1521 had disappeared by 1523.[55]

The company's special patron-saint feast was the Assumption of the Virgin (15 August), the special feature of which is related in a 1485 statute concerning lauda singing:

. . . [the captains] are obligated to execute the singing of laude on every obligatory feast, to the praise and honour of God and Our Lady, in the church of Santa Croce of Florence. And furthermore, we desire that on the vigil of the Assumption of Our Lady, the flaming star ('la stella accesa') be placed in the middle of the church, and laude are to be sung on that evening, according to a good and ancient custom.[56]

This large, candle-lit star was apparently a resident fixture in the church, for a 1523 inventory lists 'one large star in the middle of the church', as well as '25 angels for the star'.[57] In 1485, the *sindaco*, who managed the lauda-singing, was constrained to pay the 'laldieri' through the general treasurer, and was subject to immediate dismissal if he was remiss in his duties relating to the laude.[58]

The records of another laudesi company provide us with the name of one Santa Croce singer. In 1490, the Company of Sant'Agnese paid a partial salary to one of their *tenori*, Giovambattista di Currado, because he had gone 'to serve at Santa Croce', scrupulously noting that 'he could not be here and there at the same time'.[59] This is the only indication that

---

[54] ASF, CmRS, Capitoli 53, Cap. X, Cap. VII.

[55] ASF, CmRS 1373, no. 1, fasc. F, fos. 1–2; the 1523 inventory also lists 'iiii libri da dire l'uficio'.

[56] ASF, CmRS, Capitoli 874 [1485–1538], fo. 5ᵛ; Appendix I, doc. 2.

[57] ASF, CmRS 1373, no. 1, fasc. F, fo. 3ʳ⁻ᵛ. According to Monti, the star contained an image of the Virgin in the centre, and was suspended between the Asini and Guidacci chapels near where the company conducted its devotions; *Le confraternite*, i. 164–5. A 1395 inventory of the Company of San Zanobi lists two *stelle* to be hung in the church during feast days, one bearing the arms of the guilds, the other described as large and painted, upon which were hung angels and seraphims, which was also to be suspended 'nel mezo della chiesa' near the altar of St Zenobius; SZ 2170, fasc. 4, fo. 23ʳ. On these illuminated stars as devotional objects to be borne in procession, see Henderson, 'Piety and Charity', 52, 71 nn. 42–5, and Barr, *The Monophonic Lauda*, 19.

[58] ASF, CmRS, Capitoli 874, fo. 15ʳ [1485]: 'Cap. VI: E più vogliamo che detto sindacho sia tenuto diligentemente fare chantare le lalde chom'è usato, chon pacto che non possa paghare lui proprio danari a' laldieri né altri, ma faccigli paghare al nostro chamarlingho generale. E se detto sindacho manchassi de fare chantare dette lalde s'intenda essere dis[messo] . . .'.

[59] SA 4, fo. 36ᵛ [July–Dec. 1490]: 'Giovambattista di Currado . . . non ci cantò perchè serviva a Sancta Croce, et non potea essere et là et qui a un tempo medesimo.'

the Santa Croce laudesi may have been maintaining a polyphonic chapel similar to those of the other Florentine companies at this time.

Within fifty years, however, the company had abandoned lauda-singing. They revised statutes again in 1538, and, citing the dwindling membership, income, and devotion, and inadequate numbers of singers, decided to provide a dowry of L. 25 per year to the daughters of needy members in place of lauda singing.

THE SAN GIOVANNI QUARTER

The Company of San Zanobi

According to 1326 statutes, the company was founded on the vigil of the feast of St John the Baptist in 1281.[60] During most of the fourteenth century, the company, like the old Romanesque cathedral in which it met, was named for the city's oldest patron saint, St Reparata. The new cathedral of Santa Maria del Fiore having risen up around it, the last of the old cathedral was destroyed in February 1375,[61] and by 1377 the company was holding its business meetings in the sacristy of the new church.[62] By *c.*1420 the company had shifted its special patronage (and name) to St Zenobius; the cult of the city's first (fourth-century) bishop had been rejuvenated in 1331 when Giovanni Villani reported that the saint's relics were exhumed with great festivity,[63] and by 1337 the company's primary feast-day was in honour of 'San Zenobio, nostro padre'.[64]

Although in 1427 the company's assets were well below those of Orsanmichele and San Piero Martire (see Table 1), its ritual life, perhaps through association with the Cathedral, was no less splendid. Weissman's analysis of membership during the early 1330s shows that for a laudesi company, a relatively high percentage (40%) of San Zanobi members had family names, and the company had a strong city-wide appeal (30% of the membership was from outside the immediate quarter of San Giovanni).[65] Among fifteenth-century members were the painter Cosimo

[60] SZ 2170, fasc. 1, fo. 3ʳ; the 1326 statutes (and additions made between 1334 and 1377) are edited in Orioli, *Le confraternite medievali*, 20–43. The sources for the legendary (and unlikely) existence of this laudesi company in 1183, and again in 1233, are early Servite chroniclers; the Servites attribute the origin of their order (1233) to seven young noblemen whom they claim were members of a laudesi confraternity at the cathedral. These dates have been refuted by Meersseman, *Ordo fraternitatis*, ii, 922–3, n. 4.

[61] C. Guasti, *Santa Maria del Fiore* (Florence, 1887), 237.   [62] Orioli, *Le confraternite*, 41.

[63] *Cronica*, Bk. x, 168.   [64] D'Accone, 'Le compagnie', 263–4.

[65] Weissman, *Ritual Brotherhood*, 68. 279 individuals joined the company during the early 1330s. Of the 31% listed by occupation, 5% were *sottoposti* labourers, 27% independent contractors or middlemen in the production of cloth, 12% barbers, moneylenders, or other providers of local services, 25% local tradesmen or sellers of foodstuffs, 20% sellers of luxury items or traders in fine arts, 4% bankers, professionals, or major guildsmen, and 5% clergy.

Roselli (a *festaiuolo* in 1475), and, from at least 1474, Lorenzo de' Medici, followed by several other members of the family.[66] A significant aspect of the company's membership is what appears to have been an informal school of lauda poets. Of the Florentine authors of laude listed by Tenneroni, concordances are to be found only among members and singers of San Zanobi: Antonio Pucci, a captain in 1377; Cristofano di Miniato, a laudese in 1456; Ser Firenze, a laudese in 1483; Berto delle Feste, a laudese in 1494–5; and the most prolific of Florentine lauda poets, Feo Belcari (1410–84), a captain in 1435, and member through at least the 1440s.[67]

The earliest reference to lauda-singing in the company documents is in fact the earliest known bequest for a lauda vigil, made in 1313 by Michele *setaiuolo* (silk merchant), to be celebrated on the feast of St Michael (29 September) 'with lighted candles and laude'.[68] The unusually detailed statutes of 1326 describe an active and well-established laudesi programme of festal and ferial services, and a *scuola* for teaching laude.[69] For the ferial services, the chamberlains were obliged to

. . . come every evening to the said church at the time when the office of Compline is finished, and light three candles which are to remain lit until the laude are completed. And they are to prepare the proper lectern, book, and altar-cloth, and the other necessary things. And those of the company who gather . . . in the aforesaid church to sing laude ought [also] to intercede and say an Ave Maria when someone of the company has died, is sick, or is abroad . . . And they are to do similarly for peace, and no one is to rise or leave before the priest who is giving confession gives the benediction, and having given the benediction everyone is to say 'amen'.[70]

Perhaps the clearest indications of a strong performing tradition at San Zanobi are the several laudarios that the company owned by 1333, at

[66] SZ 2170, fasc. 5k, fo. 68^v: Cosimo di Lorenzo Rossegli dipintore; ibid., fo. 64^v: Lorenzo di Piero di Cosimo de' Medici [28 Dec. 1474]; 2177, fasc. 19, fo. 22^r, where Lorenzo's son, Piero, is listed as a captain in Sept. 1491; 2170, fasc. 5k, fo. 193^r, which notes the entrance of Pierfrancesco di Lorenzo de' Medici into the company in 1505.

[67] Tenneroni, *Inizii*; addenda by L. Frati, *Archivum romanicum*, 1 (1917), 441 ff. A. Pucci (6 laude), SZ 2170, fasc. 1, fo. 16^r; Cristofano di Miniato (1), 2171, fasc. 6A/3, fo. 138^v (= fra Cristofano da San Miniato, who in 1431 was hired by the company as Lenten preacher), 2186, fasc. 48, fo. 54^v; Ser Firenze (2), 2179, fasc. 28, fo. 58^r.; Berto delle Feste (1), 2171, fasc. 5, fos. 40^r, 41^r; Feo Belcari (*c.* 120), 2186, fasc. 48, fos. 152^r, 153^r. Belcari, a prominent lay religious figure and poet, was the most prolific lauda poet in the Florentine tradition of the *travestimento spirituale* (or sacred *contrafactum*, a sacred text sung to a borrowed, often secular melody, usually indicated by the rubric *cantasi come* . . .).

[68] SZ 2170, fasc. 4, fo. 1^v: '. . . facciano con candele accese le laude e la vigilia predetta' (financed by the annual rent from several houses left to the company).

[69] Orioli, *Le confraternite*, 22–4, 29 (statutes 3, 6, 8, and 20), translated and discussed in Ch. 2, *passim*.

[70] Ed. in Orioli, *Le confraternite*, 24.

which time one of them, 'the most beautiful and grand, with illumina-tion', had been used long and hard enough to require repair.[71] In fact, the company decided in 1339 to acquire yet another and grander collection, the quality of which was obviously a matter of corporate pride; a select committee was appointed to oversee the commission of

. . . a book for singing laude, which should be large, written in large letters, noted, and storiated . . . and the entire company agrees that the book should be made as beautiful as possible, and it was submitted to the captains to appoint the three best men of the company as officials to make the said book . . . and to spend whatever is necessary at the expense of the company and others who would like to give some help to make the said book.[72] (See Plate 11.)

The company undoubtedly shared in the Cathedral clergy's pride in their institution as the devotional centre of the city, a pride that for company and chapter alike was most readily expressed through liturgical splendour.[73] But how different the means of ritual celebration might be between these two is evident in the company's instrumental practice. It was most unusual in fourteenth-century Europe to find a religious service conducted in a cathedral (or any church) at a consecrated altar with the participation of ordained clergy which included as well the performance of instruments so widely associated with secular music— vielles, rebecs, and lutes. Together with the company's performance of vernacular laude during the Offertory procession at Mass, these extra-ordinary lay privileges may be regarded as an index of the clergy's respect for this form of lay devotion. Instrumentally-accompanied lauda-singing at San Zanobi was also undoubtedly prompted by the more ostentatious model of Orsanmichele just down the street, from whom the company borrowed its players. Chellino della Viola (who played at Orsanmichele between 1361 and 1383) was designated as a festal singer in 1352, but in 1365 'Chellino, who plays the vielle', was contracted to play on the vigils and evenings of twenty-five feast-days throughout the year at the rate of one florin per six months.[74] Between c.1375 and 1440, salaried Orsanmichele players like the vielle/rebec-players Maestro Luigi di Matteo, Pagolo di Ser Ambruogio, and Bartolo di Giovanni, and the lutenist Jacopo di Lorenzo all served the Company of San Zanobi on a more infrequent and *ad hoc* basis, and primarily for the two main patron-

[71] SZ 2182, fasc. 36, fo. 75ᵛ [Dec. 1333]: 'demo a detto maestro che riconciò per charte di bambascia perché rasciughasse il libro delle laude cioè il più bello e maggiore con lle fighure'.
[72] Appendix I, doc. 13. An ensuing record of expenses by the appointed officials indicates that the book was completed, and was probably the festal laudario listed in the company's 1394 inventory.
[73] On the ancient rivalry between the canons of the Cathedral and the church of San Lorenzo, see Gaston, 'Liturgy and Patronage', 112.
[74] The complete document is edited in D'Accone, 'Le compagnie', 265.

saint feasts of St Zenobius and St Reparata (8 October).[75] A few of the entries are noteworthy for what they reveal about performing practices and circumstances. In 1421 the company retained Pagolo for their ferial services, when he was paid to 'play the rebec and sing the laude during the evening [service]'.[76] In 1395 Bartolo di Giovanni and a fellow instrumentalist were paid for playing not only on the feast of St Zenobius, but in procession on 1 June when the miraculous painting of Santa Maria Impruneta was brought to town.[77] In 1406 and 1408, the rebec-player Lampreda (Andrea di Giovanni) was paid s. 30 'to play during the preaching of Lent', a practice that is recorded nowhere else.[78]

In the early 1440s, at about the time the company was discontinuing both ferial singing and the use of indoor instruments, it began regularly to hire *trombadori* and *pifferi* to play for the feast of St Zenobius; in 1442, payments were made to *pifferi di palagio* (city employees), four *trombadori*, and the Cathedral's recently formed polyphonic choir (the singers of San Giovanni), who sang at the evening lauda service.[79]

With singers as with instrumentalists, the Company of San Zanobi could not rival the Orsanmichele practice. San Zanobi's hiring practices were in fact more typical of the city's other laudesi companies: one or two singers per service throughout the fourteenth and into the early years of the fifteenth century; three to four per service from *c*.1415 to the 1460s (five to seven in the larger companies for special feast days); and by *c*.1470 larger polyphonic ensembles ranging between five (in the smaller companies) and eleven singers (see Table 5). San Zanobi was served by a single ferial singer, the wool-weaver known as 'Ciancha' (Giovanni di Giuliano) until 1405, when he was joined by another freelancing artisan singer, the goldsmith Nofri di Giovanni.[80] Two decades later account

---

[75] The last recorded payment to an indoor instrument-player was on 25 Nov. 1442 to 'Churado che suonò la viuola . . . per santo zanobi prossimo passato, la vilia e la sera'; SZ 2177, fasc. 16, fo. 35ʳ.

[76] '. . . suona la ribecha e canta le laude la sera in Santa Maria del Fiore'; D'Accone, 'Le compagnie', 267–8. A solo singer playing his own accompaniment on a stringed instrument was a common performing ensemble in the secular, monophonic repertoires of the late Middle Ages; for iconographic evidence see E. A. Bowles, *Musikleben im 15. Jahrhundert* (Leipzig, 1977), iii, pt. 8 of *Musikgeschichte in Bildern*, ed. H. Besseler and M. Schneider.

[77] The painting was periodically brought to Florence from its suburban residence and carried in procession during times of civic tension; R. Trexler, 'Florentine Religious Experience', 11–12.

[78] SZ 2183, fasc. 39, fo. 12ʳ: '. . . per sonare a la predica di quaresima'; 2178, fasc. 23, fo. 119ᵛ [1408].

[79] SZ 2177, fasc. 16, fo. 32ʳ [3 June 1442]; 's. 18 per dare a' trombetti quando s'apicchorono gli allori al campanile, s. 33 per dare a' pifferi di palagio, s. 4 d. 2 per dare a quello de la tromba, ⟨. .⟩ 12 per dare a' cantori di San Giovanni venono alle laude . . .' (angle brackets indicate illegible portion of MS). The singers were also hired by the company in 1440 (SZ 2171, fasc. 6A, fo. 49ᵛ), 1463, and 1464 (SZ 2171, fasc. 6C, fos. 117ᵛ, 122ᵛ).

[80] Their *c*. 40-year careers as laudesi included long tenures at the three largest companies (Orsanmichele, San Zanobi, and San Piero Martire), which may well have extended to the *Oltrarno* companies as well, where documentation on singer's activities does not begin until after Ciancha and Nofri disappeared from the scene in the early 1420s.

TABLE 5. *Company of San Zanobi: salaried musicians, 1345–1512*

Year	Singers				Instr.	Total
	Ferial	Festal	Lenten	Undesig.	Festal	
1345				'boys'		2+
1350–2		1–2		1	1 V	3–4
1386				2		2
1395					1 R, 1 V	2+
1404		3+				3+
1406					1 R (Lent)	2+
1408					1 R (Lent)	
1414	3				1 R	4+
1421	3	2–3			1 R	6–7
1428	3	2			1 R	6
1431–2	3	2				5+
1430–40				2		
1433	5					5
1439	5					5
1442				2	1 V	
1445				2	7	7
1446		4		2	2 S, 1 T	7
1451		6		2		6
1460		6		2		6
1463		9		2		9
1470		6 S, 3 T		2		9
1475		6 S, 5 T		2		11
1480		5 S, 3 T		2		8
1481		4 S, 3 T		2		7
1491		5 S, 4 T		2		9
1495		5 S, 4 T				9
1503		5 S, 4 T				9
1512		4 S, 4 T				8

books indicate that the company retained three ferial singers, and two to three singers and a rebec-player for feast days, but the company's 1427 tax report for some reason lists only two ferial singers: Vettorio d'Agnolo Bordoni, who claimed cloth-burling and lauda-singing as his professions, and the glove-maker Guasparre d'Ugolino Prosperi, who was the company's highest paid singer and *precentor*.[81] The pair sang for the company

[81] Catasto 291, fo. 67ʳ, where among the company's financial obligations are 'Ghuaspare d'Ugholino e Antonio d'Agnolo [= Vettorio d'Agnolo Bordoni] che chantano le laude, L. 51

between 1421 and 1445, and were also hired as a pair at Orsanmichele in 1418, where they served together until at least 1436.

The 1428 statutes of the company affirmed that 'in no manner is the singing of laude every evening, according to ancient custom, to be neglected', but the same statute admits to the company being under financial strain.[82] Payments to singers between 1427 and 1443 were periodically lowered, then restored, and in 1433 Guasparre's salary was restored (from s. 50 to s. 60) on the condition that his son join him in singing for the price of his father's new salary.[83] The company discontinued ferial singing in 1433, and thereafter no company singer received more than s. 20 per month, except Guasparre, who for the eighteen-year remainder of his service was paid s. 30 per month to prepare for the services and sing on feast-days.[84]

The dramatic changes in the musical devotions of San Zanobi during the 1430s and 1440s appear to reflect a larger shift in the corporate devotional life of the city. Under increased financial and political pressures which rendered increasingly difficult the maintenance of traditional practices unsupported by bequests (like ferial singing and the use of indoor instruments), and the cumulative effect of decades of bequests stipulating pious activities on specific feast days, Florentine laudesi practices shifted decidedly away from the generic ferial service to festive services tailored to the needs of individual Florentines.[85] In spite of the public and corporate appearance retained in this festive display, the increased emphasis upon it was brought about primarily by increasingly private and personal testamentary actions, and might be best understood as part of a larger shift towards private spheres of activity taking place in Florentine society at that time.[86] The new devotional emphasis on the festive liturgy, which in Medicean Florence tended towards spectacle in some of the laudesi companies and expansion into larger polyphonic chapels in most of them, was paralleled by what appears to be an equal

l'anno . . .' (i.e. L. 30/yr., or s. 50/mo. for Guasparre; L. 21/yr., or s. 35/mo. for Vettorio). SZ 2171, fasc. 6A, fo. 14ᵛ [1 Sept. 1421]: 'Ghuasparre d'Ugolino Prosperi che canta le laude i [sic] [ap]par[e]chiare la sera, e [ap]parechiare el dì della festa al descho, soldi sessanta per ogni mese'.

[82] SZ 2170, fasc. 2, fo. 45ʳ: '. . . Raguardando il bisogno della nostra compagnia la quale è ora asai in bisogno'. Entire statute edited in Appendix I, doc. 14.

[83] The son was probably Prospero, who was fourteen at the time, and later a rebec-player at Orsanmichele in 1436–7. SZ 2186, fasc. 48, fo. 84ᵛ: 'Stanziorono a Ghuasparre d'Ugholino e al figluolo lire tre el mese, el quale era istato rechato a s. 50 el mese, fecono [sic] per partito ch'egli tenesse el figluolo alle lalde e tornasese [sic] nel pregio suo di prima, cioè, L. tre el mese.'

[84] D'Accone, 'Alcune note', 96, where he cites documents that seem to indicate the abandonment of ferial singing in 1443. In fact this seems to have occurred already a decade earlier, when the five singers' salaries were all lowered with the declaration that '. . . ogni proposto debbi essere la sera della festa alle nostre lalde', and thereafter references to singing 'ogni sera' disappear from the records; SZ 2186, fasc.48, fo. 80ʳ.

[85] The company's feast of San Zanobi is discussed in Ch. 2 under 'Patron-Saint Feasts'.

[86] See Ch. 6 n. 6.

and opposite expansion of Lenten singing. Beginning in 1443, the above mentioned Guasparre was required to 'sing laude on the evening of feasts and throughout Lent', and as in the other laudesi companies Lenten singing became a significant (and for some *Oltrarno* companies exclusive) musical activity only in the fifteenth century. Payments to musicians for Lenten musical activities prior to the 1430s were rare; during that decade they were made primarily to pairs of clerics for singing the lament on Good Friday and, at other times, for singing the Passion or laude on the same evening.[87] After *c.*1440, with ferial services long gone, the company's laudesi assumed responsibility for singing various combinations of Lenten laude, the Good Friday lament, and the Gospels throughout the long penitential season (undoubtedly in conjunction with sermons).[88]

No stable musical practice is discernible during *c.*1445–70. Probably owing to the gradual adoption of three-, and later four-part polyphonic practice, along with the persistence of one- and two-part singing, numbers of singers for a given service varied between four and nine, and boy singers became more common. This is also the period during which polyphonic singing appears to have become more familiar to a broader range of Florentine lay singers. For a three-month term beginning in May 1446, the company was served by its first documented polyphonic ensemble, the weavers Agnolo di Lucca and Sandro di Giovanni, with Jacopo d'Arigo as their tenor ('per loro tenore').[89]

Beginning in 1470 the San Zanobi archives provide the most detailed and explicit record of the larger polyphonic chapels that began to appear among the Florentine companies, and until *c.*1495 the San Zanobi chapel was comprised almost exclusively of lay, artisan singers, as it was, for example, in 1475 (Table 6). Into the early sixteenth century the company maintained a polyphonic choir of between eight and eleven singers, with three to four singers designated as *tenori* (or *tenoristi*), and five to six singers designated as *sovrani* (or *sobbrani*, *chanti*, or *fanciulli*).[90] It is likely, however, that a similar arrangement obtained during the 1460s as well,

[87] SZ 2186, fasc. 48, fo. 54ᵛ [29 Mar. 1431]: 'stanziorono L. 1 a Ser Simone e Ser Lapo preti perchè chantorono le laude in Santa Maria del Fiore venerdì santo . . .'; ibid., fo. 89ᵛ [25 May 1433]: '. . . a due cherici d'Orto Samichele grossi otto perchè cantarono [il] lamento venerdì sancto e 'l dì delle feste tutta quaresima in Sancta Liperata [Reparata]'; ibid., fo. 148ʳ [15 Apr. 1436]: '. . . a Ser Giuliano prete in Santa Reparata e a uno cherico che chantorono el passio venerdì santo . . . [L. 1]'.

[88] On 8 Nov. 1444, L. 4 was paid to 'Francesco [di Bartolomeo] and Iacopo [di Domenico, cieco] laudesi . . . perchè cantorono e' lamento el venerdì santo . . . e in detta quaresima chantorono cierte volte el vangielo'; SZ 2177, fasc. 16, fo. 55ᵛ.

[89] SZ 2177, fasc. 16, fo. 83ʳ. All three are listed as 'lauldesi' for May–July, 1446.

[90] Similar numbers of singers were employed by the Cathedral's polyphonic choir during this period. The four to five *tenoristi* hired by the Cathedral choir were varying combinations of one to two altos, tenors, and basses; D'Accone, 'The Singers of San Giovanni', 328–31. Frequently, only tenors and altos were hired, and, when needed for four-part music, the bass part might be provided by a higher voice (often an alto) able to sing well in the lower register; ibid. 324, 349.

TABLE 6. *Company of San Zanobi: salaried musicians in 1475 and 1505*

1475	Years	Profession	Other tenures	Total years
sopranos:				
Santi di Cino	1474–5		SPM	8
Bartolomeo di Marco	1473–5	lance-maker	SPM	8
Giovanni di Rosso	1475	cloth-spinner	SA	2
Sandrino di Manovello	1475			1
Francesco di Bernaba	1475	chorister		1
Jacopo di Bernaba	1474–5, 1494–5	chorister		4
tenors:				
Sano di Giovanni	1473–1505	lantern-maker	SPM, OSM	50
Sandro di Giovanni	1469–75	wool-washer	SPM, OSM	20
Vanni di Piero Bandelli	1445–75	baker	SPM	34
Bernardino di Francesco	1467–75	goldsmith	SPM, SA	14
Piero da San Giorgio	1474–1505	weaver	SPM, OSM, SA, SSP	47

1505	Years	Profession	Other tenures	Total years
sopranos (s. 12–14/mo.):				
Francesco de Laiole	1505		SS. Annunziata	2
Bartolomeo di Sano	1501–5	lantern-maker		4
Giovanni d'Antonio Minori	1505			1
Zacharia d'Antonio Minori	1505		SS. Annunziata	3
Martino d'Agniolo Favilla	1505			1
tenors (s. 25/mo.):				
Sano di Giovanni	1473–1505	lantern-maker	SPM, OSM	50
Vanni d'Ulivante	1505			1
Agniolo d'Antonio Favilla	1491–1512		OSM, SSP	30
Piero da San Giorgio	1474–1505	weaver	SPM, OSM, SA, SSP	47

for in spite of the lack of designated voice-types during that decade, similar numbers of singers were employed, and several of them were designated polyphonic singers either concurrently at other companies, or at San Zanobi after 1470.[91] A 1470 deliberation seems to allude to a prior situation, and points up as well the desire for larger ensembles and the tendency to hire boys and young men during this period:

The said captains . . . according to the statutes of the said establishment and desiring that it be duly provided, have . . . brought into the company numerous singers (*moltissimi cantori*), and as the better and more qualified [singers] they elect and appoint the following boys as *sobbrani* [6] and *tenori* [3] . . .[92]

In 1481, the company decided to hire 'three tenors and four sopranos with a contralto',[93] but for the next two decades nine singers remained the normal size of the laudesi ensemble. The company's musical activities were not disrupted by the political upheavals of the 1490s, but they were directly affected. After the death of Lorenzo de' Medici in 1492, and the Medici expulsion in 1494, there ensued the austere theocracy of the Dominican reformer Girolamo Savonarola (1494–98), during which the only polyphonic music to be heard in the Florentine churches were laude.[94] It was during this period that the company began to hire the former members of the Cathedral's disbanded polyphonic choir, and the role of the artisan laudesi in the company's chapel was for a time greatly reduced and pre-empted by Cathedral priests and boy choristers. With the re-establishment of the Cathedral's polyphonic chapel in 1501, the composition of the San Zanobi chapel became almost exclusively clerical, and must have made company services appear to be an extension of the Cathedral clergy's liturgical duties.[95] In fact, this indeed appears to have been the case, for a 1501 Cathedral record outlining the duties of the choir includes performance at the company's lauda services:

. . . the said chapel [of two tenors, two contraltos, two basses, a teacher of figural music, and seven choristers] is obliged and bound to solemnly sing figural music every Saturday morning [at] the Mass of Our Lady at the chapel located in the said church between the two front doors, and on the evenings of all feast-days [to sing] laude at the same chapel, as they have begun to do and as is customary; and [second] Vespers on every feast day; and Mass in the choir on all solemn days in

[91] Of the company's 1463 chapel, one (Vanni) was a *tenore* for the company in 1470 and 1475, and Filippino di Francesco Bocchi, a carpenter, was a *tenore* for the Company of Sant'Agnese in 1466–7 (SA 100, fo. 81ᵛ). Of the 15 laudesi who sang for the company during 1467–9, six continued into the 1470s as designated polyphonic singers.

[92] Complete document ed. by D'Accone, 'Alcune note', 99. However, at least two of the tenors were much older—Vanni (who had sung for the company since 1445), and Sandro (who was singing for Orsanmichele in 1450 and as a *fanciullo* for San Piero Martire beginning in 1455).

[93] '. . . tres tenores [s. 20/mo.] et quatuor sovrani [s. 14/mo.] cum choltro [sic]'; ibid. 100.

[94] D'Accone, 'The Singers of San Giovanni', 346–9.

[95] See, e.g., the company's 1502 roster in D'Accone, 'Alcune note', 101.

the said manner, that is, in figural music, and on those solemn occasions to sing all those things that seem [fitting] to the Reverend Chapter of Canons of the said church, especially [during] Holy Week all those *canti* and responsories that are customarily sung as well as any others deemed [necessary] by the aforesaid Reverend Chapter . . .[96]

The chapel referred to was that patronized by the Company of San Zanobi, and traditionally devoted to the Virgin Mary, and though the Cathedral choir had been performing the Lady Mass at this altar for some time, their recently initiated lauda performances clearly remained under the company's administration. Statutes drafted in 1508 express the company's continuing commitment to 're-elect or dismiss . . . our laudesi according to their merits or demerits', and to sing the customary laude on the obligatory feast-days at the usual company altar.[97] The company's 1505 chapel, once again dominated by non-clerical singers, reveals the continuing vitality of the native Florentine laudesi tradition (see Table 6).[98] Like the Cathedral, the company paid a higher stipend to a *maestro di cappella* during the early sixteenth century. Ser David d'Alessandro, a Cathedral singer/priest who appears in the company records during 1502–20, was elected laudese in 1503 with the option of singing for s. 20 per month, or singing and teaching laude to the boys for s. 40.[99] In 1512, when the company choir consisted of four *tenoristi* and four sopranos, the higher stipend (s. 50) was being paid not to a cleric, but to Agnolo del Favilla, a professional laudese who served as *maestro di cappella* for the companies of San Zanobi (1491, 1494–5, 1512, 1520–6), Orsanmichele (1515–21), and Santo Spirito (1505, 1518–22).

Already by the second decade of the century, however, the musical activity of the lay companies was declining, and the traditional artisan laudesi of the past dwindled to a small number of professional lay singers like Agnolo, who could compete with the greater numbers of clergy trained in polyphonic performance. In 1511 the captains recorded a decision to dismiss their laudesi under the financial pressure of a new

[96] Original document edited by Seay, 'The 15th-Century Cappella', 55; trans. by D'Accone in 'The Musical Chapels at the Florentine Cathedral and Baptistry during the First Half of the 16th Century', *Journal of the American Musicological Society*, 24 (1971), 3. The Cathedral choir was actually reinstated in 1498, three days after Savonarola's arrest, with former members of the Cathedral's boys' choir, but included adult members (mostly Cathedral chaplains) only in 1501. Shortly thereafter, the musical chapels at the Baptistry and Santissima Annunziata were also reorganized, and, as was the case during most of the late 15th c., Cathedral, Baptistry, and Servite services tended to share musicians but under separate administrations; D'Accone, 'The Singers of San Giovanni', 349–50; 'The Musical Chapels', 2–13.

[97] ASF, Capitoli 154 [1508 statutes], fo. 16ᵛ.

[98] SZ 2170, fasc. 5, fo. 193ʳ. Francesco de Layolle (1492–*c.*1540), who as a boy sang laude *in sul'organo* at Santissima Annunziata (1505–7) became one of the first Italian composers of the Renaissance whose careers reached beyond their native soil.

[99] SZ 2176, fasc. 13, fo. 189ʳ [3 Sept. 1503]: 'Ser Davite di Sandro per s. 40 il mese cho'incharicho ch'egli ⟨insegni⟩ chantare le lalde a' fanc[i]ugli, e non inseg⟨n⟩ando no[n] più che s. 20 il mese'.

communal tax,[100] but in fact the company continued to hire a *maestro di cappella* and an undesignated number of singers until October 1526, after which time there is no mention of them in the company's detailed registers.[101] After 1526 the company apparently hired clerics to perform Masses and Offices in fulfilment of bequests that had previously required lauda vigils, and thereafter the Company of San Zanobi survived as a 'compagnia delle laude' in name only, until its final suppression in 1785.[102]

The Company of San Gilio[103]

When the Company of San Gilio was founded in 1278, it was associated with the Romanesque church of the same name. The church was destroyed in 1418, and replaced by a late Gothic structure designed by Bicci di Lorenzo, by which time it had been surrounded by the buildings of the great hospital of Santa Maria Nuova.[104]

The company was founded under the auspices of a short-lived mendicant order, one of a number that had been established in the wake of the Franciscans and Dominicans, only to be abolished by the Council of Lyons in 1274. The Order of the *Fratres de Poenitentia Jhesu Christi*, or more commonly the Friars of the Sack (Sacchites), was founded in Provence shortly before 1251; by 1274 there were seventy-six houses throughout Europe, living under the rule of St Augustine and constitutions based upon those of the Dominican order.[105] It is not known when they came to Florence, but they surely brought with them their Provençal saint, whose name both their church and the laudesi company bore in 1278. The abolished orders which, like the Sack Friars, previously possessed papal approval were to be dissolved gradually; the remaining friars could live out their lives under their professed rule, but were forbidden to receive new members, acquire new houses or land, alienate existing property, receive non-friars for burial, or to preach or hear confession.[106] The Florentine house of the Order was still functioning in 1286, but the last known Sack Friar was reported living at Rouen in 1309.[107]

---

[100] SZ 2177, fasc. 18, fo. 200ᵛ [5 Oct. 1511].

[101] SZ 2177, fasc. 18, fos. 196 ff.; SZ 2181, fasc. 34, fos. 229 ff. During 1520–6, Agniolo (and occasionally Ser Michelangiolo or Raffaello Paternostraio) received L. 7 s. 14 to be distributed among the singers.

[102] SZ 2182, fasc. 35; 2181, fasc. 34; 2183, fasc. 42; 2196, fascs. 74–5.

[103] Or Sant'Egidio; St Giles (d. *c.* 710), a hermit who founded a monastery in Provence. He was immensely popular in the Middle Ages, and was the patron saint of cripples, lepers, and nursing mothers. The feast of St Giles is on 1 Sept. D. H. Farmer, *The Oxford Dictionary of Saints* (Oxford, 1987), 184–5.

[104] W. and E. Paatz, *Die Kirchen von Florenz*, 6 vols. (Frankfurt am Main, 1952–5), iv. 5.

[105] Emery, 'The Friars of the Sack', 325–6.   [106] Ibid. 327.   [107] Ibid. 331, 328.

That the Company of San Gilio was founded under the wings of an abolished order that could provide neither preachers nor confessors is a witness to the determination of Florentine lay devotion to assume the form of laudesi companies attached to the mendicant orders. The company certainly outlived the order, for a 1329 petition by lay companies to the city lists San Gilio among the other laudesi companies, its surviving laudario (Mgl^2) was compiled in the late fourteenth century, and the company filed a tax report in 1427.

In 1284 the company drafted a detailed set of statutes (with later additions), which refer to the usual laudesi activities of festal and ferial lauda vigils and Sunday morning processions (every second Sunday of the month).[108] Several statutes convey the impression that in 1284 their lauda-singing was an in-house affair that did not yet involve the hiring of professional singers:

Concerning the laudesi who come to the lauda [service]: All company members who can, should come to San Gilio in the evening to sing laude, and those who cannot [should] say three *Paternostri* with the *Ave Maria*.

All those who sing the laude ought, in singing, to obey the captains . . .

Also we ordain that each company member, when he sees the candles lit in the evening in the church of San Gilio for the singing of laude, should enter the said church, and in singing and responding should obey their captains . . .[109]

Festal and ferial services were distinguished by number and size of candles, and the solemnity of a feast day was further distinguished according to whether candles were 'al ferro et ad mano' (in candle-holders and in hand), or simply 'al ferro'.

The chamberlains of this company are obliged to come every evening to the church of San Gilio and prepare the lectern and the book of laude and other things which are used for the singing of laude, placing two lighted candles into the candlesticks before the altar, and one [lighted candle] with a candlestick before the *gonfalone* when it is unfurled on the ferial days, [to burn] while the laude are sung. And Christmas, Epiphany, January 1st, Resurrection, Ascension, Pentecost, All Saints, the four feasts of the Virgin, and the feast of St Giles, and their vigils, should be solemnly conducted *al ferro* and *ad mano*. The feast days and their vigils which are conducted only *al ferro* are these: the octave of Candlemas [the special feast day of the company], St Agnes, St John the Baptist, the twelve Apostles, St Zenobius, St Mary Magdalene, St Lawrence, St Martin, St Stephen, St Sylvester [the day of the company's *ufficio generale*], and the second Sunday in May, because the company was founded on that day. And on

---

[108] BNF, Banco Rari 336 (olim Palatino 1172): 'Capitoli della Compagnia di S. Gilio . . .'. The date of foundation on the second Sunday in May 1278 is on fo. 20v. Incomplete edition in Monti, *Le confraternite*, ii, 144–58; complete edition in Schiaffini, *Testi fiorentini*, 34–54.
[109] Schiaffini, *Testi fiorentini*, 37, 39.

these days that are conducted *al ferro* and *ad mano*, and [also] when it is only *al ferro*, [the chamberlains] are to place four candlesticks with four lighted *cerotti* or *torchietti* [medium-sized candles] on the altar and two before the *gonfalone*, if it has been unfurled, [to burn] while the laude are sung.[110]

The San Gilio laudesi evidently shared their *gonfalone* (and probably their indulgences and privileges as well) with another lay company in the church, the *Raccomandati di Santa Maria* (those recommended to the Divinity through the intercession of their patroness), for one statute prohibited the captains of either company from carrying the *gonfalone* outside the church except on Candlemas.[111]

As with the Company of Santo Spirito, San Gilio's only extant fourteenth-century document is a large and elegant laudario, Mgl². [112] An inventory compiled shortly after 1420 lists three laudarios, 'one book of laude for every evening', 'one small book of old laude', and what must be a description of Mgl², including the date of its origin: 'one new book of illuminated laude, with gold embellishment throughout, and some notated sequences and some hymns. Made in 1374.'[113] The manuscript contains a calendar (one month to a page, like a Latin service-book), an index that divides the laude into groups with rubric titles, 106 *laude* without music (28 *unica*), the *Te Deum*, *Salve Regina*, a Litany of Saints and Rogations, the *Pater noster* and *Ave Maria*, and, like the Santo Spirito laudario (Mgl¹), a collection of twelve Latin sequences for the major feast days (all with music, four of them polyphonic).[114] The San Gilio laude are arranged in generally the same pattern as Mgl¹ (i.e. laude to Christ,

---

[110] Ibid. 44.

[111] Ibid. 53. Another statute prohibited the officers and members of the laudesi company (which in the statutes is referred to as the 'Compagnia di Sancto Gilio') from involvement in the services or affairs of the *raccomandati* without permission from captains or friar of the latter; ibid. 47. On the *raccomandati* in San Gilio, see A. M. Terruggia, 'In quale momento i disciplinati hanno dato origine al loro teatro', in *Il movimento dei disciplinati nel VII centenario del suo inizio* (Perugia, 1965), 436, where she asserts that this was a disciplinati company.

[112] Mgl²: Florence, Banco Rari 19 (*olim* Magl. II. I. 212); this unedited manuscript is indexed in A. Bartoli, *I manoscritti italiani della Biblioteca Nazionale di Firenze* (Florence, 1879), i, 172–96; and in P. D'Ancona, *La miniatura fiorentina* (Florence, 1914), ii, 96–9. The miniatures are examined by Vincent Moleta, 'The Illuminated *Laudari*', 43–50; and selected texts are edited by C. Del Popolo, 'Il laudario della Compagnia di Sant'Egidio', 5–26. For a physical description of the manuscript, see *Répertoire international des sources musicales* (RISM), ser. B, iv/1, *Manuscripts of Polyphonic Music, 11th–early 14th Century*, ed. G. Reaney (Munich, 1969), 790–1.

[113] ASF, CmRS 1340, fasc. C, Book 1, fo. 1ʳ: 'uno libro nuovo di laude miniato, tutto d'istorie messe d'oro, et certe sequentie notate, et con cert'ynni. Fu fatto nel mccclxxiiij. Uno libro di laude per ogni sera. E uno libro piccolo di laude vecchio.' To accommodate these festal and ferial laudarios the company also owned 'uno leggio grande di noce con ferri da porre al ferro', and 'uno leggio piccolo di chuoio per ogni sera, con iiii gambi'; ibid., fo. 2ʳ.

[114] Moleta, 'The Illuminated *Laudari*', 44, where he notes that the decorative scheme of the miniatures, though incomplete, is more uniform than in Mgl¹. Moleta dated the MS. 1360–80 on the style of the miniatures, identified with the Camaldolese miniaturist, Don Simone; ibid., 46. Music was intended for the laude, but the stave-lines remain blank. The Latin sequences are discussed in Ch. 4.

the Virgin, then the saints), and are grouped by rubrics in the index of the manuscript as follows:

Laude to Christ	nos. 1–24
Passion laude	nos. 25–34
Laude to the Virgin Mary	nos. 35–52
Laude to the Apostles	nos. 53–67
Laude to the Holy Martyrs	nos. 68–75
Laude to the Holy Confessors	nos. 76–87
Laude to the Holy Virgins	nos. 88–96
Miscellaneous laude, without rubric	nos. 97–106

Like the San Frediano laudario compiled at about the same time, this elegant manuscript probably reflects a period of prosperity attained primarily through bequests made in the long wake of the recurrent Black Death.

In 1427 a tax report was filed by 'La chonpagnia di sia [*sic*] della Vergine Maria de' rachomandati di San Gilio di Firenze', apparently the company with which the San Gilio laudesi had shared their *gonfalone* in 1284. But listed among the company's annual expenses are the following items: 'expenses for candles used at Candlemas, L. 10, and for wax used in the laude services, L. 12, and for two singers, L. 30; in total L. 52 . . .'.[115] The amount spent on wax and salaries for the singers indicates that the company was still conducting ferial lauda services, and the Candlemas service had been the special feast of the San Gilio laudesi in 1284. It appears, then, that the *raccomandati* and laudesi companies of San Gilio, whose organizational differences were probably not significant to begin with, had merged into a single company sometime between 1284 and 1427.[116] The consolidation may well have been forced by the straitened economic conditions of early fifteenth-century Florence. By 1427 the company's annual assets were a little over fl. 358, greater than those of Santo Spirito (285 florins) but less than those of Sant'Agnese (593 florins).

Although the company continued to function until its suppression in the late eighteenth century, the company's sparse documents from the late fifteenth and sixteenth centuries are inconclusive regarding its lauda-singing activities during that period, and indicate only that the company continued to refer to itself as a laudesi company.

---

[115] ASF, Catasto 291, fo. 72ʳ: 'Ad ispesa per la Donna di febraio per candele L. 10, e per ciera si loghora alle laulde L. 12, e per due cantori L. 30, in tutto L. 52 . . .'.

[116] Late 15th-c. documents variously refer to the company as 'de' Rachomandati' and 'delle laude', sometimes combining them in the title (e.g. 'la compagnia della vergine Maria delle laude de' rachomandati'); ASF, CmRS 1340, fasc. A, fos. 17–19 [1480–4]. The early 15th-c. inventory bears the title 'de' raccomandati'.

The Company of San Bastiano

When the laudesi company associated with the Florentine Servite church of Santissima Annunziata was founded as a 'Societas Beatae Mariae Virginis' in 1263, its host organization had barely moved beyond its own lay origins. The Servants of St Mary, or Servites, originated in 1233 with seven Florentine cloth merchants who had belonged to a lay company (the Brothers of Penance) associated with the church of Santa Reparata, but only began to be organized into a religious order by St Peter Martyr during his visit to Florence.[117] Peter founded a Marian society with the help of the original lay brothers, then organized the latter under the rule of St Augustine. Papal approval of the order was granted in 1256 by Alexander IV, and in 1274 the Servites averted the suppression for which they were slated by the Council of Lyons through the diplomatic intervention in the Roman Curia of the Order's general, St Philip Benizi (1233–85).

The company's identity with the Marian society founded by St Peter Martyr is doubtful, for the company's 1451 statutes relate its foundation on the Nativity of the Virgin (8 September) 1263.[118] The founder of the company was supposedly St Philip, and a brief set of Latin statutes, the 'Capitula Societatis Beatae Mariae Virginis', are attributed to the newly founded company.[119] These statutes contain no indication that the company sang laude at this time, but in 1273 St Philip granted the privileges of the Servite order to the 'Societas laudum ecclesie S. Marie conventus Florentini'.[120]

The company is next mentioned in the 1329 petition to the city from the ten current Florentine laudesi companies, but there is no sign of the company in the 1427 tax reports. The next, and last, of the company's extant documents is its 1451 set of statutes, by which time it had assumed the title of the 'Compagnia delle Laude della Vergine Maria e di sancto Philippo e di sancto Sebastiano, e di sancto Gherardo', or simply, 'San Bastiano'.[121] The statutes, drafted by 'frate Mariano, lectore in theologia', indicate that laude were sung only on feast days: Sundays, plus Christmas, Lent, Easter, the first day of Pentecost, the four feasts of the Virgin, and the feasts of St Philip (Benizi) and St Sebastian. The company met in

---

[117] J. M. Ryska, 'Servites', in *The New Catholic Encyclopedia*, xiii, 132. Early Servite chroniclers claim that these seven merchants were members of a laudesi company which met at the Church of Santa Reparata.

[118] ASF, CmRS, Capitoli 6, fo. 3ᵛ.

[119] Ed. in A. Morini and P. Soulier, *Monumenta Ordinis Servorum Sanctae Mariae*, i (Brussels, 1897), 107–8.

[120] Davidsohn, *Forschungen*, iv, 430.

[121] ASF, CmRS, Capitoli 6, fo. 2ʳ; on fo. 3ᵛ it is indicated that the name (and patronage) of St Sebastian was 'newly assumed'.

their residence on the first and third Sunday of the month at sunrise before Mass. On the first Sunday members recited the 'salmi graduali e i penitentiali', a litany, special prayers, and the *Benedictus, Te Deum*, or *Magnificat*; and on the third Sunday the Office of the Dead, 'with Vespers and laude', psalms, and prayers. On the 'extraordinary' feast days, Matins of the feasts of the Virgin, the *Te Matrem laudamus* and special prayers were recited in the morning, and in the evening the Vespers of the Virgin with the *Ave Maris Stella, Magnificat*, and prayers. [122] A statute dealing with bequests required the officers '. . . to go and remain at the lauda [service] every time they [the laude] are said . . . and the *correctore* [a friar] is to remain seated in the midst of the company [and] is authorized to see to any deficiencies in the said laude . . .'. [123] The *correctore* was to hear confession after the laude were sung in the evening, and then to lead the company in singing 'some hymn, like *Ave Maris Stella, Salve Regina, Te Matrem laudamus, Te Deum laudamus*, or other hymns . . .'. [124] The treasurer was responsible for payments covering 'the salaries of men and boys [the singers] and *sonatori*, and for [managing the] lauda-singing', and four *festaiuoli* were elected to provide flowers, food, and *trombetti* for special feast-days, above all the Nativity of the Virgin and the feast of St Sebastian (20 January). [125]

These statutes bear the strong stamp of the Servites' fervent devotion to the Virgin, but they are unique among laudesi statutes of the period for the infusion of disciplinati characterisitics: a hierarchical and authoritarian tone, a greater adherence to the Latin liturgy, and a strong penitential cast. [126] In fact, the company had become a disciplinati company by the time it drafted new statutes in 1520–34, [127] and the lauda-singing conducted by the friars at Santissima Annunziata from at least *c*.1480 suggests that the company had probably yielded up the devotion altogether by this time. [128]

[122] The texts of most of the Latin liturgical items prescribed here are copied into the back of the manuscript, fos. 26ʳ–49ʳ.

[123] ASF, CmRS, Capitoli 6, fo. 6r: '[The Captains] . . . debbino e sieno tenuti d'andare e stare alle laude ogni volta si dicessino e stare a sedere e mettere in mezzo il corectore della co[m]pagnia diputato a provedere a' manchamenti di dette laude . . .'.

[124] The complete document is transcribed, translated, and discussed in Ch. 2, 'Ferial Services'.

[125] ASF, CmRS, Capitoli 6, fos. 8ʳ, 11ᵛ: 'Cap. IV . . . Item per candelle, falcole, salari d'uomini e fanciulli et sonatori, et per fare cantare le laude quello [*sic*] sarà di bissongno . . .; Cap. IX . . . in fiori et loro mortina, ispagho, bullette, acchattatura di fiaschi, trombetti, e per fare la colectione a' fratelli in Trebiano, pane, et meleranze, et per calatura di cera . . .'

[126] On the commingling of laudesi and disciplinati spirituality, see Weissman, *Ritual Brotherhood*, 58.

[127] ASF, CmRS, Capitoli 364 [1520–34].

[128] During 1480–1, the convent hired Ser Firenze di Lazzero, 'prete da Cortona', to teach lauda-singing to the convent's novices; D'Accone, 'Alcune note', 90 n. 22; also id., 'Alessandro Coppini and Bartolomeo degli Organi' 49–75. Bartolomeo accompanied lauda-singing *in su l'organo* at Santissima Annunziata, and several famous Florentine musicians sang laude here as boys, among them Francesco de Layolle (1505–7), Bernardo Pisano (1507), and Jacopo Peri (1573–6).

The Company of San Marco

Richa mentions a 'Compagnia di Santa Maria detta di S. Marco' that was founded around the year 1250, which indicates that the San Marco laudesi may have originated as a Marian company around the time of St Peter Martyr's preaching in Florence.[129] Richa also cited part of a document dated 26 May 1299, in which the General of the Silvestrine Order conferred upon the same company the right to participate in the spiritual goods of his order.[130] Weissman reported that in 1317 the 'confraternity of San Marco' was suppressed by the city because it was 'on the verge of becoming an unofficial guild of *sottoposti* wool workers'.[131] If this is the same company as the San Marco laudesi listed among the city's laudesi companies in a 1329 petition, then the suppression was only temporary.[132]

A century later the San Marco laudesi are mentioned for the last time in their 1427 tax report under the title of 'La chonpagnia delle laulde di Sa[n] Marcho', when it was the poorest of the city's laudesi companies, with total assets of about fl. 42.[133] At that time the company owned several pieces of land, and 'palls, books, and other goods which are lent for the love of God to whomever wants them'. Annual, presumably obligatory, expenses were for '. . . a *rinovale* every year on the [feast]-day of St Matthias for him who bequeathed the abovementioned land, and to perform laude in San Marco'.[134] It is likely that the precarious existence of the company was ended during one of the suppressions that were periodically inflicted on the Florentine lay companies during the fifteenth century.

The Company of San Lorenzo

Few documents remain from the relatively short history of this laudesi company associated with the great Florentine collegiate church. The earliest is a testament of Neri Baldighieri dated 4 March 1314, which names the 'sotietas beate Marie Virginis laudum que cohadunatur [sic] in ecclesia Sa[ncti] Laur[entii]'.[135] In 1329, the company is listed among the

---

[129] G. Richa, *Notizie istoriche delle chiese fiorentini, divise ne' suoi quartieri*, 10 vols. (Florence, 1754–62), vii. 113.

[130] Ibid. 114, and J. Henderson, 'Confraternities and the Church in Late Medieval Florence', *Studies in Church History*, 23 (1986), 77–8.

[131] Weissman, *Ritual Brotherhood*, 63–4.

[132] This petition is discussed in Ch. 2 n. 26.   [133] ASF, Catasto 291, fo. 70[r].

[134] Ibid., fo. 70[r]: 'A fare ogn'anno uno rinovale il dì di Santo Matia per cholui che llasciò la sopradetta terra, e fare dire le laulde in Sa[n] Marcho.'

[135] ASF, Diplomatico Patrimonio Ecclesiastico, 4 Mar. 1313/4. The company is made an alternative recipient of a house.

ten Florentine laudesi companies in a petition to the city, and in 1338 the bishop of Florence granted a forty-day indulgence to the 'Societas Beati Laurenti Martyris' for hearing Solemn Mass and other Divine Offices, hearing the word of God preached, managing bequests, and for singing laude during the evening in the church of San Lorenzo.[136] In the eighteenth century, Richa recalled that the San Lorenzo laudesi company, known to him as the Compagnia del Sacramento, was the oldest of three companies that had met beneath the vaults of the church, in the 'ancient manner of the first Christians'.[137]

In 1427, the 'Chonpagnia delle Laulde della chiesa di Sa[n] Lorenzo' filed its tax report, listing total assets of about fl. 123.[138] The company had probably always been small, though in 1427 it was not quite the city's smallest laudesi company (San Frediano, fl. 76; San Marco, fl. 42). The *catasto* document mentions several obligatory *rinovali* but does not mention laude. A document that appears to be a different version of the 1427 *catasto* of church properties, however, mentions a bequest to the company of half a house in the San Lorenzo district, a part of the proceeds of which were to go to 'lo Starnina, che canta le laude'.[139] From 1422 to 1424, the Company of San Piero Martire retained a ferial singer named Luca Amadei, and nicknamed 'Starnino', who was listed as a resident of the San Lorenzo neighbourhood.[140]

In the heart of Medici family territory, and on the eve of Cosimo's expulsion from Florence the Company of San Lorenzo was suppressed in 1432 by order of the Florentine republic. Most of the Florentine lay companies experienced temporary suppressions during the fifteenth century, but the San Lorenzo laudesi, probably under more than mere suspicion of harbouring seditious or tax-manipulating factions, was forced to turn over its belongings to its host church, and thereafter disappeared from among the Florentine laudesi companies.[141]

---

[136] Appendix I, doc. 23.

[137] Richa, *Notizie istoriche*, v. 91. On the basis of Richa's testimony, Paatz assumed that the San Lorenzo laudesi were associated with the Cappella del Sacramento, first mentioned in 1338 and presumably known to Richa, but the location of which Paatz was unable to determine; *Die Kirchen von Florenz*, ii, 517.

[138] ASF, Catasto 291, fo. 67ᵛ.

[139] Mgl. XXXVII, MS 298; ed. in D. Moreni, *Continuazione delle memorie istoriche dell'Ambrosiana Imperiale Basilica di S. Lorenzo di Firenze*, 2 vols. (Florence, 1816), ii, 380–1 (doc. 11).

[140] SMN 322, fos. 101ᵛ, 103ᵛ.

[141] P. N. Cianfogni, *Memorie istoriche dell'Ambrosiana R. Basilica di S. Lorenzo di Firenze* (Florence, 1804), 154–5; Moreni, *Continuazione*, 33.

THE SANTA MARIA NOVELLA QUARTER

The Company of San Piero Martire

The laudesi company associated with the great Dominican convent at Santa Maria Novella was descended from the first of the Florentine Marian congregations founded by St Peter Martyr in 1244.[142] Sometime between 1267 and 1288 the company was transformed from a 'societas Sanctae Mariae Virginis' to a 'compagnia delle laude', and thereafter was rivalled only by Orsanmichele in wealth and the strength of its lauda-singing tradition. According to Meersseman, it was the prototype of the other Florentine companies that arose in the 1270s and 1280s.[143] Among the *Decameron*'s satirical portraits of the fourteenth-century Florentine religious community, the laudesi company at Santa Maria Novella is singled out by name, presumably because of its familiarity to Boccaccio's story-telling circle.[144] With the exception of Orsanmichele, the Company of San Piero Martire was the last to abandon ferial lauda-singing (in 1478) and among the last of the lay companies to abandon the ancient devotion altogether. During the third quarter of the sixteenth century, responsibility for supporting the lauda-singers shifted to the sacristy of Santa Maria Novella.[145]

More so than at other Florentine churches, the powerful Dominican establishment at Santa Maria Novella exerted a relatively strong influence on its laudesi affiliate. The aggressive intellectual climate surrounding its great *studium*, which produced scores of able preachers, left its mark on the lay company. Officers of the company usually included several friars, who were frequently *maestri* in grammar or theology, and the company maintained a school for the children of company members which, in 1316, was taught by 'Ser Filippo Nardi della gramatica'.[146] In 1325, two years after the canonization of Thomas Aquinas, the great Dominican theologian had joined the company's host of patron saints, and the company recorded a payment for the copying of a lauda and a

---

[142] Meersseman, *Ordo fraternitatis*, ii, 923–4.

[143] Ibid. 976, but there is no evidence that San Piero Martire was a laudesi company before 1288, when others were already in existence.

[144] Day 7, story 1.

[145] F. D'Accone, 'Repertory and Performance Practice in Santa Maria Novella at the Turn of the 17th Century', in M. D. Grace (ed.), *A Festschrift for Albert Seay* (Colorado Springs, Colo., 1982), 76.

[146] SMN 291, fo. 7ᵛ; Davidsohn, *Forschungen*, iv, 430; Monti, *Le confraternite*, ii, 156–7. The school's *maestro* in 1395, Ser Niccolò d'Andrea, also sang for the company between 1395 and 1402; D'Accone, 'Le compagnie', 257; SMN 294, fos. 120ᵛ, 181ᵛ. A number of friars received religious education as children in the laudesi company's school; Orlandi, *Necrologio* i. 251, and his *Il VII centenario della predicazione di San Pietro Martire*, 74. This connection with the company as children undoubtedly contributed to the adult friars' interest in company membership and the bestowing of bequests.

motet in honour of Saint Thomas.[147] The convent's ambitious artistic programme, in competition with that of the Franciscans at Santa Croce, may account for the unusual number of painters among the company's membership,[148] and for the company's selection in 1285 of the great Sienese painter Duccio di Buoninsegna to provide an altar painting; see Plate 3.[149]

The friars and lay brothers also enjoyed an unusually close relationship in the matter of bequests. The Company of San Piero Martire received a large number throughout the fourteenth and fifteenth centuries, many of which involved only a token payment to the company of one or two lire, while the remainder went primarily to the friars.[150] The lay company, it appears, was acting in the capacity of a professional executor, managing the proceeds from landed property and perhaps helping the friars side-step the delicate issue of material ownership by a mendicant order. As Henderson has shown, however, the company began to lose money through communal taxation and administrative problems, and the Dominicans' stake in the company's assets (they received 93% of the company's payments on commemorative services) was such that between 1441 and 1447 the friars successfully petitioned Eugene IV to obtain ownership of the company's property.[151] Thereafter the friars assumed a more dominant role in the company's affairs; the Chapter of Santa Maria Novella chose the four captains (two friars and two lay members), and, conversely, the company's close ties to the convent made it an important access route for aspiring Florentine citizens seeking patronage rights in Santa Maria Novella.[152]

---

[147] SMN 292, fo. 27ᵛ [27 Sept. 1325]: 'demo per fare scrivere lauda e 'l motetto di Sa[n] Tommaso . . . s. 9'.

[148] Davidsohn, *Forschungen*, iv. 430; Monti, *Le confraternite*, i, 155–6.

[149] The contract for the painting is edited in Meersseman, *Ordo fraternitatis*, ii. 1041. This painting, the 'Rucellai Madonna' (now in the Uffizi, Florence), is of great historic importance, and is discussed in Ch. 5.

[150] SMN 306 and 326, *passim*. John Henderson reckoned that between 1290 and 1389 the company received 60 bequests, mostly pieces of property; 'Confraternities and the Church', 76.

[151] Ibid.; and his 'Piety and Charity', 119–26.

[152] Two such Florentines were Guasparre dal Lama and Giovanni Tornabuoni, both of whose appointments as captains of the company (1472–3, and 1486/1490, respectively) were preceded by generous acts of patronage, and followed by the successful procurement of chapel sites. On Guasparre, whose chapel was near the west door and was embellished by Botticelli's *Adoration*, see R. Hatfield, *Botticelli's Uffizi 'Adoration': A Study in Pictorial Content* (Princeton, 1976), 16 and 25. Giovanni successfully outbid Francesco Sassetti for rights to the high altar and chapel, and his subsequent decoration of this area included Domenico Ghirlandaio's magnificent frescoes; P. Simons, 'Patronage in the Tornaquinci Chapel, Santa Maria Novella, Florence', in F. W. Kent and P. Simons (eds.), *Patronage, Art, and Society in Renaissance Italy* (Oxford, 1987), 234, where in the course of her discussion of Giovanni's manœuvres she states that the company '. . . had long occupied a prestigious and key administrative position in the convent and seems to have had special authority over the high-altar area'.

The oldest extant documents referring to the company's lauda-singing activity are two letters of indulgence. The first, issued in 1288 by Andrea Mozzi, bishop of Florence, granted twenty days for 'gathering in the evening for laude', forty days for meeting every second Sunday of the month to process with lighted candles, and forty days to hear sermons during the evening in Lent.[153] In 1304 Cardinal Nicola da Prato increased the lauda-singing indulgences to forty days to meet in Santa Maria Novella 'every day without interruption, for singing laude in the evening', and 100 days to process (as above) either in the morning or evening and 'render devout laude'.[154]

A company account book covering the years 1312–40 preserves the oldest extant record of payments to Florentine lauda-singers. In 1312, payments were made on three occasions to 'fanciulli che cantano', and again in 1330 to 'due fanciulli'.[155] Several, probably older, singers are mentioned by name: in 1325 and 1327, 'Lore, che canta le laude' (s. 10); in 1332, 'Masino, righattiere [used-clothing dealer], che chanta' (s. 10); in 1332 and 1333, Dato Bernardi, 'laudese'; and in 1338 and 1340, Giorgio 'che canta'.[156] These precious few references nevertheless indicate that from the early fourteenth century laudesi were paid, that both boys and adults were hired, and that laude were apparently performed by either one, generally older, singer, or several boys.[157]

There are no extant account books from the years between 1341 and 1389, but documentation resuming in 1390 indicates that the practice of hiring a pair of adult singers had become the norm, and would remain so into the early years of the fifteenth century (see Table 7). In 1406, the captains reaffirmed this traditional configuration when they decided that they 'might not elect more than two singers . . . nor give them for their salary and their labour more than s. 40 per month.'[158] The actual duties of these singers were set forth in a laudesi contract drafted at the same time as the above decision:

Lorenzo d'Andrea of the parish of San Pagolo of Florence and Piero di Niccolò of the parish of San Frediano are singers . . . for the period of one year . . . with these duties and conditions, that they are to come every evening to the lauda [service] to set up, and every day of a solemn feast to set up the company desk [to

---

[153] The letter is edited in Meersseman, *Ordo fraternitatis*, ii. 1042–3.
[154] Ibid. 1047–8.   [155] D'Accone, 'Le compagnie', 256.
[156] SMN 292, fos. 43ʳ, 46ʳ. Further documents in D'Accone, 'Le compagnie', 257.
[157] Who, depending upon the solemnity of the occasion, could have been either young lay singers from the artisan community, or clerically trained *biscantatori*, for whom the laudesi companies' motet collections were probably intended; see Ch. 4 nn. 56–7.
[158] SMN 321, fo. 58ʳ [13 June 1406]: 'Item che [i] capitani . . . non possano tenere né elegere più che due cantatori, con salaro, [a'] quali cantatori non possano dare né fare dare per loro salaro né per loro fatica più che soldi quaranta il mese per uno, e se contro acciò si faciesse, non vaglia e non tenga.'

TABLE 7. *Company of San Piero Martire: salaried musicians, 1312–1580*

Year	Salary (/mo.)	Singers				Total
		Ferial	Festal	Lenten	Undesig.	
1312					2 boys	2
1325–40					1–2	1–2
1390–6	s. 30				2	2
1402–5	s. 30				3	3
1405–12	s. 30–50				4	4
1414		4	2			6
1417	s. 30–60	3	3			6
1419					7	7
1422–4	s. 20–60				6	6
1446	L. 184/yr. total	4	2–3			6–7
1455–6	s. 30–40	2	3	2		5
1457–61	s. 30–40	4	2	2		6
1464		5	2	1 S, 1 T		7
1465			2		6–8	6–8
1467			2		8	8
1469					9	9
1471	s. 20–40	4	2	2		6
1472		4	4	2		8
1475	s. 20–40	4	5			9
1477					8	8
1478	s. 20	7				7
1510	L. 7 total				8	8
1549					3	3
1557–80			2–3 S, 2 T			4–5

receive candle payments], and to sing laude as we ask it, and to do every other thing well and promptly as we ask it and according to custom.[159]

By 1408, Piero had become *precentor*, for he was receiving a higher salary than the other singers, and in 1414 was recorded as receiving a payment for 'incantare et precantare' (see Table 8).[160] As *precentor*, Piero was probably responsible not only for the sacristan duties stipulated in his 1406 contract, but also for distributing payments to the other singers and for some sort of leadership in the performances. Other companies also

[159] Appendix I, doc. 11; Lorenzo was a wool-worker (*lanaiuolo*) who also sang for Orsanmichele in 1403, and Piero was a professional laudese whose 42 years of recorded singing activity (1399–1441) embraced at least three companies (see Table 8).
[160] SMN 295, fos. 170ᵛ, 172ᵛ [1408]; SMN 321, fo. 109ᵛ [1414].

instituted this informal post of *maestro di cappella* during the early fifteenth century, and its appearance may reflect both the companies' increasing distance from their ritual activities as they delegated to their hired singers what their own lauda 'governors' had previously done (and assumed a more administrative role with respect to their bequests), and the need to co-ordinate the larger numbers of singers that the companies began to hire at this time. As was the case at the other large companies, San Piero Martire began to hire more than the usual pair of singers during the early years of the fifteenth century, and by the time Piero was a designated *precentor* in 1414 the company retained six salaried singers (Table 8).[161]

TABLE 8. *Company of San Piero Martire: salaried musicians in 1414 and 1472*

1414	Salary	Years	Profession	Other tenures	Total years
ferial singers:					
Piero di Niccolò	s. 50/mo.	1399–1424	laudese	OSM, SF	42
Antonio di Petro	s. 30	1409–15	laudese	OSM, SZ, SSP	38
Vanni di Martino	s. 40	1408–16		OSM	19
Martino di Vanni		1413–17		OSM	5
festal singers:					
Salvestro Tati	s. 40	1414–15		OSM	2
Domenico di Salvestro Tati		1414–15		OSM	3
1472	**Salary**	**Years**	**Profession**	**Other tenures**	**Total years**
ferial singers:					
Ser Firenze di Lazero	s. 40	1471–80	priest	SZ (T), SS Annunziata	12
Vanni di Piero Bandelli	s. 40	1455–79	baker	SZ (T)	34
Bartolomeo di Giuliano del Friza ('Frizzi')	s. 40	1456, 1468–74		SZ	45
Tommasino di Manovello	s. 40	1471–3		SZ (S)	4
festal singers					
Sano di Giovanni	s. 20	1472–6	lantern-maker	SZ (T), OSM (T)	50
Bernardino di Francesco	s. 40	1467–80	goldsmith	SZ (T), SA	14
Giovanni d'Antonio ('Rada')	s. 30	1471–2	furrier	SZ, OSM, SA	42
Andreino di Cristofano	s. 20	1472–85	shoemaker	SZ (S, T), SA (T)	19

[161] SMN 321, fos. 109ᵛ–110ʳ.

The 1406 contract quoted above indicates that ferial and festal singers were one and the same at that time, but by 1414 the hiring of separate singers for these services undoubtedly contributed to the increased size of the chapel, and may have been a practical necessity created by the proliferation of festal services and the consequent difficulty in securing broad time commitments from the city's actively freelancing laudesi. In fact, all six of the company's 1414 retinue were in the simultaneous employment of Orsanmichele, so that Vanni and his son Martino were retained by San Piero Martire strictly as ferial singers, Salvestro and his son Domenico strictly as festal singers, while Piero and Antonio probably continued the older practice of singing for both services.

The second quarter of the century was generally a difficult period for the lay companies; under suspicion of sedition, periodic suppressions by the city had begun in 1419, and widespread economic contraction contributed to the abandonment of ferial services by most of the laudesi companies and a levelling off of laudesi salaries and numbers of singers hired. But the company's assets were relatively strong in 1427 (11,362 florins), and during the next twenty years the company received six bequests, more than any other Florentine laudesi company.[162] Thus the company was able to maintain a respectable chapel of five to seven singers between 1415 and 1465, and a detailed 1446 statute reaffirms the practice of ferial singing (at a time when all companies but Orsanmichele had abandoned the service), as well as its stable number of four ferial singers:

Also it has been provided that the customary laude sung in the said church of Santa Maria Novella ought to be sung in the place used and appointed for that purpose, every evening, in the customary devout manner and fashion, by good singers or laudesi, conducted and elected by the said captains. And these laudesi should be at least four [in number], and according to the judgement of the captains, one of these laudesi is to be appointed to set up and put away the lectern every evening, light the candles, set up the benches, and do all the other things that in the past have been customary. And the said laudesi may have at the most L. 2 a month, according to the will of the captains. And the said laudesi should be re-elected by the said captains twice a year, that is, in July and January, and who does not win a decision by four black beans,[163] is understood to be cancelled and dismissed. And every evening, when the laude are finished, the confession with the usual absolution is to be done by a friar of the convent of Santa Maria Novella, to whom [the confession] will be entrusted by the prior of the said church. And every time the said laudesi are found to be failing in their duty, they

---

[162] ASF, Catasto 686, fo. 46ᵛ; compared to Orsanmichele (4), fo. 33ᵛ; San Zanobi (1), fo. 108ᵛ; and Santo Spirito (1), fo. 25ʳ. No bequests for this period are recorded in this volume for the other companies.

[163] Black (for) and white (against) beans were used by most republican institutions of the period in an effort to assure anonymous and impartial voting procedures.

may and ought to be corrected or censured by retention of part of their salary at the discretion of the said captains.[164]

During the last third of the century, the company's musical chapel expanded yet again, to between seven and nine singers, but it is not entirely clear that this was motivated by the creation of polyphonic ensembles, as it was at the other companies. The clear references to polyphonic singing in the San Piero Martire company documents before 1500 are few, such as payments of L. 1 made to two boys and a tenor for singing laude during Easter between 1488 and 1490.[165] But since the early fifteenth century the company had been employing singers who in the records of other laudesi companies were designated as *biscantatori*, *tenoristi*, and, after *c*.1470, *sovrani* (or *chanti*).[166] Of the company's eight singers in 1472, five were designated *tenoristi* at three other companies, including the priest Ser Firenze di Lazero, who during 1480–1 is mentioned in the records of the Servite church of Santissima Annunziata as a *maestro* 'who teaches laude' (see Table 8).[167] In spite of the Santa Maria Novella friars' indifference to polyphony in the fifteenth century,[168] the company probably pursued its own musical course, in step with the other Florentine companies of its kind.

Without ferial services, which the Company of San Piero Martire discontinued in 1478, lauda-singing had become a much less attractive profession to the moonlighting artisans who had sung in the laudesi companies for nearly two centuries. After *c*.1480 the artisan laudese assumed a more restricted and less lucrative role in small polyphonic choirs dominated by young singers.[169] Until at least the 1520s, the

[164] Appendix I, doc. 12. Notwithstanding the company's internal problems during this time, its increasing subjection to management by the convent must have afforded a degree of stability unavailable to the other, more independent laudesi companies in the city.

[165] SMN 301, fos. 133^r, 137^v: 'A dua fanciugli con uno tinore che chantorono le laude per le feste di Pascua'. Also fos. 141^v, 143^v.

[166] e.g. Martino di Vanni Martini and Domenico di Salvestro Tati, who sang together for the company as ferial singers during 1414–15, also sang together for the Orsanmichele festive services as *fanciulli biscantatori* during 1412–15 (OSM 21, fo. 12^r). References to Florentine laudesi as *tenori* first appeared in the 1440s, when San Piero Martire documents are lacking, but when they resume in 1455, one of the first singers mentioned, Francesco d'Antonio, was later a *tenore* at the Company of Sant'Agnese. The special designation of a high polyphonic part as *sovrano* or *cantus* first appears in the records of the Company of San Zanobi in 1470 (the records of Orsanmichele are missing for the period 1454–1507).

[167] SMN 299, fo. 59^v; and D'Accone, 'Alcune note', 90 n. 22. In 1481 the companies of San Piero Martire and San Zanobi employed an identical number of (seven) singers, and of the four sopranos and three *tinoristi* employed by the Company of San Zanobi, three of the high voices (Duccio di Giovanni, Maruccio di Tommaso, and Matteo di Giuliano Ardinghelli) and two of the lower voices (Piero da San Giorgio and Andrea Cristofano) also sang for the Company of San Piero Martire between 1480 and 1482. SZ 2176, fasc. 13, fo. 146^v.

[168] D'Accone, 'Repertory and Performance Practice', 71.

[169] The increase of boy singers (sopranos and altos) at this time is probably related to the recent establishment of a choir school at the Cathedral; D'Accone, 'Alcune note', 113–14.

company regularly employed seven singers, frequently referred to only as 'sette fanciulli che cantano'. However, among the seven *fanciulli* in 1483, for example, there were at least four in trades (a hosier, cloth-dyer, weaver, and maker of pack-saddles), indicating that *fanciullo* did not designate boys strictly, but might include *giovani* (young men).[170] From the early 1490s the San Piero Martire chapel was under the direction of the weaver Piero di Giovanni da San Giorgio, who sang throughout the city and performed a similar *maestro di cappella* role at the Company of Santo Spirito.[171]

The relative absence of instruments from the company's services is remarkable for such a wealthy and prestigious institution as San Piero Martire, and might be attributed to the relatively conservative musical environment at Santa Maria Novella. While instrumentally accompanied lauda-singing flourished at the companies of Orsanmichele and San Zanobi, the practice at San Piero Martire was like that of the other laudesi companies associated with mendicant orders (which San Zanobi and Orsanmichele were not). Instrumentalists (*suonatori*), primarily *trombadori* (brass-players) and/or *pifferi* (wind-players), were always hired for the main patron-saint feast of St Peter Martyr, and sporadically for other important feasts. The company usually hired two *trombadori* for their namesake's feast-day (to play for both the service and the commemorative meal), and from 1472 to 1503 four *trombadori* were paid s. 11 each.[172] Payments to instrumentalists are occasionally recorded for the feasts of St Dominic, St Thomas, Assumption, Christmas, and Easter,[173] and sometimes players of indoor instruments were hired to play either at the meals ('per la cena') or the services ('alle laude') of these feasts. For the feasts of San Piero Martire in 1423 and 1459, rebec-players were hired along with laudesi and *pifferi* or *trombadori*.[174] In 1467 'two players of harp and lute' were hired to play at the lauda services during the feast-days of

---

[170] D'Accone, 'Alcune note', 91. The four artisans were the *tenorista* Andrea di Cristofano *calzaiuolo*, Mariotto *tintore*, and the sopranos Maruccio di Tommaso *tessitore* (also at SZ and SSP), and Duccio di Giovanni *bastiere* (also at SZ).

[171] Ibid. 91–2; id., 'Repertory and Performance Practice', 76. Also called Piero di Giovanni Maschalzoni (SMN 301, fo. 148ᵛ). During his 47 years of documented lauda-singing, Piero also sang with the companies of Sant'Agnese, Santo Spirito, and Orsanmichele, and San Zanobi where he sang *tenorista* to his son Francesco's soprano during 1491–2 (SZ 2171, fasc. 6B, no. 5, fos. 32ʳ–56ʳ, *passim*). His brother Niccolò was a *tenorista* for the Company of Sant'Agnese during 1484–94.

[172] SMN 298, fo. 117ʳ [1463]; 299, fo. 59ʳ [1472]; 302, fo. 92ʳ [1503].

[173] See also Ch. 2, 'Patron-Saint Feasts'; SMN 292, fo. 61ᵛ: s. 4 to 'tro[m]badori per la matina di Santa Maria a dì xii d'aghosto' [1340]; 295, fo. 185ʳ: L. 1 s. 2 'per dare a' pifferi per la festa della Donna d'aghosto' [1410]; 322, fo. 66ʳ: s. 16 d. 6 to 'Lionardo tronbetta e compagni . . . quando sonorono per lla festa di S. Maria se fe' a mezo il mese d'agosto passato' [1423]; 322, fo. 76ʳ: L. 4 'per dare a cantatori e sonatori che cantorono e sonorono tre sere alle laude per lla Pasqua della Resuresione del nostro Signore' [1421].

[174] SMN 322, fo. 113ʳ: '. . . pro dando pifferis, sonatoribus ribecarum, captoribus [*sic*] laudum' [1423]; 298, fo. 91ᵛ: 'Alla festa di Sancto Pietro martire L. undici s. 10 d. 8 per trombetti, festaiuoli, mortina, spago, laudesi, e suòni di ribegha' [1459].

Christmas,[175] and for the company feast in 1487 players of 'zufoli' (small flutes) and laudesi were hired to perform at the commemorative meal.[176] The liturgical splendour of these same feast days was also enhanced by extra singers, usually three or four boys throughout the fifteenth century, so that a late fifteenth-century celebration of the feast of St Peter Martyr might have included a dozen or more singers, four *trombetti*, and several players of lute, harp, or rebec.[177]

Although there is little evidence of extensive singing during Lent at Orsanmichele, the musical activity in the Company of San Piero Martire during this time was more typical of the Florentine laudesi companies. There are few payments for Lenten singing recorded before *c*.1425. In 1393, there were payments to 'Baccio . . . who sings the Passion with the vielle', and Maestro Niccolò, who sang the lament of the Virgin on Good Friday,[178] and in 1415 to the 'singers who sing the lament on Holy Friday in Santa Maria Novella'.[179] The documents resuming in 1455 indicate a regular Lenten practice of laying off all but a pair of singers, usually two of the company's ferial laudesi. Considering that the monthly salary of a ferial singer was L. 2 around mid-century, the L. 6 paid to each of the Lenten singers at this time clearly implies extensive singing, which could involve the singing of the Gospels as well as the Passion.[180] The record of the Passion performance for the following year contains the company's first explicit reference to polyphonic performance, when payment was made to 'Francesco cloth-cutter . . . because he held (sang) the tenor at the Passion during Lent', and to 'Ulivante di Bartolomeo, laudese . . . to sing the Passion during Lent with the above Francesco'.[181] Thereafter, the practice of hiring two Passion singers, often two friars, or a friar and a lay singer, is recorded through the early sixteenth century.

The company continued to maintain its lauda services during the second quarter of the century, when inflation, political turmoil, and waning interest in the devotion forced even a large company like San

[175] SMN 297, fo. 53ᵛ: 'A duo sonatori d'arpa e liuto pelle feste di Natale alle laude, s. xiiii' [1467].

[176] SMN 301, fo. 127: L. 2 s. 4 were paid to four 'trombetti' for the feast of San Piero Martire, and s. 16 'a' sonatori de' zufoli et laudesi per la cena' [1487].

[177] e.g. the meal for the feast of San Piero Martire in 1475, which included expenses for a laudesi *collazione*, four *trombetti*, three *fanciulli* 'who sing' (and who probably joined the company's laudesi for the vigil and morning lauda service), the *festaiuoli*, candles, food, one and a half barrels of wine, and 500 palm fronds; SMN 299, fo. 83v. For the same feast in 1496 the *maestro di cappella*, Piero, part of whose job it was to hire 'più laudesi com'è consuetudo' for feast days, received payment to be distributed to the seven regular laudesi as well as the 'cantori forestieri'; SMN 301, fo. 191ʳ.

[178] D'Accone, 'Le compagnie', 258.

[179] SMN 296, fo. 133ʳ: '. . . chantatori che disono [*sic*] i' lamento venerdì santo i[n] Santa Maria Novella'.

[180] SMN 298, fo. 116ʳ [2 May 1463]: '[per] cantare e' vangeli e la passione la quaresima'.

[181] SMN 297, fo. 40ʳ [1464]: 6 lire each to 'Francesco tessitor di drappi . . . perchè tene il tenore alla passione di quaresima', and 'Ulivante di Bartolomeo laudesi . . . per cantare la passione la quaresima col sopra detto Francescho'. On Ulivante's family of singers, see Ch. 4 n. 23.

Zanobi to abandon lauda-singing.[182] After the last recorded service of
Piero da San Giorgio and an unspecified number of singer-companions
in 1527,[183] subsequent records reflect higher salaries being paid to a
smaller group of singers. The company elected new choirmasters in 1530
and 1545 without specifying the number of other singers,[184] but in 1542
and 1549 three singers are listed.[185] The tailor Bastiano di Tommaso Arditi
first appears in the company records in 1545, and from 1549 he was master
of this tiny chapel until the singers were dismissed in May 1580.[186] Owing
perhaps to the complex financial relationship between the company and
the convent, the dismantling of the company was apparently a rather
protracted event, for the company was officially suppressed by a *Motu
proprio* of Pope Pius V on 21 January 1568, and the suppression subsequently confirmed by Sixtus V in 1585.[187] In 1555 the company voted
to dismiss its lauda-singers, and use their salaries to pay the novices of the
convent to sing Marian antiphons in place of the laude,[188] but this was
apparently temporary, for Bastiano and his friends continued to sing
until December of 1580. At this time the sacristy of Santa Maria Novella
assumed responsibility for the performance of laude when it began to
employ boy singers who, either alone or in pairs, sang laude with organ
accompaniment.[189] Since at least 1510 San Piero Martire essentially had
ceased to be a lay company, for its voting membership consisted entirely
of friars, and in 1580 it ceased to exist in name as well.

The Company of Ognissanti

The sole document testifying to the existence of this company is the
prologue of an undated laudario copied into a Magliabechiano catalogue

[182] See Ch. 6. Since lauda-singing continued in this company during the second half of the 16th c.,
its relatively substantial resources and close ties to the Dominicans at Santa Maria Novella may have
allowed it to maintain the devotion during the first half, when most other companies abandoned it.
  [183] SMN 316, fo. 233ʳ.
  [184] SMN 316, fo. 12ʳ [22 Dec. 1530]: 'Prefati Capitanei . . . elegerunt in laudensem et magistrum
cappelle laudum canendum in dicta ecclesia Sandrum Laurentii Smeraldi cum salario unius floreni
quolibet mense . . .; fo. 92ᵛ [30 Apr. 1545]: 'Item dicti domini Capitanei . . . elegerunt et
deputaverunt Honofrium Bernardi, clericum florentinum . . . in laudensem et pro laudense, cum
eius debito et consueto numero omnium aliorum laudensium, ad canendum et cantandum omnibus
diebus festivis et consuetis in ecclesia S. Marie Novelle de Florentia et in aliis locis et temporibus, ad
minus quatuor laudes pro quolibet die . . . cum salario omnium aliorum laudensium . . . librarum
octo monete cuiuslibet mensis . . .' This salary of L. 8 per month was lowered from that of L. 9
established in a 1538 decision (fo. 27ᵛ), but was considerably higher than salaries being paid to
laudesi through the early 16th c.
  [185] SMN 316, fo. 62ᵛ [9 Sept. 1542] lists frati Alexio de Strozeis, frati Vincentio Dominici, and
Antonio Pauli de Giocondis; fo. 129ʳ [24 Apr. 1549] lists Bastianum Tommasi sutorem, Francischum
Raffaelis, and Stefanum Antonii.
  [186] SMN 316, fos. 77ᵛ–78ʳ; D'Accone, 'Repertory and Performance Practice', 76.
  [187] S. Orlandi, 'La Madonna di Duccio di Boninsegna e il suo culto in S. Maria Novella', *Memorie
domenicane*, 73 (1956), 216.   [188] See Appendix I, doc. 36, which is fully translated in Ch. 6.
  [189] D'Accone, 'Repertory and Performance Practice', 76.

of the Florentine National Library, where the manuscript (Mgl. XXXVI. 28) is reported missing since 1883.[190] A description of the contents is tantalizing: a liturgical calendar, 160 laude with music, a litany (which names saints particular to Florence), and various prayers and liturgical versicles from the Roman missal. The prologue is as follows:

This book belongs to the Company of the Laude, who sing in the Church of the Friars of Ognissanti in Florence, of the Order of the *Humiliati*. This company was established and begun by the authority and will of Messer Frate Guglielmo, Master-General of the aforesaid order of the *Humiliati*, in 1336, on the 11th day of the month of November. These are the laude which were written, published, and ordained for the noble and holy men of the aforesaid company . . .[191]

THE SANTO SPIRITO QUARTER

The Company of Sant'Agnese[192]

The 'Compagnia di Santa Maria del Carmino' was among the oldest of the Florentine lay companies, and was the most prominent of the laudesi companies in the Santo Spirito quarter (also known as the *Oltrarno*, since it was across the Arno from the main part of the city). The company's 1280 statutes are the oldest extant of such documents in Florence, yet these are not the original statutes, but a series of additions (made between

[190] Cited in Mazzatinti, *Inventari*, x, 178–9; three transcriptions varying in completeness and certain details may be found in B. Becherini, *Catalogo dei manoscritti musicali della Biblioteca Nazionale Centrale di Firenze* (Kassel, 1959), 89–90; C. Burney, *General History of Music* (London, 1782), ii, 327 (reprinted and discussed in Ziino, 'Laudi e miniature', App. B, and 68–9, where he proposes a connection between this and the Sant'Agnese laudario discussed in his study), and in the Maglia-bechiano catalogue of the Florentine Biblioteca Nazionale Centrale (MS XXXVI. 28). On the mistaken identification of this laudario as Mgl¹ by Liuzzi and F. Ludwig, see Barr, *The Monophonic Lauda*, 129.

[191] Becherini, *Catalogo dei manoscritti*, 90. Charles Burney saw this manuscript during his 1770 visit to Florence. His transcription of the lauda 'Alta Trinità beata' (see Music Example 5), which he published in his *General History of Music*, appears to have been made from this manuscript; *A General History of Music* (London, 1776–89); ed. F. Mercer, 2 vols. (New York, 1957), i. 630–1. Davidsohn, *Forschungen*, iv. 431 lists a 'Societas S. Marie ecclesie Sanctorum Apostolorum' that was mentioned in a 1277 testament, which Henderson believes was the Ognissanti laudesi company, but this seems doubtful in light of the later, documented date, the absence of an Ognissanti company in the Florentine laudesi companies' 1329 petition to the city, and the lack of a clear reference to a laudesi company *per se* in the 1277 document; cf. Henderson, 'Piety and Charity', 431.

[192] St Agnes was a widely honoured Roman virgin and martyr, whose name is still in the canon of the Mass (21 Jan.). She has always been regarded as the special patroness of bodily purity. Her cult became associated with the Carmine church when in 1268 the Florentine bishop, Giovanni di Mangiadori, donated a relic of the saint (a foot) to the new church, which was eventually kept in a reliquary situated upon the company's altar; G. Bacchi, 'La compagnia di S. Maria delle laudi e di S. Agnese nel Carmine di Firenze', *Rivista storica carmelitana*, 2 (1930–1), 143–4.

1280 and 1298) to an older document which has not survived.[193] According to eighteenth-century records of the Carmelite friars which predate a disastrous fire in 1771, the entrance to the company's meeting-room bore the inscribed date of the company's foundation—1268,[194] but this inscription more likely refers to the foundation of the Carmelite church, the first cornerstone of which was laid that year.[195] In fact, the company's sixteenth-century statutes recall its origins as a *Societas fidei* during the era of St Peter Martyr's Florentine preaching: 'The venerable and religious company of the standard entitled Madonna Santa Maria delle Laude et Santa Agnese di Firenze . . . had its beginning around the year of the Lord 1245 . . .'.[196] Since construction of the Carmine church began only in 1268, a date before which lauda-singing in Florence cannot be documented, the company probably did not adopt this devotion until the necessary altar was available in the new church. Bacchi recorded an undated notice from the convent archives which stated that 'the Company of Sant'Agnese began in 1269, beside the walls of the second church'.[197]

No company account books prior to the fifteenth century have survived, but the later records of this company, together with those of the other two *Oltrarno* companies (Santo Spirito and San Frediano) reveal a character of laudesi activity markedly different from that of the other companies across the river. The Santo Spirito quarter contained its own major business and processional centre along the Via Maggio, its own great families, and a strong artisan and working-class population. Likewise, the *Oltrarno* laudesi companies elected their leaders from among the quarter's leading families, staged spectacles and feast-day celebrations that in scope and character were unique to the quarter, and in their musical activities were distinctly modest, conservative, and insular in comparison to the leading companies in the other quarters of the city. There were many laudesi who resided in this quarter and sang only for

[193] Mgl. VIII. 1500, fasc. 9; ed. G. Piccini, 'Libro degli ordinamenti de la Compagnia di Santa Maria del Carmino', in *Scelta di curiosità letterarie inedite rare dal sec. XIII al XVIII* (Bologna, 1867; repr. 1968), 9–47 (second pagination series). A more accessible and recent edition is Schiaffini, *Testi fiorentini*, 55–72. Moreover, the addition of new statutes in 1280 presupposes an earlier period during which the old ones had become inadequate.

[194] U. Procacci, 'L'incendio della chiesa del Carmine del 1771', *Rivista d'arte*, 14 (1932), 167.

[195] A. Bossi, *Ricostruzione grafica delle fasi storiche della chiesa del Carmine* (Florence, 1974), Introduction (without pagination). This date is based on the convent's documents in the ASF, although no evidence is provided for the assertion that the Company of Sant'Agnese was founded in 1264. The Carmelite order originated as an eremitical community of devout pilgrims and holy men living on Mt. Carmel during the 12th-c. Latin kingdom of Acre. With the 13th-c. decline of this kingdom the Carmelites migrated west, and their original rule, written between 1206 and 1214 by St Albert, Patriarch of Jerusalem, was modified in 1247 to permit foundations in cities, at which time they began to engage in the mendicant apostolate; J. Smet, 'Carmelites', *New Catholic Encyclopedia* (New York, 1967), iii. 118.

[196] Appendix I, doc. 1.

[197] Bacchi, 'La compagnia di S. Maria', 2 (1930–1), 143, where he cites ASF, Conventi Soppressi 113, no. 530.

the *Oltrarno* companies, generally for lower wages, and often under terms which required greater involvement in the affairs of the companies (membership, extra duties, and residence in a company-owned house in lieu of wages). The assets of all three *Oltrarno* companies were well below those of Orsanmichele, San Piero Martire, and San Zanobi (see Table 1). Nevertheless, the early fifteenth-century assets of the Company of Sant'Agnese were twice those of Santo Spirito laudesi (which in turn were four times those of the Company of San Frediano), and the company's fifteenth-century productions of its annual Ascension feast were lavish (L. 332 in 1466) and spectacular events that must have been the pride of the quarter and the amazement of the city.[198]

The surviving additions to the company's statutes (1280–96) reveal an active ritual life centred on lauda-singing. Festal and ferial lauda services evidently took place prior to 1280, and the extant statutes prescribe the addition of lauda instructors to teach laude at the *scuola* and direct the singing during the evening services and the morning processions.[199]

No fourteenth-century company document of any kind has survived, with one possible exception. Agostino Ziino has recently assembled and published a collection of Trecento laudario fragments, most of which contain musical notation and illumination executed in Florentine workshops. Among these are several that Ziino argues were once part of a laudario belonging to the Sant'Agnese laudesi, in particular an elaborate miniature at the head of the lauda 'Sancta Agnesa da Dio amata', and another depicting the All Saints lauda 'Facciam laude a tutti i santi'.[200] The lower half of the Sant'Agnese miniature contains two scenes from the saint's life, while in the upper half she is shown seated on a throne holding a lamb (one of her iconographic symbols), and flanked by two

---

[198] On the Carmine Ascension play, see C. Barr, *The Monophonic Lauda*, 25–9, and her 'Music and Spectacle in Confraternity Drama of Fifteenth-Century Florence: The Reconstruction of a Theatrical Event', in T. Verdon and J. Henderson (eds.), *Christianity and the Renaissance* (Syracuse, NY, 1990), 376–404. This was the one occasion for which the company regularly hired *trombetti* ('sonatore di suoni grossi') and *pifferi* ('sonatori di suoni sotili'). Polyphonic music was sung from within the 'nuvola', an Ascension 'cloud' that was suspended above the main altar in the centre of the church, for in 1466 a payment was made to the carpenter/laudese Filippo di Francesco '. . . che fu l'angelo del tinore della nughola' (SA 100, fo. 81ᵛ).
[199] The relevant documents are ed. in Schiaffini, *Testi fiorentini*, 64, 63–4, 72, and are translated and discussed in Ch. 2, *passim*.
[200] 'Laudi e miniature fiorentine del primo trecento', *Studi musicali*, 7 (1978), 61–9. R. Offner, *A Critical and Historical Corpus of Florentine Painting* (New York, 1957), section III, vii. 56. Ziino's conclusions have been recently discussed and corroborated by Barr, *The Monophonic Lauda*, 125–8, where she also discusses the composition and iconography of these miniatures (which are reproduced as plates 13–14). The St Agnes lauda is found primarily in Florentine sources (Mgl¹: Liuzzi, *La lauda*, ii. 384–6; with concordant music; and Mgl², no. 90, but with much simpler decorative schemes); while 'Facciam laude' is transmitted by seven Tuscan and Umbrian sources, and received an elaborate miniature in Mgl¹ as well (reproduced in colour as a frontispiece in Liuzzi, *La lauda*, ii). See Plate 1, and Ch. 2 n. 56.

angel musicians playing a vielle and a psaltery. The same *agnus* symbol may be seen in the second roundel from the top in the left margin of the other plate, which also shows two bearded figures in the centre foreground wearing the Carmelite habit.

The next surviving testimony to the company's musical activities is its 1427 tax report, which lists a number of bequests for lauda vigils made after *c.*1370,[201] but no details regarding musicians and salaries. These first appear in company records of the 1440s, and indicate that Sant'Agnese musical practices conformed more or less to the larger pattern of Florentine laudesi activity. Ferial services had been abandoned by the 1440s, and two to three singers were hired for feast-days (including Lent), until the 1470s, when a larger, polyphonic ensemble of six to seven singers is recorded into the early sixteenth century. Sant'Agnese differed from the larger companies across the river primarily in that it had less to spend on extra singers and instrumentalists for special feast days, and could maintain only the smallest possible polyphonic ensemble in the late fifteenth and early sixteenth century (see Table 9).

TABLE 9. *Company of Sant'Agnese: salaried musicians, 1441–1519*

Year	Salary (/mo.)	Singers		Total
		Festal	Lenten	
1441	L. 5/Lent		2	
1442	L. 5/Lent		1 S, 1 T	
1444		1	2 S, 1 T	1
1442–50	s. 30	1		1
1449–50	s. 66		2 friars	
1457	L. 7, s. 3 total	2 S, 1 T		
1466–8	s. 10–13	3		3
1469	L. 3/Lent		2 friars	
1474	L. 10–15	5		5
1479	s. 15	2 S, 2 T		4
1489	s. 15	3 S, 2 T		5
1490	s. 15	2 S, 3 T		5
1494	s. 15	2 S, 3 T		5
1492–3	s. 10–15	3 S, 3 T		6
1519		3 S, 3 T		6

[201] ASF, Catasto 291, fo. 69ʳ; for ex., see Appendix 1, doc. 6, and its translation and discussion in Ch. 2, under 'Bequests'.

Though the company's greater number of bequests for lauda vigils assured a broader range of festal singing than at the other *Oltrarno* companies, Sant'Agnese nevertheless conformed to another characteristic of laudesi activity in that quarter—a particular emphasis upon Lenten singing. Payments to small ensembles of Lenten singers dominate the early records, and two are of particular significance since they provide the earliest explicit references to lay polyphonic singers as well as the first recorded use of the term *tenore* among the Florentine laudesi records. For Lent in 1442 the company hired the furrier Bruno di Giovanni and 'Daniello, *tenore*', and in 1444 they hired three singers in what constituted a common ensemble of the time—two boys (probably *biscantatori*), one named Felone, who also sang the laments, and one Benedetto, who sang the Gospels, and the 69-year-old butcher Domenico di Fruosino, 'who sang *tenore* throughout Lent, with both of the above two boy singers'.[202]

The parochial quality of *Oltrarno* laudesi activity is evident in the company's hiring practices during the middle decades of the century. During 1442–50 the company was served by a father and son who lived near the Carmine church and apparently sang only for Sant'Agnese: the weaver Niccolò di Betto, who was 44 in 1442, and his son Romolo, who must have been under 17 when he began singing laude with his father in 1444, since he was not mentioned in Niccolò's 1427 tax report.[203] Niccolò's last recorded payments were through May 1450, when he was receiving s. 30 per month, and when he was apparently continuing a conservative *Oltrarno* practice of solo singing for the feast-days outside Lent (see Table 10).[204] In 1445, the company recorded the death of the weaver Antonio di Benedetto di Butino (b. 1366), who also resided in the quarter and sang only at Sant'Agnese, and who had served the company in a manner reminiscent of the earliest years of lauda-singing:

Antonio di Benedetto di Butino of the parish of Santa Maria di Verzaia . . . was a great zealot, benefactor, and laudese continuously and resolutely for more than fifty years [without pay], diligent in all company matters, much honoured and well loved by the entire company . . .

---

[202] SA 24, fo. 101[r] [Mar. 1442]: 'A spese detto L. 4 s. 19 ebe Bruno di Giovanni pelleci ⟨aio⟩ perchè nella quaresima presente à chantato le laude cioè chon Daniello per tinore . . .'. Ibid., fo. 183[r] [10 Apr. 1444]: 'A spese . . . paghai e 2 fanc[i]uletti che chantorono le laude in questa quaresima, l'uno à nome Felone che chantò i llamenti, l'altro à nome Benedetto, che chantò i vangeli . . . a Domenicho di Frosino ch'à chantato tenore tutta la quaresima . . . chon tutte e 2 sopradetti chantori fanc[i]uletti . . .'. Domenico (b. 1375) is one of those laudesi who lived and apparently sang only in the Santo Spirito quarter; see his *catasto* profile in Appendix III.

[203] SA 24, fo. 123[r]; fascs. 9–14, *passim*. ASF, Catasto 67, fos. 392[v]–393[r], which records the birth in 1427 of a son Betto, who 50 years later also sang laude for the company (SA 115, fo. 13[r]).

[204] SA 114, fo. 20[r]: 'Nicholò di Betto detto Nicholò Bughani nostro lalldese . . . per salario di mesi sei passati cioè chominciati a dì primo di settembre 1449 a ragione di L. una s. dieci [il] mese . . . L. 9' (followed by payments for Mar.–May).

TABLE 10. *Company of Sant'Agnese: salaried musicians in 1442, 1466, 1479, and 1493*

1442	Salary	Years	Profession	Other tenures	Total years
Niccolò di Betto Bugani	s. 30/mo.	1442–50	weaver		8
Romolo di Niccolò Bugani	s. 22	1442–50			8
Antonio di Benedetto di Butino	none	1395–1445			50
1466					
Guelfo di Bartolomeo	L. 20/yr.	1466–7	barber	SF, SSP	12
Antonio della Puccia	L. 6/yr.	1466–7		SF, SSP	23
Bernardino di Francesco	L. 6/yr.	1466–7	goldsmith	SZ (T), SPM	14
1479					
sopranos:					
Antonio di Zanobi del Papa	s. 15/mo.	1479		SZ	29
Francesco d'Antonio di Ventura	s. 15	1478–9		SZ, SPM	37
tenors:					
Giovanni di Jacopo	s. 15	1478–9	weaver	SPM, SF, SSP	26
Jacopo di Ser Bartolomeo da Radda	s. 15	1479–94		SSP	14
1493					
sopranos:					
Raffaello di Giovanni	s. 10	1492–4	sawyer		3
Batista di Bagatino	s. 12	1493–4			2
Donato di Jacopo	s. 10	1493–4	grain merchant		2
tenors:					
Jacopo di Ser Bartolomeo da Radda	s. 15	1479–94			14
Niccolò di Giovanni Mascalzoni	s. 15	1484–94			11
Andrea del Fieravante	s. 15	1491–4		SZ (S)	5

He was a type not encountered among the laudesi rosters of the larger companies, a committed company member who volunteered his services (including his voice) only within the neighbourhood where he lived and worked. For this he was honoured in the company's greatest fashion:

. . . so the captains decided he should be honoured, and therefore this day they conducted a grand and honourable lauda vigil with all new things [referring primarily to the candles, of which there were to be over 6 lb.].[205]

The few Sant'Agnese singers who are recorded as having sung else-where during this period sang primarily at other companies in the district. Antonio della Puccia and the barber Guelfo di Bartolomeo sang (usually together) for all three *Oltrarno* companies, and during 1466–7 were joined by Bernardino di Francesco, who thereafter moved on to the larger companies (and wages) across the river where he sang as a *tenore* for the next thirteen years (see Table 10). All three were to come on the obligatory feast days 'between the 23rd and 24th hour'.[206] Guelfo's contract for this tenure sets forth in detail his special duties as *precentor*, and reveals the level of involvement expected by the more closely knit *Oltrarno* companies:

Guelfo di Bartolomeo, barber, employee (*famiglio*) of our company, and singer of laude, shall have as salary . . . L. 20 for one year [of service] when the following obligation is fulfilled. And which year began on 1 November 1466, and shall finish on the said day in 1467. And which obligation is to be this: that the said Guelfo in the said year shall diligently come on every obligatory feast to say [sing] laude in the church of the Carmine of Florence, between the 23rd and 24th hour, to set up the lectern, and also to clear [it] away, and when he is remiss he shall be docked s. 5 for each time. And besides singing the laude, he shall diligently assemble the captains, other officials, or men of the company, . . . and in the event that he does not do [these things] or is remiss through his [own] defect or negligence, whether in singing the laude or assembling the captains, for every day s. 5 shall be withheld from his salary.[207] (see Plate 12.)

During the 1470s and 1480s, the company began to hire a small polyphonic ensemble of four to five singers, with two *tenori* and two to three sopranos, which indicates that the company probably clung to an older repertoire of two- and three-part music during this period. During the decade of the 1470s, in particular, the company was hiring a higher percentage of singers from across the Arno, most of them *tenori*; this was probably a period during which there were too few resident polyphonic singers in that quarter at a time when the companies were beginning to require greater numbers of them. The situation had changed again by *c*.1485, after which time few of the Sant'Agnese laudesi are recorded as having sung outside of the quarter (see Table 10).

[205] Appendix I, doc. 15. For a more detailed profile of Antonio, see Appendix III.
[206] The '24th hour' varied from 5.15 p.m. (21 Dec.) to 8.39 p.m. (21 June); N. Barbieri, 'Note di cronologia: le ore a Siena dal XIV al XVIII secolo', *Bulletino senese di storia patria*, 90 (1983), 148–51. It is perhaps a little revealing of a lay company's character that they would use this more precise time-keeping system developed in the 14th-c. Italian communes, rather than the ecclesiastical hours of the church in which they were situated.   [207] Appendix I, doc. 16.

In 1490 the company began hiring three *tenori* and two to three *laudieri*, perhaps the smallest possible ensemble that would allow the performance of four-part music. Nevertheless, in light of the company's later, sixteenth-century complaints about the financial difficulty of maintaining lauda-singing, one senses that even the smallest of polyphonic chapels must have been an economic strain in the face of inflation and the inadequacy of bequests made at an earlier time when only one or two singers were required. Moreover, the company's Ascension play, though involving incidental lauda performances, had for some time diverted its resources away from the liturgical context where the lauda had been primary.[208] Perhaps for these reasons the captains decided in 1492 to shore up the devotion by creating a special 'lauda account', setting aside L. 47 per year which, it was pointedly stipulated, was to be spent only on the company's lauda-singing.[209] But these hardships were about to be overshadowed by more profound changes in the religious and political life of the city.

In October 1494 the company records cease abruptly, resume tentatively in April 1498, but show no payments to singers until 1506. The period of silence between October 1494 and April 1498 corresponds exactly to the rise and fall of Savonarola, whose censure certainly fell hard upon Sant'Agnese for its lavish spectacles and close ties to the Medici. Since 1469 Lorenzo, and later his sons Piero and Giuliano, and nephew Giulio, had been benefactors and honorary members and officers of the company.[210] Within days of Lorenzo's death in April 1492, the company spent L. 10 for a *rinovale* (to be conducted *in perpetuum*) at the company's Annunciation chapel 'per la buona memoria di Lorenzo di Piero di Cosimo de' Medici'.[211]

The records of payments to singers resuming after 1506 are very sparse, undoubtedly owing to 'the ruin and great disruption of our

[208] On the role of laude in the Ascension play, see Barr, 'Music and Spectacle', and on the *sacre rappresentazioni* in general, *The Monophonic Lauda*, 27–8; and B. Becherini, 'La musica nelle sacre rappresentazioni fiorentine', *Rivista musicale italiana*, 53 (1951), 193–241.

[209] SA 4, fo. 48ᵛ [no day or month]: '. . . el ficto che dà l'anno alla compagnia Nicholò fante ungaro che dà l'anno L. 47, debbano andare solamente a conto delle laude, et questo sia l'assegnamento che hanno dette laude, et per altri detto ficto non si possa spendere'. The rent (or lease) paid by this Hungarian infantryman (!), perhaps on property bequeathed to the company, would just cover the salaries of six singers at s. 10–15/mo.

[210] Bacchi, 'La compagnia di S. Maria', 3 (1931–2), 119–21. Beginning in 1469, Lorenzo donated 24 bushels of flour every year for distribution to the poor of the Carmine neighbourhood, and in 1485 Lorenzo and his male descendants were elected to receive all the benefits while incurring none of the responsibilities of membership: '. . . Lorenzo di Piero di Cosimo de' Medici e tutti i discendenti di casa sua per linea mascolina siano ed esser debbano esentati e riservati da ogni e qualunque debito che avessimo o potessimo per l'avvenire avere degli avi loro et essendo tra che si intendano e che chosì siano netti nello specchio senza pagare cosa alcuna et questo si è fatto per i meriti e beneficii [che] hanno fatto e ogni dì fanno alla nostra compagnia . . .' [16 June 1485]; ibid. 120. See also Weissman, *Ritual Brotherhood*, 169–73. The Savonarola regime and Medici involvement in Sant'Agnese affairs is discussed more fully in Ch. 6.   [211] SA 4, fo. 48ᵛ [17 Apr. 1492].

company' reported in 1508.[212] In 1506 the company did not hire their singers individually, as in the past, but contracted the 'company of *fanciulli* of Sant'Alberto' to sing laude on the obligatory feast-days in order to fulfil bequests.[213] The boys, however, were apparently unfamiliar either with polyphonic performance or the lauda repertory, and since the company desired polyphonic laude for feast-days, a company member, Antonio di Lucha, was hired to 'hold the tenor and to teach laude to the boys'.[214] In this manner the company struggled throughout this difficult time to fulfil the terms of bequests. The last recorded payment to a full retinue of singers was in 1519, and the last recorded payment to any laudese was made in 1533 to Piero di Bartolomeo and companions.[215] By 1537 the company had ceded its liturgical obligations (including lauda-singing) to the friars, and the company became a formal neighbourhood group devoted to the management of dowries, a hospice for widows, and its annual feast.[216]

The Company of San Frediano[217]

The small church of San Frediano, from which the company took its name, stood at the opposite end of the Piazza del Carmine from the great Carmelite church, and was a Cistercian priory from 1236 to 1514, when it was remodelled and became an Augustinian convent.[218] After its suppression in 1783, the church was sold and rendered unrecognizable through incorporation into a private *palazzo*, which has led some modern scholars to assume that the company was associated with the nearby church of San Frediano in Cestello.[219]

The oldest company statutes were drafted at the time of its foundation on 1 January 1324.[220] The mission of this small company differed

---

[212] SA 115, fos. 158 ff.; the document is translated and discussed in Ch. 6, and edited and partly translated in Weissman, *Ritual Brotherhood*, 180.

[213] SA 4, fo. 114ʳ. This company also met in the Carmine church, and patronized a nave altar near that of Sant'Agnese.

[214] Barr, *The Monophonic Lauda*, 23. Antonio's son Lorenzo ('lo spato') sang tenor for the company during 1507–19.

[215] SA 1, fo. 106ʳ [29 Mar. 1533], L. 14 for singing laude and the lament during Lent.

[216] SA 1, fos. 30 ff., which specifies that the friars were performing lauda vigils for the company in fulfilment of bequests.

[217] A 6th-c. saint who became an anchorite, and later bishop, in Lucca, where he formed a clerical community. He was honoured for his holiness and miracles. In the 15th c. a nickname, 'la Bruciata' (referring to roast chestnuts) was appended to the company's title, which was derived from the terms of a 1415 bequest that required roast chestnuts to be given out after laude had been sung for soul of the deceased.

[218] O. Micali and P. Roselli, *Le soppressioni dei conventi a Firenze* (Florence, 1980), 139.

[219] e.g. C. C. Calzolai, *San Frediano in Cestello* (Florence, 1972). The latter church was not begun until c. 1450., as the Carmelite convent of S. Maria degli Angioli.

[220] BNF, Palatino 154, fo. 1ʳ. On the prevailing conditions of food shortages, harvest failures, epidemics, and increased cost of living in Florence at this time, see J. Henderson, 'The Parish and the

somewhat from other Florentine lay religious companies in that its charitable and devotional activities were directed primarily to the 'poor and the dead of the said parish'.[221] This parochial orientation was reinforced by the fact that the church of San Frediano, and not the Carmine, functioned as the headquarters of the parish.[222] In turn the members tended to be residents of the immediate neighbourhood, and captains were required to reside in the Gonfalone, or Ward, of the Green Dragon (comprised of the large parish of San Frediano and the smaller parish of Santa Maria a Verzaia). With the exception of certain officers who tended to be wealthy *Oltrarno* merchants,[223] the membership reflected the strong working-class character of this district. Only on the vigil and feast of the company's patron saint were the captains obliged to 'honour the feast of Messer Santo Fridiano [18 November] and his vigil in every way possible, singing laude, and with candles, and with the other things that pertain to a feast'.[224] In the extant company records of the period between 1333 and the 1370s, there is no mention of lauda-singing, and a 1356 inventory lists no laudarios or other lauda paraphernalia.[225]

The company was overwhelmed by the devastation of the Black Death; on one day alone in May 1348 the company buried '38 morti grandi' and '17 picholi'. But San Frediano had recovered by *c*.1360, and sometime between 1365 and 1373 actually became a laudesi company through the acquisition of a laudario, lectern, and altar paraphernalia.[226] The reasons for this change are worth pausing to consider. The devotion of lauda-singing was still strong and popular in late fourteenth-century Florence, and all the more so since the awesome encounter with death during the protracted years of the plague. The experience undoubtedly inspired the lay companies to reaffirm or expand their ritual capacity for commemorating the dead, which had always been central to laudesi

Poor in Florence at the Time of the Black Death: The Case of S. Frediano', *Continuity and Change*, 3 (1988), 251.

[221] *Continuity and Change*, 3 (1988), 251.

[222] Although some convent churches, like S. Croce, S. Maria Novella, and S. Marco, did serve this purpose; Brucker, 'Urban Parishes', 18 n. 4.

[223] e.g. Chiaro d'Ardinghello and the silk merchant Orlandino Lapi, both of whom left bequests for lauda vigils to the *Oltrarno* laudesi companies (Appendix I, docs. 4 and 6, and Plate 9). Both were recorded as captains of San Frediano in 1350; SF 29, fo. 29ᵛ.

[224] BNF, Palatino 154, fo. 1ʳ: 'VII. Come s'onori la festa de Santo Fridiano. Siano tenuti i capitani d'onorare la festa di Messer Santo Fridiano et la sua vigilia in ogne modo che potranno chantando laude et con luminare et con altre cose che a festa si recheggiono.'

[225] SF 29 and 88, *passim*; 39, fo. 45ʳ (a 1356 inventory listing primarily burial items).

[226] The company recorded expenses for lauda paraphernalia (including the copying of an illuminated laudario) during 1368–73 (see Ch. 2, 'Bequests'), but Henderson ('Piety and Charity', 357 n. 70) noted that on 30 May 1365 the company petitioned the city for the same right to elect their own syndics as had the other laudesi companies in 1329, an indication that San Frediano probably had become a laudesi company in or just before 1365.

devotion. But a lay company was also a business, notwithstanding its religious function, and it was managed by professional businessmen who must have appreciated the nature of bequests, both as a means of assuring a company's survival in a most uncertain world, and as a kind of market in which the many Florentine lay companies competed. A successful merchant and San Frediano leader like Chiaro d'Ardinghello, who had close ties to the Carmine and the Sant'Agnese laudesi, may well have prompted the company in this direction, and he certainly provided them with their first recorded bequest for a lauda vigil in 1377.[227] Thereafter the company's condition improved as membership increased and more bequests (at least nine within the following century) were made, although it remained among the city's smallest laudesi companies.[228] The Company of San Frediano was not listed among the laudesi companies that petitioned the city in 1329, but in the 1427 *Catasto* was referred to as 'La chonpagnia delle laulde di San Friano'.[229] The company purchased another laudario in 1396,[230] and the numerous expenses for altar repair and decoration in the following decades reveal the expansion of the altar-oriented ritual life characteristic of laudesi devotion. The ritual capacity of the company was further expanded by bequests that brought two more chapels under their patronage, the Chapel of St Michael in 1436, and the Chapel of the Annunciation in 1479.[231] In 1452, according to an inventory made that year, the company owned 'three books of laude, one large, one medium, and one small'.[232]

Following the completion of its new laudario in the spring of 1374, the company recorded its first expenses in the execution of a laudesi tradition— a *collazione* for the singers on the company's patron-saint feast day in

---

[227] Appendix I, doc. 6; cf. Ch. 2, 'Bequests'. It is perhaps no coincidence that Chiaro's bequest for a lauda vigil was made while Florence was under papal interdict, when the celebration of divine offices was forbidden. Lay company services did not fall under this censure, and an anonymous Florentine chronicler of the 14th c. reports the formation of 'processions with the disciplinati, carrying the standard of the Church throughout the land, singing laude and litanies and other prayers. Many such companies were newly formed at the time, companies of men, boys, and children. Also, at that time other societies of laudesi originated as well, singing . . . in the evening for the glory of God'. Monachi Patavini, *Chronicon de Rebus Gestis in Lombardia Praecipue et Marchia Tarvisina*, in *Rerum Italicarum Scriptores*, viii (Milan, 1726), col. 699; trans. in Barr, *The Monophonic Lauda*, 12. The only known laudesi company that can be said to have originated at this time in Florence is the Company of San Frediano.
[228] The company's bequests are recorded in ASF, *Acquisti e Doni* 41, fos. 1^r–9^v [1488].
[229] ASF, Catasto 291, fo. 71^r.
[230] SF 31, fos. 5^r, 7^v.
[231] SF 4, fos. 1^v–5^v; the first came through a bequest by Michele di Simone, *bottaio* (barrel-maker) which provided for a chaplaincy at the altar of St Michael. The chaplain, chosen by the company, was to say Mass at the altar every day, to help sing high Mass and Vespers in the church, and to celebrate the feast of St Michael (for which instrumentalists were hired). On the Annunciation Chapel, see SF 5, fo. 22^r.
[232] SF 4, fo. 70^r.

November.[233] After 1387 the feast-day was regularly referred to as 'la festa della scuola', which indicates that the company may have observed another laudesi custom of holding lauda schools on Sundays after Mass.[234] In a rare show of the city-wide activity more typical of larger laudesi companies, the company had by 1429 begun celebrating its St Fredianus feast in the special manner soon taken up by the neighbouring Sant'Agnese laudesi, with a '*collazione* for all the laudesi of Florence every year'.[235]

TABLE 11. *Company of San Frediano: salaried musicians, 1394–1457*

Year	Salary (/mo.)	Singers				Total
		Ferial	Festal	Lenten	Undesig.	
1394	s. 10				1	1
1405–19	L. 4–6/yr.	1				1
1419–45	s. 20	1				1
1441	L. 4 (Lent)			2		
1455–6	L. 8/yr.		2			2
1457			3			3

After a few scattered payments to individual singers in the 1390s, the earliest record of regular payments to singers begins in 1405, and for the next forty-four years the company was served by a single, solo singer, a position whose occupancy changed only once (see Table 11). In this most parochial of Florentine laudesi companies, solo, monophonic singing persisted the longest, and the company's laudesi were long-standing members, frequent office-holders, parishioners, and *famigli* who performed a variety of tasks. From 1405 to 1419 Lorenzo di Matteo ('Posserello') sang for the company's festal and ferial services.

Lorenzo di Matteo, called Posserello, who provides the service of lauda-[singing], for God and as payment for the service and labour borne in preparation of the said laude, which are said [sung] every evening in the church of San Fri[di]ano, for the past period up to the first of January of the said year 1411, L. 4, and for the future [for] performing the said service and labour of the said laude

[233] SF 30, fo. 114ʳ [1374]: 'demmo per uno mezzo barile di vino che ssi chonperò per fare onore a' chantatori della festa e per frute e per bichieri a dì 19 di novembre . . . L. 1 s. 13 d. 6.'.

[234] Ibid., fos. 129ᵛ (1387), 131ᵛ (1389).

[235] ASF, Catasto 293, fo. 31ᵛ [1429], adds to its 1427 expenses for a singer and wax, a 'cholazione a tutti i laldieri di Firenze ognianno . . . L. 6'. Both this and the Sant'Agnese feast (by 1446) were established by bequests, the latter perhaps in an effort not to be outdone by the former.

. . . the said Lorenzo is to have every year for the above cause L. 6 per year beginning . . . on the first of January 1411.[236]

The rare payments to other singers during this period were generally in fulfilment of the laudesi custom of hiring extra singers on feast-days, which San Frediano certainly did on its patron-saint feast when the *collazione* always included several laudesi.

The longest tenure as laudese was served by Lodovico di Francesco, who from 1419 to 1449 was paid L. 12 per year. The company's 1427 tax report, which shows its total assets at only fl. 76, lists the following two expenses:

Per year to Francesco laudiere who sings laude in the said church . . . L. 12

Per year for 12 lb. of candles which are used every evening at the lauda [service] . . . L. 6[237]

Lodovicho was particularly active in company affairs, holding the offices of treasurer (1426, 1428) and syndic (1426, 1436). Only once, during Lent of 1441, is he recorded as having sung elsewhere (across the *piazza* for the Company of Sant'Agnese), and on this occasion the company elected from its active membership the wide-ranging laudese Nocho d'Alesso to sing laude every evening of Lent 'for the devotion of the people' (and L. 8).[238] The records of the company after mid-century are very sparse, but significant changes are discernible. By 1455 the company had discontinued ferial singing, and was now hiring two to three singers for the obligatory feasts and vigils (Table 11). During 1456–9 the company's laudese and *famiglio* at L. 20 per year was the barber Guelfo, who later sang for the other two *Oltrarno* laudesi companies, and he was joined by two other singers at L. 6 per year.[239] Whether polyphony was being performed in the company's services during this time is unclear; in a conservative company with a strong monophonic tradition it is possible that these ensembles of two and three singers were a continuation of an older tradition of hiring additional singers on feast-days, even for monophonic lauda performances. And the majority of company laudesi hired during this time of transitional performance practice were active only in the

[236] Appendix I, doc. 20. This modest sum was his base salary for ferial singing; sporadic payments during 1410–11, totalling L. 10, indicate that Lorenzo probably received *ad hoc* payments for festal services in addition to his base pay. When singers performed at a lauda vigil in fulfilment of a bequest, some companies, like Sant'Agnese and San Frediano, paid their singers in this manner.

[237] ASF, Catasto 291, fo. 71[r].

[238] Nocho's contract is edited in Appendix 1, doc. 24. He is listed in the company's 1442 *borsa*; SF 4, fo. 23[v].

[239] Ibid., fo. 82[v] [21 Dec. 1456]: 'Capitani . . . nel luogo della loro usata residenza [elect] . . . ii laudese et a dire et cantare la sera delle feste comandate insieme con Guelfo nostro et della decta compagnia laudese nella chiesa di San Friano . . . L. 6 per anno'.

Oltrarno, and most only at San Frediano, where the *ars mensurae* was probably not yet well established. One possible exception was the weaver Giovanni di Jacopo da Brucianese, who was paired with Guelfo during 1455 and 1456; he sang with the Company of Sant'Agnese as a *tenore* in 1478–9, and certainly as a polyphonic singer with the companies of Santo Spirito and San Piero Martire in the early 1480s, but it is unlikely that the same skill was required of him as a young singer starting out at a small company in the 1450s.[240]

During the last third of the century, at a time when most laudesi companies pressed ahead with larger polyphonic ensembles, San Frediano's slender assets forced them into subsistence. Singers, no longer salaried, were hired *ad hoc* only on those handful of annual occasions when bequests required lauda-singing. In 1495 the company simply hired the Orsanmichele laudesi in order to fulfil Fra Giovanni Lozzi's bequest for a lauda vigil and *collazione* on the feast of St Fredianus,[241] and the same bequest was fulfilled in 1503 by two singers who performed six laude with organ accompaniment.[242] This frugal policy of lauda-singing *in su l'organo* may have begun earlier, for during the 1460s and 1470s the company recorded payments to an organist, and in 1468–9 paid an annual salary of L. 8 per year to Piero di Matteo 'who plays the organ in San Frediano'.[243]

By the time the company drafted a new set of statutes in 1565, it had come full circle with respect to lauda-singing; just as in the company's 1324 statutes, the only mention of the devotion was with respect to the feast of St Fredianus, with the difference that in the sixteenth century it was maintained solely by the obligation of a bequest.[244]

The Company of Santo Spirito

The Compagnia delle laude di Santo Spirito (also called *della Colomba,* or *del Piccione*, after the company's symbol, the dove of the Holy Spirit), was located in the church of Santo Spirito, the largest convent of

[240] SF 4, fo. 76ʳ; 110, fo. 11ᵛ, where his salary is recorded as having been paid to his father.

[241] SF 110, fo. 82ʳ [22 Nov. 1495]: 'A' ladieri d'Orsamichele . . . L. 2 sono per fare la vigilia a fra Giovanni pinzochero di San Pagholo chome per suo leghato lascio'. The terms of this bequest are set forth in Appendix I, doc. 5, and discussed in Ch. 2, 'Bequests'.

[242] SF 5, fo. 129ᵛ. Frank D'Accone has shown that lauda-singing *in su l'organo*, as it was designated in Florentine documents, was practised by the friars of Santissima Annunziata in the 1480s, and at Santa Maria Novella in the late 16th c.; 'Repertory and Performance Practice', 76.

[243] SF 4, fo. 108ᵛ; 110, fo. 28ᵛ. An organist was also frequently paid for the feast of St Michael (9 May), which involved only Latin liturgical items, and the practice of a 'messa chantanto cho' gl'orghani' was recorded by the company as early as 1438; SF 31, fo. 53ᵛ.

[244] ASF, Acquisti e Doni 42, fo. 34ᵛ: [In fulfilment of a bequest from Mona Caterina] '. . . si possa spendere in detta festa [of San Frediano] cioè cera, laldieri, bruciate, et colletione [*sic*], et vino . . . L. 21'.

the Tuscan-based Austin friars.[245] The company is first mentioned in a city *Provvisione* of 1322,[246] although it was probably founded during the late thirteenth century along with most of the other Florentine laudesi companies.

The only extant company document from before *c*.1420 is the early fourteenth-century laudario Mgl[1], a sumptuously illuminated and noted manuscript that is the sole source of the Florentine monophonic lauda repertory.[247] The assumption that the owners of such a manuscript must have been an institution 'of some wealth' may be true with respect to companies outside Florence, but it must be qualified with respect to the Florentine laudesi.[248] The two extant Florentine laudarios (Mgl[1] and Mgl[2]), both elegantly decorated, were in fact the possessions of two modest Florentine laudesi companies (San Gilio and Santo Spirito, respectively). A 1444 Santo Spirito inventory lists 'dua libri di laude miniate e dipinti', and as the inventories of even the smallest companies reveal, such books were *de rigueur* in the Florentine companies, for they were a requisite liturgical item at a major feast day service.[249] In his study of the miniatures in Mgl[1] and Mgl[2], Vincent Moleta observed that 'the illustration of laude in the early and mid-fourteenth-century city-states reflects a newly institutionalized phase in the production of laudari, when the lay confraternity books could now be shown to rival Latin service books in their decoration as in their liturgical range'.[250]

No company account books pre-dating the fifteenth century survive, but 1427 assets (fl. 285) reveal the company's modest proportions. During the fifteenth century, as a shrinking political arena compelled the more ambitious Florentines to seek out new power-bases, the

---

[245] The Augustinian (Austin, Hermit) friars grew out of bands of Tuscan hermits who were assigned the rule of St Augustine by Innocent IV in 1243. They were united in 1256 by Alexander IV under the title Hermits of St Augustine, with the status of mendicant friars, and by the end of the century resembled the Dominicans in organization and theology; 'Augustinians', in *New Catholic Encyclopedia* (New York, 1967), i. 1071–6. The new order had settled in the church of Santo Spirito by 1250; Anna Benvenuti Papi, 'Ordini mendicanti e città', 128–9 n. 13.

[246] ASF, Provvisione 26, fo. 8bis[r] [20 July 1322], where the company is referred to as 'Sotietatis Laudum Sancti Spiritus de Florentia'.

[247] Mgl[1]: Florence, BN, Banco Rari 18 (*olim* Mgl. II. I. 122); ed. in Liuzzi, *La lauda*, ii, with facsimiles, and transcriptions which are unacceptable for their rhythmic interpretations; Grossi, 'The Fourteenth Century Florentine Laudario', with diplomatic transcriptions and introductory study. An edition of texts is forthcoming in the series that already includes Cort, edited by G. Varanini, L. Banfi, and A. C. Burgio, *Laude cortonesi dal secolo XIII al XV*, 4 vols: i/1–2, ii (Florence, 1981–5). For a recent analysis and discussion of Mgl[1], see Barr, *The Monophonic Lauda*, ch. 4. An approximate date of Mgl[1] (*c*.1330–50) is based on a stylistic analysis of the miniatures, while its assignment to the Company of Santo Spirito is based on a thematic study of texts and miniatures: Liuzzi, *La lauda*, i. 81 (between 1310 and 1330–40); V. Moleta, 'The Illuminated *Laudari*', 29 n. 2 (*c*. 1330); Barr, *The Monophonic Lauda*, 96, 182 (n. 3) (*c*.1340–50); *Répertoire international des sources musicales*, ser. B. iv/1, 789.

[248] Grossi, 'The Fourteenth Century Florentine Laudario', 27.

[249] SSP 78, fo. 5[r].   [250] Moleta, 'The Illuminated *Laudari*', 30.

membership lists of the *Oltrarno* companies began to show greater numbers of upper guildsmen and prominent family names.[251] While these new families certainly brought the companies an economic transfusion, they also may well have determined the shift so apparent in both the Sant'Agnese and Santo Spirito companies from traditional, ferial lauda-singing to the staging of annual dramatic spectacles. A sure sign of the company's increasingly politicized environment was the entry of Lorenzo de' Medici into membership in 1467, and thereafter Medici influence was secured as it was in the Company of Sant'Agnese, by the ensuing entry of other family members.[252]

Like the other Florentine lay companies, Santo Spirito was hard hit by the economic contraction and taxation of the early fifteenth century, but appears to have revived in the 1440s with increased membership enrolment. A long list of costumes and properties in a 1444 inventory indicates that by this time the company's annual Pentecost play, the 'Festa della Sensione', had become an elaborate and spectacular affair.[253] The company had abandoned ferial services by 1446, but lauda-singing continued throughout the fifteenth and sixteenth centuries, confined primarily to Lent. In 1598 the 'Compagnia del Pippione' (*Piccione*) was still conducting lauda services during the feast-days of Lent, on the strength of a bequest made long before.

Although records of the company's professional singing activity do not begin until 1421, the strongest evidence for such activity prior to this date is its laudario. Many of the melodies in this manuscript are remarkable for their florid quality and wide range, especially when compared with the older concordant versions in the late thirteenth-century Cortona manuscript (see Music Examples 3–5). Noting the 'evident taste for luxuriant melismatic patterns' in this collection, Giulio Cattin has observed that a certain amount of 'technical accomplishment' is required in their

[251] For example, the membership lists of Santo Spirito show a rapid growth between 1444 and 1470 (30 new members in 1444), and about four of every five bore prominent *Oltrarno* family names like Frescobaldi, Ridolfi, Pitti, Corbinelli, Capponi, and Torrigiani; SSP 79, *passim*. The Florentine architect Michelozzo Michelozzi joined the Company on 3 Aug. 1446; ibid., fo. 21ᵛ.

[252] Lorenzo joined the company 10 May 1467, SSP 79, fo. 21ᵛ; on 14 May 1481 the company elected to membership Lorenzo's son Piero (b. 1472), and Lorenzo di Pierfrancesco de' Medici (b. 1463), by a vote of 43 to 1; SSP 2, fo. 4ʳ.

[253] On the feast, see A. D'Ancona, *Origini del teatro italiano*, ii. 186, and Weissman, *Ritual Brotherhood*, 169–73. By 1436 the company had begun to refer to its 'festa della colomba' as the 'festa della sensione' (SSP 58, fos. 37ʳ–43ʳ [expenses for 1436 and 1437]); the company's 1427 tax report lists only an annual expense of L. 25–30 for the 'festa della colomba' (ASF, Catasto 291, fo. 71ᵛ), but the company was certainly spending much more than this by mid-century, for its production rivalled that of the Company of Sant'Agnese, on which that company spent hundreds of lire annually. As at Sant'Agnese, this appears to have been the only occasion for which the company regularly hired instrumentalists, usually *pifferi*.

performance,[254] and documents presented in the following chapter will demonstrate the care with which the laudesi companies hired their singers. For such pieces to be in the repertory of a middling company indicates that a laudese in fourteenth-century Florence was expected to command a reasonably competent vocal technique, and the number and variety of feast-days represented by laude in this and other lauda collections reveals how substantial the musical activities of the companies were. The laudario is all the more interesting in light of company documents that demonstrate the persistence of monophonic lauda-singing into the early fifteenth century (see Table 12). The company's 1427 tax report records, along with complaints of chronic debt because of high expenses and unpaid rents from company property, an annual expense of three to six florins for 'un chantatore delle laulde'.[255]

The two- and three-part Latin motets included in the latter part of Mgl[1] (and other fourteenth-century laudarios) represent technical demands of a different order, which the lay singers probably began to meet in the

TABLE 12. *Company of Santo Spirito: salaried musicians, 1421–1508*

Year	Salary (/mo.)	Singers			Total
		Ferial	Festal	Lenten	
1421	s. 40	1			1
1426		1			1
1431		1			1
1434		2			2
1439	L. 16/yr.	2			2
1442				2	2
1445	L. 36/yr.		2		2
1447				2	2
1456				2	2
1482	s. 45			10	10
1486	L. 26/yr. total			6 S, 4 T	10
1487	L. 28, s. 12 total			6 S, 5 T	11
1503	L. 21/yr. total			3 S, 3 T, P	7
1507	L. 17/yr. total			3 S, 2 T, P	6
1508	L. 21/yr. total			4 S, 3 T	7

S = soprano, T = tenor, P = precentor

[254] Cattin, *Music of the Middle Ages*, 147–50.
[255] ASF, Catasto 291, fo. 71ᵛ [1427]: 'La chonpagnia delle laulde di Santo Spirito nominata della Cholonba . . . Anno a tenere un chantatore delle laulde al anno fl. 3 in 6 . . . La detta chonpagnia à sempre debito per le grande spese e male rischuotere.' This is corroborated by the company's own record of its 1427 tax report, which lists 'uno che chanta le laulde la sera'; SSP 1, fo. 29ʳ.

late fourteenth century. At a time when polyphony was relatively uncommon in Italian ecclesiastical establishments, it is surprising to see how common these motets were in the repertories of the Florentine companies.[256]

In 1421, the company's first recorded payments were made to Antonio di Petro, an experienced laudese who had been singing with the three major companies across the river between 1383 and 1417. Antonio resided in a parish near the church of Santo Spirito, however, and since he was in ill health by 1426, he may have semi-retired to his quarter 'to sing laude every evening in the church of St Augustine' as the company's sole singer.[257] In 1424 he and his wife became resident managers of the company's hospital, with the condition that Antonio continue singing laude in the evening ferial services without pay for this:

The company . . . elects . . . as new *spedalingo* Antonio di Petro laudese, who sings the laude, with the usual terms and conditions, and he and his wife shall enter into and execute well and with love his [new] office . . . on the condition that from this day forth he ought nor may not request any salary or commission for singing laude during the evening [services] in Santo Spirito. Whereas he formerly received s. 40 per month for his labour and compliance, thus he, being present, undertakes and promises to diligently pursue and improve in lauda-singing during the evening [services] in Santo Spirito as before, and because of the benefice of the said hospital given to him, he is obligated to us not to request a salary . . .[258]

Contracts between the company and its singers continued to involve various combinations of residency, membership, and extra duties. In 1434 the company was paying two singers, the brothers Lorenzo and Francesco di Giovanni, who in that year appear to have been living in the company hospital along with their father, Giovanni di Lorenzo. In January 1435 the two were paid L. 16 for having sung laude from Lent through October of the preceding year, and the same contract records an identical payment to Don Romualdo, a monk from the neighbouring Camaldolese church of San Felice, who very probably trained the boys as *biscantatori* and sang with them that year.[259] In April 1435 the boys and their father were dismissed from their hospital duties and privileges, but the two boys continued through 1439 to 'sing laude every evening as is customary' at L. 34 per year. They very likely took holy orders shortly thereafter, for though Lorenzo sang concurrently for San Zanobi and Orsanmichele, they are not mentioned in any subsequent laudesi records. In

---

[256] The San Gilio laudario (Mgl²) contains a similar collection, there are several references to motets in the 14th-c. records of the Company of San Piero Martire, and laudarios from Pisa and Lucca apparently contained them as well. See Ch. 4, nn. 56–7.

[257] His contract is transcribed in Appendix I, doc. 17.

[258] Appendix I, doc. 18.   [259] SSP 57, fo. 41ᵛ.

1444 another pair of singers, the carpenter Luca d'Antonio and Antonio della Puccia (both of whose laudesi activities were confined to the *Oltrarno*) became company members. Their singing tenure with the company was brief, during which their dues were credited against their salaries as singers,[260] but they remained members through 1456 while singing primarily at other *Oltrarno* companies.

The following year the company drafted a contract with two of the city's most active laudesi, who together leased a piece of land from the company in lieu of most of their salary:

. . . beginning [1 December 1445] Nocho [d'Alesso, a weaver] and Ulivante [di Bartolomeo] are obliged to come for the next two years to sing laude, and should [each] have for their salary L. 36 per year of which they must reckon the rent on a piece of land in Gangalandi which brings L. 28 per year, and L. 5 more from the Company of the Bigallo [a bequest] every year on the 5th of November . . . and the rest from annual funds of L. 3, and they are to sing every Sunday and every obligatory feast day, and the evenings of [the feasts of] St Augustine and St Nicholas, and for every time they do not sing the said laude they must be docked s. 10 . . . and they must be here in the evening at the 23rd hour . . . L. 72.[261]

There is no mention of ferial singing here, which had been discontinued by 1445, at about the same time as in the companies of San Zanobi (1433), Sant'Agnese (by 1441), and San Frediano (by *c.*1450). But the Santo Spirito singers' salaries were twice what they were a decade before, and though the larger companies spent much more than L. 72 per year on their total musicians' salaries (e.g. L. 792 at Orsanmichele in 1436, and about L. 185 at San Piero Martire in 1446), this was the highest base salary recorded for an individual Florentine laudese during the fifteenth century. This is best explained if the 'obligatory feast days' in the contract are assumed to include a heavy fare of Lenten singing, for which the Florentine companies customarily engaged a pair of singers. In fact, during the 1447 Lenten season the same pair sang for the company on 'all the obligatory feasts of this Lent, Holy Thursday, Good Friday, and all the feasts of Easter'.[262]

During the sparsely documented period between 1448 and 1482, lauda-singing on all feast-days outside Lent ceased, and the salaries were decreased while the size of the chapel increased. In 1465 the company began levying a 'lauda tax' ('l'imposta delle laude') of s. 6 on all new members,[263] and perhaps like the similar fund at Sant'Agnese it was intended to help meet the costs of both a large annual *festa* and an expanding polyphonic laudesi chapel. By 1482 the company was hiring

---

[260] SSP 79, fo. 12ʳ.   [261] Appendix I, doc. 19.
[262] SSP 78, fos. 22ʳ⁻ᵛ.   [263] SSP 60, fos. 19ʳ–22ᵛ; 78, fo. 61ᵛ.

nine to eleven singers (three to five *tenori* and six *fanciulli*) for the period of Lent (Table 12). In 1483 and 1484 the company listed nine lay singers for Lent,[264] but during the period 1488–1502 payments of L. 28–30 were made to four *fraticini* and two friars (1488), an unspecified number of *fraticini* and two *tinori* (1489, 1493–5), or most often simply to the *fraticini*.[265] Considering that the company did not maintain a regular retinue of laudesi, the friars were probably much easier to engage during the busy Lenten season when so many singers were needed at the same time throughout the city. This is the first indication that the Santo Spirito friars sang polyphony, and it is possible that its adoption by clerics, here as in some of the other Florentine churches and convents, may have been prompted by the example of the lay singers adorning the companies' festal liturgy with polyphonic music.

From 1503 to 1522 the company continued to hire singers only during Lent, but was paying less (L. 17–23 per year) to a smaller ensemble (two to three *tinori*, and three to four *fanciulli*). No friars are mentioned, and the group was under the direction of a lay *maestro di cappella* to whom the payments were made. In 1503 L. 21 was paid to the hosier nicknamed 'il Bigio' (the grey one), three *tinori*, and four *fanciulli*, for singing laude during all of Lent.[266] Thereafter the position of *maestro* alternated between Agniolo del Favilla (1505, 1518–22) and Piero da San Giorgio (1506–16), both of whom held this position at other laudesi companies during this period.[267]

The hiatus in company documents after 1522 suggests that the company experienced the same prolonged suppressions and disruptions as did the other Florentine lay companies during this politically unstable period of transition between the republic and the principate. A 1598 *memoriale* compiled by the Santo Spirito friars listed the obligations for the 'Altar of the Holy Sacrament of Matteo Corbinelli': 'the Company of the Dove must sing "laudi in musica" every feast-day [and Sunday of Lent], and afterwards a father is to give confession and recommend to God the soul of the said Matteo . . .'.[268] Although it is unusual to learn of a late sixteenth-century bequest for a lauda vigil still being performed in this manner (i.e. without Latin liturgical items having been substituted), this document most likely indicates that the company was responsible for administering the bequest by hiring singers, perhaps the friars, on this one occasion. There is no other indication that the company maintained a musical chapel or an interest in the devotion; account books for the years

---

[264] SSP 78, fo. 77ʳ; 62, fo. 46ʳ.   [265] SSP 62, fos. 47ᵛ–49ᵛ.

[266] SSP 57, fo. 21ʳ: 'al Bigio cha[l]zaiuolo . . . per avere cantato le lalde in Sancto Spirito tuta la quaresima con 3 tinore e 3 canza . . . L. 21.'

[267] SSP 78, fos. 90ᵛ–109ʳ; 57, fos. 23ʳ–24ᵛ; 62, fos. 55ᵛ–67ʳ.

[268] Appendix I, doc. 28; translated in Ch. 5, where the exact location of this and other laudesi altars is discussed.

1548–1628 record payments to the friars for Masses performed in fulfilment of bequests but no mention of laude, and the convent's 1598 *memoriale* indicates that the company had ceded other liturgical obligations to the friars.[269] Finally, the company's 1621 statutes are silent on the subject of laude, but specify the annual payment of L. 35 in dowries to the poor girls of the quarter, a popular charitable activity to which most of the Florentine laudesi companies had turned in lieu of lauda-singing during the sixteenth century.[270]

OTHER COMPANIES

A miscellaneous array of primary and secondary references point to the existence of other laudesi companies in Florence during the republican period. However, the complete absence of any primary documents belonging to these companies as well as the lack of references to these companies in the numerous extant confraternity documents would seem to indicate a short and/or insignificant existence. For some, lauda-singing may have been a marginal activity, as it was for many disciplinati companies. The majority of these companies turn out to be, upon closer examination, either mistakenly identified as laudesi, or difficult to identify as such.

All that survives of a laudesi company at the Vallombrosan church of Santa Trinita (Santa Maria Novella quarter) is a passing reference in the city's *Provvisioni Registri*.[271] Primarily on the basis of their titular devotion to Mary, Henderson has identified other laudesi companies at the churches of Sant'Ambrogio, Santa Maria Maggiore, San Pier Scheraggio, San Michele Berteldi, and San Piero Gattolini.[272]

According to Massimo Papi's research, there were laudesi companies at the churches of Santa Lucia sul Prato and San Piero Gattolini during the thirteenth century, but the documents he cites do not appear to bear this out.[273] On 28 January 1401 the Company of San Zanobi was made the executor of a commemorative bequest by Maestro Agnolo di Nuto,

---

[269] SSP 63 [1548–72]; 3 [1573–1628]. Conventi Soppressi 122, 36 [Memoriale, 1598], fo. 38^v.

[270] ASF, Acquisti e Doni 45, fo. 22^v.

[271] Vol. 72, fos. 189^{r-v} [18 Dec. 1383]. Davidsohn, *Forschungen*, iv. 440 recorded a reference to a 'Sotietas S. Trinitatis' in 1300, which may or may not be the laudesi company. I am indebted to Dr John Henderson for this reference; see his 'Piety and Charity', 419.

[272] Dr Henderson identifies these pre-16th-c. laudesi companies in his Appendix I (393 ff.), as well as a number of 16th-c. laudesi companies in his Appendix II (437 ff.) on the basis of the appellation 'di stendardo' (see also ibid. 35). While there is reason to suppose that these indeed may have been laudesi companies, their identification as such cannot be established or dismissed with certainty.

[273] M. Papi, 'Confraternite ed ordini mendicanti a Firenze', 728; 'Per un censimento delle fonti relative alle confraternite fiorentine: primi risultati', in D. Maselli (ed.), *Da Dante a Cosimo I* (Pistoia, 1976), 115–16.

'dottore et medicho fisico', to the 'Compagnia delle laude di S. Giovanni Batista'.[274] In fact, the company was one of the four primary Florentine Bianchi companies that were spawned by a great flagellant procession in 1399.[275] Penitential laude were an important part of the Bianchi movement, sung originally during their peace processions, and while the Bianchi companies were not laudesi companies, it was probably their association with laude that inspired Maestro Agnolo, less than two years after the procession, to call it a 'compagnia delle laude'.[276] The company of the Blessed Sacrament meeting in Santa Lucia sul Prato was another of the four Bianchi companies, which may account for Papi's abovementioned attribution as a laudesi company.[277]

Finally, a fourteenth-century laudario of Florentine provenance (Fior), containing several unique laude to St Eustace (but no music), has been attributed to a 'Compagnia di Sant'Eustachio' associated with the Benedictine church of Sant'Ambrogio.[278] It remains to be shown, however, that the laudario actually belonged to this company, or that this company was a laudesi group.

---

[274] SZ 1, fasc. 4, fos. 12ᵛ–13ʳ: '. . . Ancora lascio nel detto testamento alla compagnia delle laude di S. Giovanni Batista, che si raguna nella chiesa de' Frati del Marrone di Firenze, la metà di un suo podere'. The company met in the church of San Piero del Murrone (San Giovanni Quarter), a friary of the small Celestine order established in 1274 and devoted to St Peter Morone (Celestine V, c.1210–96).

[275] Weissman, *Ritual Brotherhood*, 50–5.

[276] For a discussion and edition of Bianchi laude, see Bernard Toscani, *Le laude dei Bianchi* (Florence, 1979), a critical edition of selected laude from MS Vaticano Chigiano L. VII 266.

[277] Weissman, *Ritual Brotherhood*, 51 n. 30.

[278] MS Fior = the Cecconi codex in the Florentine Archivio della Curia Arcivescovile; first edited by E. Cecconi, *Laudi di una Compagnia fiorentina del secolo XIV fin qui inedite* (Florence, 1870); recently discussed, indexed, and collated with five other medieval laudari by R. Bettarini, 'Notizia di un laudario', *Studi di filologia italiana*, 28 (1970), 55–66; see 56 n. 8 concerning the attribution to the Company of Sant'Eustachio, previously made by Cecconi.

4

The Professional Laudese

CONDITIONS AND PATTERNS OF ACTIVITY

In Florence, the development of the paid, professional laudese occurred primarily in the fourteenth century. The earliest Florentine laudesi statutes, from the last two decades of the thirteenth century, imply that laude were executed at this time by amateur singers chosen from among the company's ranks. The 1284 statutes of the Company of San Gilio concerned with lauda-singing make no special distinction between the laudesi and other company members.[1] In 1291, the Company of Sant'Agnese appointed special lauda instructors who officiated at both Sunday processions and evening services, on which occasions they were to 'send in front those singers [cantori] whom they choose'.[2] These are certainly not references to paid singers, for they imply more than one or two, and even the larger Companies of San Piero Martire and San Zanobi did not begin employing more than a pair of laudesi until the fifteenth century.

Nevertheless, in the fourteenth century, paid professionals who were not members of the companies began to appear, along with the first use of the term 'laudese' to denote an increasingly distinct and self-conscious genre of activity. Their appearance, along with liturgically sophisticated service-books, a standardized and more technically demanding musical repertory, and the proliferation and elaboration of liturgical services, signified the professional development of the Florentine laudesi companies in general. The reasons for this development are various, but may be traced to the rapid growth of a popular religious devotion under the management of guildsmen.

The Florentine laudesi companies had built a secure institutional framework for the devotion of lauda-singing by the turn of the fourteenth century. There followed bequests for lauda-singing, the earliest recorded in 1313, and these in turn must have engendered an increasingly professional attitude towards the devotion. The sixteenth-century statutes of

[1] These documents are translated and discussed in Ch. 3, 'Company of San Gilio'.
[2] Ed. in Schiaffini, *Testi fiorentini*, 64.

the Company of Sant'Agnese are explicit about the role of bequests in its thirteenth-century formation:

And besides this, because some of them, out of devotion, met in the said church of the Carmine to sing *laude spirituale*, they took the name 'delle laude', and because they received alms and bequests, it was decided that the captains and officials should meet on certain prescribed days to conduct works of mercy and distribute alms.[3]

The satisfactory fulfilment of a bequest was both a religious and a legal matter, and upon it depended the attraction of new bequests, which surely must have been a matter for stiff competition among the city's numerous companies. The establishment of the professional singer was aided by the occasional bequest that provided a salary or alms for a laudese.[4] The *scuole*, too, are perhaps best understood in this environment of increasing professionalization as an attempt to improve the quality of congregational responsorial singing; the *scuole* appear to have been taught neither by nor for the paid singers, but rather for company members, especially new ones and children, who were encouraged to learn the refrains.[5] The paid singer probably learned the soloistic singing of the lauda strophes not in the *scuole*, but in the traditional guild system of masters and apprentices (often involving a father/son relationship).

The professional attitude of the fourteenth-century laudesi companies was inherent in the mentality of both members and singers. The great majority matriculated in one or another of the twenty-one Florentine guilds, and of these many were masters of, or apprentices in, a small, independent *bottega* that performed a specialized function in the highly complex Florentine wool industry.[6] The success of the system depended upon a high degree of specialization of component functions, high standards of quality, and a rigorous system of quality control:

The Florentine sense of quality was a product of the city's craft tradition and the exceptional skills of her artisans. The industrial and craft guilds had developed a system of quality control to protect their trades; every Florentine realized that the maintenance of high standards benefited the city's economy. This appreciation of quality, and a corresponding disdain for the shoddy and the inferior, became a characteristic feature of the Florentine mentality and mode of perception.[7]

---

[3] Appendix I, doc. 1.

[4] In a 1325 bequest to the Company of San Piero Martire, Falcone Alberti left s. 10 to 'Lore che canta le laude' (SMN 292, fo. 28ʳ); a 1376 bequest to the same company by Mona Cionella provided an unspecified amount 'alle lalde dela nostra conpagnia e resto della rendita [of a farm] per chandele e per salario per laldessi' (SMN 306, fo. 23ʳ); a 1386 bequest to the Company of San Zanobi required that 'La compangnia di Santa Reparata dee ispendere livre dieci e' quali danari àvesi della pigione delle case di Santa Crocie feciegli ispendere . . . e dare a parte a' cantatori . . .' (SZ 2176, fasc. 12, fo. 28ᵛ).   [5] See Ch. 2, 'The *Scuole*'.

[6] The 26 stages of cloth manufacture, from fleecing to folding, are described in F. Edler, *Glossary of Mediaeval Terms of Business: Italian Series, 1200–1600* (Cambridge, Mass., 1934), 324–330.

[7] Brucker, *Renaissance Florence*, 220.

uiso che paradiso pieno di niente.

Facciam

laude ac

tucti sancti colla uergine ma

giore di bon core con dolci can

1. Florence, Biblioteca Nazionale, 'Facciam laude ac tuct' i santi'. All Saints lauda from Mgl[1]

2. Bernardo Daddi, *Madonna*, and Orcagna, Orsanmichele Tabernacle. Florence, Orsanmichele

3. Duccio di Buoninsegna, *Rucellai Madonna*. Florence, Uffizi.

5. Orsanmichele Madonna depicted on title-page of bequest-book

4. Master of the Biadaiolo Codex, Orsanmichele grain market and

6. Florentine, 14th century, *Madonna 'Gratiarum Plenissima'*. Florence, Santa Maria del Fiore.

. The Bigallo Master, *St Zenobius with SS Eugenius and Crescentius*. Florence, Museo dell'Opera del Duomo.

8. Coppo di Marcovaldo, *Madonna del Popolo*. Florence, Brancacci Chapel,

9. Bequest of Chiaro d'Ardinghello to Company of Sant' Agnese, 1377.

10. Letter of indulgence from the bishop of Florence to the Company of Santa Croce, 7 February 1296/7 (App. I, doc. 21). Florence, Archivio di Stato.

11. Decision by officers of the Company of San Zanobi to acquire a new

12. Laudese contract, Company of Sant'Agnese, 1466 (App. I, doc. 16).

That lauda-singing should become a specialized and professional activity was a most natural development in this environment.

There is some evidence that lauda-singing, like many other activities in Florence lacking guild status and organization,[8] was nevertheless practised and regarded as a legitimate profession. At least two singers, Maso di Niccolò and Vanni di Martino, listed their profession as 'laudese' in their 1427 tax reports, and a third, Vettorio d'Agniolo Bordoni, listed it as one of two professions, along with cloth-burling.[9] Piero di Niccolò served as a captain of the Company of San Frediano in 1441, and his name and profession ('laudese') appear several times at the top of the company's *borsa*, followed by other guildsmen.[10] During the fifteenth century, the perception by the Florentine laudesi that they constituted a professional group of sorts must have been reinforced during the annual patron-saint feasts of the Sant'Agnese and San Frediano companies, when they invited 'all the lauda-singers of Florence' for commemorative meals sponsored by these two laudesi companies.[11]

The company officers elected the singers and drafted contracts with them which generally stipulated a monthly salary (including the amount docked for each appointment missed), length of service (usually three or four months), and duties (festal and/or ferial service, sacristan duties). In the fourteenth century sacristan duties (setting up and clearing away for the services, and supervising attendance and payment of musicians) were performed by a chamberlain or specially appointed sacristan, but in the fifteenth century a laudese was paid extra to assume these tasks.[12]

The legal prose of these documents occasionally admits a few statements revealing a company's concern with the quality of the singer. When the Company of San Frediano elected Nocho d'Alesso and Antonio d'Adamo to sing during Lent of 1441, the contract stated that

. . . having elected and arranged for two [singers] to sing laude in the said church every evening throughout Lent, for the devotion of the people, some [of the captains] having seen and heard [them] to their satisfaction, they allocate L. 8 which . . . are to be given to Antonio d'Alesso and [Antonio d'Adamo] . . . on the condition that they provide the singing for all of the said Lent.[13]

---

[8] Ibid. 58–9.

[9] See Appendix III for the 1427 *Catasto* profiles of these and several other singers.

[10] SF 4, fo. 37ʳ. This same traditional format, by which a guildsman listed both his name and his guild, was used in the Florentine laudesi companies' contracts with their singers. A singer's official guild title was usually replaced in these documents by his designation as a 'laudese', or, less often, 'cantore' or 'cantatore'.

[11] Ch. 2, 'Feasts of Patron Saints'; Ch. 3, 'The Company of San Frediano'.

[12] The difference is apparent, for example, in the two sets of statutes drafted by the Company of San Zanobi (1326, ch. VII, ed. in Orioli, *Le confraternite medievali*, 24, and 1428, ch. XVI, doc. 14. By the early 16th c. the companies had begun hiring a *maestro di cappella* who was often responsible for finding the other singers, but it is not clear whether or not they were also responsible for the sacristan duties.

[13] Appendix I, doc. 24.

In 1492, the captains of the Company of Sant'Agnese gave one of their singers a raise of s. 4 per month when they decided that his ability had sufficiently improved:

. . . Giovanni di Francesco, linen-weaver in Piazza Santo Spirito, has served as 'laudiere' of the said company for some time at the rate of s. 10 per month, and having much improved his voice and singing better, [and] having cause to retain him to sing . . . [the captains] henceforth increase [his salary] s. 4 . . .[14]

In the following year, the same company granted an official appointment and retroactive pay to a singer who had been serving on probation for six months:

. . . the captains, seeing that Domenico di Lionardo, 'tavolaccino' [servant of the magistracy], has already sung as a laudiere for six months with the hope of being hired, and the above captains understanding that [they would do] well to hire him because he is a good laudiere, by their solemn resolve and by six black beans decided to hire the said Domenico as laudiere on this day at the rate of s. 10 per month, with the usual fines [for absences], and they allocate L. 3 for the said six months that he sang without having been elected.[15]

In 1518, the captains of Orsanmichele recorded a decision that revealed their concern not just with the qualities of an individual singer, but with the balance of their entire polyphonic ensemble:

[The captains] have considered with respect to the laudesi in the said oratory that there is one *tenorista* too many relative to the singing of the boys, and that not to reduce [by] one the said *tenoristi* would require . . . an increase in the number of boys. The above officials, desiring to reduce an expense rather than increase it . . . deprived of his office Giovanni di Bernardo, called 'l'Abbate', at present a *tenorista* in their said oratory.[16]

The companies usually appointed several officers to oversee the singing, as in 1351 at the Company of San Zanobi, when three were 'in charge of the singers, and in charge of lauda-singing on the feast-days'.[17]

This concern among the companies for the quality of their musicians, and the inevitable competition among the city's many laudesi, coupled with the obvious technical demands of the lauda repertoire even in the *Oltrarno* (the provenance of Mgl[1]), all suggest an arena of activity not untouched by the 'Florentine sense of quality'. A further, negative, incentive to 'product quality' was the vulnerability of musicians' salaries to the budgetary concerns of the companies. The Company of Orsanmichele lowered their singers' salaries in 1379 because

. . . those who sing every evening in the oratory . . . are very well paid, and [seeing] that such a salary is not merited by such little work . . . it was decided

[14] Appendix I, doc. 25.
[15] Appendix I, doc. 26.
[16] Ed. in D'Accone, 'Alcune note', 106.
[17] Appendix I, doc. 27; Ch. 2, 'The *Scuole*'.

that the chamberlain of the said company may not in any manner pay the said laudesi [more than] L. 3 each per month . . .[18]

In fourteenth-century Florence there were at least a dozen active laudesi companies, plus growing numbers of disciplinati companies that occasionally required the services of laudesi (especially during Holy Week), and their liturgical calendars became steadily busier through bequests for festal services that continued throughout the fourteenth and fifteenth centuries. The continual round of feasts great and small, and especially the ferial singing that was conducted every week-night for over a century and a half in most of these companies, established a strong tradition of lay professional lauda-singing, which was to endure into the sixteenth century through continual adaptation to changing musical practices and styles.

Although the account books of only half these laudesi companies survive (and these with many lacunae), it is clear that the most active singers freelanced widely. A few were omnipresent; between 1441 and 1464, the weaver Nocho d'Alesso sang at all six companies for periods of service that ranged from a single season of Lent (in the Oltrarno companies) to at least three years (at Orsanmichele and San Zanobi).[19] This free-lancing tendency is evident in the earliest records from around the mid-fourteenth century, which survive only for the companies of San Zanobi and Orsanmichele: both companies were served by Niccolò di Lippo (1351–87), Nuccio di Neri (1351–67), and Chellino Benini della Viuola (1352–83). Many names appear only for a brief period in the records of one company, but these short careers constituted a peripheral activity. The companies were most often served by singers (and instrumentalists) whose period of service to an individual company might vary from several months to many years, but who usually sang for two or more companies, and whose singing careers stretched from their adolescence to their seventies, usually lasting between ten and fifty years. The tenorista Sano di Giovanni (a lamp-maker) served the companies of San Zanobi (1473–1505) and San Piero Martire (1472–6), and in 1518 was given a pension by Orsanmichele for a long and faithful tenure:

The officials . . . have considered Sano, tenorista and singer, to be very old and to have sung in the said oratory fifty years or more, and to be of an advanced age and never to have been remiss in his duties in the said oratory . . . decide that the said Giovanni, at present a tenorista in their said oratory, for the short remainder of his life . . . is to be given and paid what is commonly called half pay every

---

[18] Ed. in D'Accone, 'Le compagnie,' 272.
[19] Nocho was apparently a member of the Company of San Frediano in 1442, when he appeared in the Company's borsa (SF 4, fo. 23ᵛ), an indication that he probably resided in the Oltrarno, as did most singers who sang for the companies in that quarter of the city.

month, that is . . . he shall have for the future L. 2 each month . . . and for this support and help the said Sano is not obliged for the future . . . to sing, or [he may] sing only as much as he wishes.[20]

The wool-carder known as Ciancha (Giovanni di Giuliano) served the same three companies for forty-one years between 1383 and 1424. The weaver Piero di Giovanni da San Giorgio sang for five companies during a forty-seven-year period between 1474 and 1521, and Francesco d'Antonio di Ventura began singing as a boy for the Company of San Zanobi in 1442, and is last recorded as a soprano for the Company of Sant'Agnese in 1479.

Singers were often in the simultaneous employment of several companies. The companies hired separate sets of singers for festal and ferial services, which were complementary, so that a singer might be engaged for festal services at one company while performing ferial duties at another, and find time to sing for the special patron-saint feasts of yet other companies (which occupied unique time-slots on the liturgical calendar and often called for extra singers). After c. 1440, by which time most companies had abandoned ferial services (except San Piero Martire and Orsanmichele), freelancing and shorter terms in the service of individual companies appears to have become more characteristic of Florentine laudesi activity.

The geographic separation and stronger neighbourhood character of the *Oltrarno* companies (Santo Spirito, Sant'Agnese, and San Frediano) were the conditions for the development of distinctive laudesi practices in that part of the city. A number of laudesi sang, and apparently resided, only in that quarter; the singing activities of Antonio di Giovanni della Puccia (1456–67) and the barber Guelfo di Bartolomeo (1455–67) were confined entirely to the three *Oltrarno* companies, and those of the carpenter Luca d'Antonio (1444–56), Domenico di Fruosino Paragliasini (1431–45), and Jacopo di Ser Bartolomeo da Radda (1479–93) to the companies of Sant'Agnese and Santo Spirito. The close neighbourhood ties in this quarter are evident in the careers of certain singers confined to a single *Oltrarno* company. Lodovico di Francesco served the Company of San Frediano from 1419 to 1449, where he was also a member and occasionally an officer. The weaver Niccolò di Betto Bugani (1444–50), and his sons Betto and Romolo, sang only for the Company of Sant'Agnese, as did Antonio di Benedetto di Butino, who was honoured at his death in 1445 for having served the company for over fifty years as a 'zealot, benefactor, and laudese'. It is also clear from the circumstances of these and other *Oltrarno* singers that they were generally more involved in the affairs of the companies they served. They tended to

---

[20] Ed. in D'Accone, 'Alcune note', 105–6.

reside in the quarter, often renting a house from the company, to be members, and to serve a company in other capacities as a *famiglio*.

Some singers appear to have begun singing with an *Oltrarno* company, and thereafter to have sung only for the larger companies across the river. The goldsmith Bernardino di Francesco is first mentioned in the Sant'Agnese accounts in 1466, but from 1467 to 1475 served as a *tenore* for the companies of San Piero Martire and San Zanobi; and Ulivante di Bartolomeo began at Santo Spirito in 1446, but from 1450 to 1464 is mentioned only in the accounts of the three larger companies across the Arno. It appears, then, that both strong neighbourhood ties and the competition for tenure with the larger companies may have allowed only the better and more ambitious singers to venture outside the *Oltrarno*. Most of the Florentine laudesi, and all the company instrumentalists, were active primarily in the larger, city-wide companies in the main part of the city. In comparison, the smaller *Oltrarno* companies offered fewer services, somewhat lower wages, and a relatively closed and parochial aspect to non-residents.[21]

A strong family aspect was common to all Florentine laudesi activity. Numerous instances of fathers, sons, and brothers are discernible among the fourteenth- and fifteenth-century lists of singers, a phenomenon which undoubtedly reflects a close-knit guild society in which specialized trade skills were often a matter of family pride and patrimony. Father/son pairs appear frequently, and it was probably in this form of master/apprentice relationship that laudesi skills were most frequently transmitted. During 1365–7 the Company of Orsanmichele employed two such pairs: Domenico Cecchi and his son Cristofano, and Nuto Tendi and his son Francesco performed together as ferial singers, and Nuto and another son, Giuliano, sang together for the company in 1373. Between 1412 and 1414, two fathers, both of whom were singing for the companies of San Piero Martire and Orsanmichele at that time, introduced their sons to the trade at about the same time in both companies. Vanni di Martino, who had been singing for both companies for about a decade, sang with his son Martino for the ferial services of the Company of San Piero Martire during 1413–17 (with two sons in 1415), and for the festal services of Orsanmichele during 1412–16, while Salvestro Tati and his son Domenico sang festal services for both San Piero Martire (1414–15) and Orsanmichele (1412–15). The activities of the two families intersected at Orsanmichele, where between 1412 and 1415 the two sons were paid

---

[21] *Oltrarno* musical practices appear to have been more conservative: monophonic song survived longer, no instruments of accompaniment were employed, and polyphonic ensembles in the late 15th c. were smaller and slower to be established. Once ferial singing was abandoned after about 1440, a characteristic feature of the *Oltrarno* companies was their particular, in some cases exclusive, focus on Lenten lauda services.

s. 25 per month to sing together as 'fanciulli biscantatori e laudesi' for festal services. As in other trades, a son trained in a craft was an asset to his father; when the Company of San Zanobi was cutting back laudesi salaries in 1433, Guasparre d'Ugolino Prosperi regained his *precentor* wage under the following condition:

[The captains] allocate to Guasparre d'Ugolino and to his son L. 3 per month, which [salary] had been reduced to s. 50 per month, [and] they agree by a vote of five black beans to reinstate his original wage, that is, L. 3 per month, if he will bring his son to the lauda services.[22]

Fathers and sons continued to sing together in the polyphonic ensembles of the late fifteenth century. At San Zanobi in 1491, Bartolomeo d'Ulivante and Piero da San Giorgio were among the company's four *tenori* (at s. 20 per month), and their sons Ulivante di Bartolomeo and Francesco di Piero were among the five *sovrani* (at s. 14 per month). It appears, as well, that the family tradition of lauda-singing may have passed from father to son through four generations of Ulivantes and Bartolomeos.[23]

Pairs of brothers, both as boys and adults, also appear frequently in companies' payments to singers. Orsanmichele recorded payments to Bartolomeo and Antonio di Lodovico during 1395–6; this is the only mention of Antonio, while Bartolomeo continued to sing for all the major companies for the next forty-one years. The boys Francesco and Lorenzo di Giovanni sang for the Company of Santo Spirito during 1434–9, while the boys Matteo and Donato di Giuliano Ardinghelli sang for Santo Spirito in 1482, but during 1479–85 pursued separate tenures as *sovrani* in the larger companies. Both pairs of boys, along with the abovementioned sons of Vanni di Martino and Salvestro Tati, disappeared rather suddenly from the companies' payrolls after periods of considerable activity as young laudesi. It is quite possible that they took holy orders, having gained access to a clerical career on the merits of singing talents developed on the Florentine laudesi 'circuit'.

The obvious tendency of laudesi to circulate among the companies in pairs was not, however, governed solely by family ties. Pairs of laudesi, related or not, some of whom journeyed together among the companies, were the norm during a period stretching from the earliest documents to

---

[22] The document is transcribed and discussed in Ch. 3, 'Company of San Zanobi'.

[23] The Ulivante cited here as a soprano is very likely the grandson of an Ulivante di Bartolomeo who is first recorded as a laudese with the Company of Santo Spirito in 1446. The singing activities of four possible generations are as follows:
1. Ulivante di Bartolomeo: SSP, 1446; OSM 1450–3; SPM, 1458–64 (where he sang with two other sons, Bernardo, in 1461, and Giovanni, in 1464); SZ, 1460
2. Bartolomeo d'Ulivante: SPM, 1463–6, 1484–6; SZ, 1491–5 (*tenore*)
3. Ulivante di Bartolomeo: SZ, 1491 (*fanciullo/sovrano*); OSM, 1520–1
4. Baccini Ulivantis: SPM, 1510; Bartolomeo d'Ulivante (SZ, 1520).

the 1460s. Nuccio di Neri and Niccolò di Lippo sang as a pair for San Zanobi in 1351, then again for Orsanmichele in 1361; Guelfo di Bartolomeo and Antonio della Puccia sang as a pair for the companies of Sant'Agnese (1466–7) and San Frediano (1455–6); and Ghuasparre d'Ugolino Prosperi and Vettorio d'Agnolo Bordoni were paired for long tenures at Orsanmichele (1418–36) and San Zanobi (1421–45). Family pairs were merely the most convenient formulation in the manifestation of a broader tendency that ultimately must have been governed by considerations of performance practice.

PERFORMING FORCES AND REPERTOIRE

From the late thirteenth to the early sixteenth century, the performance practices of the Florentine laudesi changed naturally in response to the shifting currents of musical and poetic styles. What follows is a rough sketch of those changes, an attempt at periodization, as suggested by what company documents reveal about varying numbers of singers and instrumentalists. This sketch will include a consideration of the musical repertoire associated with the laudesi companies, which is certain with respect to the monophonic lauda, but much less so with respect to the polyphonic repertory.

Keeping in mind that the lines to be drawn here represent broad temporal zones of change, four periods are proposed:

(i) The late thirteenth century, the earliest years of the Florentine laudesi companies, from which time no company account books survive. Monophonic laude were performed primarily by able, and probably unpaid, company members.

(ii) The fourteenth century through the first decades of the fifteenth century, during which monophonic practices prevailed, though probably not to the exclusion of polyphonic singing. The earliest bequests for lauda vigils and the first payments to singers are recorded during this time. Most Florentine laudesi companies employed one or two singers, and by the late fourteenth century pairs of laudesi had become the norm. The larger companies of Orsanmichele and San Zanobi hired players of instruments that were also favoured in the secular music of the time (rebec, vielle, lute, portable organ, and harp), and Orsanmichele hired exceptional numbers of singers throughout this period.

(iii) c. 1415–70, a complex period of change during which the numbers of paid singers constantly shifted but gradually increased. The first explicit references to singers of polyphonic music (*biscantatori* and *tenoristi*) appear in company records during this time. Between c. 1430 and 1450 the companies ceased hiring all accompanying instruments except the organ, and they abandoned the ancient ferial services, a sign of waning zeal for traditional laudesi devotion.

(iv) *c.* 1470 through the sixteenth century, when the companies established small choirs of five to eleven singers (*sovrani* and *tenoristi*), adequate for the performance of three- and four-part polyphonic laude.

Woven throughout this overview are several other considerations, that, for their derivation from the larger currents of Florentine musical tradition, transcend while yet shaping the particular traditions of the lauda. They are all related to an 'unwritten tradition' of music that held particular sway in Florence during the republican period: the varying dependence of the lauda repertoire upon *contrafacta* (in this case, the application to lauda texts of melodies originally associated with other, usually secular, texts), the tendency of the repertoire to hover between oral and written musical traditions, partaking of both, and a resilient tradition of solo song (and the attendant considerations of florid singing, embellishment, improvisation, and instrumental accompaniment).[24]

Late Thirteenth century

As stated at the beginning of this chapter, laudesi statutes drafted during the last two decades of the thirteenth century indicate that the soloistic strophes of laude were performed by company members. These were probably unpaid amateurs who were usually selected, undoubtedly on the basis of their natural vocal ability, by the company officers in charge of lauda singing and teaching. These singers were almost certainly not performing a polyphonic repertory, and since more than one laudese is referred to in a performance involving congregational participation in the refrains, it is evident that the soloistic performance of the current monophonic lauda repertory could, and probably did, involve more than a single soloist.[25]

The repertoires of the companies during this time probably consisted primarily of the simpler, syllabic and neumatic laude that prevail in the late thirteenth-century Cortona manuscript (Cort), and among the Marian laude of Mgl[1] (see Music Examples 1, 3, and 5). But certainly a tradition of improvised embellishment, crystallized in the florid laude copied down in Mgl[1] during the early fourteenth century, was developing as an oral tradition during this time, probably under the influence of local, popular, and unwritten vocal practices (see Music Examples 2 and

[24] Eloquently described by Nino Pirrotta in a number of articles, most of them published in *Music and Culture in Italy from the Middle Ages to the Baroque* (Cambridge, Mass., 1984), esp. nos. 5 ('New Glimpses of an Unwritten Tradition'), and 6 ('The Oral and Written Traditions of Music').

[25] In fact, during the 14th and 15th cc. it was somewhat exceptional for a laudesi company to employ a single soloist, a practice that appears to have been more prevalent in the services of disciplinati companies; see Barr, 'Lauda Singing and the Tradition of the Disciplinati Mandato'.

4). Given the early date of the Cortona manuscript and the frequent references to laudarios in the oldest extant documents of the Florentine laudesi companies, notated laudarios were probably in use during this time.[26] It is clear, as well, from the frequent expenses for repair of these books, in addition to late thirteenth-century statutes directing that festal and ferial laudarios be placed on festal and ferial lecterns for services, that these books were indeed used by the singers.

Fourteenth Century to Early Fifteenth Century

A number of factors having to do with both performing forces and repertoire define the identity of this period. With one exception, the Florentine companies hired no more than one or two singers during this time, a practice that continued through the middle of the fifteenth century in the more conservative *Oltrarno* companies. The two companies in closest proximity to the secular, civic ceremonial life of the city, San Zanobi (at the Cathedral) and Orsanmichele (administered by the commune), employed the instruments of accompaniment most commonly associated with late medieval secular music.[27]

The musical practice at Orsanmichele was exceptional in every respect; from 1361, the time of its earliest extant records regarding musical practices, the company retained separate retinues of festal and ferial singers (three each) long before the other companies, and a vielle-player for all of the festal services.[28] However, the presence of three, or even more, singers is still consonant with a monophonic practice. The model of ecclesiastical chant choirs using multiple singers was readily visible to the companies. Throughout this period most of the Orsanmichele singers also sang in pairs for the other companies (where monophonic practices seem more certain), and Orsanmichele may well have been engaging in a competitive bid to out-do the other companies and stage a ceremonial display appropriate to its station as the city's leading lay devotional institution.

[26] SMN 292, *Uscita*, 1312–40, is the oldest extant Florentine laudesi account book, and among its earliest entries (fo. 1ᵛ [1 Jan. 1313]) is a payment of L. 2 s. 9 d. 6 'per miniare e per notare e per leghare i' libro de la compangnia'. In 1317 the company recorded an expense for its 'libro grande [delle laude]', and its 'libro nero de le laude' had been used long enough to require repair; ibid., fos. 9ᵛ, 11ʳ.

[27] The last explicit references to such instruments (rebec, vielle, lute, and harp) were in 1437 at Orsanmichele (when the company employed two rebec-players, Pagolo di Ser Ambruogio and Prospero di Guasparre; there is a lacuna until 1450, when the only instrumentalist was the organist, Antonio Squarcialupi); and in 1442 at San Zanobi (the vielle-player Currado).

[28] After *c.*1380 these numbers increased, so that by 1415 there were 6 ferial singers, 4 festive singers, and 3 salaried instrumentalists (an organist and two vielle/rebec-players). As D'Accone has suggested ('Le compagnie', 279), these exceptional numbers may reflect a polyphonic practice, a possibility that is considered below in light of other factors.

From those instances when the documents allude to the function of indoor instruments (primarily string instruments), it is clear that they served primarily to accompany the performance of laude. Throughout the fourteenth century, the Orsanmichele instrumentalists are referred to as 'players at the lauda service (*sonatores ad laudes*) in the oratory of the said company', and in 1415 the rebec/vielle-player Pagolo di Ser Ambruogio and the lutenist Jacopo di Lorenzo were paid as 'players and laudesi in the said oratory'.[29] In 1408 the company recorded a payment to Filippo di Ceccho, '*piffero* and singer of laude'.[30] During the 1360s, the singer Nuccio di Neri and Chellino della viuola, 'who sing laude on feast days', were usually grouped together and paid a special salary, a situation which perhaps suggests a common ensemble of the time.[31] During the Christmas season in 1421, the Company of San Zanobi paid Pagolo to 'play the rebec and sing laude during the evening in Santa Maria del Fiore', and two years earlier the company recorded another payment to Pagolo 'and his fellow instrumentalists and singers because they played for the feast of St Zenobius at the lauda service'. In 1393, on one of the rare occasions when the use of indoor instruments was recorded in the Company of San Piero Martire, a payment was made to 'Baccio, who sang the passion with the vielle'.[32]

Quite independent of the lauda repertory and performing practices were the civic *pifferi* and *trombadori*, who were part of a different tradition of outdoor ceremonial music, and served a quite different function in the activities of the laudesi companies (primarily in fanfares and processions). The two traditions of soft, indoor and loud, outdoor instruments evident in the company services parallel, and are directly related to, their secular civic functions. The Florentine *pifferi* and *trombadori* performed in a freelance capacity for the lay companies and on other occasions such as weddings and the feast days of the guilds, but were sustained primarily

[29] OSM 22, fo. 66^r. While the Orsanmichele accounts often listed the singers and instrumentalists separately, just as often no distinction was made, and all were listed together under the heading 'laudesi'; e.g. OSM 209, fo. 6^v (1388). Similarly, Pagolo is variously referred to in the San Zanobi records as a 'sonatore' and a laudese, and though these designations may in fact indicate separate activities, they still indicate that an instrumentalist like Pagolo was expected to sing as well.

[30] OSM 213, fo. 13^r. It is unclear whether or not Filippo's playing was independent of his singing. *Piffero* was used both in the narrow sense of a wind-player and in the broader sense of an instrumentalist.

[31] OSM 4, fos. 5^r, 33^r [1366]; 5, fo. 16^r [1367]. In 1352, the Company of San Zanobi hired Chellino as 'chantatore de la chonpagnia' to perform on all the feast days which had been 'written down on a *foglio*' (SZ 2182, fasc. 36, fo. 171^v). This 'foglio' was evidently recopied, and perhaps updated, in 1365, when the contract of 'Chellino che suona la viuola' was copied at the head of a long list of feast days for which he was obligated, no doubt, to both play *and* sing; D'Accone, 'Le compagnie', 264–5.

[32] D'Accone, 'Le compagnie', 268 [25 Mar. 1419]: '. . . e compagni sonatori e chantatori perchè sonorono per S. Zanobi a le laude', and 258. Whether or not it was a passion lauda he was singing and accompanying is unclear, though likely.

by communal positions with the Signoria, the Parte Guelfa, and the Merchant Court. Similarly, the leading indoor instrumentalists (and on one occasion, a singer, Bernaba di Cristofano) of Orsanmichele also performed for the Signoria. In fact, the practice of instrumental accompaniment of laude may have originated at Orsanmichele through its close connection to the commune after the latter assumed administration of the lay company in the mid-fourteenth century. Luigi di Matteo and Pagolo di Ser Matteo (and possibly Chellino, who preceded them) were obliged by a single contract to play for both institutions, and the practice, as well as the players, appears to have been borrowed by the Company of San Zanobi from Orsanmichele. Because it was the most free of all the lay companies of ecclesiastical influence, Orsanmichele was a likely environment for the grafting of a secular instrumental practice on to laudesi devotional practices.

The development itself, whether or not it originated at Orsanmichele, speaks for the fundamentally secular, rather than ecclesiastical, roots of the monophonic lauda repertory. Michel Huglo saw little connection between the melodies of Mgl[1] and the extant repertoire of ecclesiastical chant.[33] In particular, he noted that the cadence formulas (and their modal implications) were quite different. The secular origins of the lauda repertory are suggested by its reliance upon the popular form of the ballata, the connection of lauda-singers and instrumentalists with secular institutions (the commune), and the involvement of lauda poets like Antonio Pucci, Franco Sacchetti, and Guittone d'Arezzo with secular poetry. Salimbene documented the evident familiarity of thirteenth-century Franciscan friars with secular poetry and music, and their disposition to adapt it to sacred purposes.[34] However, the lauda repertory was in a constant state of flux, and probably evolved, like other lyrical genres, by processes that ranged freely between the poles of strict *contrafactum* and original composition. Within freely treated poetic and musical structures, singers, poets, scribes, and if they were distinct, composers, continually adapted, altered, and recomposed what was already familiar to them, a process that must have been closely linked to the manner in which memory functioned. The eclectic nature of this musical repertoire is revealed in an apt description by Giulio Cattin:

Close analysis reveals in them an unexpected variety: from refined modulations to the flavour of popular song, from simple and austere processional intonations to dance-tunes, from narrative and dramatic chants with insistently repeated notes . . . to a tone which is sometimes excited, sometimes relaxed, serene, and confident. More technical examination uncovers the presence of echoes of

---

[33] Private correspondence, autumn, 1986. A different view was advanced by Liuzzi, *La lauda*, i, 225.
[34] Salimbene de Adam, *Cronica*, ed. G. Scalia, 2 vols. (Bari, 1966), 262–3.

litanic structures, with a single formula constantly repeated from verse to verse both in the refrain and in the couplet. There are also forms parallel to the hymnodic couplet, with no repetition of melodic segments (melodic scheme ABCD); some traces of sequential structure in the melodic equivalence of mutations . . .; and occasional remnants of troubadour preciosity, along with a frequent occurrence of the modes of ecclesiastical chant (at least in the oldest examples) . . . Finally, there are some hints of development towards a modern major/minor tonality . . .[35]

With respect at least to the monophonic repertoire of the period, performing ensembles might then vary from one to three or more singers, with or without the participation of an accompanying instrument. All the instruments employed by the laudesi companies were suitable and traditional instruments of accompaniment in the vernacular repertoires (both monophonic and polyphonic) of the late Middle Ages, all of them permitting the simultaneous execution of singing and playing.

The repertory of the Tuscan lauda in this period is preserved primarily in confraternity laudarios, that is, in manuscripts structured according to the liturgical needs of the lay company services and devoted exclusively to the performing repertoire of the lay companies. Of the five extant sources of Tuscan provenance, three are from Florence, and one each from Pisa and Lucca.[36] In addition to these, a number of loose folios from Trecento Tuscan laudarios, most of them executed in Florentine workshops and bearing music and sumptuous decoration, reveal both the artistic and material wealth of this tradition.[37]

---

[35] *Music of the Middle Ages*, 141.

[36] The Florentine sources are Mgl[1] (early 14th c.), with music for the laude, illumination, and Latin motets, sequences, and hymns (Company of Santo Spirito); Mgl[2] (1374), text only, illumination, Latin motets, sequences, and hymns (Company of San Gilio); and Fior (mid-14th c.), text only, no decoration. From Pisa, Ars (14th c.), with empty stave-lines (the music was never copied), illumination; from Lucca, Luc[1] (mid-14th c.), a fragment of a large laudario, with music, a careful script and decorated initials, no illumination.

The Umbrian lauda tradition, with its mystical, penitential, and dramatic qualities, is distinct from (though not independent of) the Tuscan tradition, and therefore outside the scope of this study. See V. de Bartholomaeis, *Laude drammatiche e rappresentazione sacre* (Florence, 1943); A. Fortini, *La lauda in Assisi e le origini del teatro italiano* (Assisi, 1961); G. Varanini, et al., *Laude cortonesi dal secolo XIII al XV*, vols.I/1–2, II (Florence, 1981), with a study of the melodies by G. Cattin; and C. Barr, *The Monophonic Lauda*, ch. 3. On the laude of Jacopone da Todi, see R. Bettarini, *Jacopone e il laudario urbinate* (Florence, 1969).

[37] The folios, scattered throughout European and American art collections, are reproduced, transcribed, and studied in A. Ziino, 'Laudi e miniature'. Most were previously published in R. Offner, *Corpus of Florentine Painting*, who attributed the miniatures to two different schools of Florentine painting: the *bottegha* of Pacino di Bonaguida, and that of the Master of the Dominican Effigies (who worked in Santa Maria Novella). Ziino notes the possible involvement of another *bottegha*, that of the Master of the 'Panegyric of Robert of Anjou'. The musical notation in all the extant, notated laudarios of this period is quadratic and non-mensural, like that employed in the large choral chant-books of the time (e.g. Plate 1).

A comparison of these sources reveals a repertory that was compact and uniform in its overall features, but extremely varied with respect to detail. There is a high rate of concordance among the laude preserved in them,[38] and in portions the particular sequence (for liturgical reasons) is identical, but there is extreme variation in orthography, order and number of strophes, relationship between refrain and strophe, and, where the comparison is possible, the melodies. The situation is similar to that of the other vernacular monophonic repertoires: oral and written traditions 'mix', or run 'parallel', and there is a tendency to reuse melodic material through *contrafacta* and recurrent melodic motifs.[39] But the fourteenth-century Tuscan lauda repertory evolved in a milieu fundamentally different from the courtly context of the troubadour, trouvère, minnesinger, and cantigas repertoires.[40] The competitive urban environment, the relatively high literacy of the Tuscan communal populace, the bookkeeping habits of merchants and artisans, and the regulated, institutional environment of the lay companies all contributed, especially in Florence, to the special strength of a written tradition. The scant documents of the fourteenth-century laudesi companies indicate a continual activity of copying, illuminating, and repairing laudarios,[41] and a remarkably high percentage of the extant Tuscan sources mentioned above contain music. It is clear, moreover, that laudarios were used by the singers in performance.[42] The strength of the written tradition is also evident in the relatively low instance of *contrafacta*,[43] the high percentage

[38] Concordances between a given laudario and the other major Tuscan and Umbrian sources are listed in Grossi, 'The Fourteenth Century Florentine Laudario', *passim* (Mgl¹); Liuzzi, *La lauda*, i (Cort) and ii (Mgl1), *passim*; and charted in Staaff, *Le Laudario de Pise*, pp. xxvii–xxviii (Ars); Bettarini, 'Notizia di un laudario', 61–3 (Fior); A. M. Terruggia, 'Aggiunta al laudario frammentato dell'Archivio di Stato di Lucca', *Studi e problemi di critica testuale*, 12 (1976), 26 (Luc¹); G. Varanini, 'Il manoscritto Trivulziano 535: Laude antiche di Cortona', *Studi e problemi di critica testuale*, 8 (1974), 52–65, and Varanini *et al.*, *Laude cortonesi*, iv. 150–69.

[39] A. Ziino, *Aspetti della tradizione orale nella musica medioevale* (Lanciano, 1973), 9; also publ. in *L'Etnomusicologia in Italia*, ed. D. Carpitella (Palermo, 1975).

[40] The manuscript tradition of the cantigas, however, like the circumstances under which they were composed and performed, presents a unique situation in comparison to these other vernacular repertoires.

[41] A number of 14th-c. Florentine laudesi documents concerning laudarios are transcribed in M. L. D'Ancona, *Miniatura e miniatori a Firenze dal XIV al XVI secolo* (Florence, 1962), 217–20.

[42] In 1367, the Company of Orsanmichele recorded a payment to a stationer 'per più fogli e charte e una coverta per libro grande de' laudesi . . . '; OSM 56, fo. 51ʳ. Grossi, 'The Fourteenth Century Florentine Laudario', 27, states that Mgl¹ was a 'presentation' or 'votive' volume clearly not intended for use, because of its 'expensive adornments coupled with its textual inaccuracies', but textual accuracy was not a high priority of laudario scribes, and elaborate laudarios were certainly being used in the company's festal services precisely because their visual splendour contributed to the solemnity of a feast day.

[43] See A. Ziino, 'Adattamenti musicali e tradizione manoscritta nel repertorio laudistico del duecento', in *Scritti in onore di Luigi Ronga* (Milan, 1973, 653–69). Among the 88 laude of Mgl¹, 8 of the melodies are used for two different texts, whereas among the 160 extant troubadour melodies (and over 1,100 poetic texts) 'at least 68 of the extant melodies have texts which served as models for

of manuscripts copied at the time the repertoire they contained was being performed, and the pervasiveness and formal standardization of the ballata as the poetic model for the lauda.[44]

However, oral traditions among the Florentine laudesi remained strong, both in this century and the next, showing signs of deterioration only in the late fifteenth century with the advent of printing. Oral transmission and memorization undoubtedly were the indispensible tools of the singers as the repertory was taught by the old to the young, the veterans to the novices. The melodies were the common fund of the Florentine, even the Tuscan, laudesi, easily memorized as they sang them at the predictable and recurrent intervals of the liturgical year throughout their long careers. The lauda texts, however, might contain numerous strophes which were selected and re-ordered according to the needs of individual companies and services, so that even in the Florentine tradition texts alone (Fior and Mgl[2]) were copied down more often than text and melody together (Mgl[1]).[45] The melodies that were copied down have all the earmarks of an oral tradition, and 'most likely represent only some of the many melodic versions in circulation at that time'.[46] Three such versions of a lauda on the subject of the Trinity, 'Alta Trinità beata', feature significant variants in orthography and melody (cadence pitches, ornamental figures, transposition of melodic phrases), and the version in Cort is even notated a fourth lower than the other two melodies (see Music Example 5). Two versions (in Cort and Mgl[1]) of a lauda for the feast of the Assumption, 'Ave donna santissima', cadence on different pitches in three out of four lines in the strophe, and reveal significant melodic variants throughout the soloistic strophe (see Music Example 3).[47] Once again, one is struck by the analogy between lauda and sermon, for like the lauda the late medieval sermon hovered between written and

other poems'; F. M. Chambers, 'Imitation of Form in the Old Provençal Lyric', *Romance Philology*, 6 (1937), 104; Ziino, *Aspetti*, 10.

[44] A. Ziino, *Strutture strofiche nel laudario di Cortona* (Palermo, 1968), 32; 'Adattamenti', 653 ff. On the ballata form during this period, see also N. Pirrotta, 'Ars Nova and Stil Novo', in *Music and Culture in Italy*, 26–38; id., 'Ballate e "soni" secondo un grammatico del Trecento', in *Saggi e ricerche in memorie di Ettore Li Gotti*, 3 vols. (Palermo, 1961), iii. 42–54; L. Meierhans, *Die Ballata* (Bern, 1956); B. R. Suchla, *Studien zur Provenienz der Trecento Ballata* (Göttingen, 1976). The musico-poetic schemes of the monophonic lauda repertory have been classified and analysed in Liuzzi, *La lauda* i. 42–4 (Cort), 88–92 (Mgl[1]), and more recently in Barr, *The Monophonic Lauda*, 82–93 (Cort), 106–15 (Mgl[1]).

[45] For a given lauda, the varying number of strophes transmitted in Tuscan laudarios is discussed in Terruggia, 'Aggiunta al laudario', 12, 16–17.

[46] Ziino, 'Laudi e miniature', 58.

[47] The texts of both these popular laude are contained in most of the major Tuscan and Umbrian sources. For 'Ave donna santissima' all sources transmit the first two strophes, but thereafter the number and choice vary significantly: Mgl[1] (8); Luc[1] and Ars (8; but strophes differ from Mgl[1]); a second version in Ars (23); Fior (3); Mgl[2] (53; the final strophe contains the name of the lauda poet, Garzo); and the three Umbrian laudarios Cort, Aret, and Triv appear to transmit the same 21 strophes; Terruggia, 'Aggiunti', 16–17.

oral traditions, relied upon a fund of standard, patterned materials that circulated freely, and was constantly renewed in 'performance', and is therefore imperfectly represented by extant written sources.[48]

The practice of *contrafacta*, while not as prevalent as in the northern vernacular repertories nor the fifteenth-century lauda repertory, was still a notable feature of the Trecento lauda, and was surely applied more frequently than the sources suggest. The melody of a lauda to St Anthony of Padua, 'Ciascun che fede sente', served the same texts in Cort and Mgl[1], as well as the text of a lauda to St Andrew, 'A tutt' or dobbiam laudare' in Luc[1] (text also in Ars), and the text of a lauda to yet a third saint, 'Sancto Agostin doctor' (Mgl[1]; text also in Fior and Mgl[2]) (see Music Example 4). The melodic plasticity of this repertory, evident in all the above examples, was a characteristic feature of a lyrical genre that required that a singer be able to adapt a melody to different texts (either *contrafacta* or different strophes of the same lauda), and yet allowed him the freedom to nuance his performance according to memory, ability, and taste.[49]

Apposite to variations in melodic detail in the lauda repertory is a certain amount of melodic stereotype and repetition. Clearly this must have aided memorization of the large repertory that an active Florentine laudese had to command. This tendency towards melodic economy is evident at all structural levels: in small, ornamental clusters and cadential formulas (usually sung to a single syllable), in the recurrence of a number of intonations,[50] and in the borrowing of music for entire lines, refrains, and compositions (*contrafactum*).

Among the laude in the *sanctorale* section of the Mgl[1] are a number of highly florid melodies 'that must have required considerable virtuosity on the part of the performers'.[51] These virtuosic lauda are quite unlike anything in Cort, and may well have grown out of the interaction between a local, Florentine tradition of florid singing, and the impulse of the prosperous Florentine laudesi companies towards a liturgical splendour that was understood to bring prestige to the company and honour to their sacred patrons. In several cases in Mgl[1], certain saints, for whom a simpler, syllabic/neumatic lauda already existed, were honoured with a second, florid lauda. The two laude to St Dominic, whose order was

[48] Cf. Ch. 1, 'Preaching', and Rouse, *Preachers, Florilegia, and Sermons*, 65. Of particular interest in this context is P. Howard, ' "Non parum laborat formica ad colligendum unde vivat": Oral Discourse as the Context of the *Summa Theologica* of St. Antoninus of Florence', *Archivum Fratrum Praedicatorum*, 59 (1989), 89–148.

[49] Ziino, 'Adattamenti', 659; R. Monterosso, 'La tradizione melismatica sino all'Ars Nova', *L'Ars nova italiana del Trecento*, 3 (Certaldo, 1970), 45–8.

[50] Ziino, 'Adattamenti', 657 n. 4.

[51] N. Pirrotta, 'Ars Nova and Stil Novo', in *Music and Culture in Italy*, 35. Cattin likewise has noted the 'technical accomplishment' required of singers to perform these florid laude in Mgl[1]; *Music of the Middle Ages*, 147.

particularly strong in Florence, provide a striking contrast between the austere, syllabic 'San Domenico beato' and the much longer and rhapsodic 'Allegro canto, popol cristiano' (see Music Examples 1 and 2).[52] St Augustine was held in special veneration by the friars and lay brothers of Santo Spirito, and the lauda 'Gaudiamo tucti quanti' pays multiple honours to the saint by virtue of its new text, its virtuosity, and its derivation from the older lauda, 'Sancto Agostin doctor' (see Music Example 4). The latter originated as a *contrafactum* of the lauda to St Anthony, but 'Gaudiamo tucti quanti' provided the patron saint of Santo Spirito with an essentially new piece through a process of adaptation, or perhaps more accurately, improvisatory singing, which took as its point of departure the *incipits* and finals of phrases, and the requirements of a different poetic structure.

The florid style is less evident in the older corpus of Cortona melodies *cum* text that are preserved in Mgl[1], but even here it can be found. The version of 'Ave donna santissima' in Mgl[1] reveals several characteristic traits of the Florentine repertory in comparison with the older Cortona version (Music Example 3): the expansion of the shorter melismas in the older version (which often fall on important or accented syllables), filling in of thirds ('-ten-', line 2), the addition of figures based on lower neighbouring notes ('ce-' in line 3), and a taste for appoggiaturas (both from above, 'virtù', line 3; and below, '-ma', line 2).[53] This impulse towards melodic arabesque is also evident in the Mgl[1] and Burney versions of 'Alta Trinità beata', while the differences between these two versions (text corruptions aside) reflect how different two performances of the same melody might have been (see Music Example 5).

A comparison of the number of strophes transmitted by the two versions of 'Ave donna santissima' (eight in Mgl[1], twenty-one in Cort) reveals another significant aspect of the Florentine collection: Mgl[1] (along with Fior) often gives shorter readings than the other sources.[54]

---

[52] One should note also the difference in range: a 9th in 'San Domenico', although individual lines are usually contained within a 5th; a 12th in 'Allegro canto', with individual lines of an octave or greater. Also interesting is the exact repetition of the refrain in the *volta* (last three lines of the strophe) of 'San Domenico', which signalled to the congregation the return of the refrain; in 'Allegro canto' the relationship is freer, and suggests, along with the florid nature of the refrain, the possibility that the refrains of these more florid laude were performed by soloists. This may have been the reason for pairs (or in the case of Orsanmichele, three or more) singers in 14th-c. Florentine practice. Fior and Mgl[2] both contain the text of the more traditional 'San Domenico'; 'Allegro canto' is an *unicum*, but surely it must have been in the repertory of the Company San Piero Martire.

[53] Also significant in this comparison is the near identity between the music of the refrains, and the much greater difference between the strophes (esp. line 5), which may indicate congregational participation on the refrain of the Mgl[1] version of this traditional Marian lauda. The strophe, on the other hand, shows signs of soloistic variation.

[54] Of the 20 texts shared by Cort and Mgl[1], 19 of the Mgl[1] versions contain fewer strophes; see Liuzzi, *La lauda*, i. 84. The Tuscan sources in general (with the exception of Mgl[2]) appear to contain

The reduced scope of these poems in Mgl[1] must have been conditioned by the greater emphasis on music in this collection.[55] In general, the contrast between the musical practices represented by these two collections suggests a development with an interesting parallel to the much earlier history of responsorial chant. The reduced number of strophes, the increased virtuosity of the music, the professionalization of the singer, and the growing distance of the congregation from participation in the singing all appear to be a vastly accelerated version of the process whereby the responsorial chants of the Mass and Office lost their psalm verses, grew in soloistic virtuosity, and became the exclusive provenance of trained singers.

One important aspect of the Florentine laudarios remains to be considered. Both Mgl[1] and Mgl[2] contain a small collection of monophonic and polyphonic Latin 'sequentie'.[56] The polyphonic motets are in two and three parts, in a relatively homorhythmic Ars Antiqua style, and were intended for performance on the most important liturgical feasts. The presence of these motets in lay company laudarios raises the question as to who performed them, for the *ars mensurae* of these works constituted a performing tradition distinct from the improvisatory freedom and rhythmic refinement of the monophonic lauda repertory. The Company of San Piero Martire owned a collection of motets in 1323, at which time it seems more likely that the performers for these works were drawn not from the secular sphere of the laudesi, but from an ecclesiastical institution where training in mensural music was more likely to be available. It may well have been for the performance of these motets that the Company of San Zanobi recorded an expense in 1349 on behalf of the 'biscantatori di San Lorenzo',[57] and that several companies recorded early fourteenth-

shorter versions than the Umbrian laudarios, which might indicate a more traditional nature of Umbrian practice.

[55] Pirrotta, 'Ars Nova and Stil Novo', 35.

[56] These pieces follow the laude in the manuscripts, and are in fact a collection of popular hymns and sequences to be sung on major feast-days. In neither case do these Latin works appear to have been a part of the collection's original plan; they are appendices, and are in different, although 14th-c., hands. The polyphonic pieces are catalogued in RISM B. iv/1, 789–91, and edited in *Polyphonic Music of the Fourteenth Century*, xii, ed. K. von Fischer and F. A. Gallo (Monaco, 1976), 107, 116–22, 125–8. Facsimiles are published by Gallo and G. Vecchi in *I più antichi monumenti sacri italiani* (Monumenta lyrica medii aevi italica, i/1; Bologna, 1968), plates LXVI–LXXXII. All the Latin works in Mgl[2] (fos. 71[r]–98[r]) have been indexed by C. Del Popolo, 'Il laudario', 11. The polyphonic works are discussed by A. Ziino, 'Una ignota testimonianza sulla diffusione del mottetto in Italia durante il XIV secolo', *Rivista italiana di musicologia*, 10 (1975), 20–31. The polyphonic motets in Mgl[1] (6) and Mgl[2] (4) comprise 10 of a total of 16 known motets in Italian Trecento sources, most of them in Ars Antiqua style. Moreover, it appears that both Ars and Luc[1] contained similar collections of Latin polyphony.

[57] SZ 2182, fasc. 36, fo. 130[v]: 'Ispese in fare onore a' biscantatori di San Lorenzo e altri cantatori istavano quando si fecero angnoli . . . s. vii'. On the church of San Lorenzo as an important Trecento musical centre, see F. A. Gallo, 'Lorenzo Masini e Francesco degli Organi in S. Lorenzo', *Studi musicali*, 4 (1975), 57–63.

century payments to anonymous *fanciulli*, all for feast-days when poly-phony was most likely to have been performed.

However, certain changes in the lauda repertory of the late fourteenth century suggest that the technique of polyphonic performance may have become a part of the lauda-singer's art. The most significant change is signalled by several manuscripts which transmit lauda repertory in a manner that became characteristic in the fifteenth century. These sources contain only the texts of laude, but they are also accompanied by the rubric 'cantasi come' ('is sung like'), followed by the title of another (usually secular) song of similar poetic structure, the tune of which was to be applied to the lauda text.[58] In these collections, the *contrafactum* indications link the laude texts with the music of the Florentine poly-phonic repertory of the late Trecento.[59] Another testimony to polyphonic settings of the lauda repertory, which became standard in the fifteenth century, is by the Florentine cleric, singer, and composer Andrea Stefani. In an extant autograph manuscript, Stefani noted the titles of five laude he composed at the time of the Bianchi processions in Florence (1399–

[58] Florence, B. N., Magliabechiano-Strozziano XXXVIII. 130, ed. G. Varanini, *Rime sacre* (Florence, 1970), is a private devotional book that belonged to Neri Pagliaresi (*c.*1350–1406), secretary and confidante to St Catherine of Siena. It contains, among other devotional texts, 15 laude copied down between *c.*1380 and 1408 and bearing the rubric 'questa si canta come quella che comincia così . . .', or 'cantasi questa . . .'.

Rome, Biblioteca Vaticana, MS Chigiano L. VII. 266 [Ch 266], is discussed and partly edited by Toscani, *Le laude dei Bianchi; cantasi come* laude are indexed by Luisi, *Laudario giustinianeo* i. 198–204. This MS contains 700 laude copied down by the Florentine Filippo di Lorenzo Benci between *c.*1448 and 1464, but many of them dating from the time of the Bianchi movement in Florence (1399–1400), in which Filippo's father (a wool merchant) participated.

A third *cantasi come* source of this period is Riccardiana 2871; G. Corsi, 'Madrigali inediti del trecento', *Belfagor*, 14 (1959), 329–40.

The Pagliaresi and Chigiano manuscripts represent the two final surges of lay devotional zeal in Tuscany, both of which made significant contributions to the lauda repertory. The Gesuati (not to be confused with the Jesuits) were established *c.*1366 as a lay congregation in Siena by Giovanni Colombini; his mystical and penitential zeal was popularized by his cousin, St Catherine, and the lauda poets of his circle, chiefly Bianco da Siena. The Bianchi movement was the last of the mass penitential processions that periodically swept Italy during the late Middle Ages. The movement was cut short by an outbreak of the plague in 1400, but in Florence it spawned four lay confraternities and added new impetus to lauda composition.

[59] In Mgl.-Strozz. XXXVIII. 130, 4 of the 15 secular ballate given as *cantasi come* models for the laude are listed in K. von Fischer, *Studien zur italienischen Musik des Trecento und frühen Quattrocento* (Bern, 1956): no. 379 (anon., 2^2); no. 299 (Landini, 2^2); no. 356 (Andrea di Firenze, 2^2); no. 210 (Gherardello, 1^1). The first figure in the parentheses refers to the number of voices, while the superior figure indicates how many of the voices are texted in the original source. Of the 31 lauda *contrafacta* listed in *Polyphonic Music of the Fourteenth Century*, xii. 188, 21 appear as *cantasi come* sources in Ch 266 and 10 in Ricc. 2871. Of the 25 different secular works (some were used for more than one lauda text), 23 are 2-part (20 ballate, 3 madrigals), 22 are texted in both parts, and 17 are by Landini, 3 by Niccolò da Perugia, and one each by Giovanni da Firenze, Andrea da Firenze, Jacopo da Bologna, Jacopo Pianelaio, and Guilielmus de Francia. The Trecento lauda *contrafacta* are examined in Corsi, 'Madrigali inediti', 329–40, and E. Diederichs, *Die Anfänge der mehrstimmige Lauda vom Ende des 14. bis zur Mitte des 15. Jahrhunderts* (Tützing, 1986), 48–86.

1400), with the rubric: 'All these are set to music in three parts and copied in a notebook in my hand with all the words . . .'.[60]

The existence of a late fourteenth-century repertory of polyphonic laude in Florence is not unexpected, given the relationship of the lauda repertory with contemporary secular music both before and after this time. However, the difficulty in linking this polyphonic lauda repertory with the Florentine laudesi companies stems from the increasingly broader context of this repertory. From the late fourteenth century through the fifteenth, the lauda loses some of its local, devotional, and strictly confraternal character, and, perhaps through its newly acquired polyphonic attire, begins to mirror the stylistic diversity of the broader cultural arena into which it passes.

But it is just within this broader context that one might observe the popular poetry of the lauda associating with the simpler and more 'popular' styles of polyphony that were in the ascendant at this time.[61] With this we return to the question of the laudesi companies, which D'Accone proposes may have been 'the medium through which the democratization of polyphonic performance occurred in Florence during the *Ars Nova*'.[62] There are good reasons for this supposition. The polyphonic repertory of the Florentine Trecento is musically not so far removed from the contemporary lauda repertory as it might seem. Kurt von Fischer has argued that the polyphonic repertory is rooted in 'simple indigenous types of music-making, arising from an originally instrumentally accompanied monody'.[63] The latter practice was prevalent at

---

[60] Florence, Bibl. Marucelliana MS C. 152, fo. 54ᵛ: 'Tutte queste sono intonate a tre canti e figurate in su n'un quaderno di mia mano con tutte le parole . . .'; quoted and discussed in Toscani, 'Contributi alla storia musicale delle laude dei Bianchi', 169. As Diederichs has suggested (*Die Anfänge*, 48), the style of Stefani's polyphonic laude, which are not extant, might be deduced from the style of his extant secular works (2 ballate and 1 madrigal, ed. in *Polyphonic Music of the Fourteenth Century*, x ed. W. T. Marrocco (Monaco, 1977), 51–5), especially the simpler, note-against-note style of his ballata 'I' sentì matutino'. Andrea was apparently among the other schoolmasters responsible for organizing brigades for the Bianchi processions in Florence, each of which had two lauda-singers in their midst; Toscani, 'Contributi', 168.

[61] See two essays by N. Pirrotta, 'Music for a Text Attributed to Frederick II' and 'New Glimpses of an Unwritten Tradition', in *Music and Culture in Italy*, 39–71, where he discusses the rise of popular styles of polyphony in Tuscany and the Veneto during the 14th c., and a 'growing disaffection among some of the most sophisticated listeners for what I call the scholastic tradition of music, art polyphony' (66). On the popular roots of Trecento polyphony, see K. von Fischer, 'On the Technique, Origin, and Evolution of Italian Trecento Music', *The Musical Quarterly*, 47 (1961), 41–57.

[62] 'Le compagnie', 280.

[63] 'On the Technique', 47; he also notes the 'absence of a traditional tenor foundation in early Italian trecento music', 'the large role monophony must have played as a starting point for the madrigal [the earliest poetic form set to polyphony]' (49), and in general 'a technique, or rather practice, of polyphony that developed naturally and that exhibits affinities with traits found in traditional Mediterranean folk music (such as drone effects and parallel progressions)' (53). Cf. Pirrotta, who also sees in instrumentally accompanied indigenous song the roots of popular polyphony; 'New Glimpses', 63–6.

Orsanmichele, and to a lesser extent at San Zanobi, during the fourteenth century. Common to both repertoires was a florid style of singing, and they reveal significant similarities in the melodic patterns of the *fioriture*.[64] Nevertheless, the polyphonic works selected as models for lauda *contrafacta* were generally two-part ballate with a relatively simple musical setting, which perhaps testifies to the popular impulse at work in the *contrafactum* process.[65] The reliance of the Trecento lauda upon the poetic form of the secular ballata undoubtedly influenced the shift from monophony to polyphony in the late fourteenth-century lauda, for the ballata itself underwent this transformation at that time. The earliest musical settings of ballate by Trecento composers were monophonic, and only around 1370 did polyphonists begin to apply their art to this most popular of Trecento poetic forms. Even after the vogue for polyphonic ballate was in full flower, the literary tradition of the ballata remained distinctly more popular than the caccia and madrigal traditions.[66]

The significant relationships between the musical repertoires of the Trecento lauda and secular ballata, above all the *contrafactum* link, support the likelihood that certain Florentine laudesi companies adopted polyphonic performance in the late fourteenth century. In particular, the two companies with the closest ties to secular culture, Orsanmichele and San Zanobi, retained a practice of accompanied monody which, leading scholars have argued, is the basis upon which Trecento polyphony developed.

These same two companies emerge in the search for specific ties between the laudesi companies and the Florentine polyphonic repertoire. Orsanmichele was distinguished not only by its greater number of singers and regular use of string instruments for accompaniment, but in the regular employment of organists who were a part of the larger Florentine tradition of organist/composers exemplified by Francesco

---

[64] Discussed in B. Wilson, 'The Florid Tradition in Trecento Florentine Music', paper presented at the annual meeting of the American Musicological Society, Baltimore, MD, Nov. 1988, where connections between the repertoires, composers, and institutions of lauda and secular polyphony are explored.

[65] G. Cattin, 'Contributi alla storia della lauda spirituale', *Quadrivium*, 2 (1958), 49–50; and K. von Fischer, 'Quelques remarques sur les relations entre les laudesi et les compositeurs florentins du trecento', *L'Ars nova italiana del Trecento*, 3 (Certaldo, 1970), 251. Diederichs has transcribed six secular Trecento compositions (4 by Landini, 1 by Niccolò da Perugia, 1 anon.) and underlaid them with the texts of their lauda *contrafacta*; *Die Anfänge*, 284–95.

[66] F. A. Gallo, 'The Musical and Literary Tradition of Fourteenth-Century Poetry Set to Music', in V. Günther and L. Finscher (eds.), *Musik und Text in der Mehrstimmigkeit des 14. und 15. Jahrhunderts* (Kassel, 1984), 74–5. Gallo observes that Florentine composers, in contrast to their choice of cacce and madrigal texts, chose ballata texts, mostly anonymous, without literary claims, and which were available in large quantities. Moreover, the main literary collections of ballata texts are 'manuscripts containing a "popular" type of repertory ["siciliane", and "giullaresco"-type poetry]'.

Landini.[67] Two Florentine composers appear in the membership lists of the Company of San Zanobi: Ser Gherardello (1343 and later), and Bonaiuto Corsini (1375, 1387).[68] The most obvious link between the two milieux was Franco Sacchetti (c. 1330–1400). Like Antonio Pucci, he exhibited a typically Florentine breadth of activity which embraced letters, politics, mercantilism, and lay devotion. His poetry was well known to Florentine composers, and Sacchetti, who was himself a composer, carefully noted the names of composers who set his texts to music.[69] At least four of his texts set by Florentine composers served also as models for nine lauda *contrafacta*.[70] Sacchetti himself was qualified and motivated to manage the process of polyphonic lauda *contrafacta*, and he was well placed for their introduction into laudesi worship, for after c. 1380 he was actively involved in the affairs of Orsanmichele. In 1398 he served as a captain, and shortly after this time he designed a vast biblical programme for the interior decoration of the oratory, which included twelve stained-glass windows and the entire vault system.[71]

During the late fourteenth and early fifteenth centuries, the Florentine laudesi companies, diverse in size, wealth, and openness to secular influence, exhibited a similar variety of musical practices. The smaller and conservative *Oltrarno* companies of San Frediano and Santo Spirito retained the most ancient practice of unaccompanied monody, hiring only a single soloist. Monophonic laude were occasionally performed with the accompaniment of instruments (which also may have provided

[67] Wilson, 'The Florid Tradition'. It is noteworthy that Antonio Squarcialupi, organist at Orsanmichele (and member of San Zanobi) during the second quarter of the 15th c., was owner of the Squarcialupi codex, which is by far the major source of those Florentine Trecento works which served as models for lauda *contrafacta*.

[68] K. von Fischer, 'Quelques remarques', 249. Giovanni da Firenze also may have been a San Zanobi member c.1342–62; ibid.

[69] Gallo, 'The Musical and Literary Tradition', 75. Sacchetti wrote canzoni, sonnets, madrigals (14), cacce (2), frottole, capitoli, ballate (18), and canzoni a ballo; R. Scrivano, 'Franco Sacchetti', *Grande dizionario enciclopedico* (Turin, 1971), xvi. 468. On his musical settings, see von Fischer, *Studien zur italienischen Musik*, 77–8, and E. Li Gotti and N. Pirrotta, *Il Sacchetti e la technica musicale del Trecento italiano* (Florence, 1935).

[70] The four texts are the madrigal 'Nel mezo già del mar' (set by Niccolò da Perugia; 2²), the music of which served for the lauda 'Nel mezo a due ladron' (Ricc. 2871, fo. 61ᵛ); the ballata 'Non creder, donna' (Landini, 2²), the music of which served 3 laude: 'Ciascun che 'l regno' (Ricc. 2871, fo. 61ʳ), 'Preghian la dolce Vergine' (Ch 266, fo. 204ʳ), and 'Volgi li occhi' (ibid., fo. 204ᵛ); the ballata 'Altri n'arà la pena' (Landini, 2²), the music of which also served the lauda 'Preghian la dolce Vergine'; and the ballata 'Né te né altra voglio amar già mai' (Landini; music not extant), the music of which served 4 laude: 'Altro che te non voglio amar già mai' (ibid., fo. 74ʳ), 'Con sicurtà ritorna, o peccatore' (ibid., fo. 203ʳ), 'O Signor Jesù, i' ti vo cercando' (ibid., fo. 206ʳ), and 'Come se' da laudar più ch'altrui assai' (ibid., fo. 208ʳ).

[71] E. Borsook, *The Mural Painters of Tuscany* (2nd edn., Oxford, 1980), 54–5. Sacchetti was also responsible for the design of the *Stabat Mater* for the Passion altar, the theme of an extremely popular poem for which he composed a vernacular setting, 'Stava madre dolorosa, a la croce lagrimosa' (Tenneroni, *Inizii*, 246). The Sacchetti family name appears frequently in the Orsanmichele records beginning c.1367 (OSM 56, fos. 37 ff.).

a simple and/or improvised polyphonic accompaniment) at the Company of San Zanobi, and the companies of San Piero Martire and San Zanobi regularly hired pairs of singers during this time. By 1415, the oratory of Orsanmichele must have been the pre-eminent musical establishment of the city, with its six ferial singers, four festal singers, rebec-player, lutenist, and organist. Certainly it would have been the first company to adopt a polyphonic practice, which then would have been easily transmitted to the other companies for which the Orsanmichele musicians regularly performed.[72]

c.1415–1470

The performing forces of the laudesi companies changed significantly, and at varying rates, during this period. Orsanmichele continued to hire at least six ferial singers and an organist, although it discontinued the use of other accompanying instruments between c.1430 and 1450. San Zanobi and San Piero Martire both began to hire more than a pair of ferial singers right around 1415. San Zanobi paid three ferial singers during c.1415–45, and with the abandonment of ferial services in 1445 then retained five to seven singers during c.1445–70. San Piero Martire paid three to four ferial singers during the entire period, with four becoming the norm by 1448.[73] The performing forces of the insular *Oltrarno* companies changed more slowly. The companies of Santo Spirito and San Frediano retained a single laudese until c.1430 and 1446, respectively. Santo Spirito hired two singers during c.1430–1456, at which time there is a lacuna in the documents until 1482. San Frediano recorded payments to two to three singers in the late 1450s, after which time the company ceased to retain salaried singers. The Company of Sant'Agnese employed two to three singers from 1440 (when company documents commence) throughout the period, and three laudesi had

---

[72] The pairs of laudesi singing for the companies of San Zanobi and San Piero Martire during this period may have been performing the polyphonic setting suggested by the lauda *contrafacta* repertory: two-part ballate texted in both parts. Certainly two-part textures with either a vocal or instrumental lower part were possible options at this time. Filippo Villani reported that from the early 14th c. pairs of singers performed polyphony at the Florentine Cathedral, and the presence of a *cantore* and a *tenorista* there is documented from 1407 until the establishment of a polyphonic chapel in 1438; D'Accone, 'Music and Musicians at Santa Maria del Fiore in the Early Quattrocento', in *Scritti in onore di Luigi Ronga* (Milan, 1973), 114.

[73] The larger laudesi establishments were comparable in numbers to the polyphonic chapel at the Cathedral and Baptistry, which from its founding in 1437 through the following decade retained a *maestro di cappella* and 3–5 singers. Several members of the Cathedral choir, including the *maestro*, also served at Orsanmichele during the same period, and at least one member of the choir, Goro di Maso, sang for both Orsanmichele (1432–7) and San Zanobi (1435–6). However, laudesi and Cathedral choirs must have differed significantly with respect to the types and abilities of singers (the Cathedral hired primarily professional singer/composers from northern Europe), and the repertory they performed.

become standard by the 1460s. By 1445 all but two companies had discontinued ferial services, and none was hiring stringed instruments for accompaniment.

These growing numbers are certainly a witness to the acceleration of developments already evident in the late fourteenth and early years of the fifteenth century: the penetration of polyphonic practice into the laudesi services, and the establishment of the *cantasi come* tradition which linked the lauda to an increasingly broad range of polyphonic models. The earliest explicit references to polyphonic performance in the laudesi documents come, as it happens, from an *Oltrarno* company, Sant'Agnese, in 1442 (a *tenore* and a laudese) and 1444 (a *tenore* and two *fanciulli*), and slightly later from San Zanobi, in 1446 (a *tenore* and two laudesi). Most, if not all, of the above were secular singers, and certainly the larger companies must have predated an *Oltrarno* company in the polyphonic performance of laude. In fact, members of the polyphonic chapel established at the Cathedral in 1437 sang for the companies of Orsanmichele and San Zanobi during the 1430s.

Complementary to the gradual conversion of fifteenth-century laudesi services to polyphony was the dissemination of the lauda into a broader cultural realm in which polyphony, especially in its simpler forms, was cultivated. Always eclectic in its response to popular tastes, the lauda of this period exhibited no single form or style, but continually mirrored the varied and changing aspects of the broader musico-poetic world in which it now circulated. In the numerous *cantasi come* manuscripts of this period[74] there emerged an entirely new and vast repertory of lauda poetry which displayed the diverse poetic schemes of popular fifteenth-century poetry (barzellette, canzonette, frottole, and related forms) and few concordances with fourteenth-century laudario collections.[75] With

[74] None of these sources contains music. Among the major *cantasi come* sources of this period are *Ch 266, *Ricc. 2224 (1433), *Mgl. II. VII. 4 (*c.* 1453), Ricc. 1502, Mgl. 367, Mgl. 690, *Vaticano Rossiano 424, Mgl. C. VII. 30, Ricc. Edizioni rare 196 (discussed and indexed by G. Cattin, 'I "cantasi come" in una stampa di laude della Biblioteca Riccardiana (Ed. r. 196)', *Quadrivium*, 19 (1978), 5–52). Much of the above *cantasi come* repertory (507 laude) was issued in a series of four Florentine prints between 1486 and *c.* 1512, reprinted by G. C. Galletti, *Laude spirituali di Feo Belcari, di Lorenzo de' Medici, di Francesco d'Albizzo, di Castellano Castellani e di altri, comprese nelle quattro più antiche raccolte con alcune inedite e con nuovi illustrazioni* (Florence, 1864). Galletti[1]: *Laude di Feo Belcari . . .* [Florence, *c.* 1490]; Galletti[2]: *Laude fatte e composte da più persone spirituale a onore dello onnipotente Iddio e della Santa Maria e di molti altri Santi o Sante, raccolte ed insieme ridotte da Iacopo di Maestro Luigi de' Morsi cittadino Fiorentino* [Florence, 1486]; Galletti[3]: *Laude facte e composte da più persone spirituale . . .* [Florence, *c.* 1495]; Galletti[4]: *Libro di Laude a petizione di ser Piero Pacini di Pescia* [Florence, *c.* 1502–8; reprinted in Venice, 1512]. Much of this repertory is indexed in A. D'Ancona, *La poesia popolare italiana* (2nd edn., Livorno, 1906; repr. Bologna, 1974), 475–95. (The asterisks above indicate those manuscripts discussed and inventoried in Luisi, *Laudario giustinianeo*, i. 131–248, *passim*.)

[75] For example, Luisi has shown that only three of the 100 laude in Mgl[2] turn up in the many fifteenth-century collections examined by him (i.e., in MSS and prints containing laude related in any way to the Giustiniani tradition of laude); *Laudario giustinianeo*, i. 135–7. Even those lauda texts in late 14th- and early 15th-c. sources that were linked through *contrafacta* to Trecento polyphonic

this formal and stylistic diversity, the lauda now gained access to an expanded musical field; a lauda might now be 'sung like' a variety of popular Italian secular songs, or 'la passione', 'le stanze d'Abram',[76] 'a ballo', 'I vangeli di quaresima', 'Gli strambotti', 'al modo di Cicilia',[77] French chansons,[78] 'chanzona tedesca a piacevole modo', 'al modo de Benolio cantore' (or another unknown composer), or simply to its own tune ('ha modo proprio').[79] Most of this diverse musical repertoire upon which the lauda texts drew does not survive, and in fact may never have been written down.

The *cantasi come* tradition of this (and the next) period was overwhelmingly Florentine, and its chief poets were the Florentines Feo Belcari (1410–84), Francesco degli Albizzi, Ser Michele Chelli, Lorenzo de' Medici, and his mother Lucrezia Tornabuoni de' Medici. But there was another tradition that paralleled, intermingled with, and strongly influenced the Florentine lauda tradition.

music continue to appear only sporadically in early 15th-c. sources (Mgl. II. VII. 4; Ricc. 2224, Ricc. 2894, Ricc. 2929) before disappearing completely by *c.* 1450. In this respect, Ch 266 is a hybrid, being both a late source of many 14th-c. laude and an early source of laude that survived to appear in the 16th-c. collections of Petrucci and Razzi. Its hybrid nature is also revealed in the mixture of newer and older poetic forms.

[76] Presumably the well-known *rappresentazione sacra* by Feo Belcari, the 'Rappresentazione di Abramo e Isac' (1449).

[77] Ch 266, fo. 218ᵛ: the lauda 'Tu sse' Signiore dello paradiso' was to be sung 'in the manner of a *siciliana*'. This reference may be added to others examined by Pirrotta in his essay on a genre of unwritten popular song which first surfaced in written tradition in the Veneto during the 14th c., and represented a 'vogue of eclectic exoticism that was spreading among professional and semi-professional singers'; 'New Glimpses of an Unwritten Tradition', in *Music and Culture in Italy*, 58.

[78] These appear throughout this period, from Ch 266 to the late 15th-c. prints published by Galletti. The *c.* 18 chansons which appear in known sources are in the form of the rondeau (*quatrain* and *cinquain*), and are well represented in Italian sources; the attributable works are by the leading northern composers of the 15th c. (Binchois, Hayne, Dufay, Lannoy, Caron, among others). One song with a German text, a *villancico*, and a number of popular Latin works (like the ubiquitous 'Verbum caro factum est') were also *contrafacta* sources for 15th-c. lauda poets. G. Cattin, ' "Contrafacta" internazionali: musiche europee per laude italiane', in V. Günther and L. Finscher (eds), *Musik und Text in der Mehrstrimmigkeit des 14. und 15. Jahrhunderts* (Kassel, 1984), 417–35.

[79] A number of musical models for *cantasi come* laude have been located and catalogued by F. Ghisi, 'Strambotti e laude nel travestimento spirituale della poesia musicale del Quattrocento', *Collectanea historiae musicae*, 1 (1953), 45–76, and G. Cattin, 'I "cantasi come" in una stampa di laude', 5–52. Cattin's extensive research into the 15th-c. lauda *contrafacta* repertoire has led him to the conclusion that during *c.* 1440–90 (the 'periodo belcariano', after the foremost lauda poet of the time), the relationship between the lauda text and its model was 'approximate, if not arbitrary'. Apparently, the lauda poet was most interested in the abstract qualities of the music: its melodic beauty, vocality, capacity to convey a particular mood, and often (but not necessarily) its widespread familiarity. In the case of models in a different language, the resemblance of the lauda text to the original model was generally limited to the the refrain, at most, or to such mnemonic devices as certain aspects of rhyme, the incipit of the poem (consisting of the first several words or a line translated strictly into Italian), or often the copying in Italian of certain linguistic sounds in the original. Both immediately prior to this period (in the late 14th- and early 15th-c. *contrafacta*) and following it, poets pursued a stricter relationship between lauda and model. ' "Contrafacta" internazionali', 435; id., 'Musiche per le laude di Castellano Castellani', *Rivista italiana di musicologia*, 12 (1977), 185–6.

The majority of manuscripts that preserve fifteenth-century laude in musical settings are directly or indirectly traceable to the Veneto.[80] Most of them contain both sacred (liturgical and non-liturgical) and secular works, and appear to have originated in a clerical environment. All of them were copied between c.1420 and 1500, and together preserve a highly diverse repertoire of lauda settings, the style and composition of which span the entire century. The culmination of this written tradition of lauda settings related to the Veneto are the two books of laude issued by the Venetian printer Petrucci in 1507 and 1508. The poet (and musician, though none of his musical compositions is extant) who by far figures most prominently in this north Italian lauda tradition is the Venetian statesman Leonardo Giustiniani (1387/8–1446). By the time of Giustiniani's death, the strength of the Venetian lauda tradition was such that the Venetian laudesi companies, the *Scuole Grandi*, began seriously to upgrade the standard of music at their ceremonies.[81] This admittedly loose bundle of evidence nevertheless points to a strong lauda tradition that developed in the Venetian territory with dramatic speed in the early fifteenth century, and warrants some consideration here for its impact upon the Florentine tradition.[82]

Four of these musical lauda sources originated in the Veneto: Venice, Biblioteca Nazionale Marciana, MS Cl. IX. 145 [Ven] (c.1420–60);[83] Bologna, Biblioteca Universitaria, Ms. 2216 [BU] (c.1440);[84] Bologna,

[80] Most of this lauda repertory is briefly discussed, catalogued, and provided with musical incipits in P. Damilano, 'Fonti musicali della lauda polifonica intorno alla metà del sec. XV', *Collectanea historiae musicae*, 3 (1963), 59–90. These sources are also briefly discussed by F. Ghisi, 'Strambotti e laude', 49–67. The most thorough and recent study is by E. Diederichs, *Die Anfänge*. She focuses upon 4 sources: BU, BL, Ven, and Pav, and provides a large appendix of musical transcriptions (pp. 281–433).

[81] J. Glixon, 'Music at the Venetian Scuole Grandi, 1440–1540', in Iain Fenlon (ed.), *Music in Medieval and Early Modern Europe: Patronage, Sources, and Texts* (Cambridge, 1981), 193–208; and F. Luisi, *Laudario giustinianeo*, i. 413–523. Like the Florentine companies, most of the Venetian *scuole* were founded during the late 13th and early 14th cc., but unlike their Florentine counterparts did not begin to hire professional singers or perform polyphonic works until the 1440s.

[82] The primacy of the Venetian lauda (and its chief poet Giustiniani) in the early 15th c., and its importance for the Florentine tradition later in the century, are acknowledged by Cattin, 'Contributi alla storia della lauda spirituale', 52–3, and B. Becherini, 'Musica italiana a Firenze nel XV secolo', *Revue belge de musicologie*, 8 (1954), 109. Of the 186 laude determined by Luisi to belong to the Giustiniani tradition, 42 appear in Cod 266.

[83] Inventory by G. Cattin, 'Il Manoscritto Veneto Marciano Italiano IX 145', *Quadrivium*, 4 (1960), 1–57; K. Jeppesen, 'Ein venezianisches Laudenmanuskript', in G. Bosse (ed.), *Theodor Kroyer Festschrift zum Sechzigsten Geburtstag* (Regensburg, 1933), 69–76. Examined in detail by E. M. Cambon, 'The Italian and Latin Lauda of the Fifteenth Century', Ph.D. thesis (Tulane University, 1975, music). Transcriptions by Cattin, *Laudi quattrocentesche del Cod. Veneto Marc. It. IX 145* (Bologna, 1958); Diederichs, *Die Anfänge*, 281–433, *passim*; and Luisi, *Laudario giustinianeo*, ii, *passim*. Ven is in two parts: VenI (c.1450–60), containing works in the early style of Dufay; VenII (c.1420–40), containing works in the style of 'primitive' polyphony. Both sections contain motets, liturgical pieces, and laude. The manuscript is a small (10 × 6.5 cm.) anthology which probably originated in a Franciscan establishment in Venice.

[84] Inventory by H. Besseler, 'The Manuscript Bologna Biblioteca Universitaria 2216', *Musica*

Civico Museo Bibliografico Musicale, MS Q 15 [BL] (*c.* 1420–35),[85] and Washington, DC, Library of Congress, MS. ML171 J6 [Wc] (*c.* 1460).[86] A fourth source, Pavia, Biblioteca Universitaria, MS Aldini 361 [Pav] (*c.* 1470–80), is the only known source to have concordances with the laude in Ven.[87] Two other sources (in addition to Wc) come from Benedictine communities that had come under a reform movement initiated by a Venetian nobleman in the monastery of Santa Giustina in Padua: Montecassino, Biblioteca dell'Abbazia, MS 871 [MC] (*c.* 1430–80);[88] and Capetown, South African Public Library, Grey Collection 3. b. 12 [Grey] (*c.* 1500).[89]

disciplina, 6 (1952), 39; facs. ed. by F. A. Gallo, *Il codice musicale 2216 della Biblioteca Universitaria di Bologna* (Monumenta Lyricae Medii Aevi Italica, 3; Bologna, 1970); studies by F. A. Gallo, 'Musiche veneziane del Ms. 2216 della Biblioteca Universitaria di Bologna', *Quadrivium*, 6 (1964), 107–11; J. Palumbo- Lavery, 'BU 2216: The Manuscript, its Repertory, and the Transmission of Polyphony in the Early Fifteenth Century' (Ph.D. thesis, Princeton University, in progress). Transcriptions by Diederichs, *Die Anfänge*, and Luisi, *Laudario giustinianeo*, ii. Mostly copied before 1440 in the vicinity of Venice; remainder copied shortly thereafter in Brescia. Contains Mass ordinary sections, motets, French and Italian secular pieces, laude, and miscellaneous liturgical pieces.

[85] M. Bent, 'A Contemporary Perception of Early Fifteenth-Century Style: Bologna Q 15 as a Document of Scribal Editorial Initiative', *Musica disciplina*, 41 (1987), 183–99; G. de Van, 'Inventory of Manuscript Bologna Liceo Musicale, Q 15 (olim 37)', *Musica disciplina*, 2 (1948), 231–57; H. Besseler, 'Bologna, Kodex BL', in *Die Musik in Geschichte und Gegenwart*, ii, cols. 95–9. Transcriptions by Diederichs, *Die Anfänge*, and Luisi, *Laudario giustinianeo*, ii. Copied *c.* 1420–35; primarily a liturgical manuscript with secular works and laude copied into unused portions (usually the bottom of a folio).

[86] G. Cattin, 'Polifonia quattrocentesca italiana nel Codice Washington, Library of Congress, ML 171 J6', *Quadrivium*, 9 (1968), 87–102; F. A. Gallo, '*Cantus planus binatim*: Polifonia primitiva in fonti tardive', *Quadrivium*, 7 (1966), 79–89. Transcriptions by Luisi, *Laudario giustinianeo*, ii, no. 58. A private manuscript belonging to the Benedictine monk Gianfranco Preottoni, who resided at San Giorgio in Venice (*c.* 1465), and later at Pavia (1480). Related to VenII, and, like Pav, contains a music treatise. The manuscript originated in a Benedictine monastery under the Santa Giustina reform movement discussed below.

[87] G. Cattin, 'Le composizioni musicali del Ms. Pavia Aldini 361', in *L'Ars nova italiana del Trecento*, 2 (Certaldo, 1968), 1–21 (inventory and transcription); F. Ghisi, 'Di una lauda nel codice pavese Aldini', in G. Reese and R. J. Snow (eds.), *Essays in musicology in Honor of Dragan Plamenac on his 70th Birthday* (Pittsburgh, 1969), 61–4. Transcriptions in Luisi, *Laudario giustinianeo*, ii. Like Ven, a small book (15 × 11 cm.) containing mostly 2–part polyphony, probably for the private use of a cantor or music instructor.

[88] I. Pope and M. Kanazawa, 'The Musical Manuscript Montecassino N871', *Anuario musical*, 19 (1966), 123–53; complete transcription and study by Pope and Kanazawa, *The Musical Manuscript Montecassino 871: A Neapolitan Repertory of Sacred and Secular Music of the Late Fifteenth Century* (Oxford, 1978). From the vicinity of Naples, probably originating at the Benedictine convent of St Angela di Gaeta. Although probably copied during the 1480s, the retrospective repertoire spans the period *c.* 1430–80, and contains Franco–Flemish Latin works, *canti carnascialeschi*, and laude (mostly 3-part) in the form of *strambotti* and *canzone*.

[89] G. Cattin, 'Nuova fonte italiana della polifonia intorno al 1500 (Ms. Capetown, Grey 3. b. 12)', *Acta musicologica*, 9 (1973), 165–221. Transcriptions by Cattin, *Italian Laude and Latin Unica in Ms. Capetown, Grey 3. b. 12* (Corpus mensurabilis musicae, 76; Neuhausen-Stuttgart, 1977), and Luisi, *Laudario giustinianeo*, ii. Copied *c.* 1500, possibly in the Paduan area, the manuscript contains 85 pieces (only one is monodic) which stylistically span most of the 15th c. Contains many liturgical items (esp. for Holy Week) and lauda *unica* in 2, 3, and 4 parts, and a number of lauda texts from the Giustiniani tradition are set.

Several interesting developments surround the establishment of the Venetian lauda tradition in the early fifteenth century. The Gesuati, originally a Sienese lay congregation that included a number of lauda poets in their circle, had brought their lauda tradition north from Siena in the late fourteenth century, and their most famous lauda poet, Bianco da Siena, died in Venice in 1412.[90] A devotional climate favourable to the lauda developed with the Benedictine reform movement initiated in 1409 by the Venetian nobleman Ludovico Barbo.[91] Having begun in the Paduan monastery of Santa Giustina, the Congregatio Sanctae Iustinae soon included most of the Italian Benedictine establishments. The reform was predicated upon a negative attitude towards polyphony, but soon relaxed in favour of simpler styles of polyphony. This reform impulse attained a much broader influence through Gabriele Condulmer, the Venetian patrician who became Pope Eugene IV in 1431,[92] and through Lorenzo Giustiniani, the poet's brother, who served Eugene IV and became the first Patriarch of Venice in 1451.[93]

The poetic forms of this Venetian lauda repertoire are those popularized in the elegant and widely diffused verse of Giustiniani: the strambotto, capitolo, ode, and frottola, as well as the classical ballata. The majority of the musical settings of this period are in two parts, a fewer number in three, and most are anonymous. The diversity of musical styles reveals the particularly eclectic nature of the lauda at this time: 'primitive' organal textures (VenII), simple note-against-note polyphony, cantilena textures in which the lower part(s), while supportive, are generally texted and singable, and more 'modern' works in the style of early Dufay, with a tendency towards repetition of melodic formulas, parlando-like tone repetitions at the beginnings of phrases, and a syllabic, homo-rhythmic declamation.[94] There is relatively little evidence of polyphony in the Franco-Flemish style. The florid tradition of the Italian Ars Nova

[90] Diederichs, Die Anfänge, 257.

[91] G. Cattin, 'Tradizione e tendenze innovatrici nella normativa e nella pratica liturgico-musicale della Congregazione di S. Giustina', Benedictina, 17 (1970), 254–99; id., Italian Laude and Latin Unica, pp. ix–xi; Diederichs, Die Anfänge, 255–8; Luisi, Laudario giustinianeo, i, 526. Barbo was abbot of the monastery beginning in 1408.

[92] It was this same pope who established and subsidized the polyphonic chapel and chant school for training boy singers at the Florentine Cathedral in 1438, and in whose service Dufay composed his homophonic hymn settings. Significant in this light is Pirrotta's evidence that Padua, and particularly the Santa Giustina abbey, was an important centre in the late 14th c. for the cultivation of siciliane and the popularization of polyphony; 'New Glimpses', in Music and Culture in Italy, 71.

[93] Lorenzo assumed the abbacy of S. Giorgio in Alga in 1408, vacated by Barbo when the latter succeeded to the abbacy of S. Giustina in Padua. Together with Barbo and Condulmer, he is considered one of the three pillars of Venetian spirituality in the 15th c. He later wrote a treatise on monastic life (Doctrina et non puocho utile a quelloro che novamente intrati sono nella religione del vivere religiosamente [Venice, 1494]) which included a chapter on the discipline of lauda-singing entitled 'Come debano essere facti coloro hi [sic] quali sono presenti alle divine laude et che a Dio psalmizano' (cap. XVII); Luisi, Laudario giustinianeo, i, 526.

[94] Diederichs, Die Anfänge, 251–4.

continues, but is modified, and is most apparent in frequent cadential flourishes which suggest a continuing tradition of vocal improvisation. Evident in much of the repertoire, in fact, is the earliest trace of an essentially Italian style of Renaissance polyphony, the 'nuovo stile frottolistico',[95] which an increasing presence of the Franco–Flemish tradition was gradually transforming from a popular, unwritten state into the written, artistic tradition of the frottola that was to emerge at the end of the century. The new style was characterized by a predilection for syllabic and homorhythmic text treatment, for a monodic texture in which a cantabile superius was sustained by a homophonic support, and a rhetorical correspondence between the verbal and musical phrase, with clearly marked cadences.[96] The style was, in other words, strongly conditioned by the demands of the poetic text. Nevertheless, some of the musical settings show signs of having been borrowed from secular *contrafacta* models.[97]

A brief tour of the musical settings and manuscript tradition of four lauda texts generally attributed to Giustiniani will serve to demonstrate the character of the repertory during this period. 'L'Amor a me venendo', 'O Iesù dolce, o infinito amor', 'Con desiderio io vo cerchando', and 'Madre che festi colui' are among the most widely diffused laude of the fifteenth and early sixteenth centuries, and their successive settings serve as an index of changing musical styles. All four laude passed quickly into the Florentine lauda tradition, perhaps even during the poet's lifetime, for they all appear in Ch 266 and the succeeding Florentine *cantasi come* sources.

'L'amor a me venendo' appears in twenty-seven literary sources,[98] and four musical settings in Ven (2²), Pav (2²), Petrucci[1] (Venice, 1508; 4⁴),

---

[95] Becherini, 'Musica italiana', 114.

[96] P. Damilano, 'Fonti musicali', 74–5; F. Ghisi, 'Strambotti e laude', 49, 67; Diederichs, *Die Anfänge*, 18. The repertory of 2-part (as well as later 3- and 4-part) settings discussed below is well represented in the editions by Luisi, *Laudario giustinianeo*, ii, and Cattin, *Italian Laude and Latin Unica*. A number of 2- and 3-part laude are also edited in Cattin, 'Contributi', 57–72, and id., 'Le composizioni musicali del MS Pavia Aldini 361', 9–20.

[97] Cattin observed this with respect to the lauda repertoire in Grey: '. . . texts of versification quite different from the originals forced to music destined to quite another end; new syllables and vowels added to words; words broken in half and started over again . . .'; *Italian Laude and Latin Unica*, p. x.

[98] The information on the manuscript tradition of these laude is from Luisi, *Laudario giustinianeo*, i, tables 33, 35, 37–9, and the four texts are edited in i. 291 ('L'amor'), 255 ('O Iesù'), 292–3 ('Con desiderio'), and 260 ('Madre'). The musical settings, including a number of selected *contrafacta* reconstructions, are edited in vol. ii. On Luisi's problematic transcriptions and criteria for selection of *cantasi come* reconstructions, see the review of *Laudario giustinianeo* by J. Glixon, *Journal of the American Musicological Society*, 41 (1988), 170–9. There is, of course, no guarantee that a surviving musical setting was the particular one intended by the *cantasi come* rubric, nor is it clear whether a monophonic tune or the whole polyphonic fabric of the *contrafactum* model was to be borrowed, but the Florentine companies' capability of polyphonic performance and the opportunism of the *cantasi come* tradition suggest that a variety of musical settings (particularly those with compatible verse structures) were fair game.

and Razzi[1] (Florence, 1563; 3[3]).[99] A particular musical setting was associated with the lauda relatively early in this period, for already in Ch 266 it served as a *cantasi come* source for another lauda.[100] In the Florentine *cantasi come* prints of the late fifteenth century (Gall[1−4]), 'L'amor' appears once with a *cantasi come* source, and in turn as a *cantasi come* source for three other laude.[101] The music for this lauda in Ven and Pav may well preserve a setting that was generally associated with the text during this period, for the two pieces are essentially the same (see Music Example 6). The remarkably conservative, organal texture of Ven presents a written version of a simple musical style which may have long served as a basis for an improvised and rudimentary polyphony. The more refined version in Pav retains the melodic outline of both parts in Ven, but eliminates some of the parallel progressions and intervals by fleshing out the melodic lines with passing notes. In Pav, the text underlay is altered, and the melodic design of the cadences restructured, so that musical and textual rhymes correspond (especially for 'venendo' and 'languendo'). The essential identity between the two polyphonic settings suggests the possibility that the piece circulated orally in this manner, and that the *cantasi come* reference in Ch 266 was to a polyphonic setting and not just to a melody.[102]

The inaugural lauda in most of the Venetian lauda collections is 'O Iesù dolce', which appears in thirty-three literary sources, and in musical settings in Grey (2[2]), Wc (tenor only), Panc. 27 (3[1]), Petrucci[1] (4[1]), and Razzi[1] (2[2]). This lauda text was strongly associated with its own musical setting. Only once does it appear with a *cantasi come* direction for it to be sung to another melody,[103] but throughout the fifteenth century twenty-one other laude were to be sung to the music associated with 'O Iesù dolce'.[104] The two-part settings in Grey and Razzi[1], and the three-part setting in Panc. 27 (with added contratenor) are all versions of the same

[99] For bibliography on the Petrucci and Razzi prints see below (nn. 129, 134), where these sources are discussed more fully in the context of 16th-c. music.

[100] 'D'amore tutto m'acciendo', Ch 266, fos. 293[r−v].

[101] 'L'Amor' was to be sung to the tune of 'Donna sti mie' lamenti' (Gall[2], 222, where 'L'amor' is attributed to Bianco da Siena), and was itself the musical source for 'Dolce madre Maria' (Gall[2], 100; F. Belcari), 'Dir pur così vorrei' (Gall[2], 230; A. di M. Muzi), and 'Maria piena d'amore' (Gall[4], 485; anon.).

[102] Cattin expressed his doubt about the polyphonic performance of 15th-c. *cantasi come* laude in ' "Contrafacta" internazionali', 436–7, but in late 15th-c. Florence the pervasive *cantasi come* repertoire in conjunction with polyphonic laudesi chapels would seem to suggest otherwise. Most of the 3- and 4-part settings of all 4 laude discussed here belong stylistically to the next period, and are discussed below.

[103] In an early 16th-c. print, *Laudi spirituali di diversi: Del modo di confessarsi e della purità di coscienza* (Ricc. Edizioni rare 196) (Florence, 1512), fo. 18[v]: 'O crudel donna poi che lassato m'hai'.

[104] It was a *cantasi come* model for 5 laude in Ch 266, and for 17 in the Galletti prints (with two in common to both sources), with attributions to F. D'Albizzo (9), F. Belcari (3), M. Lucrezia de' Medici (1), B. Malatesti (1), S. Pallaio (1), and L. Giustiniani (1).

piece, and once again probably represent a musical setting with which the text was commonly linked in the *cantasi come* tradition (see Music Example 8). The moments of awkward text underlay in all three versions indicate that the music was originally composed for another text, but some of these problems in Grey (for example, at 'inestimabil') have been smoothed out in the other versions. The cadential embellishments in Grey, as in other early lauda settings, tend to disappear in later settings (though probably not from performance). The Grey and Panc. 27 version show some affinities, especially in light of the unique interpolation in the Razzi setting (Music Example 8, phrase beginning 'che fuggend'io'), but Panc. 27 is probably an attempt to update the piece by the addition of a third, lower voice. Nevertheless, all three settings exemplify a style of two-part polyphony that must have prevailed throughout the present period: frequent unisons and octaves (especially at the beginning and end of phrases), declamatory repeated notes at the beginning of phrases, frequent parallel thirds, and a prevailingly syllabic and homorhythmic style of text-setting in which the verbal phrases are marked by clear musical cadences.

'Con desiderio io vo cercando' is preserved in twenty-four literary sources, and five musical settings, in BU (22), Mgl. II. XI. 18 (1^1), Panc. 27 (3^3 and 4^4), and Grey (4^4). According to Gall[2] (p. 217) both this lauda and the secular 'La vita della sgalera' served as *cantasi come* models for the lauda 'Tu che puoi quel che tu vuoi'. The musical settings are not related. The BU version differs somewhat from the other two-part settings of the time in the overlapping of phrases (textual and musical), the greater independence of the voices, the alternation between duple and triple rhythmic groupings, the florid character of the cantus, and the under-third cadences (see Music Example 10). The style seems to be a fusion of Trecento polyphony with certain aspects of the newer style: the commencement of phrases with declamatory repeated notes, and a predilection for imperfect consonances. The 'note coronate', which serve to highlight important text, such as the name of Christ (mm. 16–20), appear also in a handful of laude from this period, most of them associated with Giustiniani.[105] The single melody in Mgl. II. XI. 18 appears to be the tenor of a two-part setting in which the text has been awkwardly applied to a borrowed melody.

[105] See e.g. 'Mercè te chiamo' (attr. to Giustiniani), also in BU, fos. 27^v–28^r; ed. in Luisi, *Laudario giustinianeo* ii. 236–7; a contratenor is added to the same piece in MC, pp. 348–9; in Pope and Kanazawa (eds.), *The Musical Manuscript*, 336–8. Partial transcriptions of both versions are in Ghisi, 'Strambotti e laude', 58–9. Another two-part setting of a Giustiniani lauda, 'Benedeto ne sia lo zorno' (Grey, fos. 61^v–62^r; Luisi, ii. 21–2) contains numerous 'note coronate' on the words 'Ahmè Jesù'. See also 'Dilectoza cortezia' (BL, fos. 9^v–10^r) with 'corone' on 'Sancto Jhesu'. On the 'corone' as an indication for improvised embellishment, see C. Warren, 'Punctus Organi and Cantus Coronatus in the Music of Dufay', in A. W. Atlas (ed.), *Papers Read at the Dufay Quincentenary Conference* (Brooklyn, NY, 1976), 128–43.

There are twenty-five extant literary sources for 'Madre che festi', and two musical settings, in Ven (2²) and Petrucci[1] (4⁴). Of all four Giustiniani laude discussed here, the text and music of 'Madre' became the most popular in the Florentine tradition. The music served as a *cantasi come* source for twenty-three other laude, including twenty in Ch 266, and seven by Belcari in Gall[1].[106] In Gall[2] (p. 234), 'Madre' was assigned three *cantasi come* directions: it could be sung to the music of either of two popular French chansons, 'J'ay pris amours' and 'Mon seul plaisir', or to its own well-known tune ('Questa lauda ha modo proprio').[107] The two-part setting in Ven exemplifies the 'new frottola style' described above, and the musical setting is so well suited to the text that it appears to have been composed as the original *modo proprio* for this lauda (see Music Example 11).

The prominence of these relatively simple two-part settings during this period do not preclude, however, the possibility that improvised embellishment was added in performance. In fact, a number of lauda-related compositions from this period contain passages which suggest that the tradition of florid singing so evident in Florentine Trecento music (both lauda and secular) continued into the fifteenth century. Moreover, the fifteenth-century florid style appears to be strongly associated with the poetry of Giustiniani.[108] Rubsamen identified the four unusually florid works in Petrucci's *Frottole libro sexto* (Venice, 1505) as the 'Iustiniane' referred to in the index of the collection, and, based on an unornamented version of one of the four found in Escorial MS IV. a. 24 (*c.*1460–70), he identified a mid-fifteenth-century style of *Justiniane*:

. . . a three-voice composition for solo voice and instrumental accompaniment, in which long *colorature* alternate with shorter declamatory phrases in the elaborately melismatic discantus. The metrical scheme is generally irregular,

---

[106] Five of the Belcari laude also appear in Ch 266. In Ms. Ross. 424, fo. 200ʳ, 'Madre' is attributed to the Florentine improvisatory singer, Maestro Antonio di Guido, an indication perhaps that the piece became associated with him through performance.

[107] On the *contrafacta* of the chansons, see Cattin, ' "Contrafacta" internazionali', 419. Luisi has reconstructed 6 musical settings in *Laudario giustinianeo*, ii. 165–79: one setting of 'Mon seul plaisir' (Dufay/Bedingham, 3¹, Pavia Aldini 362, fos. 24ᵛ–25ʳ), and 5 settings of 'J'ay pris amours' (Isaac, 3¹, BN, Banco Rari 229, no. 8; J. Japart, 4¹, ibid., no. 152; J. Martini, 4¹, ibid., no. 179; id., 3¹, Panc. 27, fo. 41ᵛ; and Isaac, 4¹, Magl. XIX. 178, fos. 2ᵛ–4ʳ.

[108] W. Rubsamen, 'The Justiniane or Viniziane of the 15th Century', *Acta musicologica*, 29 (1957), 172–84. Rubsamen documents the existence during and after the poet's lifetime of a Venetian melodic style ('l'aere venetiano') associated with Giustiniani's poetry. Pietro Bembo wrote in the early 16th c. that the Venetian poet 'was held in greater esteem for the manner of song with which he sent forth his poems than for his mode of writing'; ibid. 174. A 1460 document indicates that *arie veneziane* required special skill in performance; ibid., 174. Rubsamen edits both the ornamented and unornamented version of one of the *Justiniane* ('Aymè sospiri', 180–2), both versions of which are also ed. by Luisi, *Laudario giustinianeo*, ii. 268–70. For a different interpretation of the significance of Petrucci's ornamented version (an instrumental intabulation), see J. Haar, *Essays on Italian Poetry and Music in the Renaissance, 1350–1600* (Berkeley, Calif., 1986), 42–3.

alternating freely between duple and triple, although triple meter may prevail throughout. Because of the melismas and the nature of the poetry, the irregular phrases are much longer than those in the frottola. Holds or rests demarcate the ends of phrases, presumably in order that the lower, instrumental parts may recognize the close of a florid passage in the voice part. Since the upper voice plays the leading melodic role, there is little or no imitation between the parts, and all voices generally start and finish a phrase simultaneously. The tenor also has melodic character, whereas the contratenor or bass furnishes harmonic support.[109]

Rubsamen also observed in these pieces a recourse to an older style of cadential formula, and the tendency of the upper two parts to proceed in parallel thirds and sixths. If one were to consider only the cantus and tenor of these pieces (the reverse of the process already evident in the Panc. 27 version of 'O Jesù dolce', where a third lower part was added to an original two-part setting), with the text (quite easily) applied to the tenor as well, the resulting pieces would closely resemble ornamented versions of such two-part laude as 'O Jesù dolce' (Music Example 8). To put it more directly, these simpler, two-part laude may have offered to able singers the option of a basic musical framework which could be embellished in performance according to a long tradition of improvised ornamentation, a tradition which in the Veneto was occasionally committed to notation. Rubsamen observed that the florid style of the *Justiniane* he examined was rooted in a Trecento melismatic tradition that had been carried over into the early fifteenth century to be cultivated on a more harmonic basis.[110] In fact, the continuity of this tradition is evident in the similarity of melodic stereotypes between the *Justiniane* repertoire and those of the Trecento polyphonic and lauda repertoires. Also significant in this context is the evidence that the above mentioned 'corone' that tend to appear in musical settings of Giustiniani laude might have been indications for improvised embellishment.[111]

Of the four *Justiniane* (all *canzonette*) identified by Rubsamen, three served as *cantasi come* models for Florentine laude and are especially well represented in mid fifteenth-century *cantasi come* sources.[112] In particular,

[109] Rubsamen, 'The Justiniane', 177.

[110] Ibid., 178. The florid style, which according to Rubsamen is evident in Italian sources until *c*.1475, is also apparent in several pieces in Ven: 'O Francisce, pater pie' (VenI, fos. 36ᵛ–37ʳ), and 'O dolce amor Yhesu' (VenII, fos. 129ʳ–130ᵛ; attr. to Giustiniani), which is more neumatic in style, but appears to be an originally melismatic melody in the style of the *Justiniane*, but with added text.

[111] Warren, 'Punctus Organi'. One of these pieces, 'Mercè te chiamo', was considered by Rubsamen to be a *Justiniana* that might be ornamented in the manner of the Petrucci pieces. The piece appears not only in two important lauda sources, MC and BU, but in the Escorial MS in which Rubsamen located the unornamented version of his *Justiniana*; 'The Justiniane', 177, 183.

[112] 'Aimè sospiri' is listed in Gall² as a *cantasi come* source for a lauda by Belcari, 'Omè, Signor, donami pace' (reconstructed by Luisi, *Laudario giustinianeo*, ii. 268–9). 'Io vedo ben ch'amore è traditore' (the initial strophe of which, 'Aimè, ch'a torto', is set in the Petrucci version), is listed in

'Io vedo ben che'l bon servire è vano' (for which Petrucci's incipit is 'Moro de doglia', the first strophe) was a *cantasi come* model for ten laude in Ch 266 and Gall[1]. Among these, a lauda by Belcari, 'Ave del Verbo eterno genitrice', was linked to the music of Giustiniani's *canzonetta* sometime before 1453.[113] Another *canzonetta* attributed to Giustiniani is referred to in Gall[3] as 'Donna esto mio lamento, Vinitiana', and served as a *cantasi come* source for four different laude, among them 'L'amor a me venendo' (Gall[2], 222).

The preceding discussion has outlined two fifteenth-century lauda traditions: the Venetian (strongly associated with the poetry of Giustiniani, and a written tradition of *modo proprio* musical settings), and the Florentine (much influenced by the Venetian, but dedicated to an unwritten musical tradition of *cantasi come* references).[114] However, the problem remains as to what extent this lauda repertoire was cultivated in the Florentine laudesi companies. Extant lauda collections of this period provide few clues; the musical sources emanate primarily from ecclesiastical institutions outside Florence, and the Florentine *cantasi come* sources appear to have been private collections. And in the more abundant fifteenth-century documents of the companies there are only scant references to lauda collections, compared to the numerous references among the sparser fourteenth-century documents. The burden of purchasing and maintaining laudarios may have shifted from the companies to the singers as manuscript books and, later in the century, printed books lacking notation and illumination may well have been within the means of individuals. What appear to be private lauda collections lacking any company affiliation may have been the personal collections of freelancing laudesi. Earlier in the century members also may have prepared and donated these private collections. A 1463 inventory of the Company of Santo Spirito listed 'one book of laude . . . with the signature of Piacito di Luca Piaciti'.[115] In 1467, the Company of Sant'Agnese owned five laudarios, one of them an illuminated book containing 'molte laude antiche', and another containing 'molte laude zolfate e fighurate basso'.[116] 'Laude antiche' most likely refers to a fourteenth-century repertoire, and implies that the other three

---

Ch 266, Ross. 424, and Gall[1] as a *cantasi come* source for another Belcari lauda, 'I' sento il buon Gesù dentro nel core' (Luisi, ii. 230–3). 'Chui dicesse e non l'amare' does not appear in the *cantasi come* sources.

[113] Ms. Magl. II. VII. 4, fos. 11[r–v]. 'Io vedo ben' was also a *cantasi come* source for another lauda in this manuscript, 'Ciaschun fedel cristiano', fos. 13[r]–13[v]. The manuscript belonged to a notary living in Castel San Giovanni and is dated by him 3 Dec. 1453; Luisi, *Laudario giustinianeo*, i. 132–3. 'Ave verbo' is listed in Gall[1] with the same *cantasi come* source.

[114] These two traditions are contrasted in an essay by Luisi, *Laudario giustinianeo*, i. 525 ff.

[115] SSP 78, fo. 44[v]: 'i libro del[le] lalde . . . chon sengno Piacito di Luca Piaciti'.

[116] SA 115, fo. 164[r]; Barr, *The Monophonic Lauda*, 186–7 n. 56, and ead., 'A Renaissance Artist', 110.

laudarios (and certainly the apparently polyphonic collection mentioned above) are more current, fifteenth-century collections.

The strongest evidence linking the repertoire of this period to the companies is circumstantial. Four of the Florentine *cantasi come* lauda poets were associated with the Company of San Zanobi, three of them as laudesi.[117] The most prolific lauda poet of the period was Feo Belcari, a pious layman who was associated with the Medici and served as a city prior in 1454. His father, a wool merchant also named Feo, served the company in the early fifteenth century, and Feo di Feo Belcari is first mentioned as a captain in 1436, and thereafter in the company *borsa* until 1444.[118] Belcari was evidently familiar with the Venetian lauda texts and the music associated with them, and through his numerous *cantasi come* references to Giustiniani poetry and music may have been a key figure in popularizing the Venetian repertoire in Florence, and certainly among the Florentine laudesi.

Finally, without evidence to the contrary, it might be assumed that the *cantasi come* laude and their musical settings passed into the laudesi company services since the performing forces of the companies matched the requirements of two- and three-part polyphony, and simply because the *cantasi come* practice was so pervasive in Florence. It is impossible to imagine that company members and the wide-ranging laudesi would not have been attentive to the latest styles of poetry and music, particularly in light of the influx of wealthier Florentines into the lay companies during this period.

c. 1470–1570

During the late 1460s the Florentine companies began to hire larger numbers of singers, and after *c.*1470 a stable practice emerged within each company of hiring small polyphonic choirs ranging in size from 5 singers (Sant'Agnese), 7–8 (San Piero Martire), 9–11 (San Zanobi, Santo Spirito), to 11–12 (Orsanmichele). The choirs were divided into two

[117] See Ch. 3, 'Company of San Zanobi'. Cristofano di Miniato, who sang for the company in 1456, wrote 'Vergine alta Regina' (attrib. in BN, MS Palatino 99), *cantasi come* 'Galantina Morosini' (Gall², 213; Mgl. VII. 30, fos. 65ᵛ–66ʳ). Ser Firenze sang for the company in 1483, as well as for San Piero Martire during 1471–80, and appeared in the documents of the church of Santissima Annunziata as a *maestro* 'che insegna le laude' in 1480–1; he is credited with 'Ben ch'adirato si mostri 'l Signore', *cantasi come* 'Questo mostrarsi adirato di fore' (Poliziano, Gall⁴; with music 'intonata da Bartolomeo organista', cf. Ghisi, 'Strambotti', 76); 'E' servi tuoi, Maria, vengono a te' (Gall⁴, MS Ross. 424, fo. 120ᵛ); and the *modo proprio* music for 'Conosco ben che pel peccato mio' (F. degli Albizzi, Gall² and Gall⁴; music in Razzi, 1563; Ghisi, 'Strambotti', 70) and 'Iesù splendor del cielo et vivo lume' (Savonarola, Ross. 424, fo. 202ʳ⁻ᵛ). Berto delle Feste sang for the company in 1494–5, and wrote 'La vita non mi piace' (Gall⁴).

[118] Feo di Jachopo Belchari, *lanaiuolo*, is recorded as a *sindaco* and *procuratore* for the company in 1405 and 1406; SZ 2183, fasc. 39, fo. 1ʳ, and 2171, fasc. 6A, fo. 25ᵛ. Feo di Feo di Jachopo Belchari: SZ 2186, fasc. 48, fos. 152ʳ, 153ʳ; 2177, fasc. 16, fos. 30ᵛ, 52ᵛ.

groups, designated as *sovrani* (or laudesi, and occasionally *fanciulli*) and *tenori*. The latter included tenors, altos, and, less often at first, basses. Boys and adult falsettists both sang alto and soprano, and certain adult singers were capable of singing either alto or bass.[119] The balance, typical of such choirs which were multiplying throughout Italian cathedrals and courts, favoured the highest voices: one or two each of the lower parts supported from three to six *sovrani*.[120]

This same period witnessed increasing numbers of clerics and *fanciulli* (probably clerically trained) in the laudesi chapels. In 1488 the Company of Santo Spirito hired four 'fraticini' as sopranos and two 'frati' as tenors, and for the next fifteen years recorded payments only to 'fraticini' and 'tinori'. During 1482–4 San Piero Martire paid seven *fanciulli* 'who sing the laude', and San Zanobi and Orsanmichele both hired Cathedral singers. This certainly reflects the establishment in the company services of three- and four-part singing, and with that, the advent of a written musical tradition. The waning of an unwritten lauda tradition in Florence inevitably reduced the role of the traditional lay singer, whose greatest asset had been a prodigious memory and experience of the repertoire, rather than formal musical training. However, lay singers adapted, as before, to the latest musico-poetic styles, and they continued to dominate the company payrolls. Laudesi services provided the early professional musical experience to a nascent school of native composers, such as Bernardo Pisano and Francesco de Layolle, and the companies were frequently served by independent laudesi choirs with lay *capomaestri* like Agniolo del Favilla, the weaver Piero da San Giorgio, and the tailor Bastiano di Tommaso Arditi.

Like the artisan singers, the unwritten musical tradition of *cantasi come* laude continued during this period. Belcari lived until 1484, and was the dominant poet in the four printed editions (Gall[1–4]) issued between 1486 and *c.*1508. In the early sixteenth century *cantasi come* sources a new

[119] In 1468, the singer Jachetto di Marvilla approached Lorenzo de' Medici about the re-establishment of the Cathedral chapel, offering '. . . to bring you a good tenor who has a large voice, high and low, sweet and sufficient; and three very high treble singers with good, full, and suave voices; and myself for contra[tenor]. And meanwhile, when we wish to sing *a quattro voce*, Bartholomeo could be the bass. And when we have arrived in Florence, we shall send to France for a contra[tenor] who is a good bass as well'; D'Accone, 'The Singers of San Giovanni', 324. Apparently, 3-part singing was still the norm at this time. The number and nature of the Cathedral singers is relevant to laudesi practices, for San Zanobi hired Cathedral singers prior to this time, and again beginning in the 1490s, and in matters of liturgy the companies frequently emulated ecclesiastical practices.

[120] The ratios of *tenori* to *sovrani* in the various companies were as follows: Sant'Agnese, 2:2 (1479), 3:2 (1489, 1494), 3:3 (1492, 1519); Santo Spirito, 4:6 (1486), 5:6 (1487), 4:2 (1488), 4:3 (1503, 1509); San Zanobi, 3:6 (1470), 5:6 (1475), 3:5 (1480), 3:4 (1481), 4:5 (1491, 1494, 1503); Orsanmichele, 6:5 (1508), 7:5 (1520). These numbers do not appear to have changed appreciably during the 16th c., except for an increase in the number of sopranos: Orsanmichele, 5:6 (1569, 1572), 5:9 (1574), 5:8 (1589–92), and a *maestro di cappella* and organist at all times.

generation of post-Savonarola poets emerged who had been strongly influenced by the Dominican friar's vision of a morally rejuvenated Florentine society.[121] Chief among these was Castellano Castellani (1461–1519/20), a Dominican theologian and follower of Savonarola.[122] Cattin has recovered a number of the *cantasi come* models of Castellani's laude; he observes in the *travestimento* process more rigorous criteria for the identity in versification and rhyme, possibly the result of a deteriorating tradition of memorization and the difficulty of relying upon a widespread familiarity with secular models drawn increasingly from the realm of written music.[123] Italian secular music itself was attaining a stable and written form at this time, and among Castellani's works 'it is difficult to find a lauda composed independently of a *carnascialesco* [carnival] text or a frottolistic composition'.[124] As at other times in the history of the lauda, this habitual recourse to secular music assured the sacred texts a broader circulation and a ready source of music, but the Savonarolan lauda poets sought a more complex end in the *contrafactum* process. The tendency of poets like Castellani to parody in a religious tone the carnival songs that were associated with the extravagant Laurentian period undoubtedly had been promoted by Savonarola, and he appealed to many of the Florentine Platonists who 'served and fought for [Savonarola] with the best weapons they had, with frottola, canzona, political tract, and philosophical dialogue'.[125]

It is in this large secular repertoire of the frottola that Pirrotta sees the surfacing, in the late fifteenth century, 'in written tradition of forms and modes which until then had been employed in oral tradition'.[126] The appearance of Florentine sources preserving musical settings of laude as well as the secular music to which the laude were linked by *cantasi come* indications was due in part to the development of conditions favourable to the cultivation of artistic polyphony. Franco–Flemish polyphony and

[121] Among these sources are Gall⁴ (Florence, *c.*1502–8), the first section of Ricc. Edizioni rare 196 (Florence, 1512), devoted entirely to the laude of Castellano Castellani; the second section of MS Ross. 424 (after *c.*1490), with laude by Castellani, Savonarola, 'il Tholosano', and fra' Roberto da Gagliano di San Marco (where Savonarola was prior). Other Savonarolan poets are Bernardo Giambullari and Girolamo Benivieni; Becherini, 'Musica italiana', 114–15.

[122] Cattin, 'Musiche per le laude de Castellano Castellano'; id., 'I "cantasi come" '. Castellani wrote laude, sonnets, and *sacre rappresentazioni*, among other works.

[123] 'Musiche per le laude', 185–6. Nevertheless, the lauda *contrafactum* (or 'travestimento spirituale') tradition continued well into the 17th c., when melodies of secular *arie* provided the lauda with music.

[124] Ibid. 186.

[125] D. Weinstein, *Savonarola and Florence: Prophecy and Patriotism in the Renaissance* (Princeton, NJ, 1970), 205.

[126] 'The Oral and Written Traditions of Music', in *Music and Culture*, 75–6. I use the term frottola here in one of the two senses in which it was used in the early 16th c., to refer generally to the secular forms in vogue at that time: the barzeletta (the frottola in the strict sense; the successor to the refrain form of the ballata), and the non-refrain forms of strambotto, sonnet, ode, and capitolo. On the forms, see W. Prizer, 'Performance Practices in the Frottola', *Early Music*, 3 (1975), 228.

performers were now familiar to Florentines, the Cathedral school commenced instruction in polyphony in 1478, and a new school of Florentine composers appeared shortly after this time.[127] But the musical style of the three- and four-part frottole and laude of the period was a consolidation of native stylistic tendencies evident in the earlier two-part works considered above, but with an expanded harmonic framework and greater formal symmetry.

The Florentine sources of lauda settings during this period are Panc. 27 (early sixteenth century),[128] and Razzi[1], the retrospective collection of one- to four-voice settings gathered by the Dominican friar Serafino Razzi in his *Libro Primo delle laudi Spirituali* (Venice, 1563).[129] Biblioteca Apostolica Vaticana, MS Ferrajoli 84 (*c.*1541–59) is a Tuscan source, probably from a Dominican convent, and contains only the melodies for laude by Castellani and others.[130] The major non-Florentine sources of lauda settings are Grey; MC; Paris, B. N., MS Rés. Vm^7 676 (1502);[131]

[127] D'Accone, 'Alcune note', 113–14.

[128] B. Becherini, *Catalogo dei manoscritti musicali*, 94. Becherini speculates that the repertoire of lauda settings in this manuscript, not found in other Florentine sources, is related to the memory of Savonarola; 'Musica italiana', 116. The closest source in shape and number of concordances (22) is Grey; Cattin, *Italian Laude and Latin Unica*, p. x. Like Grey, Panc. 27 is a retrospective collection of lauda settings compiled around the turn of the 16th c.

[129] *Libro Primo delle Laudi Spirituali da diversi eccell. e divoti autori, antichi e moderni composte. Le quali si usano cantare in Firenze nelle chiese dopo vespro o la compieta con la propria musica e modo di cantare ciascuna Laude, come si è usato da gli antichi, et si usa in Firenze. Raccolte dal R. P. Fra Serafino Razzi Fiorentino, dell' ordine de' Frati Predicatori. Con Privilegij della Illustriss. Signoria di Venetia, et del Duca di Firenze, et di Siena. In Venetia, ad instantia de' Giunti di Firenze. M. D. LXIII* (repr. Bologna, 1969). 92 laude (*c.*70 anonymous), with music for 1–4 voices. Many of these works appear in a later collection, *Santuario di Laudi, o vero rime spirituali per le feste di ciaschedun santo . . . composte dal Padre F. S. Razzi del Sacro Ordine dei Predicatori . . . Firenze, appresso Bartolomeo Sermartelli e Fratelli, 1609*. Many of the *cantasi come* indications are directed to a music supplement at the back of the collection containing 31 settings for 1 and 2 voices. Florence, BNF, Palatino 173 is Razzi's autograph of both texts and music in four books dated between 1586 and 1596. Razzi's taste as editor was eclectic: some of the 2-part settings are over a century old (e.g. Music Example 8), while the 4-part settings are related to the more recent style of composers like Verdelot; see Fabbri, 'Laude spirituali di travestimento nella Firenze della Rinascenza', 154; and C. Barr, 'The Ubiquitous Fra Serafino Razzi: Some Thoughts on his travestimenti spirituali', *The Musical Quarterly*, forthcoming. Many of the texts in the above collections not authored by Razzi himself are by his contemporaries at San Marco, an important centre of lauda poets since the priorate of Savonarola. As a theologian, Razzi also made a considerable contribution to Counter-Reformation theological literature.

[130] A. Ziino and F. Carboni, 'Laudi musicali del XVI secolo: il manoscritto Ferrajoli 84 della Biblioteca Apostolica Vaticana', *Cultura neolatina*, 33 (1973), 273–329. Monodic versions preserved here and in later sources of 'laude filippine' (a Counter-Reformation lauda tradition established in Rome by Filippo Neri at the Congregazione dell'Oratorio), such as Matteo Coferati's *Corona di sacre laudi* (Florence, 1675, 1689, 1710), were probably intended for soloistic performance with organ accompaniment. This practice of soloistic lauda-singing 'in sul organo' was cultivated in clerical services at Santissima Annunziata and Santa Maria Novella in the 16th c., and perhaps at the Company of San Frediano in the late 15th c., but among the Florentine companies part-singing seems to have prevailed, even when an organist was involved, as at Orsanmichele in the late 16th c.

[131] A performance manuscript from the Mantua/Ferrara region. N. Bridgman, 'Un Manuscrit italien du début du XVIe siécle à la Bibliothèque Nationale (Département de la musique, Rés. Vm^7

Perugia, Biblioteca Comunale Augusta, 431 (G 20; *c.*1490);[132] Udine, Biblioteca Comunale, MS 165, fondo Joppi (*c.* 1500)[133] and, above all, the two Petrucci lauda prints, Petrucci[1,2] (Venice, 1508).[134]

The music of both the *modo proprio* settings in the above sources and the traceable *cantasi come* sources of laude is homophonic, faithful to the phrasing and declamation of the text, extremely economical with respect to the music provided for the poetic form, and primarily in three and four parts. Cattin has located the music for about thirty of Castellani's fifty-four attributable laude with *cantasi come* indications, much of which can be found in Razzi 1563 and a major source of secular polyphony by Florentine composers, BNF, Banco Rari 230 (*c.* 1500).[135] The latter contains an anonymous three-part setting of 'I' son più mal maritata', the well-suited *cantasi come* source of Castellani's lauda 'Pecorelle pien d'errore, ritorna'.[136]

The advent of the newer three- and four-part frottola style is evident in the later settings of the four Giustiniani laude discussed above. In each case, the music of the older two-part settings has been displaced by entirely different settings for three and four voices contained in the above musical sources. The settings of 'L'amor a me venendo' in Petrucci[1] (4[4]; by Dammonis) and in Razzi[1] (3[3]; Music Example 7) are models of musical economy.[137] Dammonis provides twelve measures of music, of which measures 9–12 are derived from measures 5–8. Only the first two

676)', *Annales musicologiques*, 1 (1953), 177–267, with corrections and additions in *Annales musicologiques*, 4 (1956), 259–60; W. Prizer, 'Paris Bibliothèque Nationale, Rés. Vm.⁷ 676 and Music at Mantua', *Atti del XIV Congresso della Società Internationale di Musicologia, Bologna, 1987* (Turin, 1990) ii. 235–9.

[132] A. Atlas, 'On the Neapolitan Provenance of the Manuscript Perugia, Biblioteca Comunale Augusta, 432 (G 20)', *Musica disciplina*, 31 (1977), 45–105.

[133] Containing 2- , 3- , and 4-part laude by Pietro Capretto (Petrus Hedus), intended for performance by a Paduan *disciplinati* company. Discussed in Cattin, 'La lauda in ambiente veneto e le composizioni di Pietro Edo', delivered at the Convegno internazionale di studi per il V centenario della nascita di Giorgione (Castelfranco Veneto–Asolo, 1978). The music is ed. by Luisi, ii. 306–15.

[134] Petrucci[1]: *Laude Libro Primo. In. Dammonis Curarum dulce lenimen. Impressum Venetiis per Octavianum Petrutium Forosemproniensem. M. D. VIII* . . . This volume is dedicated entirely to the compositions (his only known music) of Frate Innocentius Dammonis, a member of the Congregazione di San Salvatore in Venice; Luisi, *Laudario giustinianeo*, i. 528; the previously unedited works of Dammonis (including some rather elaborate polyphonic laude in 4 and 6 parts) are edited in Luisi, ii. 316–65. For a recent excellent discussion of Dammonis' laude, see J. Glixon, 'The Polyphonic Laude of Innocentius Dammonis', *Journal of Musicology*, 8 (1990), 19–53. Petrucci[2]: *Laude Libro Secondo, Impressum Venetiis per Octavianum Petrutium Forosemproniensem. M. D. VII* [1508 NS]. Most of the above repertoire is edited, with a long introductory essay, by K. Jeppesen, *Die mehrstimmige italienische Laude um 1500* (Leipzig, 1935; repr. Bologna, 1971).

[135] Olim Mgl. XIX. 141; B. Becherini, *Catalogo dei manoscritti*, 60 ff. According to the numbering in Cattin, 'Musiche per le laude di Castellano Castellani', BR 230 contains 3- and 4-part music for 9 Castellani laude (nos. 2, 7, 14, 25, 27, 33, 46, 47, 51), Razzi contains music for 11 Castellani laude (nos. 6, 8, 10, 15–17, 28–9, 39, 44, 46), as well as 4 *modo proprio* settings (nos. 28–9, 32, 49), and Petrucci *Laude* I contains 1 *cantasi come* source (no. 8) and 2 *modo proprio* settings (nos. 9, 44).

[136] Cattin, 'Musiche', 219–29, where this and several other musical settings are edited.

[137] The Dammonis version is published in Jeppesen, *Die mehrstimmige italienische Laude*, 152, and Luisi, *Laudario giustinianeo*, ii. 56.

lines of the refrain are set, but the music is intended to serve the four-line refrain and the eight-line strophes (of which there are eight). Razzi, on the other hand, provides sixteen measures of music for the entire refrain, which is then repeated for the strophe (Music Example 7, mm. 1–9 for the first six lines, mm. 10–16 for the final two). Among the later settings of 'O Jesù dolce', the two-part setting in Razzi[1] is derived, with significant variants, from a much older fifteenth-century version, and the Panc. 27 version provides an updated version of similar music by the addition of a third lower voice which provides harmonic support (see Music Example 8). Dammonis provided a new and relatively spacious setting in Petrucci[1], with music for the entire refrain, and repeat indications for the strophe (Music Example 9: mm. 1–20 for the first four lines, the two *mutazioni*; mm. 21–33 for the next two lines, the first *volta*; and mm. 34–46 for the second *volta*). Panc. 27 provides two new settings of 'Con desiderio io vo cercando'; a three-part setting (also in Grey) and a four-part setting, each of the entire strophe and, like other laude in this manuscript, with the text provided only for the cantus.[138] Yet another setting in Grey, for four voices, provides music for the first three lines of the strophe.[139] Finally, a four-part setting of 'Madre che festi' by Dammonis provides new music for the entire strophe.[140] Gall[1] (p. 1) indicates that the text of 'Madre' could be sung to the music associated with Belcari's lauda, 'Da che tu m'hai Dio il cor ferito', of which there survives both a four-part setting by Dammonis and a two-part setting by Razzi.[141]

It seems fairly certain in this period that the polyphonic ensembles of the laudesi companies, in which many trained singers participated, were capable of performing *a libro* the repertoire discussed above. The companies of San Zanobi and Orsanmichele hired a *maestro di cappella* whose obligations included teaching laude.[142] As in the previous period, the performing forces of the Florentine companies match the requirements of the contemporary repertoire. The Udine manuscript discussed above contains a more polyphonically complex repertoire of three- and four-voice laude by Petrus Hedus which were performed by a lay company in Padua. There is also some evidence that the companies may have used (or continued to use) *cantasi come* lauda collections during this period. In

---

[138] Both are ed. in Luisi, *Laudario giustinianeo*, ii. 30–3; and the 3-part setting is ed. in Cattin, *Italian Laude*, no. 22.

[139] Luisi, ii. 34–5, and Cattin, *Italian Laude*, no. 5.

[140] Ed. in Luisi, ii. 61–2, and Jeppesen, *Die mehrstimmige italienische Laude*, 126 (no. 75).

[141] The Dammonis setting is ed. in Luisi, ii. 180–1, and Jeppesen, *Die mehrstimmige italienische Laude*, 100–1. The Razzi setting of 'Madre' is edited by Becherini, 'Musica italiana', 117. A musical setting of Belcari's 'Da che tu' (probably the Razzi version) was also the *cantasi come* source for a Castellani lauda, 'Da che tu m'hai, Gesù, mostro la via'; ed. in Cattin, 'Musiche', no. 8.

[142] Ch. 3, nn. 45 and 99.

1569, Orsanmichele recorded a payment to Ser Jacopo di Raffaele from Campi for '. . . 230 laude copied by him in [the] new book of the said oratory at the rate of s. 13 d. 4 for each lauda . . .',[143] and it is unlikely that such a large collection of texts afforded space for musical notation as well.

Polyphony in Florence was not under the exclusive patronage of courts, as in most other principal Italian cities, and D'Accone has noted that 'thus reflecting the democratic aspirations of the city, polyphony in Florence lost its restrictive associations and eventually came to form a part of even the ordinary citizen's cultural interests'.[144] This popularization of polyphony is impossible to imagine apart from the highly visible and numerous performances of the Florentine laudesi companies, and it is equally difficult to imagine that they did not draw upon the written and unwritten repertoires discussed above. Lauda-singing was entirely in the hands of clerics by the end of the sixteenth century, at which time the Counter-Reformation had given a new impetus to this ancient practice, but the numerous printed collections that continued to appear throughout Italy in the seventeenth century were a faint echo of the lay practice that had thrived in another age.[145]

[143] OSM 31bis, fo. 58ᵛ [1569]: '. . . a ser Jaco[bo] Raphaelis de Campio . . . pro laudibus n° 230 per eum scriptis in libro novo dicti oratorii ad rationem s. 13 d. 4 pro quolibet lauda . . . L. 153 s. 6 d. 8'.
[144] 'The Singers of San Giovanni', 350.
[145] A complete list of these sources is provided in Luisi, *Laudario giustinianeo*, ii. pp. xxiii–xxviii. Some of them are briefly surveyed by W. Prizer, 'Lauda spirituale,' *The New Grove Dictionary*, x, 542, and Fabbri, 'Laude spirituali di travestimento', 149–58.

5

Ritual Space and Imagination

LAUDA-SINGING AND DEVOTION

LAUDA-singing was premised on a belief that was characteristic of devotional religion in early modern Europe, a belief in the ability of the sacred to 'materialize' itself. At root was a 'sacramental view of the world, in which grace was expressed in material forms', with the consequence that the power of the sacred could be imputed to objects and thereby transmitted to humans.[1] This concrete and familiar quality of the sacred infused laudesi devotion with a strong orientation to the particular and the local. Divine power, or *virtù*,[2] was manifested in certain objects or places, and therefore a laudesi company was affiliated with a particular church, and conducted its lauda-singing devotions at specified altars, before certain images, and in relation to individual saints with whom the company cultivated essentially personal relationships. Only through such a specific, carefully maintained ritual locus could sacred *virtù* and human devotion (lauda-singing) be effectively exchanged in the kind of contractual relationship that was familiar to Florentine merchants and artisans. In such a world, the average Christian 'based his hopes on a personal relationship to a proven source of power in a world of localized *virtù*'.[3]

The great Florentine churches were the most obvious manifestations of this localized *virtù*, for their walls contained the sacred images, consecrated altars, relics of the holy dead, and the prayers and sacraments administered by the holy living. Proximity to these, both in life and

---

[1] Scribner, 'Interpreting Religion in Early Modern Europe', 94. See also R. Kieckhefer, 'Major Currents in Late Medieval Devotion', 81, where he contrasts liturgical religion (associated with special times) and contemplative religion (which transcends time and place) with devotional religion, which 'attends mainly to the veneration of sacred places or to the objects that make these places holy. Relics, images, and consecrated Hosts are the mainstay of devotional practice'.

[2] *Virtù* is used here in the same (and now obsolete) sense given as the first definition of the English 'virtue' in the *Oxford English Dictionary* (2nd edn., Oxford, 1989): 'the power or operative influence inherent in a supernatural or divine being'. This is in contrast to a later, Renaissance usage denoting both moral worth (*honestas*) and inner, personal strength; J. Seigel, 'Virtù in and since the Renaissance', in *Dictionary of the History of Ideas*, ed. P. Wiener (New York, 1973), iv. 476–86.

[3] Trexler, 'Florentine Religious Experience', 29.

death, was highly desirable, and the laudesi companies were typically affiliated with the greatest Florentine centres of sacred power.

The companies usually owned several sepulchres in the church, either beneath the vaults of the church (Santa Croce), in front of the chapter room (Santo Spirito), next to the campanile (San Zanobi), or, preferably, near the main altar (Sant'Agnese).[4] Business meetings and the *scuole* might be conducted beneath the vaults in the refectory, or in an oratory, sacristy, or another room within the church equipped with an altar. The monthly processions and the lauda services, which papal and episcopal indulgences stipulated must take place in a church, occurred at an altar patronized by the company, or less often at another altar determined by a bequest or a special liturgical occasion.

Nearly every Florentine laudesi company was the patron of an altar, sometimes two, within its host church. A company's relationship to an altar was often intensified by the presence of relics associated with the company's patron saint, which underscored the role of these companies in promoting the special saints of their host church.[5] The location of the altar varied among companies, and might be found in the nave, transept, or apse. The companies' ongoing expenses for construction, repair, and decoration on the one hand, and on the other for liturgical accessories, clergy to recite Masses and Offices, and for their own lauda vigils, reveal a breadth of activity that embraced the responsibilities of both patron and chaplain.

The laudesi companies' relationship to their images was among the most intense expressions of localized *virtù* in this society. A company's painting of the Virgin or another saint was its most important possession, and great care was given to the commission and maintenance of the painting, and above all to the lauda-singing devotion that contributed directly to the efficacy of the image. Trexler has stressed this reciprocal role, noting that Florentines were conscious of their role as supplicants in a relationship whereby devotion to an image tapped, as it were, the divine power with which such holy objects were believed to be laden.[6] Such a perception was, furthermore, particularly mercantile:

A belief that succor was to be found by manipulation of the physical image, by gifts in exchange for favours, and a belief that a change in emotional states was due to the same image were natural to a practical merchant society based on *ragione*.[7]

---

[4] St Antoninus gave three reasons for the desirability of intramural burial: the intercession, the church's patron saints, the prayers of the faithful provoked by the sight of the tombs, the assurance of a rest undisturbed by demons; *Summa Theologica* (Verona, 1740; repr. Graz, 1959), 3. 10. 3.

[5] The foot of St Agnes was kept in a reliquary on that company's altar in Santa Maria del Carmine, and the head of St Zenobius (who was buried in the crypt of the Cathedral) reposed in a reliquary on the altar of the Company of San Zanobi.

[6] Trexler, 'Florentine Religious Experience', 23.   [7] Ibid. 33.

The power of an image was sustained by devotion, the strength of the devotion by the sacredness of the image.

Images were firmly placed before the eyes of lay worshippers when the Synod of Trier declared in 1310 that an image or picture of some kind should be installed on or behind every altar.[8] The theological stance of the late medieval Church regarding images was framed by St Thomas Aquinas:

There is a twofold movement of the mind toward an image: one toward the image as a thing in itself, another toward the image insofar as it is a representation of something else . . . and it is in its latter capacity as a sign that reverence should be shown to an image.[9]

But in practice, especially lay practice, this 'twofold' distinction was not easily made. Theologians acknowledged that worship done to an image reached and terminated in the person represented, so that there was no practical distinction between the types of worship done to an image and a person; 'he who worships an image worships the reality of him who is painted in it' had been the position of the church since Nicea II (787).[10] Thomas himself maintained that in order for devotion to achieve its purpose, it must have a sensible human appeal, as well as sound dogmatic content; the need to concretize the spiritual in the sensible was a consequence of the fundamental unity of body and soul.[11]

From this perception of sacred image it was a short step to the widespread belief, not only of the laity, that the divine power of a saint could reside in the image itself, which might work miracles or possess sensory attributes.[12] Furthermore, devotion expressed through such acts as lauda-singing contributed directly to the *virtù* of the image. This interdependence between devotion and image is evident in Giovanni Villani's description of the miracles attributed to the Madonna of Orsanmichele:

. . . out of custom and devotion, a number of laity sang laude before this figure, and the fame of these miracles, for the merits of Our Lady, so increased that people came from all over Tuscany in pilgrimage, just as they come now for all

[8] 'Ut imagines Ecclesiae fiunt supra Altare. Praecipimus, ut in unaquaque Ecclesia ante vel post, vel super Altare sit imago, vel sculptura, vel scriptura, vel pictura expresse designans, et cuilibet intuenti manifestans, in cujus Sancti meritum et honorem sit ipsum Altare constructum.' Otto von Simson, 'Über die Bedeutung von Masaccios Trinität-fresko in S. Maria Novella', *Jahrbuch der Berliner Museen*, 7 (1966), 122 n. 9.

[9] *Summa Theologica*, 2a2ae, 84. 1–3; trans. A. D. Lee, 'Images, Veneration of', *The New Catholic Encyclopedia* (New York, 1967), vii. 372. For a 15th-c. formulation of this view, see St Antoninus, *Summa*, 3. 12. 9, col. 542.

[10] Lee, 'Images'.

[11] *Summa*, 1a2ae, 101.3 ad3; P. F. Mulhern, 'Devotions, religious', *New Catholic Encyclopedia*, iv. 834.

[12] Trexler, 'Florentine Religious Experience', 18–19.

the feasts of Our Lady, bringing various wax images, for great miracles accomplished.[13]

That Florentine citizens might thus influence, and even initiate, manifestations of divine power testifies to the personal and participatory nature of their worship, and to the strong contractual basis underlying all relationships in this society. St Thomas alluded to the proximity of sacred and secular relationships when he distinguished between two kinds of worship: *latria*, the adoration due to God alone, and *dulia*, the honour or homage due to distinguished persons, including Mary and the saints.[14] It is this contractual exchange of human devotion for divine power, of clientage for patronage, that was implicit in the laudesi activity of singing (or playing) before a devotional image. The act itself is made explicit in several Orsanmichele documents. The company's 1297 statute concerned with 'the feasts for which one ought to conduct vigils beneath the loggia of San Michele in Orto' stated that the captains 'are obligated to conduct the solemn vigils of lauda-singing before the figure (*figura*) of the Virgin'.[15]

A 1333 statute concerned with preaching beneath the loggia indicates that lauda-singing (which followed the preaching) was not the only activity directed to their famous Madonna, for in addition 'the laudesi are to be confessed every evening before the image of Our Lady upon the pilaster, [in the same way] as the laude are sung'.[16] The close relationship between music and devotion upon which laudesi devotion was premised is particularly apparent in the new musical service instituted by the company in 1387. As part of their duties, the municipal instrumentalists came on the major feast-days and Sundays 'to play devoutly and solemnly render *mactinata* [morning salutation] while the image of the gracious Mother of God is unveiled'.[17]

The devotional habits of the Florentines with regard to images show that sacred relationships were prey to the same instability that plagued secular ones. Writing in the 1380s, Franco Sacchetti was a member of Orsanmichele and therefore well placed to comment upon the Florentines' fickle devotions to images of the Virgin:

How many changes there have been in the figure of Our Lady! There was a time when everyone ran to Santa Maria Cingoli. Then one went to Santa Maria della Selva. Then the fame of Santa Maria Impruneta grew. Then at Fiesole to Santa Maria di Primerana, and then to Our Lady of Or San Michele. Then all were deserted.[18]

---

[13] G. Villani, *Cronica*, Bk. VII, 154.
[15] Ed. Castellani, *Nuovi testi fiorentini*, 669.
[17] See Ch. 3, 'Company of Orsanmichele'.

[14] Lee, 'Image', 372.
[16] La Sorsa, *La compagnia*, 199.
[18] Trans. in Trexler, *Public Life*, 70.

The popular pressure to acknowledge these images was considerable, and the mendicant orders drew the hostility of Florentines when they rejected the efficacy of the Orsanmichele Madonna.[19]

The secure place of images within the church, the widespread belief in their power, and the honour that came from owning an efficacious image help explain the widespread patronage of religious art in the society of republican Florence. The religious companies were important patrons, and Meiss was referring to the laudesi activity of singing before painted images of the Virgin when he claimed that 'no phenomenon of town life was more expressive of its democratic and lay tendencies, and none impinged more directly upon the art of painting'.[20] The Florentine companies usually owned more than one painting, and the images of various saints mentioned in company inventories were presumably used on special feast-days and may well have been commissioned through bequests. The Company of San Zanobi owned at least six paintings ('[i]magini') during the fourteenth century: an image of the Virgin and Child (1335), a St Andrew and a St Christopher (1358), and three more Virgins (1394), one with Sts Mary Magdalene and Margaret, one with Sts Nicholas and Francis, and one with Sts John the Baptist and Philip.[21]

Two of the greatest extant works of late medieval Florentine art were commissioned by laudesi companies. In 1285, the Sienese artist Duccio di Buoninsegna painted a Madonna for the Company of San Piero Martire (about 3 by 4.5 m.), which is currently in the Uffizi gallery under the title of the Rucellai Madonna; see Plate 3. The splendour and importance of this painting, both now and in its own day, testify to the prestige of the lay company that commissioned it.[22] The Madonna currently framed by Orcagna's luxurious marble tabernacle in Orsanmichele was painted for that company in 1347 by another major artist, Bernardo Daddi; see Plate 2. Both the Duccio and Daddi paintings, however, were created to function as devotional images, and their great artistic merit was probably inseparable from this function in the minds of the company members. Above all they served a ritual function as focal points of lauda-singing devotion, and their expense, craft, and beauty were intended to enhance the painting's potential as a channel of virtù.

---

[19] G. Villani, Bk. VII, ch. 154; Trexler, 'Florentine Religious Experience', 22.

[20] Meiss, Painting in Florence and Siena, 60.

[21] Orioli, Le confraternite, 33 (1335 statute); SZ 2170, fasc. 4, fos. 20ʳ–23ʳ (1358 and 1394 inventories). The St Andrew is attributed in the inventory to Giovanni Cristiani, and the St Christopher to Andrea di Donato.

[22] On this painting see the essays in P. B. Pacini et al. (eds.), La Maestà di Duccio restaurata (Gli Uffizi: Studi e Recerche 6; Florence, 1990); J. H. Stubblebine, Duccio di Buoninsegna and His School, 2 vols. (Princeton, 1979), i. 21–7; J. White, Duccio, Tuscan Art and the Medieval Workshop (London, 1979), 32–45, 185–7; B. Cole, Giotto and Florentine Painting: 1280–1375 (New York, 1976), 3–6, 32–4.

Such devotional Madonnas (of which every laudesi company certainly owned at least one) were characteristic expressions of the mendicant spirituality upon which laudesi devotion was based. Mary is the major figure in the painting, and she is depicted in her dual role as the very human, familiar *Mater Dei*, and, because of this special relationship to Christ, as the more exalted *Maria mediatrix*, the compassionate inter- cessor on behalf of humanity. As Meiss has noted, these devotional images appeared first in Tuscany during the late thirteenth and early fourteenth centuries, concurrent with the founding of the laudesi com- panies, and they

. . . embody in the most distinctive and novel way those tendencies apparent in all the art of this period to establish a direct, sympathetic, and intimate emotional relationship between the spectator and the sacred figures. They usually show only a few figures, who are outwardly quiet and inactive but involved in a very emotional—usually pathetic—relationship . . .[23]

These images also shed light on the interior, mental practice of devotion. The 'mental habit' of imagery, and its function in the creation of 'devotio', has already been alluded to with respect to the preaching techniques of the friars (Ch. 1), and one would expect to discover such a reciprocal influence between iconic paintings and devotion. The fourteenth-century Franciscan mystic and lauda poet Ugo Panziera da Prato described the process of devotional imagination in the following manner:

When the mind is, for a long period of time, concentrated on Christ, bringing Christ into the imagination, Christ does not permit himself to be divested of the corporeal virtue [being] called forth by the mind. The first time the mind begins to think of Christ, in these circumstances, Christ appears in the mind and the imagination as if written. The second time He seems to be outlined. In the third, He seems to be outlined and shaded. In the fourth, He seems painted and individuated. In the fifth, He seems individuated and modelled.[24]

In his reception-theory study of fifteenth-century Italian painting, Baxandall has described this relationship between the painter, 'a pro- fessional visualizer of the holy stories', and his pious public, who were 'practiced in spiritual exercises that demanded a high level of visualiza- tion'.[25] The particular practice common to mendicant preaching, devo- tional painting, and imaginative devotion was the selection and isolation

    [23] Meiss, *Painting in Florence and Siena*, 145, and K. Weigelt, 'Über di "Mütterliche" Madonna in der italienischen Malerei des 13. Jahrhunderts', *Art Studies*, 6 (1928), 195–221.
    [24] Trans. in R. Assunto, 'Images and Iconoclasm', *Encyclopedia of World Art* (New York, 1963), vii. 819. For a more detailed discussion of the relationship between image and devotion see Meiss, *Painting in Florence and Siena*, ch. 5.
    [25] Baxandall, *Painting and Experience in Fifteenth-Century Italy*, 45.

of an image, often drawn from a historical scene (as the Madonna and Child were drawn from the Nativity), which was to be dwelt upon in the imagination for the pious effect of the image upon the spectator.[26] A handbook called the *Garden of Prayer* (*Zardino de Oration*), written in 1454 and later published in Venice, explains the process of internal visualization that is necessary in prayer:

The better to impress the story of the Passion on your mind, and to memorize each action of it more easily, it is helpful and necessary to fix the places and people in your mind: a city, for example, which will be the city of Jerusalem— taking for this purpose a city that is well known to you. In this city find the principal places in which all the episodes of the Passion would have taken place—for instance, a palace with the supper-room where Christ had the Last Supper with the Disciples, and the house of Anne, and that of Caiaphas . . .

And then too you must shape in your mind some people, people well known to you, to represent for you the people involved in the Passion—the person of Jesus Himself, of the Virgin, Saint Peter, Saint John the Evangelist, Saint Mary Magdalen, Anne, Caiaphas, Pilate, Judas and the others, every one of whom you will fashion in your mind. When you have done all this, putting all your imagination into it, then go into your chamber. Alone and solitary, excluding every external thought from your mind, start thinking of the beginning of the Passion, starting with how Jesus entered Jerusalem on the ass. Moving slowly from episode to episode, meditate on each one, dwelling on each single stage and step of the story. And if at any point you feel a sensation of piety, stop: do not pass on as long as that sweet and devout sentiment lasts . . .[27]

The devotional paintings of the time, which frequently included smaller frames narrating the important events in the life of the Virgin or the saints, depicted the most dramatic and pathos-laden of these pious moments in Christian history.

The laude that were addressed to and devoutly sung before these images constituted a lyrical act of 'dwelling' upon the internal sacred image. The Marian laude, in particular, appeal directly to the imagination through frequent allusions to the concrete and sensuous:

Laude novella sïa cantata	Let a new lauda be sung
a l'alta donna encoronata!	to the exalted, crowned lady.
Fresca vergene donçella,	Fresh virgin maid,
primo fior, rosa novella,	first flower, new rose,
tutto 'l mondo a te s'apella;	all the world appeals to you;
nella bon'or' fosti nata.	in a blessed hour you were born.

---

[26] Meiss, *Painting in Florence and Siena*, 147. Kieckhefer also alludes to this link between devotional text, image, and imagination when he observes that 'even meditational reading is typically an aid to the exercise of meditation, in which attention is fixed on an image, perhaps an ivory diptych or a privately owned panel painting'; 'Major Currents', 81.

[27] Trans. in Baxandall, *Painting and Experience*, 46.

Fonte se' d'aqqua surgente,	You are a spring of water,
madre de Dïo vivente:	mother of the living God;
tu se' luce de la gente,	You are the light of the people
sovra li angeli exaltata.	exalted above the angels.
Tu se' verga, tu se' fiore,	You are the branch, you are the flower,
tu se' luna de splendore: . . .	you are the moon of splendour;. . .
tu se' rosa, tu se' gillio,	You are the rose, you are the lily
tu portasti el dolce fillio . . .	you bore the sweet son . . .[28]

The lauda to St Catherine of Alexandria, 'Vergine donzella', draws on the *Legenda aurea* in the narration of scenes from her life (her famous martyrdom), such as might appear in the predella of an altar painting:

Stando nel palaçço gratïosa,	dwelling graciously in a palace
tutta fosti de Dio amorosa,	you were all beloved to God;
. . .	. . .
Un crudel tiranno pien d'errore	A cruel despot full of error,
per la terra mandò el banditore	sent a crier through the land
ke ciascun venisse a falli honore,	that all should come to honour him
. . .	. . .
ke venissar a dà llo tributo	that they should come to give tribute,
al suo dïo k'era sordo e muto:	to his god who was deaf and dumb;
. . .	. . .
E lo 'mperadore sacrificando,	and as the emperor sacrificed,
tutta l'altra gente sequitando,	[and] the other people followed,
la Katerina udio metter lo bando,	Catherine listened to the proclamation,
e mantenente fo maravelliata.	and was immediately astonished.[29]

Another lauda honouring all saints, 'Facciamo laude a tutt'i santi' (see Plate 1), portrays the 'celestial court' much as it might have been depicted in a fourteenth-century painting of the Virgin's Assumption:

Facciamo laude a tutt'i santi	Let us praise all the saints,
colla Vergene maggiure,	and the supreme Virgin,
de buon core cum dolçe canti,	with a good heart and sweet songs
per amore del Creatore.	out of love for the creator.
. . .	. . .

[28] Cort, no. 2, lines 1–12, 15–16 (Varanini *et al.*, *Laude cortonesi*, i/1, 90–1). The English translations in this and the following examples are taken, with a few changes, from C. Barr, 'The Laude Francescane and the Disciplinati of Thirteenth Century Umbria and Tuscany: A Critical Study of the Cortona Codex 91', Ph.D. thesis (Catholic University of America, 1965). The music and text of this lauda are also edited in R. Hoppin, *Anthology of Medieval Music* (New York, 1978), 103–4.

[29] Text and melody in Cort, no. 17, lines 11–12, 19–30 (Varanini *et al.*, *Laude cortonesi*, i/1, 154–7) and Mgl¹, no. 84 (Liuzzi, *La lauda*, ii); text alone in Mgl², Aret, Ars.

Ferventissimo Segnore,	Most fervent Lord
ke li sancti ài rimflammati	who inflamed the saints
et de gloria et d'onore	with glory and honour, you
tu li ài 'n ciel encoronati,	have crowned them in heaven.
constituisti, redemptore,	You created a redeemer
nei perpetui imperïati,	in the everlasting empire
vivendo dëificati	to live deified
con teco, alto 'mperadore.	with you, exalted emperor.
. . .	. . .
Tutta gente dican 'ave!'	Let all mankind say 'hail'
a la Vergene dei sancti,	to the Virgin, mother of the saints,
k' ella ingemgnosa kiav'è	for she is the ingenious key
ke li serra tutti quanti;	that encloses them;
ell'è porto lor suave,	she is their sweet harbour
ell'è stella de l'irranti:	she is the star of travellers;
tutta la celestial corte	all the celestial court
la resguard'a tutte l'ore.	gazes upon her continually.
Innanzi al throno imperiale	Before the imperial throne
stanno i quatro vangelista,	stand the four evangelists,
per la luce supernale	in the divine radiance
tutta la corte [n'a] vista	beheld by the entire court
che laudan perpetuale	which eternally praises
lo segnore col Batista;	the Lord with the Baptist;
'alleluya, alleluya,	'alleluia, alleluia,
agnus Dei et pastore'.	Lamb of God and shepherd'.[30]

Perhaps only the image of the crucifixion was as firmly fixed in the mind's eye of preachers, painters, and lay worshippers as this one of the Virgin enthroned. Here her dual role as nurturing mother and compassionate intercessor is exalted and rendered most apparent, and this detail from the celestial scene of her Assumption is the very subject of enthroned Madonnas such as those of Duccio and Daddi. Less apparent to the modern eye, but very much a part of this heavenly scene, was the 'canto celestiale' that accompanied it. In his *Legenda aurea*, Jacobus de Voragine quotes St Jerome when the latter describes 'with what songs she was led to her throne'.[31] Angel musicians were often included in

[30] Text and music in Cort, no. 42, lines 1–4, 13–20, 29–36 (Varanini *et al.*, *Laude cortonesi*, i/1, 294–6), and Mgl¹, no. 87 (the final stanza above, which does not appear in Cort, is taken from Mgl¹, lines 21–8, ed. in Liuzzi, *La lauda*, ii).

[31] *La leggenda aurea*, trans. A. Levasti, 3 vols. (Florence, 1924), iii. 992; St Jerome, *De assumptione Mariae Virginis*, ed. in *Patrologia Latina*, xxx, col. 130: 'Quanto magis credendum est hodierna die militiam coelorum cum suis agminibus festive obviam venisse genitrici Dei, eamque ingenti lumine circumfuisse, et usque ad thronum olim sibi etiam ante mundi constitutionem paratum, cum laudibus et canticis spiritualibus perduxisse!' This text is discussed in relation to Duccio's Madonna in B. Santi, '"De pulcerima pictura . . . ad honorem beate et gloriose Virginis Marie": vicende critiche e una proposta di lettura per la "Madonna Rucellai"', in P. B. Pacini *et al.* (eds.), *La Maestà di Duccio restaurata*, 14. Cf. the partial transcription and translation of the Assumption lauda 'Chanto celestiale' in the introduction to Ch. 1.

depictions of the Virgin enthroned, but in the Duccio and Daddi Madonnas the spiritual songs came not from the silent, gazing angels, but from the company's lauda-singers. Participants in this sacred scene by virtue of their pious songs, the laudesi not only exchanged devotion for *virtù* before their images, but reconstructed the heavenly context of this image by continually re-enacting this most joyous and popular of religious tableaux.

ALTARS AND IMAGES

The right to build and decorate chapels and altars, and access to *intra muros* burial were central to the lay person's quest for spiritual authentication in republican Florence, and numerous Florentines rich and poor could acquire these through the lay companies.[32] Moreover, the laudesi companies in particular offered not only a popular and efficacious devotion, but a devotion that cultivated sacred relationships with the saints most popular among Florentines, above all the Virgin Mary, all of which assured that the particular altars and images of these companies occupied special and familiar places in the sacred landscape of Florence.

The Company of Orsanmichele

The Bernardo Daddi Madonna set in Orcagna's marble tabernacle is the only Florentine laudesi image that may still be viewed in its original setting, essentially unchanged since the fourteenth century (Plate 2). This locus was the most important and enduring centre of Florentine lay devotion, and that it was the focus of lauda-singing testifies to the significance of this particular devotion within the larger framework of Florentine ritual life.

The company's 1294 statutes describe the care with which its two original images, on pilasters beneath the open loggia of the grain market, were to be veiled and unveiled. The miraculous 'figura' of the Virgin, whose 'devotion always increases and multiplies and advances', was to be unveiled only after two candles had been lit, and to remain unveiled for only brief periods.[33] The 'tavola' of St Michael, apparently a painting, had suffered damage in the exposed location:

---

[32] For a detailed discussion, see J. Henderson, 'Piety and Charity', ch. 4, and more recently, 'Religious Confraternities and Death in Early Renaissance Florence', in P. Denley and C. Elam (eds.), *Florence and Italy: Renaissance Studies in Honour of Nicolai Rubinstein* (London, 1988) 383–94.

[33] Castellani, *Nuovi testi fiorentini*, 660–1, XIII: 'Anche ordiniamo e fermiamo a la reverenza de la detta nostra Domna Vergine Madonna Santa Maria, perchè sempre la sua devotione crescha e multiplichi e vada inanzi . . .'.

We also decide and establish . . . that because the painting of St Michael suffers dust and damage caused by the grain market and other things done in the said piazza beneath the loggia, the captains are obliged to keep it covered to conserve its beauty and [so that] it does not decay. Except that on Saturday after Nones, the market having dispersed, they should uncover it and leave it uncovered all day Sunday, and do the same for the solemn feast-days when the market is not held there.[34]

According to a 1333 statute,

The image of Our Lady ought to be covered with a fine and elegant veil or veils of silk; and after the preaching beneath the loggia, it ought to be uncovered and shown on the Sundays and feast-days deemed appropriate by the rectors and captains, with two lighted candles. And when visitors come who wish to see it, it should be uncovered with the permission of the [company] priest or a captain, and shown for a short time and then recovered.[35]

The 1297 and 1333 statutes concerning the Madonna actually refer to two different images, the first destroyed (or at least badly damaged) by a fire in 1304, but depicted in miniatures from the Biadaiolo Codex (Plate 4) and in an Orsanmichele account book (Plate 5), and the second now in the Oratorio di Santa Maria Maddalena in Pian di Mugnone.[36] The third Madonna executed by Daddi in 1347 was apparently intended to replace the second, and more closely resembles the first image.[37] Common to the first and third images, and absent from the second, are the shape and elaboration of the throne, the goldfinch in the left hand of the Child,[38] the kneeling posture of the angels, and the incense boats held by the two angels in the foreground; cf. Plates 2, 4, and 5. Implicit in these multiple depictions of the Orsanmichele Madonna is the belief that her image, while always expressed through a particular painting or fresco at any given time, at the same time transcended and was something more than that particular painting or fresco. The Madonna 'image' could survive the destruction of a material image, for its efficacy derived less from any quality inherent in the image than from the relationship conducted through it by means of devotional exercises.

[34] Ibid. 661.

[35] For a 1416 list of feast-days (and vigils) on which the image was to be unveiled, see Ch. 3, 'Company of Orsanmichele'.

[36] On the identification of the second image by W. Cohn, B. Cole, and L. Bellosi, see Fabbri and Rutenburg, 'The Tabernacle of Orsanmichele', 388 n. 18, and fig. 4. Copies of the first image also survive in frescos in the Santa Croce Museum and the Palazzo dell'Arte della Lana, as well as the Biadaiolo Codex and OSM 470; for bibliography see Fabbri and Rutenburg, 389 n. 30. The pre-Daddi image was attributed by Vasari (Le vite, ed. Milanesi, i. 455) to Ugolino da Siena (d. 1339).

[37] Fabbri and Rutenburg, 'The Tabernacle of Orsanmichele', 388–9.

[38] A symbol of the human soul that flies away at death, but also a reference to the legend that the goldfinch acquired its red spot when it drew a thorn from the head of the crucified Christ on Calvary, and was splashed with a drop of the Saviour's blood.

In addition to the Daddi Madonna, the 1340s brought to the company its first portable altar, dedicated to St Anne, whose immediately popular cult the company supervised after the expulsion of the Duke of Athens on St Anne's feast-day in 1343, and the commission of Orcagna's great tabernacle for the Daddi image. The tabernacle itself contains an elaborate decorative scheme of marble bas-reliefs, and the subject-matter of several of the scenes (particularly that of the Assumption) has been linked to texts of the laude sung by the company.[39] By 1367, when two more altars were constructed next to the tabernacle, the importance of Orsanmichele as a ritual site brought about the removal of the grain market, and the religious and civic importance of the company's famous Madonna was acknowledged when the commune made her the special protectress of the city in 1365, 1386, and again in 1388.

The company's considerable artistic and financial investment in the Orsanmichele Madonna was critical to maintaining devotional zeal at this site, for upon this the company's fortunes depended. Despite the decline in those fortunes after the fourteenth century, Vasari could report in the sixteenth that the company's oratory was still the site of a 'grandissima venerazione'.[40]

The Company of Santa Croce

Throughout the history of their presence in the great Franciscan church, the Santa Croce laudesi were situated in the north-easternmost chapel in the church. According to Moisè, the company was first located at the Bardi di Vernio chapel (Fig. 2, no. 1), then more permanently at what is now called the Niccolini chapel (Fig. 2, no. 2).[41] Beginning in 1439, a series of church *memoriali* describe this later location as 'the chapel in the corner (opposite the door of the sacristy), dedicated to the Virgin Mary, belonging to the Company of the Laude of the Virgin Mary'.[42] In 1470, the Archbishop of Florence renewed the company's forty-day indulgence for devotions conducted at the 'altare Virginis Marie'.[43] The only company images of which we have any knowledge are a large illuminated star that was suspended in the church on the vigil of the feast of the

---

[39] Fabbri and Rutenburg, 'The Tabernacle of Orsanmichele', 400.

[40] *Le vite*, i. 455.

[41] F. Moisè, *Santa Croce di Firenze: Illustrazione storico-artistica* (Florence, 1845), 416. See also Paatz, *Die Kirchen*, i. 503, 594, 604 and M. Hall, *Renovation and Counter-Reformation: Duke Cosimo and Vasari in Santa Maria Novella and Santa Croce 1565–1575* (Oxford, 1979), 157, no. 7, where documents are presented supporting the company's patronage of this chapel.

[42] M. Hall, *Renovation and Counter-Reformation*, 156–7: 'La chappella nel chanto (rimpetto alla porta della Sagrestia) e intitolata nella Vergine Maria è della Compagnia delle Laude della Vergine Maria'. All six sources cited by Hall are in agreement on the attribution of this chapel to the company.

[43] ASF, CmRS, Capitoli 53, cap. XII.

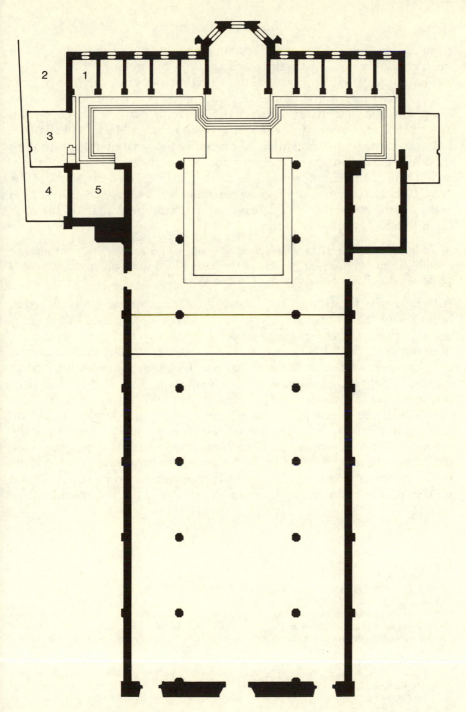

FIG. 2. Floor plan of Santa Croce

Assumption, which may have contained an image of the Virgin,[44] and the company's insignia, yellow crosses on a red field.

The company had abandoned lauda-singing by 1538, which must have weakened its traditional connection to this chapel. Beginning in 1565, Duke Cosimo and his architect/artist Vasari began a vast renovation project in Santa Croce paralleling their work in Santa Maria Novella.[45] In both cases, the renovation affected primarily the nave altars, and though the Santa Croce laudesi chapel was not among these, the same princely reshuffling of ancient patronage rights that had deprived the Santa Maria Novella laudesi of an altar was carried out in Santa Croce. Between 1579 and 1582 the company was deprived of its traditional altar by the next Grand Duke, Francesco Maria de' Medici,

. . . whom it pleased that the ancient site of our company might accommodate the illustrious Signore Giovanni of the most illustrious and most reverend cardinal Niccolini, so that a chapel might be made there.[46]

Allotted a new location by the Grand Duke, the company was forced to build a new residence just outside the church wall, 'in the place [Fig. 2, no. 4] between the chapel of the illustrious Salviati [Fig. 2, no. 5] and the illustrious Bardi and Gualterotti [Fig. 2, no. 3]'.[47] The company was certainly deprived of an altar in its new location, but was allowed to continue celebrating its *ufficio generale* on the feast of St Lucy, when they processed to the company's sepulchre 'in the middle of the church'.[48] By the turn of the century, however, the Santa Croce laudesi could no longer afford to meet the terms of the bequest that provided for the *ufficio*; in 1602 the company, complaining of minimal income, petitioned the friars to be relieved of *collazione* expenses for bread and wine, and the friars curtly reminded their lay *fratelli* of the precise amounts of bread and wine expected of them, short of which they could go find another place to sing.[49]

[44] Cf. Ch. 3, 'Company of Santa Croce'.

[45] M. Hall, *Renovation and Counter-Reformation, passim.*

[46] Appendix I, doc. 29. The date of the expulsion given in this document is 1579, but another source gives the date 1582 (ASF, CmRS 1373, no. 1, fasc. F, filza 6). The company appears to have actually vacated the site in 1582, and was probably notified three years prior and given time to make other arrangements.

[47] Appendix I, doc. 29.

[48] A 1439 *Sepoltuario di S. Croce* (ASF, Manoscritti 619, fo. 6ᵛ) records that 'sei sepolture sono della compagnia della Vergine Maria chiamata compagnia della laude . . . sanza numeri e segniato nel archo una + e per ogni corpo si mette in dette sepolture si paga soldi 20 a detta compagnia'; cited in Henderson, 'Piety and Charity', 131 n. 16.

[49] ASF, CmRS 1373, no. 1, fasc. F, filza 6.

The Company of San Zanobi

From its foundation in 1281, the company was situated in the old Romanesque church of Santa Reparata until no later than 1375, when the old church was destroyed after the new Cathedral had completely enclosed it. It is not known which altar in the old church was patronized by the company, but a 1335 statute mentions that their Madonna image was to be kept in a new tabernacle 'in the pilaster of St Bartholomew . . . in the middle of the nave', from where it was taken to the 'usual place' for services. The general location of the latter is indicated in an inventory compiled while the company was situated in the old Cathedral, which lists 'one lectern which is placed in the middle of the church where the laude are sung'.[50] The statute mentioned above offers a strong statement on the deference shown to this image by the company:

. . . we rectors establish . . . that on the pilaster of St Bartholomew in the said church of Santa Reparata in the middle of the nave, where Our Lady stands, there is to be made a wooden tabernacle as honourably beautiful as possible . . . The said rectors and chamberlains are obliged to protect and preserve and augment and improve the said tabernacle, [along] with the said figure of Our Lady, which they ought to augment and improve. And no one of the said company may touch or carry forth from the said tabernacle the said figure of Our Lady without the permission of the said rectors . . . And the said Lady may not be carried forth from the said tabernacle without procession, candles, and song . . . And so that [Our Lady] is carried to the altar in the usual place with more devotion and more people, it is to be carried on Saturday evening after laude are sung, or, if they [the officers] wish, on Sunday morning, with [all] the love and reverence that can be summoned.[51]

The figure, in this instance, was a carved image of the Madonna and Christ Child, and the tabernacle in which it was stored was equipped with a lock and key.[52]

The company's meeting-room and *scuola* were situated in a chapter room beneath the vaults of the old church, and in the south sacristy (the

[50] SZ 2170, fasc. 4, fo. 21ʳ [c. 1354–75]: 'Uno legio che ssi pone in mezo della chiesa la dove si canta le laude'. Although imprecise, the 'middle of the church' suggests an area near the main altar, or at least nearer this altar than the pillar upon which tabernacle and image were hung.

[51] Ed. in Orioli, *Le confraternite medievali*, 33. The Company owned two images of the Virgin kept in tabernacles—the *gonfalone*, which was painted with an Annunciation on one side and a Christ in Majesty on the other (and accompanied by two wooden poles, which were covered with gold crosses on a black background, the Company insignia, and used for carrying the *gonfalone* in procession), and a carved image of the Madonna and Child. The *gonfalone* was given the most deferential treatment, and both the 1326 and 1427 statutes prescribe the occasions when the tabernacle may be opened and the *gonfalone* carried forth in procession. A third tabernacle held a carved image of St Zenobius. SZ 2170, fasc. 4, fos. 20ʳ, 22ʳ.

[52] Such carved images appear to have been stored in tabernacles equipped with lock and key, as this one was, for they were probably more subject to theft than the large paintings.

canonry) of the new Cathedral; see Fig. 3, no. 1.[53] Both places were
equipped with an altar, and the sacristy in the new church included a
white altar-cloth, upon it a painting of the Virgin with Saints Mary
Magdalene and Margaret, a lectern 'where the laude are sung during the
scuola', and chairs in which the captains sat during the *scuola*.[54]

The company's 1428 statutes clearly indicate the location of the
company altar in the new church of Santa Maria del Fiore. The hired
laudesi were to come every evening and set up for the lauda service
'before the altar of Our Lady at the end of the church beside the great
door'.[55] The original Cathedral plans called for no altars outside of the
three large tribunes, but others arose under the pressure of spontaneous
popular devotions. In 1397, a committee of Cathedral *operai*, including
Franco Sacchetti, recorded a decision to move a fresco of the Madonna
and Child (Plate 6) from the wall west of the altar of St Victor (the first
altar in the south tribune) to a space of wall between the great door and
the door nearest the campanile; see Fig. 3, no. 2.[56] The original location
of the image was no longer convenient because of the crowds that had
grown along with the new devotion. An altar was constructed and given
a temporary wooden enclosure at this time, and became known, after the
name of the image, as the altar of Our Lady 'gratiarum plenissima'. The
altar was also fitted with a *baldacchino*, the image covered with a curtain
painted by Lorenzo di Bicci, and numerous subsequent decorations were
executed during the fifteenth and early sixteenth centuries.[57] By 1427 the
new altar was under the patronage of the lay brothers of the Company of
San Zanobi, the fitting overseers of a popular lay devotion to the Virgin.

During the feasts of the Purification (associated with the new Cathedral),
St Zenobius, and St Reparata (the patroness of the old Cathedral), the
lauda services took place at the altar of St Zenobius, the central altar of

---

[53] Orioli, *Le confraternite*, 35; Paatz, *Die Kirchen*, iii. 423–4; ASF, Manoscritti 625, fo. 1128ʳ.
[54] SZ 2170, fasc. 4, fo. 22ᵛ [1394 inventory].   [55] Appendix I, doc. 14.
[56] G. Poggi, *Il Duomo di Firenze* (Berlin, 1909), pp. cvi–cvii, and docs. 1004–6. Doc. 1004 [14
Dec. 1397]: 'Consiglio renduto a . . . operai della decta opera di sancta Reparata, pegl'infrascripti
cittadini, cioè Francho Sachetti [*et al.*] . . . sopra il provedimento e modo dell'adornare la figura di
nostra Donna ch'è in santa Reparata apresso della porta verso il cimitero e de l'altare di sancto
Victorio, e in che luogho si pongho più onorevole e acto. Consigliarono e dissono i detti cittadini di
comune concordia a' detti operai che alloro parea che la decta figura s'onorasse per la devotione che
vi cresce, e perchè il luogo ov'è non è acto, si levasse di quello luogho e ponessesi nella faccia della
chiesa dallato dentro tra le due porti della chiesa, cioè tra la porta magiore e la porta dalla parte del
campanile sopra ove sono al presente le due arche di marmo, cioè degli Adimari e de' Medici; e dove
sono l'arche si faccia uno altare circundato di bastoni al presente, tolte via prima le arche; e la detta
figura s'adorni con cielo d'assi di sopra e intorno, come parrà agli operai.'
[57] The *operai*'s decoration of the chapel is described and documented in Poggi, *Il Duomo*, pp. cvi–
cix, and Paatz, *Die Kirchen*, iii. 401–2. By the 18th c. the chapel had been rededicated to the
Immaculate Conception, and was subsequently destroyed in an 1841 restoration, at which time the
fresco was relocated to the chapel of St John, Evangelist and venerated as the 'Madonna dei Cherici';
Poggi, *Il Duomo*, p. cviii.

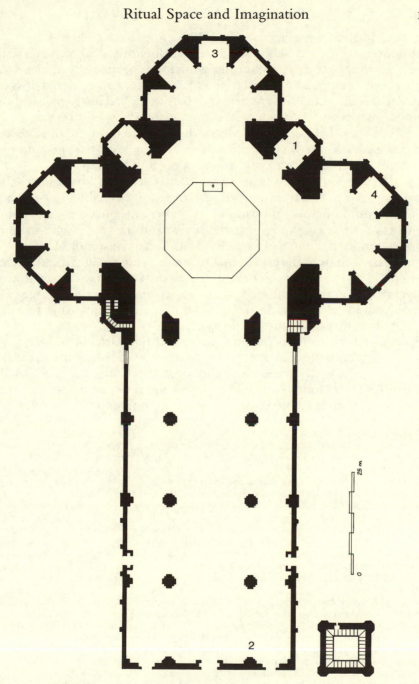

Fig. 3. Floor plan of Santa Maria del Fiore

the central tribune; see Fig. 3, no. 3.[58] Proximity to the relics of the city's first bishop, whose sepulchre was directly below this altar, was especially desirable on these occasions, during which the company's *gonfalone* was hung above the altar and a special lectern, laudario, embroidered dossals, and decorated candles were arrayed before it.[59] The *gonfalone* bore painted images on both sides, an Annunciate Mary on one side and a Maestà on the other, and included a cloth curtain and fringe, and a pair of wooden poles painted with yellow crosses on a black background (the company insignia) for carrying the banner in procession.[60]

The Baptistry of San Giovanni was also an occasional ritual site for the company. A 1353 statute set forth the terms under which a company member could borrow company property in order to 'conduct, out of their devotion, a lauda vigil for the praise and glory of some male or female saint, in the church of Santa Reparata or San Giovanni a Duomo'.[61]

In the new church, the carved image of the Madonna and its tabernacle were relocated on a column next to the altar of St Sebastian, the fourth chapel in the south tribune (see Fig. 3, no. 4), and the carved image of St Zenobius and its tabernacle were located on a column beside the altar dedicated to this saint (Fig. 3, no. 3).[62]

In addition to the six 'imagini' described in fourteenth-century inventories, several other images were acquired by the company in the late fifteenth century. Between 1487 and 1491 the Cathedral gave to the company a large, fourteenth-century painting in Byzantine style, which shows St Zenobius flanked by the Saints Eugenius and Crescentius, and

[58] SZ 2170, fasc. 1, fos. 51[r–v].

[59] The saint's relics were transferred from San Lorenzo to Santa Reparata in the 9th c., and were forgotten until their rediscovery in 1331 during the construction of the new Cathedral; G. Villani, *Cronica*, Bk. x, ch. 172; Poggi, *Il Duomo*, pp. xciv–xcv. If the company conducted its festal services at the St Zenobius altar in the old church, this altar was located in the lower level of the split-level chancel. In the new church, the company maintained an oil lamp before 'l'altare del glorioso Sancto Zenobio et sua sancta sepultura . . .', which probably refers to the crypt altar dedicated to St Zenobius; SZ 2170, fasc. 1, fo. 49[v].

[60] SZ 2170, fasc. 4, fo. 20[r] [1354 inventory]. The *gonfalone* was carried in procession only by captains, and only on the feast of the Annunciation and during city-wide processions and the visits of the important church prelates, and was removed to be hung above the altar of St Zenobius only on the feasts of that saint and the Purification. Otherwise it remained in its wooden tabernacle, which was opened only on a half-dozen prescribed feast-days; SZ 2170, fasc. 1, fos. 9[r] [1326 statute], 52[v] [1428 statute].

[61] Orioli, *Le confraternite medievali*, 35: '. . . Che qualunque persona della detta compagnia vuole o vora fare o far fare per sua devotione a laude et gloria d'alchuno sancto o santa vigilia di laude nella chiesa di Santa Reparata o di San Giovanni a duomo . . .'. On the eve of the feast of St John in 1396 the company recorded expenses to move a lectern and benches to the Baptistry (SZ 2171, fasc 6C, no. 5, fo. 246[r]), and in 1402 L. 1 was paid to the vielle-players Pagolo di Ser Ambruogio and Berzolla 'che sonorono a San Giovanni' (ibid., fo. 274[v]).

[62] SZ 2170, fasc. 4, fo. 22[r] [1394 inventory]: 'Una fighura intagliata di nostra Donna chol figliuo in chollo in uno tabernacholo di legniame dipinto in su una cholonna dietro all'altare di Sancto Bastiano . . . Una fighura di Sancto Zenobio intagliato in uno tabernacholo alla cholonna ch'è allato a Sancto Zenobio cioè all'altare di Sancto Zenobio'.

four small panels depicting events from the life of the saint; see Plate 7.[63] The painting hung above the altar of St Zenobius from at least 1475 to 1559, and probably until 1588, when the altar was rededicated to the Sacrament. In May 1486 the company commissioned Ser Piero di Lorenzo Ubaldini, a Cathedral chaplain and company member, to 'make a beautiful altar panel with an Annunciation and St John the Baptist and St Zenobius',[64] and in 1495 Andrea della Robbia executed a terracotta image of St Zenobius which was placed above the outside entrance to the company's meeting-room (the canonry, Fig. 3, no. 1).[65]

The Company of San Bastiano

The company's oratory was a small room located on the east side of the tribune in Santissima Annunziata, a room equipped with an altar and probably the site of its ferial singing; see Fig. 4, no. 1.[66] Although the location of any sanctuary chapels with which the company might have been associated is not known, two possible locations (by virtue of the chapels' dedications) are the St Sebastian chapel (Fig. 4, no. 2), and the fourth chapel on the right side of the nave, dedicated to St Gerard (a patron saint of the company) and the *Pietà*.[67]

The Company of San Lorenzo

According to Richa, the San Lorenzo laudesi were associated with the chapel of the Sacrament (probably the sixteenth-century title of this altar), located in the crypt of the church.[68]

The Company of San Piero Martire

The original ritual sites of the Florentine laudesi companies were probably temporary ones either in or near the great mendicant churches, which were under construction during the earliest period of these companies.

[63] G. Poggi, 'La tavola di San Zanobi nella chiesa di Santa Reparata', *Rivista d'arte*, 5 (1907), 112–17. According to Paatz, *Die Kirchen*, iii. 403–4, 415, this painting was located in the crypt at an original St Zenobius altar (*c.*1330–1439), and then at a new crypt altar below the tribune altar dedicated to this saint (1439–*c.*1487). The painting is now in the Museo dell'Opera del Duomo.

[64] SZ 2177, fasc. 18, fo. 159ʳ [May 1486]: '. . . a Ser Piero di Lorenzo Ubaldini chapellano di duomo ch' egli facessi fare una bella tavola d'altare chon una Nonziata e San Giovanni Batista e San Zanobi. . .'.

[65] SZ 2176, fasc. 14, fo. 35ᵛ; G. Richa, *Notizie istoriche delle chiese fiorentine*, vi. 107.

[66] Micali and Roselli, *Le soppressioni*, 74; Ricc., Moreniana 351, fo. 1ʳ. A 1520 inventory states that the company's reliquary was located in an 'armario posto nell'altare del nostro oratorio . . .'; ASF, CmRS, Capitoli 364, fo. 38ᵛ.

[67] Paatz, *Die Kirchen*, i. 79, 100.

[68] Richa, *Notizie*, v. 91; Paatz, *Die Kirchen*, ii. 517.

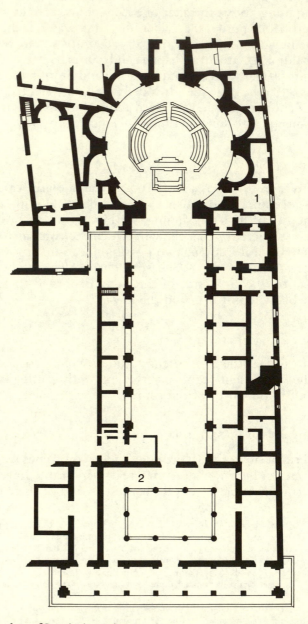

FIG. 4. Floor plan of Santissima Annunziata

The laudesi at Santa Maria Novella had commissioned their great altar painting from Duccio in 1285 (Plate 3), but from this early date the exact location of this painting and the company's ritual activities is unclear. This site has been assumed to be the easternmost chapel of the north wall, originally dedicated to St Gregory; see Fig. 5, no. 1.[69] The assumption is based on two entries in the company's records in 1316, neither of which makes the usual reference to 'la nostra cappella' or 'l'altare della compagnia', though the fact that the company furnished the chapel with a bench, floor-matting, and a metal grille would seem to indicate some kind of patronage link to the altar.[70] Another entry of that year implies that the laudesi performed directly beneath an arch at the entrance to a chapel, but does not specify which chapel.[71] Orlandi cited an equally inconclusive set of documents in arguing for the high altar as the painting's original site, while Irene Hueck has recently proposed that the late sixteenth-century location of the painting (discussed below), its earliest one that is certain, may well have been its location from the beginning.[72]

Whatever the company's relationship with the St Gregory chapel was in these early years, it would have been severed in 1335 when the estate of Riccardo di Ricco Bardi purchased the rights to the chapel from the friars for fl. 200.[73] Vasari reported in the sixteenth century that the Duccio Madonna (which he attributed to Cimabue) hung on the wall between the Bardi and Rucellai chapels; see Fig. 5, no. 2.[74] This was certainly a more spacious and advantageous site for this great panel, which could have been easily served by a portable altar. Given both the great size of the painting and the extreme competition with wealthy private patrons for the highly desirable chapels and altars in Santa Maria Novella, this

[69] J. Wood Brown, *The Dominican Church of Santa Maria Novella at Florence* (Edinburgh, 1902), 127; Stubblebine, *Duccio di Buoninsegna*, i. 21–7, where his argument that the Madonna hung on the left wall of the chapel is based on his reconstruction of the original decorative scheme of the chapel and the orientation of Duccio's painting to a view from the left. However, it is difficult to imagine singers, altar paraphernalia, and a large company of lay worshippers all able to worship before this image in such a location, and equally difficult to imagine such a large and expensive painting being commissioned for a location where it could not be seen to greater advantage.

[70] SMN 292, fo. 8ᵛ: 'per una pancha e per una as[s]e d'abete che si puose ne la chappella di San Ghirighoro per sedervi suso, e per ferri stagniati che si misero a l'uscio della detta chapella . . . L. 1 s. 11; Demo per una stuoia che si mise ne la chapella di San Grighoro . . . s. 4 d. 10'.

[71] SMN 292, fo. 8ʳ [1316]: 'Anche avemo ispeso in due [*sic*] che son al muro sula volta per istarvi a chantare le laude cho' l pio[m]bo . . .'

[72] S. Orlandi, 'La Madonna di Duccio di Boninsegna e il suo culto in S. Maria Novella', *Memorie domenicane*, 73 (1956), 205–17; I. Hueck, 'La tavola di Duccio e la Compagnia delle Laudi di Santa Maria Novella', in P. B. Pacini *et al.* (eds.), *La Maestà di Duccio restaurata*, 33–46, where she reviews the archival documents and Orlandi's argument, and argues against the high altar and the St Gregory chapel as appropriate and adequate sites for this painting. Recent assumptions about the company's patronage influence over the high altar area appear to be based on the above, inconclusive evidence; see Simons, 'Patronage in the Tornaquinci Chapel', 234, and C. Black, *Italian Confraternities in the Sixteenth Century* (Cambridge, 1989), 235–6.

[73] Wood Brown, *The Dominican Church*, 127.

[74] G. Vasari, *Le vite de' più eccelenti pittori, scultori, e architettori*, ed. K. Frey (Munich, 1911), i. 254.

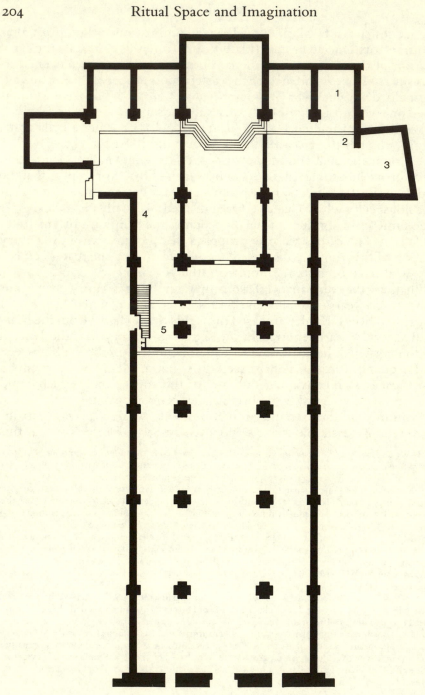

FIG. 5. Floor plan of Santa Maria Novella

site near the main altar which could accommodate both the company and its painting may well have been the company's ritual *locus* during the late thirteenth and fourteenth centuries.

In the mid-sixteenth century, however, Vasari was apparently unaware of the company's connection to the painting, and in the fifteenth century increasing references in company documents to the feast, altar, and patronage of St Peter Martyr indicate a shift away from traditional Marian devotion at the site of the Duccio Madonna towards the more specialized devotion of this Dominican saint.[75] Sources have identified this chapel with the Strozzi chapel (Fig. 5, no. 4), which was opposite a miraculous image of St Peter Martyr located on the outer, western wall of the choir.[76] However, the altar dedicated to the Dominican martyr appears to have been one of eight situated in the church's medieval rood-screen. According to a 1556 chronicle, the altar of St Peter Martyr, belonging to the Castiglione family, was on the lower level, 'on the pilaster towards the organ' (i.e., to the west); see Fig. 5, no. 5.[77] The destruction of the rood-screen (or *ponte*) during Vasari's renovation of the church beginning in 1565 undoubtedly led to the later confusion about the location of the altar, and Duke Cosimo's autocratic and preferential reshuffling of patronage rights at this time probably dislodged the company from its devotional locus for the second, and last, time.[78]

---

[75] 1447 statutes state that the company was to celebrate its Monday morning Mass for deceased members at the altar of St Peter Martyr (SMN 324, fo. 3ᵛ), and in 1373 the company recorded expenses for the repair and decoration of this altar (SMN 299, fo. 64ʳ). In 1494 the company had its 'libro delle laude di San Piero Martire' bound (SMN 301, fo. 171ᵛ). The company also referred to a 'new altar' in its residence (near the entrance to the cloisters on the west side of the sanctuary) in 1408, after which it recorded numerous expenses for the decoration of the 'altare della compagnia' (SMN 321, fo. 80ʳ; 295, fos. 165 ff.); very likely the company was celebrating its ferial services here, and its festal services in the sanctuary.

[76] Hall, *Renovation and Counter-Reformation*, 108, notes that the proximity of the image on the choir wall (destroyed in 1565) to the Strozzi chapel has led to the mistaken attribution of the latter as the altar originally dedicated to St Peter Martyr. This attribution was made in Niccolò Sermartelli's 1617 *Sepoltuario* (ASF, Manoscritti 621, fo. 29ʳ), and repeated by Wood Brown, 120, and Paatz, *Die Kirchen*, iii. 716.

[77] Orlandi, *Necrologio di Santa Maria Novella*, ii. 402–3, a transcription of V. Borghigiani, *Cronaca Analistica*, iii. 330–40, a 1556 description of the church interior prior to the Vasari renovation. Borghigiani relates that there were eight altars in the *ponte*, four on the upper level and four on ground level. On each level, two of the altars were situated against the inside wall of the nave, while the other two were directly opposite one another on the inside of the two large columns supporting the *ponte* (Hall's diagram, adapted in Fig. 5, shows these altars on the south side of these columns): 'Otto Cappelle o Altari v'erano, 4 sotto e 4 sopra al detto Ponte . . . ed al Pilastrone di verso l'Organo lo Altare di S. Pietro Martire della famiglia de Castiglioni, voltati di contro l'uno all'altro, come ora stanno i due quadri di S. Piero Martire e di S. Giacinto . . .'. With the exception of the main altar, all the altars in the church were enclosed with walls on the sides and fronted with a locking wooden gate, and included a built-in wardrobe within.

[78] According to the records of the convent's Opera, the entire *ponte* 'and all its chapels both above and below' were to be demolished, and four of the *ponte* chapels (which four is not specified) were

In 1617 the Duccio Madonna still hung in the location described by Vasari, but by 1681 it had been moved into the Rucellai chapel; see Fig. 5, no. 3.[79] It remained there until 1948 and came to be known as the 'Rucellai Madonna', but the company did not survive long enough to sing before its famous painting in this location.

The Company of Sant'Agnese

The Sant'Agnese laudesi retained a strong claim to their Carmine altars throughout their five-hundred-year existence, which makes their location a relatively easy task to determine. Probably from the foundation of the church, the company managed all aspects of decoration, repair, and liturgical devotions at the altar dedicated to St Agnes; see Fig. 6, no. 1.[80] In 1377 the company acquired the patronage rights to a second chapel through the bequest of the chapel's previous owner, the cloth merchant Chiaro d'Ardinghello.[81] The chapel of the Annunciation, 'detta la Seggiolina', was located at the rear of the church just to the left of the main door; see Fig. 6, no. 2.[82] The company's oratory (Fig. 6, no. 3) was not destroyed by the 1771 fire, and the remains of late fourteenth- and early fifteenth-century monochrome frescos indicate that the room was in use at least by that time. The two chapels and oratory in such proximity must have constituted one of the strongest and most coherent centres of lay devotion in Florence.

The company's fifteenth-century records show continual and significant expenses on altar renovation and decoration. Extensive work on the St Agnes chapel in 1437–8 included a 'nuova porta di Santa Angnesa del cimitero', indicating that the company had private access to a cemetery on the east side of the nave.[83] In 1467 a carpenter was paid

subsumed under a single title, and moved to another location; Hall, *Renovation and Counter-Reformation*, 167–8.

[79] Hueck, 'La tavola di Duccio', 33.

[80] The layout of the Carmine altars prior to a disastrous fire in 1771 was reconstructed by U. Procacci, 'L'incendio della chiesa del Carmine del 1771', *Rivista d'arte*, 14 (1932), 141–232. See also Bossi, *Ricostruzione grafica*.

[81] G. Bacchi, 'La compagnia di S. Maria delle laudi', 3 (1931–2), 103–7. The chapel was not officially ceded to the company until 1433. From 1377 to 1433 it remained in the possession of the Ardinghelli, although the company maintained it at their expense.

[82] Procacci, 'L'incendio', 166. The altar was renovated in 1590, but its paintings and frescos, like most in the other chapels (except the Brancacci) were destroyed by the 1771 fire. In 1444 the company recorded a payment for altar-cloths to be washed for 'nostri altari, cioè Santa Angnesa, Sa[n] Nicholò, e ll'Anuziata'; SA 24, fo. 226ᵛ. The bequest of Chiaro d'Ardinghello did provide for the establishment of a chapel dedicated to Sts Nicholas, Martin, Margaret, and Catherine, but the above record is the only indication that a third altar was under the company's patronage; Bacchi, 'La compagnia', 3 (1931–2), 103. The Nicholas altar (Fig. 6, no. 4) was rededicated to St Albert in the 16th c., and was under the patronage of the Marzinghi family; Procacci, 'L'incendio', 165.

[83] SA 98, fos. 137ᵛ–140ʳ.

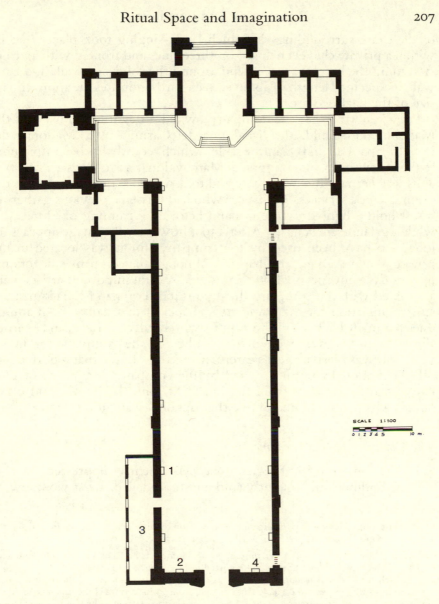

FIG. 6. Floor plan of Santa Maria del Carmine

L. 78½ to build an armchair, bench, and carved lintel inside one of the chapels 'in the place where the laude are sung'.[84] This is a rare indication

[84] SA 115, fo. 52ʳ: 'Zanobi di Domenicho legnaiuolo a San Tomaso de avere per una ciscranna a noi fatta cioè alla nostra compagnia nella chiesa di Santa Maria del Charmino, chon una ispalliera a sedere e uno ischaglione da pie' chon una chassa in detta ciscranna la quale è in detta chiesa allato alla

of the exact surroundings in which lauda-singing took place, that is, within a private chapel enclosed on three sides and fronted with a grille. Assuming the lintel was to extend around the solid side walls and back wall, its specified length of about sixteen yards indicates the approximate size of the enclosed area.

Paatz reported that the company owned a devotional image of the Madonna and Child, the 'Madonna del Carmine' (or 'Madonna del Popolo'), painted 'in Byzantine style', which recently has been attributed to the Florentine painter Coppo di Marcovaldo (c. 1270–80; see Plate 8).[85] This was perhaps the image referred to in a 1289 statute concerning the evening lauda services. An officer who had missed a previous gathering 'must hold a lighted candle in hand before the painting of Our Lady, while the laude are sung'.[86] After 1390, however, the image appears no longer to have been used by the company, for it was located in the privately owned Brancacci chapel.[87] Although the company's devotional images have not survived, we know that several important artists were associated with the company. In 1399–1400, Lorenzo Monaco painted an Annunciation for the company's chapel of that name.[88] An annual dues payment by Fra Filippo Lippi was recorded in 1431, and Neri di Bicci (1419–91) was a devoted member of the company for many years.[89] It was Neri di Bicci's careful inventory of 1466 that reported one other devotional painting owned by the company, a triptych of Our Lady with four scenes from the life of St John the Baptist and other saints, which was located above the captains' seats in the oratory.[90]

The Company of San Frediano

Since the church of San Frediano was permanently suppressed in 1783, and the building subsequently sold and remodelled, what we know of

nostra compagnia a' luogho dove si dichono le laude chon segni della nostra compagnia, e di sopra architrave fregio chornicone [sic] di bracc[i]a sedici in circha . . . L. 78 s. 10.'

[85] Paatz, Die Kirchen, iii. 209 n. 109; the Coppo attribution was based on a restoration conducted by Paola Bracco and Ottavio Ciappi and reported in La Nazione, 30 Dec. 1985.

[86] Ed. Schiaffini, Testi fiorentini, 62 [1289]: '. . . debbia tenere una candella accesa in mano dinanzi a la tavola di nostra Donna, tanto che le laude si cantino . . .'; In May 1285 the captains noted the commission of another painting (or perhaps fresco): '. . . che fosse fatta una ymagine di nostra Donna sopra l'avello de la compangnia; e la ymagine stea in cotale modo, che abbia appiede figure le quali steano ginocchioni co' le mane chiuse'; ibid. 59.

[87] At the June 1990 opening of the Brancacci chapel, with its recently restored Masaccio frescos, this painting could once again be viewed in this setting.

[88] Procacci, 'L'incendio', 28. Bacchi, 'La Compagnia di Santa Maria', 3 (1931–2), 104–5, maintains, however, that Lorenzo's painting was executed for the new St Nicholas chapel established by Chiaro d'Ardinghello's bequest.

[89] Bacchi, 'La compagnia', 3 (1931–2), 13, 17, 36; Barr, 'A Renaissance Artist', passim.

[90] Bacchi, 'La compagnia', ibid. 100.

the interior must be reconstructed from the reports of Richa and Paatz.[91] According to both, the company's primary altar, dedicated to St Fredianus, was the third one on the right (south) wall of the nave, apparently the last nave altar before the main altar in this small church.[92] The company was bequeathed the patronage rights to two other chapels in the fifteenth century, the chapel of St Michael (1436), and the chapel of the Annunciation (1479), but the location of these two chapels within the church is unknown.

In 1368 the company owned 'due' magini di san friano',[93] and thereafter the frequent altar work and acquisition of a number of images reflects its shift to the imaginative devotion of a laudesi company. By 1400, the company owned a *Pietà*, 'which is placed upon the altar-cloth of the laude', and for which a tabernacle was constructed that year.[94] In 1442 a fresco of the Virgin with Saints Anthony and Leonard was commissioned from the painter Stefano d'Antonio.[95] During the 1470s the company completely renovated the San Frediano chapel, then between *c.*1480 and 1520 commissioned several works from Florentine artists for the decoration of the new chapel. During 1484–6 payments were made to Jacopo del Sellaio for a *Pietà* with Saints Jerome and Fredianus, an extant painting now in the Bode Museum in Berlin (no. 1055).[96] Between 1495 and 1520 several terracotta figures were provided by the Della Robbia workshop: a company insignia executed in 1495 by Luca della Robbia, a group of cherubim fashioned in 1502 by Andrea for the frieze of the altar, and in 1519–20 a risen Christ by Andrea which was placed in the lunette.[97]

[91] Richa, *Notizie istoriche*, ix. 173–9; Paatz, *Die Kirchen*, ii. 138–44.

[92] Richa, ix. 177; Paatz, ii. 140. According to H. Horne, 'Jacopo del Sellaio', *Burlington Magazine*, 13 (1908), 212, Stefano Roselli's 1657 *Sepoltuario fiorentino* (ASF, *Manoscritti* 624) lists four altars, the company's then being the fourth on the right.

[93] SF 30, fo. 98[r] [1368 inventory]; On 31 Dec. of that year the company recorded a payment of L. 2 s. 10 for a 'mezina d'olio per fornire la lampana [*sic*] che sta dinanzi alla tavola di Mess[er] Sancto Fridiano'; SF 88, fo. 84[v]. Richa, *Notizie*, ix. 165, reported a fresco of San Frediano but not its location; now lost.

[94] SF 31, fos. 13[r–v], 35[v]: 'A [*lacuna*] dipintore per dipingnere e per luaglesco [*sic*] per fare la piata che si pone a la tovaglia delle lalde . . . L. 3.'

[95] SF 4, fo. 35[v]; 31, fo. 63[r]. This was the fulfillment of a bequest, and seems to have been executed primarily by Stefano (1405–83), a former assistant to Bicci di Lorenzo (who was, along with his son Neri di Bicci, a member of the neighbouring Company of Sant'Agnese). D. E. Colnaghi, *Dictionary of Florentine Painters* (London, 1928), 257.

[96] SF 110, fos. 53[v]–63[r]; 53[v]: 'A Jachopo d'Archangiolo dipintore a dì 8 di Marzo [1484] fiorini due larghi dise per dare a Zanobi di Domenico lengnaiuolo per parte del quadro della tavola della alltare di Sancto Friano nuovamente fatto . . . L. 12 s. 2.' Paatz, *Die Kirchen*, ii. 140, where he dates the commission of the painting in 1483. Sellaio (1442–93), a pupil of Filippo Lippi, also furnished a painting of the Crucifixion for the main altar. Several members of the Sellaio family belonged to the company, and Jacopo was buried in San Frediano. Colnaghi, *Dictionary*, 245, and Horne, 'Jacopo del Sellaio', 210–13.

[97] On 24 Apr. 1495, L. 33 was paid to Luca della Robbia 'per un sengnio [of the company] per detta capella . . .', SF 112, fo. 87[r]; between Mar. and Sept. 1502, L. 44 was paid to Andrea di Luca for

The Company of Santo Spirito

The company's records fail to mention the name or location of its altar in the Augustinian church of Santo Spirito. A 1598 *memoriale*, the friars' altar-by-altar record of their liturgical obligations, provides the only clue to the location of the company altar. Among the duties associated with the 'Altar of the Holy Sacrament of Matteo Corbinelli', located in the left nave (Fig. 7, no. 1), was the following:

The Company of the Dove must sing laude *in musica* on every feast-day [of Lent], and afterwards a Father is to give confession and recommend to God the soul of the said Matteo, for which they [the company] are to be given a gold florin. These laude are sung on the Sundays and feast-days during Lent.[98]

There can be no certainty that this was the company's primary altar during the previous three centuries of its existence, but it may well have been since the mid-fifteenth century, given the company's exclusive attention to Lenten lauda-singing after that time.

A detailed inventory of 1444 lists no devotional images, but in 1465 the friars of Santo Spirito traded a painting from the company altar, an Annunciation, to Santa Croce, and received in return a Madonna and Child, surrounded by Saints John, Jerome, Alexis, and James, with gold decoration.[99] The latter was placed 'in sul nostro altare', and the company received permission from the friars to have the painting signed with the company's symbol, the dove. According to a 1621 inventory, the company still retained this painting, along with several other images located in the company's hospital: a painted wood Madonna with a gold frame in a tabernacle, and two paintings of the Madonna 'all'antica'.[100]

The devotional framework is as crucial to an understanding of lauda-singing as the social context described in Ch. 1. The interior, imaginative process of devotion was implicit in the lay spirituality of republican Florence, and lauda-singing was one of the most creative and popular expressions of that spirituality. Moreover, laudesi devotion reveals both in its inner mental 'habits' and its outer manifestations a strong orientation to the concrete, the particular, and the familiar. Whether this orientation

'cherubini di tira chotti . . . per la chapella nostra di San Friano . . . per mettere nel architrave . . .', ibid., fo. 112^{r-v}; and payments were made in Sept. 1518, Apr. 1519, and the last on 1 Sept. 1520 to Andrea '. . . per una resuressione di terra cotta fatta sotto l'archo di detta chapella per adornamento fatto fare . . . L. 59 s. 10 d. 4', ibid., fos. 112^r, 200^v–201^r. Cf. Paatz, *Die Kirchen*, ii. 141, and Richa, *Notizie*, ix. 177. The latter decorations were probably part of a second renovation of the chapel in 1520, when Sellaio's son, Arcangiolo, retouched his father's altar panel, and a new carved and gilt frame was provided, at a total cost of L. 60; Paatz, ii. 140, and Horne, 'Jacopo del Sellaio', 212.

[98] Appendix I, doc. 28.
[99] SSP 78, fo. 47^v.
[100] SSP 3, fos. 114^v–117^r.

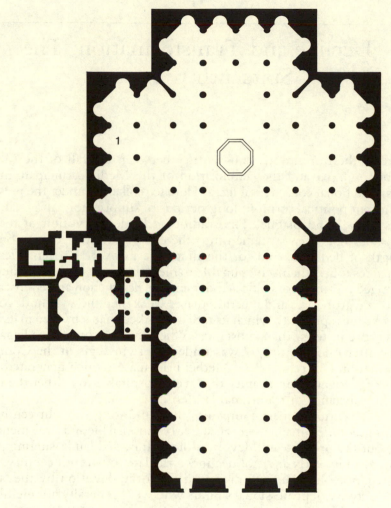

FIG. 7. Floor plan of Santo Spirito

is attributable to a practical turn of mind that was particularly urban and mercantile, or more broadly to the secular Everyman of late medieval society, it is nevertheless readily apparent in the centuries during which the companies maintained, decorated, and met at their particular altars, and conversed with their sacred advocates who stood before them in the vivid panels of Tuscan artists.

6

Decline and Transformation: The Sixteenth Century

DURING the tumultuous half-century between the fall of the Medici republic in 1494 and the stabilization of the Medici principate in the 1540s, traditional confraternal life in Florence collapsed under the pressure of constant political turmoil, long periods of suppression, and recurrent bouts of war and plague. The traditional laudesi devotion of the lay companies had been sustained into the early sixteenth century on the strength of bequests, and for the first time in over two centuries the companies found themselves unable to meet the terms of those bequests. Prolonged cessations of cultic activity and the destruction and confiscation of income properties and meeting places weakened the ancient devotion that, like the republic to which its fate was linked, had survived in its later years more in form than substance. When the lay companies began to revive after mid-century, it was under the twin aegis of the Counter-Reformation Church and the Medici principate, which generated new ideals of piety and community that were hospitable to neither the form nor the substance of traditional laudesi devotion.

The Florentine laudesi companies thrived during the fourteenth and fifteenth centuries, maintaining an active ceremonial life and large membership, but the practice and devotion of confraternal lauda-singing *per se* began to show early signs of decline in the late fourteenth century. The congregations had become distanced from the devotion by the widespread activity of professional singers who were generally not members, the production of laudarios began to taper off, new laudesi companies had ceased to appear, and existing companies became increasingly preoccupied with the liturgical pomp that Savonarola was to decry a century later.[1] The decline was fully apparent in the fifteenth century, with the abandonment of ferial singing in the 1440s and the drying up altogether of bequests for lauda vigils after mid-century. But why this decline? In spite of increased communal taxation and control, most of the

---

[1] Barr, *The Monophonic Lauda*, 24–30, cites the increased virtuosity of the laude in Mgl[1] as an early sign of decadence, suggesting that the lauda had become more a vehicle of display than of devotion.

companies continued to maintain active, in some cases expanding, ritual lives, and the musico-poetic genre of the lauda thrived.[2]

Another noticeable feature of late fourteenth-century laudesi practice is the weakening of the traditional identity between the lay companies and the lauda repertoire. In fact, beginning in this period the repertoire (both Florentine and Venetian) becomes increasingly difficult to link directly to the Florentine companies. While this condition may be partly attributable to the broader and shifting currents of poetic taste, it is more directly related to changes in the nature of Florentine politics and society which in turn forced a shift in the priorities of the lay companies.

The Florentine laudesi companies were a characteristic manifestation of early guild republicanism. They were city-wide and socially hetero-geneous, they enjoyed a certain degree of corporate autonomy for being mid-way between the authority of the Church and the commune, and they were predicated upon an easy confluence of widely accepted sacred and secular values. The erosion of corporate pluralism, in particular, appears to have begun under the city's financial burden of increasingly expensive military campaigns waged against neighbouring cities (espe-cially during the Oligarchy, c.1382–1427), and the commune's desire to regulate traditional corporate groups, like the guilds and the lay com-panies, for the purpose of more effective taxation. What began in the late fourteenth century as a whittling away of rights, privileges, and im-munities became in the fifteenth century, especially after the return of the Medici in 1433, the wilful usurpation and centralization of political power.[3] The protracted wars against Milan, and later Lucca, intensified traditional conflicts centring on taxation and eligibility to office, and required exorbitant taxes that led to the redistribution of wealth into the hands of relatively few citizens. This contributed to the consolidation of a politically dominant patrician class, a long process which had begun

[2] For the period covered in this chapter, the important works on the Florentine political system are Brucker, *The Civic World of Early Renaissance Florence*; D. Kent, *The Rise of the Medici: Faction in Florence, 1426–1434* (London, 1978); N. Rubinstein, *The Government of Florence under the Medici* (Oxford, 1966); H. C. Butters, *Governors and Government in Early Sixteenth-Century Florence* (Oxford, 1985); J. N. Stephens, *The Fall of the Florentine Republic, 1512–1530* (Oxford, 1983); F. Diaz, *Il Granducato di Toscana* (Turin, 1976). On 15th-c. Florentine society: L. Martines, *The Social World of the Florentine Humanists* (Princeton, 1963); F. W. Kent, *Household and Lineage in Renaissance Florence* (Princeton, 1977), and D. V. and F. W. Kent, *Neighbours and Neighbourhood in Renaissance Florence*.

[3] Becker, 'Aspects of Lay Piety', 180–1; the period of the Oligarchy is examined in detail in Brucker, *The Civic World of Early Renaissance Florence*, with additional comments by A. Brown, *Journal of Modern History*, 52 (1980), 335–9. The earliest sign of this tendency was the communal legislation passed in 1363, when Florence was at war with Pisa, which enabled the commune to seize all confraternity bequests and sell certain confraternity assets in order to pay for war expenses; M. Becker, 'The Florentine Territorial State and Civic Humanism in the Early Renaissance', in E. F. Jacob (ed.), *Florentine Studies* (London, 1968), 111 n. 2. On similar problems encountered by the Company of Orsanmichele during the 1360s and 1370s, see La Sorsa, *La compagnia d'Or San Michele*, 51–67, and Cassidy, 'The Financing of the Tabernacle of Orsanmichele', 3 nn. 18–22.

with the rise of the Oligarchy after the revolt of the Florentine wool workers in 1378 (the *Ciompi* revolution), and reached full bloom in the sixteenth-century principate.

During the early fifteenth century the Church's attitude towards the lay companies began to mirror the commune's desire to regulate the companies. Under the episcopates of Andrea Corsini (1411–35) and Antoninus (1446–59), company statutes came under more regular and careful scrutiny, and the companies increasingly were perceived as exercising too much initiative in the liturgy and being in competition with parish clergy.[4] In 1425 Corsini initiated a course of action that would be fully realized in the sixteenth century when he insisted that the Company of San Lorenzo grant the parish priest, rather than the company's private chaplain, ultimate jurisdiction over the cure of parishioners' souls.[5]

A concomitant development was the general change from corporate to private spheres of activity, which was evident, for example, in the shift of artistic patronage from public subsidy to the private patron after *c.*1425,[6] and the great increase of private devotional books (for layman and cleric) containing laude.[7] The pattern of giving through bequests changed as well, and Florentines appeared less interested in purchasing the ritual of clerical and confraternal institutions, and more inclined to subvent philanthropic causes that benefited the needy individuals of Florentine society.[8] Accordingly, the nature of public ritual changed, as traditional public expressions of lay devotion (like the laudesi ferial services and spontaneous mass processions) were either displaced by more private acts of philanthropy, or yielded to fewer and grander forms of festive display. By the mid fifteenth century, the companies of Sant'Agnese and Santo Spirito were expending huge sums of money on annual religious spectacles that were subsidized and monitored by the Medici,[9] and by the sixteenth century the companies were occupied with

---

[4] J. Henderson, 'Confraternities and the Church', 77–83; id., 'Le confraternite religiose nella Firenze del tardo medioevo: patroni spirituali e anche politici?', *Ricerche storiche*, 15 (1985), 77–94; Gaston, 'Liturgy and Patronage', 132–3.

[5] Henderson, 'Confraternities and the Church', 80.

[6] Brucker, *Renaissance Florence*, 227; Trexler, 'Ritual in Florence', 263–4. Goldthwaite has observed this with respect to building programmes: 'As the [Italian] communes evolved into more oligarchical and despotic states, the ruling élites began to build more assertively for themselves; . . . building shifted from the public to the private sphere . . .'; 'The Empire of Things: Consumer Demand in Renaissance Italy', in Kent and Simons (eds.), *Patronage, Art, and Society*, 165.

[7] e.g. Ricc. 1672 (the property of Tommaso di Giuliano Brancacci), Mgl II. IX. 58 (Bernardo de M. Niccolò da Rabalta), Mgl II. VIII. 3 (Frate Niccolò da Poggibonsi), and Mgl VII. 285.

[8] Trexler, 'Ritual in Florence', 209–10. Meersseman, *Ordo fraternitatis*, ii. 997–8, where he notes the weakening of ties between confraternities and their mendicant hosts as a factor in this shift away from spiritual and liturgical matters within the companies themselves.

[9] Henderson, 'Piety and Charity', 54–7.

the relatively private and politically neutral activity of providing dowries for the unwed daughters of company members.

Florentine leaders had always distrusted any large and wealthy organization with the potential for developing into an independent estate and influencing the conduct of the city's affairs. In 1348–9 Orsanmichele, the wealthiest lay company in the city, was forced to sell most of its goods to the city, which then assumed the right to elect its captains. But only during the last quarter of the century did the commune begin consistently to fear the conspiratorial potential of the lay companies during times of crisis. During the War of the Eight Saints, when Florence incurred papal interdict in 1376–8, the city considered suppressing the disciplinati companies, which were increasing their activity in the organization of peace processions.[10] However, with the cessation of priestly ritual the religious activities of the lay companies assumed a special significance, and their cathartic value under the pressure of interdict was appreciated by the city leaders. Contemporary chroniclers provide a vivid picture:

It appeared that a compunction had seized all the citizens, so that in almost every church they sang *laudi* every evening. An infinite number of men and women attended, and the costs that were run up in candles and books and necessary articles were amazing. Every day there was a processsion with relics and hymns followed by the whole population. Every company beat themselves, including children down to ten years of age. There were certainly more than 5,000 flagellants at processions, and more than 20,000 people followed the procession.[11]

Today, on the 19th of April of the year 1377, in the morning, every single company of flagellants paraded through Florence with many banners of *tavole* of Our Lady, of S. Gilio, and many crucifixes and *tavole* and standards of the companies. They went completely through the city of Florence with many beautiful and large processions of flagellants and youths, singing many beautiful *laudi* and songs . . .[12]

Finally, after the spring of 1377, the government's fear of sedition and disorder surpassed their tolerance, and all public manifestations of religion were banned.

During the early fifteenth century, as the ruling Oligarchy enacted legislation that led to the political disenfranchisement of first the guilds (1414), then the lay companies, the fears of the ruling élite that these

[10] R. Trexler, *The Spiritual Power: Republican Florence under Interdict* (Leiden, 1974), 129; Weissman, *Ritual Brotherhood*, 165. The disciplinati companies in particular attracted suspicion because their membership tended to be the wealthier and more influential Florentines, their meetings were extremely secretive, and their hooded garb allowed them to march anonymously in public.

[11] Stefani, *Cronaca fiorentina di Marchionne di Coppo*, rubric 757; ed. N. Rodolico, *Rerum Italicarum Scriptores* (new edn.), xxx. 1 (Città di Castello, 1903). Trans. in Trexler, *The Spiritual Power*, 130–1.

[12] *Diario d'Anonimo, fiorentino*, ed. A. Gherardi in *Cronache dei secoli XIII e XIV: documenti di storia italiana* (Florence, 1867), vi. 331. Trans. in Trexler, *The Spiritual Power*, 132.

groups mixed religion and politics naturally increased.[13] Such fears were likely to be justified as the merchant class, traditionally at the centre of Florentine politics, was subjected increasingly to the twin pressures of increased taxation and reduced political recourse.[14] Actual episodes of political activism among the lay companies called down the unprecedented legislation of 1419, which is worth quoting at length since it served as the basis for subsequent legislation against the companies:

... The lord priors ... desire to eliminate the cause and occasion of scandals and to remove all suspicion from the minds of the authorities so that everyone can live peaceably. They have learned that as a result of the meeting of certain confraternities, the spirits of the citizenry have been perturbed, divisions have arisen, and many other inconveniences have occurred. Desiring to provide the proper remedy, they ... have decreed ... that every confraternity, whether penitential or dedicated to singing laude ... which is accustomed to assemble in the ecclesiastical foundations of the city of Florence ... is henceforth to be dissolved and banned, and its meetings categorically prohibited. Whoever has ... the custody of any of the books or documents containing the names of the confraternity's members, or their constitutions, observances, and regulations must bring them to the chancellor of the Commune of Florence during the month of October ...

Item, the lord priors ... are authorized, between now and the end of November, to dispose of all property, both real and personal, belonging to these confraternities ... for the benefit of the souls, and for the remission of sins, of those who have given that property to those confraternities ...

Item, all of the furnishings in the buildings of these confraternities are to be totally destroyed ... and the places of assembly ... are to be used for other purposes or for habitation, or they are to be closed ... so that no congregation or meeting can be held in them.

Item, none of the confraternities may assemble or congregate in any other location, whether ecclesiastical or secular, within or outside the city of Florence ...

Item, no person, lay or clerical, of whatever dignity, status, quality, or eminence may allow any company to assemble in his house ...

---

[13] In 1414, the statutes of the guilds were altered so as to limit their scope for independent political action and to prevent them from serving as channels for corporate aims and grievances, which were beginning to be viewed by the ruling Oligarchy (and upper classes in general) as a threat to their hegemony. In 1415, Florentine guild members (esp. Wool guild members) were prohibited from attending the meetings of any confraternity without permission from the consuls of their guild. That is, guildsmen were forbidden to use the lay companies as an alternative means to formulate dissent. L. Polizzotto, 'Confraternities, Conventicles and Political Dissent: The Case of the Savonarolan "Capi Rossi"', *Memorie domenicane*, NS 16 (1985), 237–8. Polizzotto and Weissman, *Ritual Brotherhood*, chs. 4 and 5, provide detailed accounts of the Florentine lay companies' political problems during the 15th and 16th cc.

[14] On the economic problems of the laudesi companies at this time, see Henderson, 'Piety and Charity', 57–65, where he notes the deficits of most of the companies in their 1427 tax returns, and cites as general causes increased spending (through bequests), and decreased revenues (through taxation, suspension, and bad debts).

Item, no confraternity may be newly created or established in the city of Florence or within a three-mile radius . . . This provision does not apply . . . to any confraternity which is newly established with the license and consent of the lord priors . . . [Within each] confraternity which is accepted, confirmed, and approved by the above-mentioned license . . . the members thereof . . . are prohibited from . . . interfering by word or deed in matters pertaining to the Commune of Florence, to the Merchant's Court, to any guild . . . in the city of Florence, or to the administration of any of them . . .[15]

These provisions were immediately qualified by significant concessions, and no immediate action against the companies is known to have been taken, but they served as a stiff warning designed to inhibit the less acceptable activities, as well as a precedent for more aggressive actions in the future.[16] Such action was not far off, and new regulations in 1426 were enacted, like those of 1419, in the midst of grave political and financial crises, conflict within the Oligarchy, and fear of civic discord. Debates among government leaders in 1426 revealed remarkable hostility towards the companies, and for the first time specific charges were made, the most frequent being the accusation that members of lay companies used their positions as confraternal officers for the political advancement of themselves and friends, and in order to obtain preferential treatment in tax allocations. The new regulations prohibited politically qualified citizens (*veduti*), as well as brothers, sons, or grandsons of *veduti* since 1381, from any form of participation in the lay companies.

Under increasing pressure to avoid political scandal, the companies revised their statutes a number of times during the fifteenth and sixteenth centuries. In particular, those statutes concerned with election procedures of officers began to dwarf the rest of the document, as the companies went to great lengths to convince the commune officials who scrutinized these statutes that such procedures were immune to factional manipulation.[17] In 1438, the Company of San Frediano appended to its fourteenth-century statutes a long and elaborate regulation concerning elections, with the following preface:

. . . in that time [of the original 1324 statutes] there were other customs and modes of living that today do not exist, and because the times have changed, it is

---

[15] Trans. G. Brucker in *The Society of Renaissance Florence* (New York, 1971), 83–4.

[16] The 1419 legislation was implemented to the extent that a special commission was established which investigated the companies between 19 and 31 Oct., during which time the companies were probably suspended; Polizzotto, 'Confraternities, Conventicles', 239–40.

[17] Beginning in the 1420s, the archiepiscopal curia also began thoroughly to review both existing and new company statutes, and thereafter insisted upon approving them. The co-operation of secular and ecclesiastical powers in overseeing the statutes of the companies contributed significantly to the erosion of lay companies' independence. Similar developments towards ecclesiastical centralization were occurring elsewhere in Italy. Ibid. 244–5.

necessary to change other regulations and statutes, above all [those concerning] the means of electing the officials of the said company.[18]

When the laudesi company at Santa Croce drafted new statutes in 1470, a long statute was devoted to election procedures 'so as to prevent the scandals which often intrude in the election of officers in similar places'.[19] The Company of San Lorenzo, abolished in 1432 at the Medici family church shortly before the Medici were expelled from Florence, was undoubtedly the victim of a political indiscretion during this tense period.

Changes in the membership of laudesi companies during this time suggest that lay companies had indeed become attractive to politically minded Florentines, and not only guildsmen, who were increasingly excluded from traditional channels of political participation. Company membership lists, especially in the *Oltrarno* companies, show a marked increase in Florentine family names. The Company of Santo Spirito was transformed by the influx of prominent families of the quarter during c. 1440–70.[20]

Provisions similar to those of 1419 and 1426 were enacted again in 1443, 1455, 1458, and 1471. The 1458 prohibition was enacted, once again, in the midst of political crisis and reports of secret meetings, and this time resulted in a prolonged suppression for six years.[21] As with previous anti-confraternal legislation, however, the action of the law was more selective and compromising than its letter, for it was understood by the commune that the companies were also bound by law, both secular and ecclesiastical, to fulfil the terms of their bequests. The companies of San Zanobi, San Piero Martire, and Sant'Agnese continued to hire singers and conduct services during this period. No singers are named in the records of San Frediano after 1458, where the decline of lauda-singing appears to have resulted from the combined impact upon this small company of a prolonged suppression and the difficulty of maintaining the larger, polyphonic choirs that came into fashion in the 1460s.

On 10 May 1467 the Company of Santo Spirito recorded the new membership of a leading Florentine citizen. He soon appeared also in the

---

[18] BNF, Palatino 154, fo. 13r [1438]: '. . . nel qual tempo erano altri costumi et modi di vivere che oggi non sono, et perchè i tempi sono mutati è necessario mutare altri ordini et capitoli, maximamente del modo della electione degli ufficiali della decta compagnia'. This was the first statute revision or addition since 1368, and others followed in 1440, 1441, 1444, 1467, and 1468.

[19] ASF, CmRS, Capitoli 53, Cap. II: '. . . Acciò che si obvii agli scandali che spesso intervenghono nelle creationi degli ufficiali di simili luoghi . . .'.

[20] e.g. the Corsini, Ridolfi, Capponi, Pitti, Corbinelli, Frescobaldi, Torrigioni, Biliotti, and Lanfredini. The influx may have begun sooner, but the extant membership lists were compiled after 1451, and date back to 1444. ssp 79, *Debitori e Creditori*, 1451–1522, *passim*. Cosimo's favourite architect, Michelozzo Michelozzi, entered the company on 3 Aug. 1446; ibid., fo. 21v.

[21] Weissman, *Ritual Brotherhood*, 168 and n. 17; Polizzotto, 'Confraternities, Conventicles', 245.

membership lists of Sant'Agnese (1469), and San Zanobi (1474).[22] Even before his accession to power as *the* leading citizen of Florence in 1469, Lorenzo de' Medici had already initiated his novel policy with regard to the lay companies. He recognized their potential as sources of political support for Medici rule, and he exploited the opportunity by sharing with them various forms of patronage (endowments, tax exemptions, and donations of properties), and by joining the companies (he was a nominal member of at least eight lay companies), or seeing to it that family and loyal friends and supporters were elected to the major lay offices.[23]

Medici involvement in the affairs of the Company of Sant'Agnese is particularly well documented. Lorenzo was elected to the office of syndic in 1483, councillor in 1487, captain in 1489, treasurer in 1491, and captain again in 1491–2. Lorenzo's son Piero was too young to hold office, but the company waived the regulations 'because the Medici House has always been the benefactor of our company', and Piero was elected captain in 1488, and again in 1489–90. Giuliano and Giulio (Pope Clement VII) de' Medici enjoyed similar privileges, for in 1485 Lorenzo and all his male heirs were elected to receive all the benefits with none of the obligations of membership. Bartolomeo Scala, Chancellor of Florence and loyal Medici follower, entered the company in 1487 with the same privileges as the Medici family, and served as captain in 1491. From 1469 Lorenzo, and after him Piero, provided the grain for bread that was distributed annually at Christmas, and helped secure subvention for the company's annual Ascension feast. Lorenzo died on 8 April 1492, and nine days later the company celebrated a *rinovale* at their traditional altar, 'per la buona memoria' of their long-time patron.

The lay companies proved to be an effective and compliant tool in the dissemination of Medici patronage and control. During the relative political stability of this period, the laudesi companies experienced few disruptions, and succeeded in establishing polyphonic chapels which suited the ritual splendour of Laurentian Florence.

---

[22] SSP 79, fo. 21ᵛ: 'Lorenzo di Piero di Chosimo de' Medici entro nella nostra chonpagnia a dì 10 di magio, 1467'. Medici involvement in the Company of Sant'Agnese is examined by Weissman, *Ritual Brotherhood*, 170–2.

[23] Polizzotto, 'Confraternities, Conventicles', 146–7; Weissman, *Ritual Brotherhood*, 169–73; A. Brown, *Bartolomeo Scala—1430–1497—Chancellor of Florence* (Princeton, 1979), 112–13; Trexler, *Public Life*, 419–62; R. Hatfield, 'The Compagnia de' Magi', *Journal of the Warburg and Courtauld Institutes*, 33 (1970), 107–61, a fascinating examination of the activities of one lay company, whose public pageant, the feast of the Magi, ritualized Medici patronage itself. There is some evidence that Cosimo may have used similar tactics; the eminent Florentine musician Antonio Squarcialupi, a Medici partisan who in 1445 appeared in Medici correspondence reporting on the secret electoral procedures of one lay company, was an officer of the Company of San Zanobi during the 1430s and 1440s, and on several occasions was in trouble with the company. In 1436, he was declared 'libero della corezione gli fu fatto per disubidiente'; SZ 2186, fasc. 48, fo. 147ʳ.

With the expulsion of the Medici in 1494, blessing turned to curse. In the several decades during which companies like Sant'Agnese had been drawn into the web of Medici politics, they were unwittingly elevated to the rank of those parties suspected by a new regime for having been too closely aligned with a deposed one. Beginning in 1494 the lay companies were subjected to increasingly frequent bans, and their suppression became the reflex of leaders during crisis.[24] For the next four years, during which Savonarola effectively ruled Florence, it is clear that his plans for the religious revival of Florence did not include the lay companies, which he regarded with suspicion.[25] Music, however, and particularly laude and plainchant, was a matter of vital concern to the Dominican friar. His vehement preaching against polyphony in religious services contained a distinct echo of St Augustine's ancient suspicion:

. . . figural music is sooner injurious in church than useful, because there one must contemplate and pray to God with the mind and the intellect, and figural music does nothing but charm the ear and the senses.[26]

But the lauda, now in simple polyphonic settings that did not obscure the text, remained a useful symbol of popular devotion. By his own example he encouraged the composition of lauda texts set to music,[27] and Savonarola's lasting impression upon the city was kept alive in part by the number of lauda poets who had been influenced by his teachings.[28] His attitude was made explicit in a sermon delivered from the pulpit of the Cathedral:

[24] The 1494 suppressions are discussed in Polizzotto, 'Confraternities and Conventicles', 247–8; N. Rubinstein, 'Politics and Constitution in Florence at the End of the Fifteenth Century', in E. F. Jacob (ed.), *Italian Renaissance Studies* (London, 1960), 148–83, esp. 168; and Weissman, *Ritual Brotherhood*, 173–4.

[25] Polizzotto, 248–9. The numerous youth confraternities in Florence, however, became the target of Savonarolan organization; see Trexler, 'Ritual in Florence'.

[26] Excerpt from a sermon of 23 Mar. 1495, translated in D'Accone, 'The Singers of San Giovanni', 347. Harsher denunciations than this led to the abolition of polyphonic chapels at the city's leading churches: 'God says: Take away all your beautiful figural music; these gentlemen have chapels of singers which seem like a rabble . . . because there stands a singer with a large voice like a calf's, and the others howl around him like dogs, and no one understands what they are saying. Let figural music go, and sing the plainchant ordered by the Church! You also want the organs played. You go to church to hear the organs. God says: I don't hear your organs, but yet you refuse to understand . . .' (6 Mar. 1496); ibid. 348.

[27] G. Cattin, 'Le poesie del Savonarola nelle fonti musicali', *Quadrivium*, 12 (1971), 259–80; D'Accone, 'The Singers of San Giovanni', 347; L. Parigi, *Laurentiana* (Florence, 1954), 91; M. Ferrara, *Savonarola* (Florence, 1952); Savonarola's lauda texts are printed in *Girolamo Savonarola: Poesie*, ed. M. Martelli (Rome, 1968).

[28] Among them was Castellano Castellani and Girolamo Benivieni, the chief publicist of the Savonarolan movement, who at one time was a leading poet of Lorenzo's literary *brigata*, and pupil of Marsilio Ficino, Angelo Poliziano, and Giovanni Pico della Mirandola; Weinstein, *Savonarola and Florence*, 205–7, 216–20.

And now children, let us talk to you a bit. Listen to me: you sing laude here every morning and that's fine; but once in a while I'd also like to hear you sing the *canti* of the church such as the *Ave maris stella* or the *Veni creator Spiritus*; and it wouldn't hurt if the people were to sing the responses; and if I were to come to the pulpit and find that you were singing that *Ave maris stella*, I'd probably sing also . . .[29]

It is unclear just who was singing these laude, for records of payments to singers for the Company of San Zanobi cease during this period,[30] as they do for most of the other laudesi companies. The hiatus in the records of the Company of Sant'Agnese reflects the cost of Medici patronage, for it corresponds exactly to the span of Savonarola's rule (October 1494 to April 1498). Only in the Company of Santo Spirito did lauda-singing continue, undoubtedly because it was by this time entirely in the hands of the Santo Spirito friars.[31] The situation reveals the disassociation between lauda and laudesi company that had begun a century before. The lauda remained a vital form and expression of lay devotion, attaining new vigour during and after the Savonarolan period, but the laudesi companies were clearly no longer its chief guardian and sponsor.

Florence entered the sixteenth century in a state of endemic crisis which was not to subside until Cosimo de' Medici's entrenchment in power in the years 1537–40. During the last two periods of the republic (1498–1512, 1527–30), the Florentine oligarchy was deeply divided and beset by the political upheaval of the Italian peninsula caused by the military intervention of foreign monarchs. The fitful beginnings of despotic government were accompanied by the intrusion of those larger forces that would reshape Florentine society. The first Medici restoration in 1512 was accomplished by the combined forces of papal interdict and the Spanish Army (representing the Holy League established by Pope Julius II).[32] The last republic fell in 1530 to Imperial forces, and two centuries of despotic Medici rule commenced with the unstable regime of Duke Alessandro de' Medici. During the ten-month siege prior to the fall, tens of thousands of Florentines died of fighting, starvation, and plague, defending one of the last republican communes in Italy.

The consequences for the lay companies were predictable: 'Any internal or external threat to the government, whether real or imagined,

[29] Trans. in D'Accone, 'The Singers of San Giovanni', 349 n. 202.

[30] There is a hiatus between Mar. 1495 and Jan. 1498; D'Accone, Alcune note sulle compagnie', 101.

[31] Clerical involvement in lauda-singing gradually increased during the 15th c., probably in part a consequence of the need for lauda bequests to be fulfilled during times of confraternity suppression, and came to be dominated by clerics in the 16th c.

[32] Trexler, *The Spiritual Power*, 178–86; Stephens, *The Fall of the Florentine Republic*, ch. 3.

any change of regime, any seemingly unfavourable development or set of circumstances, occasioned the immediate, pre-emptive banning of adult confraternities.'[33] The situation was further aggravated by the fact that followers of Savonarola had turned to the confraternities shortly after the friar's death to keep alive his memory and ideals. Thus the bans became an index of political instability: four in 1503, four in 1504, and three in 1505. The Medici restoration began in the same manner, with one in 1513, three in 1514, two in 1515, three in 1516, and three in 1517.[34]

The companies attempted to deal with the problems of frequent suppression by appointing long-term officials to oversee the fiscal affairs of the company while it was closed. The Company of San Frediano had been suppressed in 1495, showed no signs of activity until 1502,[35] and by 1520 was in total disarray:

How great is the disorder in which this company finds itself and its properties, not being able to make good on its accounts, nor to collect from its debtors, and the proper observance of the statutes has been neglected, and all this occurred because our meetings have no order. The captains and other officials, when requested to come to the company to take care of business, do not come to exercise the duties that they ought to perform. The company, on account of this, remains abandoned and there is no one who looks after its affairs.[36]

Amidst the government's widespread confiscations of ecclesiastical and confraternity property during the siege, the company lost its meeting place, which was regained in 1531 through the intercession of a papal emissary.[37]

The Company of Sant'Agnese recorded a few, sparse payments to singers during 1506–11, the first since its suppression in 1494. Already in 1508 the suppressions had severely disrupted this company's liturgical activity, resulting in

. . . the ruin and great disruption of our company, since we could not perform the necessary business at the appropriate times . . . the business being . . . the satisfaction of the obligations and bequests of those who have willed movable and fixed property to the company in order to celebrate divine Offices, or [to distribute] charity, or to recite laude for their souls, and they await the above intercessions and help.[38]

Statutes drafted at the end of the sixteenth century allude to the instability of these years:

[33] Polizzotto, 'Confraternities, Conventicles', 251.   [34] Ibid. 250.
[35] Payments to laudesi were made in 1502 and 1503 in fulfilment of the terms of a bequest.
[36] Trans. in Weissman, *Ritual Brotherhood*, 174–5.
[37] Ibid. 192–3; during the same period the Company of San Zanobi lost a house, and the Company of San Piero Martire lost a house, a farm, three parcels of land, and five shops.
[38] SA 4, fo. 133ʳ; for ed. and partial trans., see Weissman, *Ritual Brotherhood*, 187.

. . . up to the year 1496 [the company] continued to be governed by secular and lay persons without particular statutes, according to deliberations that were made day to day. But in that year the said company was brought under new regulations and statutes which they drew up, and proceeded thus until 1515 . . . at which time all previous statutes were discarded, and new statutes were compiled . . . But because the changing and passing of time always brings new circumstances, [it was] necessary to make some corrections, limitations, and additions to these statutes in 1550 . . .[39]

The Company of San Bastiano fared no better for having become a disciplinati company prior to 1520. In 1525 the company had not met for three years 'on account of the plague and the evil times'.[40] In spite of repeated attempts to draw and sustain members by cancelling debts and lowering dues, the company languished for the next half-century, until it began to revive in the 1570s.

The Company of San Zanobi recorded sporadic payments to singers in 1498–1503, 1505, and 1512, but statutes drafted in 1508 prescribed business as usual. Laudesi were to be hired according to their merits and paid no more than L. 120 per year, the Sunday morning procession was to be led by six trumpeters, laude in honour of God, the Virgin, and St Zenobius were to be sung every evening of obligatory feasts, after Compline, at the usual company altar; and the feast of St Zenobius was to be celebrated

. . . without the display and needless pomp of the world. Thus . . . the usual laude are to be sung in the middle of the Cathedral after Compline of the vigil and the day of such ceremony, before the lectern and at the head of the above bishop and confessor [St Zenobius], which activity is to be prepared for with candles and with the angels hung from the star in the usual way, and with organ and trumpets according to ancient practice.[41]

But after three years the difficulty of the times was revealed when the captains unanimously decided that

. . . the laudesi who sing the laude in Santa Maria del Fiore are all dismissed from this day forward, and this has been done because of a tax placed upon this company by the officials in charge of taxing the religious institutions.[42]

In fact, the company continued to hire singers until 1526, but thereafter was closed for most of the next two decades, during which time the strategy of appointing an interim committee worked no better for San Zanobi than it had for San Frediano. In 1546 the company's disorderly

---

[39] Appendix I, doc. 30.   [40] Weissman, *Ritual Brotherhood*, 180.
[41] Appendix I, doc. 31.
[42] SZ 2177, fasc. 18, fo. 200ᵛ [5 Oct. 1511]: 'E più vinsono per 6 fave nere che' laldesi che chantono le laude in Sancta Maria del Fiore sieno tati [tutti] chassi da ogi in là, e questo feciono per rispetto da la 'nposta che stetta [stata] posta a detta chonpagnia dagli uficiali fatti a porre a' religiosi.'

state was the pretext under which the grand duke assumed control of the company:

Having appreciated the aforementioned pious works [accomplished by the confraternity], His Excellency wishes to participate in the spiritual benefits of the company and to be counted among our members . . . However, the aforementioned Duke, illuminated by God, and by His sweetest mother, Madonna Saint Mary, Ever Virginal, and by our Pastor and Advocate, St Zenobius, orders the aforementioned captains and counselors to add eight men as Reformers, who must, given the things that have happened in the past which have damaged the company not a little because of the bad custody and negligence of its ministers, reform and correct all errors and conserve and maintain the accounts and property of this holy house and protect the affairs of the company from decline and usurpation. And these men created and elected by His Excellency must remain in this office for life . . . and their authority must be as great as the whole body of the confraternity . . . and at least four of the Reformers must be present with the captains and counselors at all deliberations and decision-making sessions regarding the affairs of the company. And in the event that some doubt or hesitation should arise between the captains, counselors and ministers in the correction of delinquents . . . the chaplain, chancellor, or provisioner must expose such cases to the Reformers.[43]

By the middle of the sixteenth century, no lay company was untouched by the ravages of that period—radical loss of members, indifference to office-holding, loss of dues, accumulation and cancellation of members' debts, company mergers, loss of property and meeting places, and neglect of ritual and liturgical duties.[44] The laudesi companies fared better than most, but during years of cultic disruption and unfulfilled bequests, the liturgical mooring of their lauda-singing had loosened. It had become a difficult and outmoded practice to maintain, and the companies petitioned to substitute other charitable or liturgical activities. In 1538, the Company of Santa Croce complained of the

. . . very great difficulty that [now] occurs because there is no longer the abundance of singers that we once had, and in observance of this difficulty we wish to conduct in place of the singing of laude a charity of L. 25 per year to be given to the daughter [of one] of our brothers who is in need at the time of her marriage.[45]

The company also abandoned its traditional Assumption feast, when the 'lighted star' had been hung in the church and laude sung on the vigil, followed by a gathering the next morning at the company altar of all the company men holding lighted candles. But 'those times were more

---

[43] ASF, CmRS, Capitoli 155 [1555], fos. 28ᵛ–29ᵛ; trans. in Weissman, *Ritual Brotherhood*, 200–1.
[44] Ibid. 173, and ch. 4, *passim*.
[45] Appendix I, doc. 32. The text is badly damaged, and I have taken some liberties with the translation since the intent of the document seems clear.

prosperous, and people were more devout than they are at present . . .
[and] we no longer wish to be bound or obligated by the ancient
regulation'.[46] Most telling, certain details of the ceremony appear to have
faded from all memory.[47] When the company drafted its *Libro di dote*
(Book of Dowries) in 1565, lauda-singing had become no more than a
memory preserved in the ancient books of statutes:

Our ancient fathers and predecessors having considered . . . the prayers and
laude that are paid to them by us Christians, it was thus resolved that our
company should be called the Company of the LAUDE [for] they wished that
the name correspond to the activity, and therefore they ordained that besides the
divine offices, laude should be sung every feast-day by capable men and
sufficient [numbers of] singers. [But] such devotion has declined for a long
time now because there have not been enough men inclined to that office.
Therefore . . . our paternal captains together with the men of our company
carried out a new reform with the consent of our father Corrector and the Vicar
of the Archbishop of Florence, and in order not to fall short in pious and
Christian works, and being no longer able to sing laude because of the
impossibility of the [i.e. lack of] men and the wickedness of the times, they
want instead to give each year L. 25 as a dowry to a young girl who must be the
natural and legitimate daughter of one of our brothers . . .[48]

The Company of Sant'Agnese drafted new statutes in 1584, by which
time it had long since abandoned the devotion by means of an arrangement with the Carmine friars:

. . . it is said that at the time when this company sang laude, there were various
testators who bequeathed to this [company] more fixed properties with the
obligation, among others, to have a vigil or Nocturne of the Dead recited by the
friars of the Carmine after the laude, and . . . as much wax given to them as
required by the bequest. It happened afterwards that, the singers of laude not
being content with the small wages and the salary that was given to them, it was
necessary to dismiss the singing of the said laude as a thing that was not
obligatory. Wherefore it was agreed with the friars that they would recite the
same vigil, and Nocturne of the Dead, in addition to a certain number of Masses
for the Dead, and certain feasts arranged by the testators, and [the friars] would
have the same payment as that provided by the testator to be spent, and they [the
friars] should contribute the wax . . .[49]

The low ebb of this company's once fervent devotion is measured in
its willingness to pay the friars for activities that were formerly the
company's *raison d'être*. The company's activities were now centred on
the local parish—the distribution of alms, the management of the

---

[46] Ibid.
[47] Ibid.; the latter part of this document seems to allude to this problem.
[48] Appendix I, doc. 33.   [49] Appendix I, doc. 34.

hospice for women, and, with increasing attention, the management of dowries for the daughters of needy company members.[50]

When the Company of San Zanobi redrafted statutes in 1555, lauda-singing survived only as an optional devotion on the feast of St Zenobius. The 1508 statute on lauda-singing *per se* had been stricken, and to the 1508 passage quoted above describing the San Zanobi feast was appended the following:

. . . Or instead of the said laude, there [may be] sung in our oratory on the vigil and the day itself [of the feast] two Vespers with thirteen priests, in addition to our chaplain, [to be sung] after those [Vespers] of the Cathedral, with those regulations, customs, and alms for the priests that have been customary in the past; and this, whether to sing laude or Vespers, is to be decided by the current captains . . .[51]

An undated document in a seventeenth-century hand lists annual expenses which indicate that San Zanobi, like the companies of Santa Croce and Sant'Agnese, had shifted its focus to the management of bequests for dowries.[52]

By 1565, lauda-singing had come full circle in the 240-year history of the Company of San Frediano. The devotion having moved to the centre of company activities in the late fourteenth century, it had now returned to exactly the role it had been assigned in the company's 1324 statutes, when laude were sung only on the feast of St Fredianus.[53] But the late sixteenth-century character of the company could not be further removed from its origins. Once a modest company with strong roots in the local, working-class parish, officers were now required to hold the rank of 'Dottore', 'Cavaliere' (nobility), or a high-placed city official, and members had to be 'persons of good quality and reputation, and must not be or have been grave-diggers, or messengers or employees of the commune, or of any magistrate of the city of Florence'.[54]

Although lauda-singing by laymen persisted longest of all in the Company of San Piero Martire, a measure temporarily enacted in 1555

---

[50] ASF, Acquisti e Doni 44 [*Capitoli*, 1584–1643], fos. 33 f. Additions made in 1607 and 1643 reflect the growing preoccupation with the management of dowries.

[51] Appendix I, doc. 35. Company records after 1526 indicate, in fact, that for some time prior to 1555 the company had been opting for clerical services.

[52] SZ 2170, fasc. 5E [loose folio]: 'Dote L. 2871; Speziale L. 490; Monache dello Spirito Santo L. 150; Opera L. 140; Medico L. 84; Prestanze L. 40; [Total] L. 3,725'.

[53] ASF, Acquisit è Doni 42 [*Capitoli*, 1565], fo. 34ᵛ: '[in fulfilment of the bequest of Mona Caterina] . . . si possa spendere in detta festa cio[è] [in] cera, laldieri, bruciate, et collatione, et vino . . . L. 21'.

[54] Ibid., fos. 4ʳ, 23ʳ⁻ᵛ: '. . . non possa sedere alcuno altro offitiale della nostra compagnia quantumque havessi grado di dottore or cavaliere o havessi nella città offitio di qual si voglia grado . . .; [fos. 23ʳ⁻ᵛ] [novices] sieno persone de buona qualità et fama, et che non sieno o sieno stati beccamorti o messi o famigli del comune o di alcuno magistrato della città di Firenze'.

was a sign of contemporary decline and a herald of the lay singer's eventual extinction:

. . . the aforementioned captains . . . noticed that the new laudesi did not sing the laude—or rather, the number of laude—that until now used to be sung by the company's laudesi on certain days according to the custom and habit of their company. The captains wanted to maintain the honour of their company on this matter and so . . . they resolved that for the future the company's laudesi would no longer sing laude in the church of Santa Maria Novella. Instead, from the next Easter on, the novice brothers of the monastery of Santa Maria Novella would sing the antiphons of the most glorious Mother ever virgin Mary in the said church, in substitution of the said laudesi and in place of the aforementioned laude. They would receive the same salary that was given to the laudesi for the singing of the laude . . .[55]

By 1580, the company relinquished its 300-year-old devotion to the sacristy of Santa Maria Novella, and the only lay company to actively maintain the devotion thereafter was Orsanmichele. But even this great company experienced difficulty fulfilling bequests, and here too the choir consisted primarily of clerics by c.1585.[56] The Dominican friar Serafino Razzi published his *Libro primo delle laude* (Razzi[1]) in 1563, the first Florentine lauda print of the century, and if there is any truth to his claim that it revived the custom of daily lauda-singing, this revival could only have been taking place among his fellow clerics.

Decline gave way to transformation as the lay companies, weakened and disoriented by the vicissitudes of the early sixteenth century, slowly rebuilt in the vastly changed society of grand ducal Florence. The older confraternal traditions, like lauda-singing, receded into the background of company activity or disappeared altogether, and new generations of Florentines, lacking contact with or commitment to the older traditions, reorganized the lay companies according to new perceptions of piety and community based on principles of hierarchy, class distinction, and obedience. The older, city-wide companies, like the laudesi and disciplinati, tended to become élite, neigbourhood groups under the control of the duke. The laudesi companies of San Zanobi, Sant'Agnese, and Santa Croce, for example, limited themselves to neighbourhood activity by the late sixteenth century, and particularly to the management of dowries for poor girls.[57] On the other hand, the majority of the new

[55] Appendix I, doc. 36.

[56] OSM 31bis, fo. 26[r–v] [20 May 1569]: [the company was petitioning the Grand Duke to reduce the number of chaplains, specified in bequests, from 14 to 12, because it was difficult to find 14 chaplains who] '. . . voglino venire a servire per L. 12 el mese, dicendo che se l'altre chiese e ministeri di Firenze danno a' loro cappellani di salario chi XIIII et chi XV lire el mese, [e'] non voglino venire a servire Hor San Michele per XII . . .'.

[57] On this general trend among 16th-c. Italian confraternities, see Black, *Italian Confraternities*, 178–84.

companies founded in the sixteenth century reflected the stratification of Florentine society. Parish and craft companies, in growing numbers, revealed strong neighbourhood ties, and their working-class membership was determined by the exclusivity of the older companies.[58]

The lay companies' loss of their semi-autonomous and city-wide character, and their subsequent reorientation to the parish, signalled one of the most profound changes in sixteenth-century Florentine society. The success of the duke in subjugating the lay companies was greatly aided by the Counter-Reformation, a gradual process, the beginning of which is discernible in the 1530s, and through which new attitudes towards piety and church community arose and were eventually codified during the Council of Trent.[59] Confronted by the Protestant challenge, the Counter-Reformation Church promoted the authority of the Church hierarchy and the clergy (and the corresponding virtues of obedience and orthodoxy), which also had the effect of strengthening the prince's position in his state. In particular, the decrees of Trent strengthened the authority of the diocesan clergy with respect to the lay companies by requiring episcopal visitation and approval of all pious places.[60] The Florentine provincial synod of 1573 took further steps which brought all the lay companies under the increasing control of the parish clergy—lay companies of every sort were now forbidden to celebrate Mass on Sundays or feast-days without the prior permission of the local parish priest.[61] The Church actively promoted Eucharistic devotion, which effectively affirmed the authority of local clergy and strengthened the cause of orthodoxy.[62] The cult of the eucharistic host had moved to the centre of confraternal devotion by the late sixteenth century; in 1588 the altar of the Company of San Zanobi, called the altar of 'Our Lady' after the ancient patroness of the laudesi companies, was rededicated to the Holy Sacrament.[63]

The chief sponsors of traditional confraternal life, the friars, receded in the face of the advancing forces of centralized government and diocesan clergy. The torch of religious renewal, having reached its most distant bearer in the hands of the lay companies, now returned to the upper levels of the Church hierarchy. An élite corps of priests, the Jesuits,

---

[58] Weissman, *Ritual Brotherhood*, 198–235.

[59] Hall, *Renovation and Counter-Reformation*, 1–15; N. Davis, 'From "Popular Religion" to Popular Cultures', in S. Ozment (ed.), *Reformation Europe: A Guide to Research* (St. Louis, 1982), 327–8.

[60] 22nd session of the Council of Trent (1562), rubrics 8 and 9, ed. and trans. by H. J. Schroeder, *Canons and Decrees of the Council of Trent* (St. Louis, 1960), 156–7.

[61] Weissman, *Ritual Brotherhood*, 223.

[62] Ibid. 222–3.

[63] Paatz, *Die Kirchen von Florenz*, iii. 379. This was also the dedication of the chapel at which the Santo Spirito laudesi performed in the late 16th c. Weissman, *Ritual Brotherhood*, 220–35.

administered a Counter-Reformation version of the affective devotion that had originated long before among friars and laymen.

The conditions that had fostered traditional laudesi devotion no longer existed in late sixteenth-century Florence, and there is no more poignant image of this fact than the fate of the laudesi companies at the two great mendicant churches of Florence. Dominican Santa Maria Novella and Franciscan Santa Croce, once the semi-autonomous centres of civic devotion, were the targets of major architectural renovations begun in 1565, two years after the close of the Council of Trent. The renovations were initiated by the 'super patron' of Florence, the duke himself, and were intended as a demonstration of piety and devotion to the spirit of the Council, but with the aim of securing from the pope the title of Grand Duke.[64] Similarly, all aspects of the artistic design were presided over by a single man, Giorgio Vasari, whose overall scheme for each church dictated the architectural, sculptural, and pictorial elements, the co-ordination of which was aimed at the creation of a harmonious and self-consistent effect. The results, which closely reflect the Tridentine attitude towards architecture set forth in St Charles Borromeo's *Instructiones fabricae et supellectilis ecclesiasticae* (1577), were the elimination of the rood-screen, the removal of the choir behind the high altar, and a renewed emphasis upon the design and pictorial scheme of the nave altars. Ostensibly, these changes were intended to benefit the laity, whose sense of participation in the Mass was enhanced, and whose devotion might be excited by more accessible nave altars. But the effect of these changes upon the Florentine churches bears closer examination.

The medieval interiors of the mendicant churches had evolved, like republican culture, through the interaction of a 'loose, complex bundle of immunities, privileges, and liberties'.[65] The friars, the guilds (acting as *operai*), the commune, and a host of secular patrons (including the lay companies) all contributed to the gradual process of accretion whereby the churches filled with countless independently conceived and executed decorations. Acting either as a private patron or the member of a lay company, the Florentine laity could hope to leave their mark, quite literally, on the interior of a church, and to find final rest in a place rendered all the more holy by these countless acts of devotion.

The powers that had previously mattered most now mattered least in the Cosimo/Vasari renovations. Cosimo pre-empted the authority of the friars and the guilds, and patronage rights, redistributed to those families with proper wealth and connection to the duke, no longer included the right to determine the altar design, expense, or, at Santa

[64] Hall, *Renovation and Counter-Reformation*, 6–7.
[65] Becker, *Florence in Transition*, ii. 16.

Croce, the subject of the altar-piece.[66] The renovations swept aside, in a few short years, the centuries of devotional insignias left by Florentine citizens, and in the process the laudesi companies in both churches lost their traditional ritual sites. Within fifteen years after the renovation had begun in Santa Maria Novella, one of the oldest and largest lay companies in Florence, the Company of San Piero Martire, had disappeared. In 1579 the site patronized by the Company of Santa Croce for three centuries was reassigned by the grand duke to Giovanni Niccolini, the son of a cardinal, and the company was allotted a location that amounted to spiritual exile—just outside the church wall.

The Counter-Reformation church, with its architectural renovations, appears to have offered the laity an unprecedented opportunity to participate in religious devotion. But the medieval rood-screens in Santa Maria Novella and Santa Croce had not prevented the laity from passing through and practising their own vernacular liturgies at the chancel altars. Ironically, their destruction coincided with a time when lay initiative in devotion had been pre-empted. The rood-screens were gone, for their function had now been spiritualized in the Counter-Reformation church. During the Vasari renovation the Santa Croce *operai*, undoubtedly reflecting a ducal attitude, had argued that the laity could not own 'things in churches',[67] and since at least the time of Antoninus the clergy had sought to maintain 'a more rigid separation between the worlds of the laity and the clergy'.[68] Separated from the clergy, excluded from the liturgy, reoriented to the nave, and deprived of patronage rights, the laity were nudged a step back towards their ancient role as spectators in the process of their own salvation. As the church sought to regain control of the signs and symbols of its faith, one of the most ancient symbols of lay religious activism, the lauda, passed almost entirely into the hands of clerical singers.

---

[66] Hall, *Renovation and Counter-Reformation*, 87.   [67] Ibid. 23.

[68] Henderson, 'Confraternities and the Church', 81. The Company of Sant'Agnese noted in its 1584 statutes that it had turned from liturgical devotions to the charitable activity of providing dowries partly because of an ecclesiastical prohibition against the participation of laity in the *piatanze* of the friars; ASF, Acquisti e Doni 44, fo. 35ᵛ.

APPENDIX I

Documents

In the following documents, square brackets indicate editorial additions or interpolations, angle brackets illegible words and phrases, upper half square brackets marginalia.

Doc. 1. Company of Sant'Agnese. 1584 statutes. ASF, Acquisti e Doni 44, *Capitoli*, 1584–1643, fos. 5^{r–v}.

La veneranda e religiosa compagnia di di [*sic*] stendardo, intitolata in Madonna Santa Maria delle Laude et Santa Agnesa di Firenze . . . hebbe il suo principio circa gl'anni del Signore 1245, et si chiamò da stendardo perché gl'huomini e donne che di quella erono, andando segnati con una croce bianca et rossa in sula spalla destra, seguivano ogni volta che occorreva il bisogno lo stendardo della sacrosanta Inquisitione in aiuto della sacrosanta Chiesa ad istirpatione degl'heretici et heresie che allhora erano et pulullavano in questa città di Firenze. Et oltre a ciò perché si ragunavono in detta chiesa del Carmine alcuni di essi per loro devotione a cantare laude spirituale [*sic*], prese il titolo delle Laude, e perché gl'erono fatte limosine e lasciati beni fu ordinato che gli capitani et offitiali di quella si ragunassero certi giorni determinati a fare opere di pietà et distribuire elemosine . . .

Doc. 2. Company of Santa Croce. 1485 statutes. ASF, Compagnie Religiose Soppresse, Capitoli 874, 1485–1538, fo. 5^v.

. . . che debino e sieno ubrighati sotto caricho di loro conscienza a fare cantare le lalde ogni dì di festa comandata a lalde e honore di Dio e di nostra Donna nella chiesa di Sancta Croce di Firenze. Et più vogliamo che lla vigilia della Ascensione di nostra Donna si pongha la stella accesa nel mezo della chiesa e chantisi le lalde in decta sera chom'era di buona usanza antica. Et più vogliamo che e' sopradetti capitani e consiglieri possino spendere quello e quanto parrà loro a ffare cantare dette lalde.

Doc. 3. Company of San Zanobi. 1428 statutes. SZ 2170, fasc. 2, *Statuti*, 1428, fos. 47^v–48r.

XVIIII. Del fare le vigilie per chi lasciasse o volesse si facessono. Ancora ordiniamo e provediamo che se alcuno lasciasse de' nostri confratri di decta compagnia veramente o per lascio o per testamento o quanto fusse di piacere de' suoi o parenti o rede od executori, quanto a lloro piacesse o parrà come per continuata et honesta et laudabile usanza in decta compagnia fare assai volte vigilie, que' tali che avessono a fare o volessono diliberare sieno col nostro camarlingo et dieno quel numero di candele convenevole et honesto secondo rimarrano d'acordo col nostro camarlingo delle candele che vogliono per la decta vigilia, che il nostro camarlingo la sera ordinata et diputata et facto a sapere a' nostri capitani et consiglieri et quelli che possono sieno della nostra compagnia invitati et pregati sieno per l'amore di Dio.

Il nostro camarlingo faccia sonare la nostra campana di campanile Ferrantina chiamata, a quell'ora che parrà a' capitani per lo nostro messo o per altri, et suoni solo una volta quanto fusse di dire xxv Pater Nostri et Ave Marie. Et ristata si dieno dodici tocchi et non più. Al quale sonare si ragunino i decti capitani et consiglieri et altri di nostra compagnia, et similemente i parenti di decto morto, co' lloro quelli che a lloro parrà per loro honoranza. Et posto a sedere il nostro cappellano, capitani, parenti, et altri a decta vigilia venuti, il decto nostro camarlingo o proveditore avute le candele e apicchate al leggio grande, il quale si ponga inna[n]zi a l'altare della vergine Maria come et dove si dicono le laude.

Et di poi si dieno le candele di quello numero parrà a decto camarlingo, a tutti i capitani et parenti per ciascuno due, el cappellano tre, et per tutti gli altri una per uno, et accese si tenghino quanto si pena a dire la decta vigilia et laude. Et per li nostri laudesi decte quelle laude che sono facte per decta devotione, et finite come è l'usanza. Allora il nostro cappellano con tre sacerdoti i quali lui arà a cciò invitati ad aiutare cantare la sequentia de' morti, cioè Dies Ire et cetera. Et a' detti tre sacerdoti il decto camarlingo dia per ciascuno due candele. Et finita detta sequentia il nostro prete, o altri che piacesse a' decti capitani, faccia et notifichi per cui si fa la decta vigilia, et racomandigia con De Profundis, et cetera, et l'oratione. Fatte tutte queste cose si faccia la confessione generale et annunti il perdono che si concede a chi si truova di decta compagnia a decte cose fare et devotioni, et poi suonosi l'Ave Maria, et ciascuno sia licentiato data la beneditione il sacerdote.

Doc. 4. Bequest of Orlandino Lapi (13 January 1387/8). SSP 78, *Ricordi*, 1444–1521 (glued to inside front cover).

Testamentum Orlandini Lapi. Fit fides, qualiter de anno 1387, et die 13 januarii Orlandinus filius olim Lapi Orlandini setaiuolus populi Sancti Fidriani de Florentia suum ultimum condidit testamentum, in quo plura disposuit, et inter cetera re⟨liquit⟩ ⟨societa⟩ti maiorum Sanctae Mariae del Bigallo de Florentia unam dom⟨um⟩ sitam in populo Sancti Fidriani in via Clara de Florentia cum pluri[bu]s oneribus, et inter coetera cum onere solvendi libras quinque societa[ti] Laudarum del Carmino. Item reliquit fratribus del Carmino de Florentia libras duodecim, et libras quinque fratribus Sanctae Mariae Novellae, et libras quinque fratribus minoribus Sanctae Crucis, et libras quinque societati Laudarum Sancti Spiritus cum onere annuatim im perpetuum teneantur facere dic⟨ere⟩ unam vigiliam pro anima dicti testatoris et suorum mortuorum . . .

Doc. 5. Company of San Frediano. Bequest of frate Giovanni Lozzi di San Pagolo (1415). ASF, Acquisti e Doni 41, *Memoriale*, 1488, fos. 2ᵛ–3ʳ.

Sono obligati e' capitani di San Friano che pel tempo saranno ogn'anno im perpetuo la prima domenica dopo el dì di San Friano far cantare le laude nella chiesa di San Friano con una vigilia per l'anima di decto fra' Giovanni. Essi di poi aggiunto per consuetudine in decto di dare le bruciate, et fare la sera nella compagnia nostra una collatione a' preti et a' laudieri et a gl'uomini della compagnia. Spendesi comunemente in tucto L. octo in circa.

Doc. 6. Company of Sant'Agnese. Bequest of Chiaro d'Ardinghello (1377). SA 29, *Beni della compagnia*, 1488, fos. 3^{l-r} [left-right].

In caricho del Chiaro d'Ardinghello. In prima che ogni anno in perpetuo per la festa della Anuntiata, cioè a dì xxv di marzo, ànno avere e' frati del Charmino lire dodici per una piatanza ànnove a ire due de' chapitani a desinare in luogho di testimoni, e uno sindacho   L. xii

E a dì sei di dicembre ogni anno in perpetuo ànno avere i detti frati lire dieci chontanti, àssene a fare quello che 'l detto Chiaro lasciò in segreto al priore di detti frati   L. x

E a dì otto di dicembre ogn'anno in perpetuo ànno avere i sopradetti frati lire dodici per una piatanza ànnovi andare a desinare in luogho di testimoni due capitani   L. xii

E a dì xxv di dicembre il dì di Pasqua di Natale s'à a dare a' poveri del nostro ghonfalone del Dragho lire dodici di pane chotto   L. xii

E più s'à a fare del mese d'aghosto ogn'anno in perpetuo una vigilia e laude a modo usato di lire sei   L. vi

E più si fa ogn'anno in perpetuo del mese d'agosto, cioè àssi a dare alla chompagnia di San Friano di Firenze lire quattro per fare una vigilia alle laude   L. iiii

[total lire] 56

Chiaro d'Ardinghello del popolo di Sancto Friano di Firenze lasciò alla nostra chompagnia uno podere posto nel popolo di San Piero a Monticelli, luogho detto Via di Mezo chon chasa da lavoratore, e chon incharicho che qui a rischontro si vede, àssene l'anno di ficto lire cinquantacinque, e una cesta di baccelli l'anno quando facciamo la festa della Scensione, chome appare a' libro biancho chiamato specchio, a 2   L. Lv [sic]

Doc. 7. Company of Santo Spirito. *Ufficio generale* on 11 November 1424. SSP 1, *Memoriale/Ricordanze*, 1419–27, fo. 11^v.

A dì xi di novembre 1424 fu fatto detto rinovale e solene messa e ufic[i]o la mattina, presenti iiii de' capitani e molti della compagnia invitati e sopra le sepolture della compagnia denanzi al chapitolo, e poi i frati colla cerone andati intorno al chiostro e tornati per la porta grande, e demmo a frate Bernardo Giambollari sagrestano L. cinque . . . e la sera dinanzi ffacemo solenne vigilia a le lalde con 6 frati e huomini con candele in mano e libre iii di candele nuove . . . L. 1 s. 7.

Doc. 8. Company of San Zanobi. 1428 statute concerning the Feast of St Zenobius. SZ 2170, fasc. 2, *Statuti*, 1428, fos. 51^v–52^v.

XXIII. Del modo del fare le nostre feste di Sancta Maria et di Sancto Zenobio . . . Alla festa del glorioso sanctissimo Zenobio nostro padrone et protectore et advocato inanzi al altissimo Idio di tutto il popolo fiorentino, et guida di questa sancta congregatione, fraternità, et compagnia, i capitani et consiglieri che saranno nel mese di maggio nel principio di decto mese chiamino et eleggino sei festaiuoli o otto per decta festa adornare et fare. Li quali così chiamati abbino per otto dì dinanzi aconciare il decto gonfalone per decto modo di sopra et lampanaio. Et di sotto appiccare i nostri drappelloni che si faranno per li nostri capitani et consiglieri, o altri singulari persone di nostra compagnia, come parla il capitolo sequente xxiii. Proveggino di fiori, rose, viuole et quello pare a' decti festaiu[o]li per aconciare et adornare i scudi et compassi come è d'usanza. Et più di due trombetti, sonatori, laudesi abbino a invitare per le laude della vigilia, e scuola, et per la sera di decta festa come nel capitolo delle laude parla, cioè capitolo xvi [doc. 14]. Et che per detti festaiuoli non si possa fare alcuna cosa più che il modo usato sanza diliberatione di detti capitani et consiglieri per li due terzi di loro.

Et al facto dell'oferta la quale vogliamo sempre si faccia la mattina di detta festa quanto sia possibile fare alla compagnia per quello parrà a i capitani et consiglieri che allora saranno. Et quando la decta offerta si debba fare, et data l'ora et dove, et invitati tutti coloro che si poteranno invitare per parte de' capitani, et venuti et ragunati insieme i detti capitani et consiglieri, et tutti quelli saranno della compagnia nella nostra sacrestia, o veramente in altro loro [*sic*; loco] dove parrà ai detti capitani, o all'opera di San Giovanni, o alla Misericordia. Et [es]sendo tutti ragunati, il nostro sindaco et overo proveditore mettino in ordine la detta oferta, in prima i due trombetti col segno nostro, et il nostro cappellano et il proposto, et uno de' compagnia accoppiati insieme. Et seguitando accoppia accoppia come si richiede, et così tutti gli altri di rietro [*sic*] ai capitani et consiglieri. Et per decto sindaco al cappellano et a ciascuno de' capitani abbino uno torchietto di libra, et i consiglieri per ciascuno uno torchietto d'oncie otto, et a tutti gli altri di mezza libra, faccendo quella che parrà ai detti capitani fare. Et facta decta oferta, vogliamo et preghiamo che per gli detti capitani et festaiuoli sia proveduto essere alquanti dì inanzi a decta festa con messer lo proposto et li altri signori canonaci di detta chiesa fiorentina, et co[n] li operai o cchi acciò accadesse dovere parlare . . .

Doc. 9. Company of Sant'Agnese. Feast of St Lucy. SA 24, *Entrata e Uscita*, 1440–7, fo. 340^v.

Alla schuola che ssi fe' per Santa Agniesa, cioè dovevasi fare in quest'anno dominicha doppo Santa Agniesa a dì 22 di giennaio e non si fe' per certi inpedimenti, fessi ogi questo dì dominicha a dì 28 di giennaio 1446, c[i]oè la

schuola e invitoronsi tutti i chantori delle laude di Firenze, debbesi ispendere
nella chollazione insino in lire sei che chosì lasciò mona Filippa di ghrano si
spendessi della sua sustanza avuto rendite fessi doppo desinare chantassi in chiesa
alla chappella di Santa Agniesa e in rifettoro di frati si fe' la cholazione . . . mele
s. 12, finochio s. 6, 1/4 di lupini s. 2 d. 8, 1 barila di vino biancho L. 3 s. 10, 210
berlinghozzi L. 2 s. 10 . . .

Doc. 10. Company of San Zanobi. 1428 statute concerning the company *scuola*.
SZ 2170, fasc. 2, *Statuti*, 1428, fo. 45^r.

XV. Dello apparare [imparare] le laude per conservare la divotione di ciò.
Vogliamo che considerata la prima divotione et reverenzia facta per li nostri
antichi et principiatori di questa sancta congregatione, fraternità, et compagnia
fu della devotione del cantare le laude a honore di Dio et della vergine sempre
Maria et del glorioso messer Sancto Zenobio pastore fiorentino. Et però i
capitani che sono o saranno di decta fraternità debbiano avere buona diligentia et
studio intorno a cciò provedere che tutti i dì domenicali faccino insegnare le
laude a quelli tali fussono a cciò atti di nostra compagnia o di fuori . . . Et questo
facciano sempre i detti dì dopo nona e dopo mangiare nella nostra sacrestia et
residenzia.

Doc. 11. Company of San Piero Martire. Laudese contract, 13 June 1406. SMN
321, *Provisioni, deliberationi, e partiti*, 1401–14, fo. 58^v.

Item che Lorenzo d'Andrea del popolo di San Pagholo di Firenze et Piero di
Nicholò del popolo di Sancto Friano di Firenze siano cantatori . . . per tempo
d'uno anno [beginning 1 August 1406 at L. 2 per month] . . . con questi pacti e
conditioni ch'eglino siano tenuti d'aparechiare ogni sera alle laude e ogni dì di
festa solepne aparechiare il descho della compagnia bene e sollecitamente e
cantare le laude come si richiede e fare ogni altra cosa bene e sollecitamente . . . si
richiede e secondo ch'è consueto.

Doc. 12. Company of San Piero Martire. 1447 statute concerning laudesi
contracts. SMN 324, *Capitoli*, 1447, fo. 3^v.

VIII. Delle laude. Anchora fu proveduto che le laude usitate di cantarsi in detta
chiesa di Sancta Maria Novella si debbono cantare i' nel luogho acciò usato et
deputato ogni sera in nella forma et modo consueto divotamente, per buoni
cantori overo laudesi, condocti et electi per detti chapitani. E' quali laudesi
debbono essere per lo meno quatro, et che uno o laudese o altri secondo parrà a'
detti chapitani sia deputato il quale abbia aparechiare et sparechiare ogni sera el
legio, appichare le candele, et trovare et ordinare le panche et tucte l'altre chose
fare che è usato pel passato. Et possino e' decti laudesi il più avere lire due el mese
secondo la volontà de' detti capitani. Et debbono e' decti laudesi due volte l'anno

esser rafermi per detti capitani, cioè del mese di lulglio et di gennaio, et chi non
vincesse el partito per quatro fave nere se intenda esser casso et rimosso. Et che
ogni sera finite le laude, si facci la confessione colla absolutione usata per uno
frate del convento di Sancta Maria Novella, a cui sarà commesso per il priore di
decta chiesa. Et ogni volta che si trovasse detti laudesi manchare del loro uficio,
possino et debbano esser corretti o condannati in detenere del loro salario
secondo parrà alla discretione di detti capitani.

Doc. 13. Company of San Zanobi. Decision to acquire a new laudario, 8 August
1339. SZ 2182, fasc. 36, *Entrata e Uscita*, 1333–77, fo. 20^v (Plate 11).

[The company officers have decided] . . . di fare uno libro bisognia di fare grande
da chantare laude, iscritto di lettere grosse et notato e 'storiato. Fu renduto per
chonsilglio e fatto poi il partito fu vinto da tutti quelgli della chonpangnia che
v'erano che il libro fosse fatto il più bello che fare si possa, e ffu rimesso ne' detti
chapitani ch'elgli eleggiesono tre huomini, i milgliori che sapessono della
chonpangnia, per uficiali a ffare il detto libro . . . e ffare ongni spesa che bisognia
di danari della chonpangnia et delgli altri i quali vorranno fare alchuno aiuto a
ffare il detto libro.

Doc. 14. Company of San Zanobi. 1428 statutes concerning lauda-singing. SZ
2170, fasc. 2, *Statuti*, 1428, fo. 45^{r-v}.

XVI. Del cantare le laude et de eleggere laudesi di confermare o cassare . . .
Ordiniamo et vogliamo che per niuno modo mancare non debba di cantare le
laude ogni sera ⌐di festa comandata⌐ come è per antica consuetudine che per
quest[i] nostri capitoli e ordini sia conservata la detta devotione ad honore di
Dio et della vergine Maria. I capitani et consiglieri che sono o saranno per li
tempi che proveggino dicenti laudesi, *et sonatori* [stricken] a cantare le dette
laude, tanti et quanti reggino sia di bisogno con quello salario parrà et piacerà
loro, raguardando il bisogno della nostra compagnia, la quale è ora asai in
bisogno. Con questa conditione et modo: vogliamo che in ogni entrata di
capitani sieno aprovati o confermati o cassi od electi altri di chi fusse casso. Et
questo abino a fare i capitani et consiglieri o la maggiore parte di loro et di ciò si
ne faccino partito come parrà a lloro. Et di ciò parla ancora nel capitolo VI de'
capitani di detta confermatione. Et questi tali laudesi vogliamo ogni sera ⌐di festa
comandata⌐ venghino all'ora debita in detta chiesa maggiore che veghino [*sic*] sia
più abile et honesta, aparechiando il legio e l'altre cose ⟨. . .⟩ si richiegono
intorno a cciò fare, innanzi a l'altare di nostra Donna in fine di detta chiesa a llato
alla porta maggior, et così per continuo si faccia, overamente in altro luogo dove
paresse a' capitani più devotione . . .

Doc. 15. Company of Sant'Agnese. Laudese funeral, 25 September 1445. SA
24, *Entrata e Uscita*, 1440–7, fos. 252^r, 254^r.

. . . Antonio di Benedetto di Butino del popolo di Santa Maria di Verzaia . . . fu
ghrande *parziale* [deleted], zelante, e benefattore, e llaldese chontinuo più d'anni

50 fermamente, e a tutte le chose della chonpagnia sollecito, e molto vi fu
onorato e bene amato tutta la chonpagnia presente . . . [fo. 254^r]: Alla vigilia alle
laude per l'anima d'Antonio di Benedetto di Butino . . . ch'era nostro benifattore
solicito alle laude per tempo d'anni 50 o più ogni sera sanza alchuno premio . . .,
cholonne vera di questa chonpagnia e in ogni suo a[b]ito fu chostumato . . . e ffu
molto onorato in questa chonpagnia, el perchè e' chapitani deliberono si gli
facesi honore, e però gli feciano oggi questo dì una vigilia alle laude ghrande e
orevole, di tutte cose nuove e oltre a quale ch'era nella chonpagnia anche ⟨. . .⟩m
libre 6, on[cie] 4 di chandele nuove . . . L. 3 s. 8.

Doc. 16. Company of Sant'Agnese. Laudese contract, 1 November 1466. SA
115, *Lasciti e Legati*, 1466–1510, fo. 34^r (Plate 12).

Ghuelfo di Bartolomeo barbiere, famiglio della nostra chonpagnia e chantatore
delle lalde, de' avere per prezo . . . quando arà sodisfatto allo infrascritto obrigho
L. venti in uno anno. El quale anno inchominciò insino dì primo di novembre
1466, e de' finire a detto dì 1467. El quale obrigho fia questo, c[i]oè: Che 'l detto
Ghuelfo in detto anno deba chon sollecitudine ogni dì di festa chomandata
venire a dire le laude nella chiesa del Charmino di Fire[n]ze, tra lle 23 e 24 ore, e
aparechiare cl legio, e chosì isparechiare, e quando manchase deba esergli
ischontato del suo salare ⌐s. 5 per ogni volta manchase¬, e oltre al
dire le laude, deba ogni dì e ora fuse richiesto o dal proposto de' nostri chapitani
o da' sindachi che dovesi andare a raunare e' chapitani o altri ufici[ali] o uomini
della nostra chompagnia; chon sollecitudine andare e fare quanto di sopra è
detto, e in chaso nollo facese o manchase per suo difetto o nigrigenza per ogni dì
se gli deba torre s. 5 del suo salare, chosì del dire le laude chome de raunare e'
chapitani. E di questo n'abia a fare alla choscienza de' sindachi che pe[r] gli tenpi
saranno. El detto salaro deba al detto Ghuelfo paghare el sindacho di detta
chonpagnia, overo chamarlingho, ogni dua mesi chuella rata gli tocherà, c[i]oè,
che s'intenda el salaro e sarà rechonpensato in questo modo L. dodici per raunare
e' chapitani e altri ufici[ali], chom'è detto, e L. 8 s. ⟨. .⟩ per dire le laude, chom'è
detto, per tutto L. 20 . . . Antonio della Pucc[i]a nostro laudese de' avere L. sei a
dire le lalde insieme chon Ghuelfo nostro laudese, e chon Bernardino di
Francesco, uno anno [as above] . . . ogni dì di festa chomandata . . .
     Bernardino di Francescho nostro laldese de' avere L. sei per suo salaro a dire le
laude insieme chon [as above] . . .

Doc. 17. Company of Santo Spirito. Laudese contract, 17 March 1420/1. SSP 1,
Memoriale, ricordanze, 1419–27, fo. 35^v.

Ricordanza e memoria a ciascheduno della chompagnia dello Spirito Santo di
Spirito Santo [*sic*] sia che ad 17 di marzo 1420 [1421] tolsono e' chapitani e ladesi
Antonio di Pettro ladesse per chantare le laude ogni sera nella chiesa di Santo
Agostino, cioè per la chompagnia dello Spirito Santo, e deba avere L. due i[l] .
mese per suo salario d'achordo cho[n] lui, e questo dì detto di sopra chomi[n]ciò
al nome di Dio.

Doc. 18. Company of Santo Spirito. Laudese contract, 22 June 1424. Ibid., fo. 37^r.

E nel nome di Dio deto dì xxii di g[i]ugno 1424. Ragunato el corpo della compagnia . . . elessono e chiamaro e feciono spedalingo nuovo in detto spedale Antonio di Petro laldese, che canta le lalde con quelli patti e conditioni usati, e deba entrare a posta e volontà de' detti capitani e fare bene e con amore el suo uficio lui e la sua donna . . . con patto che da questo dì inanzi non deba né possa domandare salaro né provisione alchuna del chantare le lalde la sera in Santo Spirito, dov'era usato avere soldi 40 el mese per sua faticha e ubidenza, e così lui presente s'obriga e promete seguire di bene in megl[i]o di cantare le lalde la sera in Santo Spirito com'era usato, e per benificio fatto a lui di deto spedale s'obriga a noi di non doma[n]dare salare e cantare le lalde e seguire da qua ina[nzi] com'è usato per lo passato e di bene in megl[i]o e co[n] fede e amore.

Doc. 19. Company of Santo Spirito. Laudese contract, 1 December 1445. SSP 78, *Ricordi*, 1444–1521, fo. 20^v.

Richordanza chom'ogi questo dì primo di dicembre 1445 i chapitani in deti tenpi ànno tolto a salare Nocho e Ulivante a chantare le laude per dua anni prossimi. Debano venire chominciati [*sic*] sopradeto dì e debano avere per loro salare L. trenta sei l'anno, delle quali se debano chontare il fito d'un pezo di tera posta a Ghanghalandi che se n'à l'ano L. 28, e più L. cinque s'àno avere da la chonpagnia del Bighalo ogni ano a dì V di novembre 1446, e àno avere i[l] resto di chontati ogni ano che sono L. tre, e debano chantare ogni domenica, e ogni indì [*sic*] di festa chomandata, e la sera di Sancto Aghostino e di Sancto Nicholò, e manchando i[n] [o]gn⟨i⟩ volta no[n] fusino a chantare dete a chantare dete [*sic*] laude, àno a es[s]ere apuntati in s. 10 per ogni volta manchasino àno venire, e debano eserci a ore 23 la sera . . . L. 72.

Doc. 20. Company of San Frediano. Laudese contracts, 6 and 25 January 1410/1. SF 88, *Entrata e Uscita: Ricordi di Lasciti e Obblighi*, 1333–1441, fo. 105^r [6 Jan.]; SF 31, *Tratta degli Ufficiali*, 1394–1442, fo. 26^r [25 Jan.].

[6 Jan.] . . . Lorenzo di Matteo detto Posserello, il quale fa il servigio delle lalde, abia per Dio e per remunarazione del servigio e faticha dura a l'aparechio delle dette laude che si dichono ongni sera nella chesa di San Friano per ⟨il⟩ tempo passato per i[n]fino a dì primo di gennaio, anni detti 1410 [1411], L. quattro, e per l'avenire facendo il detto servigio e faticha delle dette lalde . . . el detto Lorenzo abia ongni anno per la sopradetta chagione L. sei l'anno, chominciando . . . a dì primo di gennaio 1410 [1411].
[25 Jan.]: A Lorenzo di Matteo che chanta le lalde in San Friano a dì 25 di giennaio lire quattro . . . per lla sua faticha cioè dell' aparechiare alle dette lalde . . . L. 4.

Doc. 21. Company of Santa Croce. Letter of indulgence from the bishop of Florence, 1297. ASF, Diplomatico Patrimonio Ecclesiastico, 7 February 1296/7 (Plate 10).

Franciscus, Dei et apostolice sedis gratia episcopus Florentinus, dilectis in Christo filiis, rectoribus sotietatis Sancte Crucis de Florentia ceterisque omnibus et singulis de sotietate predicta in predicta ecclesia convenientibus, salutem in Domino sempiternam. Licet cunctos in Dei servitio constitutos ubicumque fuerint sinceris affectibus diligamus, illos tamen magis amplectimur in visceribus caritatis qui devotionem suam Domino iugiter exhibentes de ipsorum actibus reddimur certiores. Exhibita quidem nobis verum supplicatio annuebat ut illis qui sotietati vestre fecerint se adscribi in ipso ingressu, nec non et vobis omnibus de sotietate predicta cum in dicta ecclesia Sancte Crucis ad processionem seu ad reddendum vel reddi faciendum laudes Deo nec non ad tractandum de ipsius sotietatis utilitatibus seu necessitatibus secundum consuetudinem quam habuistis actenus convenitis specialem indulgentiam facere dignaremus ac etiam illis qui vobis ammonitionis verbum disseminaverint faciendi vobis certam indulgentiam licentiam preberemus. Nos igitur ⟨vestris⟩ supplicationibus inclinati universis et singulis qui vestre sotietati fecerint se adscribi in ipso ingressu et etiam vobis de sotietate predicta quotienscumque ad reddendum seu reddi faciendum laudes Deo et sue matri virgini gloriose vel pro utilitatibus ipsius sotietatis seu necessitatibus in dicta ecclesia convenitis, de omnipotentis Dei misericordia et beatorum Johannis Baptiste ac Zenobii confessoris patronorum nostrorum ac Beate Reparate Virginis confisi quadraginta dies de iniuncta vobis penitentia misericorditer in domino relaxamus. Predicatoribus quoque seu vestris ammonitoribus predicte ecclesie fratribus qui vobis predicaverint vel ammonitionis documenta tradiderint predictam vobis eisdem diebus indulgentiam annuntiandi liberam concedimus facultatem. In cuius rei testimonium presentes litteras nostri sigilli fecimus appensione muniri. Datum Florentie anno Domini millesimo ducentesimo nonagesimo sexto, indictione nona, mense februarii, die septima.

Doc. 22. Company of Santa Croce. 1470 statute concerned with festal services. ASF, Compagnie Religiose Soppresse, Capitoli 53, fo. 1^r (without pagination).

I. [incomplete] . . . et per le feste comandate si dichino et o vero cantino in nella chiesa di Sancta Croce le laude ad honore di decta nostra advocata come antichamente s'è usato . . . considerato che per quelle grande devotione si generi et acquistisine grande util[i]tà spirituale et temporale. Alle quali laude intervenghino il più che se può de' capitani et de' fratelli di nostra compagnia . . . Et che in decte laude si possa spendere quello o quanto parrà a' decti capitani et a' loro consiglieri.

Doc. 23. Company of San Lorenzo. Letter of indulgence from the bishop of Florence, 1 April 1338. Ed. Cianfogni, *Memorie istoriche*, 220–1 (doc. XX).

. . . Capitaneis Societatis, et iis de Societate B. Laurentii Florentini tam maribus, quam feminis, tam presentibus, quam futuris salutem in Domino sempiternam. Si quasi per premia corda fidelium, ut suam Altissimo devotionem exhibeant excitamus statui providemus salubriter ipsorum, quod dignum est apud Dominum, et meritorum reputandum, porrectis itaque nobis pro parte vestra devotis supplicationibus inclinati, tenore presentium omnibus, et singulis, qui vestre Societati predicte fecerint se adscribi, in ipso eorum ingressu, si postmodum perseveraverint in eadem, nec non vobis omnibus de Societatis predicte vere penitentibus, et confessis, dum in dicta Ecclesia B. Laurentii conveneritis Missarum Solempnia, vel alia Divina Offitia, seu predicationes verbi Domini audituri, et de ipsius Societatis negotiis tractaturi, ac laudes de sero in dicta Ecclesia cantaturi, de Omnipotentis Dei misericordia, et B. Marie Virginis Matris eius, Beatorum quoque Johannis Baptiste, Zenobii, Reparate, ac Vencentii [*sic*] Patronorum Ecclesie Florentine meritis confidentes, auctoritate, qua fungimur, quadraginta dies iniuncta vobis, et eis penitentia, misericorditer relaxamus . . .

Doc. 24. Company of San Frediano. Election of laudesi for Lent, 26 March 1441. SF 4, *Partiti*, 1468–1510, fo. 23ʳ.

Item decto dì et hora inmantanente i detti capitani avendo electi et ordinata [*sic*] due a cantare laude nella decta chiesa ogni sera, tutta la quaresima, per devotione de' popoli, avendo veduto e udito per coloro in parte essi bene satisfatto, stantiorono loro lire otto, che a lloro sieno date, cioè, Antonio d'Alesso e *Antonio d'Adamo* [deleted] . . . con conditione che forniscano di cantare tutta la decta quaresima.

Doc. 25. Company of Sant'Agnese. Decision to raise the salary of a laudese, 23 September 1492. SA 4, *Partiti*, 1483–1509, fo. 52ᵛ.

Item e' prefati capitani, atteso che Giovanni di Francescho [lacuna] tessitore di pannilini d'in sulla piaza di Santo Spirito, ha servito per laudiere decta compagnia più tempo ad ragione di s. dieci el mese, et essendo migl[i]oratogli la boce assai, et cantare meglio, per haver cagione di fermallo a cantare, per loro solenne partito vinto tra lloro per tucte fave nere . . . gl' accrebbono per l'avenire s. quattro per tucto el tempo ⟨. . .⟩ condocto a cantare in nostra compagnia . . . sono per tucto ad ragione di s. quattordici.

Doc. 26. Company of Sant'Agnese. Election of a laudese, [no day or month] 1493. Ibid., fo. 56ᵛ.

Item e' prefati capitani decto dì atteso che Domenicho di Lionardo tavolaccino ha cantat[o] per laudiere già sono sei mesi passati con speranza d'essere condocto, et intendendo e' capitani predecti che gl'⟨è⟩ bene di conducerlo perchè è buon laudiere, per loro solenne partito e per sei fave nere vinsono e condussono decto Domenicho per laudiere oggi questo dì detto ad ragione di s. dieci el mese, et colle apuntature consuete, et stantiarono L. tre picciole per decti sei mesi che lui ha cantato sanza essere stato condocto.

Doc. 27. Company of San Zanobi. Laudese contracts, 1 November 1351 and 25 March 1352. SZ 2182, fasc. 36, *Entrata e Uscita*, 1333–8, fo. 171ʳ (loose).

Al nome di Dio e dela beata vergine Maria e di tuta la chorte di paradiso, qui apresso iscriveremo tuti i chantatori dela chonpagnia di Santa Liperata per me

Andrea di Piero Bacci, e per Andrea di Giusto astaio, e per Andrea di Donato Baciutti, uficiali chiamati sopra a' detti chantatori e sopra a le feste a fare chantare le laude della detta chonpagnia.

[A]l nome di Dio, in primo inscriveremo a dì [1] novembre Celino de la viuola chantatore dela detta cho[m]pagnia chon salaro e prezo d'uno fiorino d'oro. E detto Celino de' venire a tutte le feste che chamarlichi [*sic*] della detta chonpagnia gli asegnerano e scriverano i[n] su uno foglio.

A dì xxv di marzo ani mccclii, anche si scriveremo pe' sopra detti uficiali che aviate sopra a detti chantatori Talento Ducci orafo chon salaro e prezo d'uno fiorino e mezo d'oro [c]ominiciando al nome di Dio il detto dì di sopra. E'l deto Talento sia tenuto e deba venire a chantare ed a fare chantare laude a la detta chonpagnia si chome ne' patti si chonteghano [*sic*], e se chontra ciò facesi [*sic*] non sieno tenuti i chapitani di farli dare alchuna chosa del detto salaro.

Doc. 28. Company of Santo Spirito. 16th-century altar site. ASF, Conventi Soppressi 122 [Santo Spirito], vol. 36, *Memoriale*, 1598, fo. 28^r.

Altare del Santissimo Sacramento di Mattio Corbinelli . . . la compagnia del Pippione deve ogni festa far cantare le laudi in musica, et doppo farsi da un padre la confession con raccomandar al Signore Dio l'anima di detto Mattio, li si deve dare un fiorino d'oro. Quelle laudi si cantano la quaresima le domeniche e le feste.

Doc. 29. Company of Santa Croce. 1589 statutes. ASF, Compagnie Religiose Soppresse, Capitoli 74, 1589–1634, fo. 1^v.

[Grand Duke Francesco Maria de' Medici] . . . gli piacque che il nostro sito antico della compagnia ne fusse accomodato allo illustre signore Giovanni dell'illustrissimo e reverendissimo cardinale Niccolini per farvi una capella [8 August 1579] . . . Et havendo gli huomini di detta compagnia murato il nuovo sito fuori della chiesa di Santa Croce, posto fra la capella delli illustri Salviati e li illustri Bardi et Gualterotti, è stato necessario riformare et di nuovo ricorregere detti capitoli . . .

Doc. 30. Company of Sant'Agnese. Late 16th-century statute. ASF, Acquisti e Doni 44, *Capitoli*, 1584–1643, fos. 5^v–6^r.

. . . et per quanto si truova durorno insino a l'anno 1496 a reggersi e governarsi da persone secolari e laiche sensa capitoli particolari, secondo le deliberationi che alla giornata si facevano. Ma nel detto anno fu la detta compagnia restretta sotto alcuni ordini et capitoli da loro fatti, et così andò camminando in sino all'anno 1515 . . . Nel qual tempo levato via tutti i vecchi capitoli, furno fatti et compilati nuovi capitoli et ordini . . . Ma perchè la varietà e scorrimento de' tempi arreca sempre nuove occasioni, bisognò l'anno 1550 fare a' detti capitoli alcune correttioni et limitationi et addictioni.

Doc. 31. Company of San Zanobi. 1508 statute concerning festal services. ASF, Compagnie Religiose Soppresse, Capitoli 154, 1508, fo. 29^v.

XVIII. [Principal feasts]. [The San Zanobi *festaiuoli* must] ornare el nostro oratorio et co[m]pagnia in quello modo . . . senza fasto o pompa superflua di mondo. Et così dare opera che nel mezo della chiesa cathedrale si cantino le laude consuete dopo la compieta della vigilia et del dì di tale solenità, dinanzi al leggio et alla testa del predecto vescovo et confessore, ad tale acto preparata con lumi et con li angeli pendenti dalla stella, secondo el modo consueto et con li organi et trombetti, come è di anticho costume.

Doc. 32. Company of Santa Croce. 1538 statute concerning substitution of dowry awards for lauda-singing. ASF, Compagnie Religiose Soppresse, Capitoli 874, 1485–1538, fos. 40^{r-v}, 39^r.

. . . Da un temp⟨o⟩ q⟨. . .⟩ son⟨. . ⟩tate con grandissima difficultà advenga che no[n] ha più quella copia di cantori che per il passato havevamo ⟨. . . ⟩ vedut⟨. .⟩ la difficultà, vogliamo, in iscam⟨bio⟩ di cantare le laude, si facia un limosina di lire venticinque ogn⟨i⟩ ⟨anno⟩, la quale si hab⟨bia⟩ a dar⟨e a una figluo⟩la ch⟨. . .⟩ no de' nostri fratelli che sia bisognosa quando si marita; [fo. 39^r]: Ma perchè a que' tempi erano più prosper⟨i⟩, e le persone più divote che al presente non sono et maximamente che habbiamo inteso da e⟨. . . . .⟩ che non riccordono mai tal ⟨. . . .⟩ nia o ordine essersi ⟨. . . .⟩ la difficultà et imposs⟨ibili⟩tà ⟨. . . . .⟩, non vogliamo ancor noi esser tenuti et obligati all'antico ordine.

Doc. 33. Company of Santa Croce. Book of Dowries, 1565. ASF, Compagnie Religiose Soppresse 1373, no. 1, fasc. F [*Testi, scritte*, etc., 1403–1778], part 3, *Libro delle dote della Compagnia delle Laude*, 1565–1729, fo. 1^l.

Havendo gli antichi padri e antecessor nostri considerato . . . le preci, l'orationi, et le laude che per noi altri cristiani se li paghono, però si risolvettero principal-mente che la nostra compagnia si chiamase la Compagnia delle LAUDE, e volsero che al nome conrispondessero l'opere, et però in chiesa ordinarono che si cantassero oltre gl'uffizi divini ogni giorno di festa le laude da huomini idonei et cantori suffizienti. La onde [es]sendo da un tempo in qua mancata tal devotione per non haver più copia d'huomini atti a tal offitio, però . . . i nostri padri capitani con li huomini di nostra compagnia hanno fatto nuova riforma col consenso del nostro padre correttore et del vicario del arcivescovo di Firenze, et per non mancare in opere pie et cristiane, non potendo più come è detto fare per l'impossibilità degli huomini et malvagità de' tempi cantare le laude, vogliono in quello scambio ogni anno dare a una fanciulla lire venticinque per dota, la quale debba essere figluola legitima e naturale d'uno de' nostri fratelli . . .

Doc. 34. Company of Sant'Agnese. 1584 statute concerning decision to cede lauda-singing obligations to Carmine friars. ASF, Acquisti e Doni 44, *Capitoli*, 1584–1643, fo. 33^{r-v}.

XIII. Delli oblighi della compagnia e osservanza de' legati. . . . Trattando adunque del primo, si dice che al tempo che questa compagnia cantava o faceva cantare le laude, furno diversi testatori che lasciorno a questa più beni immobili con obligo fra l'altre cose di fare dire doppo le laude alli frati del Carmine una vigilia, overo notturno de' morti, et che si desse loro tanta cera in candele, quanta per detti testamenti è espresso. Occorse doppo, che non si contentando li cantori delle laude, delli piccoli prezzi, et salarii che si davon loro, fu di necessità dismettere il cantare le laude dette come cosa che non era d'obligo. Onde che si convenne con li frati che essi dicessino la medesima vigilia, et notturno de' morti, e di più certa quantità di messe de' morti, et certe feste ordinate da' detti testatori, et havessino el prezzo medesimo che dal testatore era ordinato si spendesse et essi mettessino la cera di loro . . .

Doc. 35. Company of San Zanobi. 1555 statute concerning festal services. ASF, Compagnie Religiose Soppresse, Capitoli 155, 1555, fos. 29^r–30^r.

XX. Della nostra festa principale. [Identical to doc. 29, but with the following addition]: . . . Overo in iscambio di dette laude, si cantino nel nostro oratorio la vigilia, et el dì proprio, due vespri con tredici preti fuor del numero del nostro cappellano, dopo quelli della chiesa cathedrale, con quelli ordine, modi, et elemosine a' detti preti s'è usato per el passato; e questo sia in arbitrio deliberare, o di far cantare le laude o e' vespri, de' signori capitani, che per e' tempi saranno . . .

Doc. 36. Company of San Piero Martire. 1555 statute concerning cancelling of laudesi. SMN 316, fo. 184^{r-v}.

Item dicti domini Capitanei . . . advertentes qualiter per modernos laudenses non sunt cantate laudes et numerus laudum que hactenus solite sunt per laudenses eorum societatis cantari diebus secundum morem et consuetudinem dictes eorum socie[ta]tis. Volentes honori dicte eorum societatis in predictis providere, ideo . . . deliberaverunt quod de cetero . . . per presentes laudenses eorum societatis non debeant amplius in ecclesia S. Marie Novelle cantari laudes, sed a proxima futura Paschate Resurrectionis in antea, in dicta ecclesia et in loco dictorum laudensium et pro dictis laudibus et in loco laudum, per novitios fratres conventus S. Marie Novelle diebus consuetis et in dicta ecclesia debeant ut supra de cetero cantari antiphonas gloriosissime Matris Marie semper Virginis, cum eodem salario et prout percipiebatur . . . quolibet mense . . . per laudenses predictos pro cantandis dictis laudibus . . .

APPENDIX II

Document Types of the Florentine Laudesi Companies

1. SERVICE-BOOKS:

Prior to the fifteenth century, most companies appear to have owned from two to five laudarios, which varied in size, function, and splendour, and at least one of which was notated and illuminated. Only three of Florentine provenance survive (Mgl[1], Mgl[2], and Fior). The laude are usually indexed, and ordered *de tempore* and *de sanctis*, with a section devoted to Marian laude. The more ornate books might include music for the laude (Mgl[1]), a complete liturgical calendar (Mgl[2]), illumination (both), and a collection of polyphonic Latin motets (both). It is unclear what kinds of lauda collections served the companies during the fifteenth century. In addition, a company usually owned collections of readings: Saints' lives, various creeds, prayers, and liturgical items, and rhymed, vernacular versions of the Gospels, laments, and the Passion which were intoned during Lent. The inventories of wealthier companies, like San Piero Martire, indicate other types of service-book as well: missals, breviaries, lectionaries, notated processionals, and motet collections.[1]

2. STATUTES (*statuti, capitoli*):

These are the charters of a company, which set forth in formal language its purpose, *modus operandi*, and the scope of its activities. A relatively high number have survived, and they are an important source of information about musical practices. These formal documents required a notary's seal and bishop's approval, were read aloud (in part) at monthly meetings, and were revised at least two to four times during the republican period in response to social and political change. They were usually composed in collaboration between the company's prior (a cleric) and the company members.

---

[1]SMN 292, fos. 56[r–v], 44[v]; SSP 78, fo. 44[v]; 1 fo. 42[r]; OSM 56, fo. 3[v]; 12, fo. 29[r]; SC CmRS 1373, fasc. 3.

3. LETTERS OF INDULGENCE:

Letters of ecclesiastical confirmation which awarded specified numbers of days of indulgence for certain devotional activities (most often processing and lauda-singing/hearing). Issued by popes, cardinals, and bishops, and highly prized by the companies, these parchment scrolls were the primary expression of the link between the lay company and the Church.

4. BOOK OF BEQUESTS (*testamenti, lasciti, obblighi, giornale*):

A record of the property (landed or otherwise) willed to the company by deceased members and non–members alike, and the terms of the bequest (which often called for a commemorative lauda service).

5. DELIBERATIONS OF THE CAPTAINS (*deliberazioni, partiti, ricor-danze, stanziamenti*):

A record of decisions reached by the captains (usually four to six in number) at their bi-monthly meetings. Subject to their vote were any unusual expenditures or actions and the election of all other officers (including the musicians) and the fixing of their salaries. They frequently set forth the musicians' contracts, describing obligations, salary, and conditions of service.

6. INCOME AND EXPENSE (*entrata e uscita*):

A general account book, usually maintained by a treasurer (*camarlingo*), the officer in charge of making, receiving, and recording payments. Primary source of the names and salaries of musicians, and the specific occasions of musical activity.

7. DEBITS AND CREDITS (*debitori e creditori*):

The account book of the company's auditor (*sindaco, procuratore*), who makes, receives, and records payments involved in the execution of bequests. This provides information similar to no. 6.

8. BOOK OF CANDLES (*libro del cero*):

Records the purchase and sale of candles used in company services. A symbol of the *lux perpetua* and eternal life, candles were an essential component of a religious service, as well as a source of light, and they were an important source of revenue for any religious institution.

9. BOOK OF MEMBERS (*libro dei uomini, delle donne*):

A list of the company's living members. There were usually separate books for male and female members, and in the larger companies for the quarters of the city.

10. BOOK OF THE DEAD (*libro dei morti*):

A list of deceased company members, whose names were read aloud at an annual requiem service in their honour.

Of the above, nos. 1–3 (and often 4) are formal parchment documents, copied by professional scribes; no. 3 is always in Latin; nos. 2 and 5 may be either Latin or Italian; nos. 5–9 are account books. Nos. 1–7 all provide information concerning musical activities. All but no. 1 are located primarily in the Archivio di Stato in Florence.

There is a remarkable uniformity in the format of each of these documents, a witness to the strength of guild (account books, statutes), liturgical (service-books), and legal (bequests) models, and to the universal organization of the mendicants through which confraternal structure developed. Given the frequent rotation (every four to six months) and broad social spectrum of the officers who maintained these books, they also reveal a broadly literate society.

APPENDIX III

Laudesi Profiles from the 1427 *Catasto*[1]

The following profiles of individual singers (and one instrumentalist) are offered here not as representatives or types of laudesi activity, but simply as portraits of individuals who filed tax reports in the year 1427. The selection is atypical in that all these individuals were heads of households, the condition for their inclusion in the *catasto*. Neither is the year typical, for it marked the beginning of a period of economic crisis, engendered by a long and expensive military struggle with Milan (*c.*1424–7), which motivated the introduction of the *catasto*.[2] Most of the following laudesi were born during *c.*1350–1400, and since none (except no. 6) lived long enough to see the introduction into the laudesi companies of three- and four-part polyphonic practice in the 1460s, they all must have been steeped in the monophonic and *cantus binatum* traditions that prevailed during their lifetime.

1. *Antonio di Benedetto di Butino* (1377–1445) was a master weaver of wool who resided in the Green Dragon district of the Santo Spirito quarter (the *Oltrarno*).[3] Antonio is recorded as a laudese only for the Company of Sant'Agnese, who honoured him at his death with a lauda vigil for having served the company over fifty years as a benefactor and laudese (without salary). In 1427 Antonio was 50, his wife 38, a son 3, and a daughter 5 months; he owned three houses in the Drago district and one in the San Giovanni quarter. His assets were reckoned at fl. 140 s. 18 d. 5, and his obligations (including a 200–fl. deduction for each person) at fl. 810.

---

[1] The Florentine *catasto* was introduced in 1427 as a system of taxation based upon a detailed register of property owned by Florentine citizens. The head of each household was required to compile a completed list of his assets (real estate, business investments, communal bonds, cash, and loans) and his debts and obligations. His assessment was calculated at 0.5% of the value of his assets, minus his obligations and deductions for dependants (fl. 200 per dependant) and living quarters. Thus it was a property, and not an income, tax. In addition, a head tax was levied upon every able-bodied adult male between the ages of 18 and 60 (2 to 6 gold soldi). Officials were also authorized to declare 'miserabile' those men and women whom age or infirmity rendered incapable of earning a living. Usually the infirm, aged, minor orphans, and widows, the *miserabili* were exempt from taxes but not from filing a return. D. Herlihy and C. Klapisch-Zuber, *Tuscans and their Families: A Study of the Florentine Catasto of 1427* (New Haven, 1985), 10–20.

[2] Brucker, *Renaissance Florence*, 82–4.

[3] ASF, Catasto 67, fo. 164^r; a weaver (*tessitore*) was usually a master who wove cloth at home from material provided by an entrepreneur who paid him by the piece and who frequently furnished the loom; F. Edler, *Glossary of Mediaeval Terms of Business*, 295.

2. *Bernaba di Cristofano Loci* (b. 1357) was a cloth shearman who resided in the Nicchio district of the Santo Spirito quarter.[4] Bernaba's career as a singer was linked primarily to the commune; in 1404 he was on the city payroll as a 'cantor dominorum priorum' at L. 4 s. 10 per month,[5] and he served the Company of Orsanmichele (under commune supervision since *c.*1350) during 1403–16 as a ferial singer at s. 50 per month, and again in 1436–7 (79–80 years old) as a festal singer at s. 40 per month.[6] In 1427 Bernaba's wife (45) had just died, and he was supporting his sons Antonio (25) and Pagolo (18). Antonio adopted both his father's trades, wool-shearing and lauda-singing. He sang for the Company of Santo Spirito during 1425–7, and served there as a *camarlingo* in 1425. Bernaba's assets amounted to fl. 188 s. 8 d. 6, and included a house and four pieces of cultivated land outside the city walls, and money owed him by eleven parties. His obligations (fl. 788 s. 10) included rent on a house and *bottega* near the church of San Felice, and debts owed to thirteen parties (among them the laudese Guasparre d'Ugolino Prosperi (below, no. 6), to whom he owed fl. 2 s. 13 d. 9.

3. *Domenico di Fruosino Ghumerello* (b. 1375) was a butcher living in the Scala district of the Santo Spirito Quarter.[7] Domenico sang for the Companies of Santo Spirito (1431) and Sant'Agnese (during Lent of 1444 and 1445, as a *tenore*). In both cases, he is among the first singers mentioned in extant account books that begin only a short time before, and since he was 52 in 1427, it is likely that most of his singing activity preceded the above dates. He, and another laudese named Daniello who sang for Sant'Agnese in 1442, are the earliest adult laudesi referred to in Florentine documents as polyphonic singers (*tenore*). In 1427 Domenico owned three small houses ('one next to the other'; one in which his family lived, the others for storing wine and straw), and sixteen parcels of land cultivated by the family. The assets of his wife Mona Tessa (48) are listed separately: two half houses in Borgo San Niccolò and a parcel of cultivated land with a 'chasellina trista' in the San Stefano parish. Their assets amounted to fl. 809 s. 4, but a household of nine (six children and a daughter-in-law between the ages of 6 and 30) and a debt brought their obligations to fl. 1,850 s. 7 d. 6. He was assessed a tax of s. 18.

4. *Filippo di Francesco Antinori* (b. 1357) filed his tax report in the Green Dragon district of the *Oltrarno*, though he is listed as residing in 'Chastelo di Pogibonzi'.[8]

    [4] ASF, Catasto 65, fos. 286$^{r–v}$; a *cimatore* was usually a small master with a private workshop, and his work was the stage of cloth refinement just prior to dyeing. F. Edler, Roover, *Glossary*, 75.

    [5] G. Corti, 'Un musicista fiammingo a Firenze agli inizi del quattrocento', in *L'Ars nova italiana del Trecento*, 4 (Certaldo, 1979), 177–9. Also listed in the employment of the Signoria was Antonio di Matteo, 'cantor cantilenarum et recitator moralium ad mensam dominorum priorum artium', at L. 3 per month.

    [6] In 1412 the Company of San Zanobi recorded a payment to 'Loci'; D'Accone, 'Le compagnie', 267–8 n. 57. During his first tenure at Orsanmichele, Bernaba at various times sang with Filippo Antinori (below, no. 4), the rebec-player Pagolo (no. 10), the brother of Maso di Niccolò (no. 8), and Vanni di Martino (no. 12) and his son Martino. In 1436–7 he sang with Vettorio d'Agnolo Bordoni (no. 13), Francesco di Niccolò (no. 5), Maso di Niccolò (no. 8), and Guasparre d'Ugolino Prosperi (no. 6) and his son Prospero, a rebec-player.

    [7] ASF, Catasto 64, fos. 259^{v}–260^{r}.

    [8] ASF, Catasto 67, fo. 495^{v}; Poggibonsi is a small town between Florence and Siena, at that time

Filippo sang for the companies of San Piero Martire (1404–6, 1411–13), San Zanobi (1406–11), and Orsanmichele (1404–8), where he also served as a *camarlingo* in 1404.[9] In 1427 Filippo (70) and his wife Mona Giovanna (62) were living alone, when his modest assets (fl. 1041 s. 7, mostly debts owed him, and four parcels of land) had apparently enabled him to have long since retired from lauda-singing. His obligations, including rent on a house and a single debt, amounted to fl. 428 s. 11. His taxable assets totalled fl. 613, and he was required to pay a tax of fl. 13.

5. *Francesco (cieco) di Niccolò degli Asini* (b. 1415) was blind and, at age 12, the eldest of three brothers (Marco, 11, and Niccolò, 9) living together in the White Lion district of the Santa Maria Novella quarter.[10] He sang for the Company of San Zanobi during 1427–30 and 1433–6 (where he is usually referred to as Francesco cieco, laldese), and for the ferial services of Orsanmichele during 1436–7.[11] The three boys lived rent-free with a certain Mona Andrea. Their assets (2/3 of a farm) were valued at fl. 470 s. 14 d. 6, their obligations at fl. 600 (i.e. the 200-fl. deduction per person), and a note in the margin reads 'sostanze nulla'.

6. *Guasparre d'Ugolino Prosperi* (b. 1377) was a resident of the Vaio district of the San Giovanni quarter.[12] He served long terms for the companies of San Zanobi (1421–45, 1451) and Orsanmichele (1418–37, 1450–3), at both places paired with Vettorio d'Agnolo Bordoni (no. 13).[13] He performed precentor's duties for the Company of San Zanobi. In 1433 his salary was lowered, then restored on the condition that his son (unnamed) come and sing for the price of his father's salary.[14] The son may have been Prospero, who was a rebec-player for Orsanmichele in 1436–7, when he was 17–18. But in 1427 Guasparre (50) and his wife Mona Chaterina (36) had other sons and daughters, and another young dependant—in all nine children between the ages of 1 and 15. Their assets were 'nulla' and their condition was judged to be 'miserabile'. Their obligations, including annual rent of fl. 6 on a house owned by the Company of San Zanobi, were fl. 2,317 s. 15. When San Zanobi discontinued ferial services in 1433, the reduction of Guasparre's salary from s. 60 to s. 30 per month must have hit this straitened family hard, and hence the offer to add his son to the lauda-singing services in exchange for a restored salary.

---

under Florentine dominion. Filippo's profession, if he had one besides lauda-singing, is not indicated.

[9] He sang with the other singers on this list at San Piero Martire (nos. 12, 13, 8); San Zanobi (no. 10); and Orsanmichele (nos. 10, 2, 12).

[10] ASF, Catasto 77, fo. 250[v].

[11] At San Zanobi, he sang with nos. 6, 13, 10, and 8, and at Orsanmichele with nos. 6, 13, 10, 8, and 2.

[12] ASF, Catasto 81, fo. 260[v]; his occupation is listed as 'ghuantaio' (*guantiere*), glove-maker.

[13] Guasparre also sang with nos. 8, 10, and 5 at San Zanobi, and nos. 6, 5, 2, and 10 at Orsanmichele.

[14] See Ch. 3, under 'Company of San Zanobi'. Guasparre and Vettorio are listed as the two principal laudesi in San Zanobi's 1427 *catasto*.

7. *Luca di Giusto* (b. 1387) was a weaver living in the Ferza district of the Santo Spirito quarter.[15] Luca is listed only once as a laudese, for the Company of Sant'Agnese in 1465. In 1427, he owned two houses in the parish of San Pier Gattolini, his 38-year-old brother had just died, and the household of 8 included Luca (40), his mother (72), his wife (40), two children (18 and 21), and three grandchildren (1, 3, and 4½). His obligations totalled fl. 2,052 s. 10.

8. *Maso di Niccolò* (b. 1377) was a laudese by profession, living in the Drago district of the San Giovanni quarter.[16] His active career embraced long tenures as a festal and ferial singer for the Company of San Piero Martire (1409–24), a festal singer for San Zanobi (1411–37), and a ferial singer for Orsanmichele (1418, 1436–7).[17] He was often paired with his brother Vermiglio, who also sang for San Zanobi (1411–18) and Orsanmichele (1410–16). In 1427 Maso (50), his wife Mona Pasqua (42), a son Giacomo (19), and a daughter Giana (8) lived in a rented house on Via degli Armati, near the church of Santa Maria Maggiore. His assets (a fl. 26 debt owed him) as against his obligations (fl. 926 s. 11) solicited the assessment of his condition as 'fatto miserabile'.

9. *Niccolò di Betto Bugani* (b. 1398), a weaver of woollen cloth, resided in the Green Dragon district (and parish of San Frediano) of the Santo Spirito quarter.[18] Niccolò appears only in the records of the Company of Sant'Agnese, between 1444 and 1450. Although the Company hired outside singers during Lent, Niccolò, and his son Romolo, sang for the Company throughout the year, and performed sacristan duties for the lauda services. Niccolò must have introduced Romolo to lauda-singing while he was in his early teens, for Romolo was not yet born in 1427 when the household comprised Niccolò (29), his mother Mona Margerita (66), his wife La Peracina (18), and his son Betto (b. 26 Aug. 1427). Betto appeared once as a laudese in the Sant'Agnese accounts fifty years later in 1477, where he is referred to as 'Betto di Nicho detto Chornachino, laldese'. Niccolò and his family shared a house on Via Santo Salvadore with two other parties (whether they owned or rented is unclear); their assets were fl. 41 s. 10 in debts owed them, and their obligations fl. 839. They, too, were pronounced 'miserabile'.

10. *Pagolo di Ser Ambruogio, chiamato Vinci* (b. 1368) was a full-time, professional instrumentalist who resided in the Drago district of the San Giovanni quarter.[19] According to the *catasto*, he was by offical trade a *piffero* in the employment of the city. However, Pagolo's first recorded activity as a rebec/vielle-player is at Orsanmichele, where his long tenure (1405–37) overlapped with that of Maestro Luigi di Matteo della Viuola (1388–1413). Pagolo may have been apprenticed to Luigi, for when the older master died in 1413, Pagolo assumed both Luigi's official posts: the Signoria appointed him as instrumentalist at its meals 'cum

---

[15] ASF, Catasto 66, fo. 296ᵛ.
[16] ASF, Catasto 79, fo. 523ʳ, where his title is 'Maso di Niccholò laldese' (Maso = Tommaso).
[17] Maso sang at San Piero Martire with nos. 12, 13, and 4; at San Zanobi with nos. 2, 5, 6, 10, 13; and at Orsanmichele with nos. 2, 5, 6, 10, and 13.
[18] ASF, Catasto 67, fos. 392ᵛ–393ʳ.
[19] ASF, Catasto 79, fo. 594ᵛ (incomplete); 408, fo. 484ʳ (1430).

viola vel aliquo musico instrumento', and the Company of Orsanmichele as 'optimum sonatorem viole, ribeche, liuti et aliorum instrumentorum', with the highest salary.[20] Pagolo was frequently hired by the Company of San Zanobi to play for special feast-days, particularly for the feasts of St Zenobius and St Reparata, and is occasionally referred to as a singer.[21] Pagolo's 1427 *catasto* fragment shows that he owned one and a half houses, which were rented out. In 1430 Pagholo (62) owned, and lived in, a small house in the neighbourhood of Verzaia di Stima, along with his wife (39) and four sons between the ages of 4½ and 26. His assets (the house) were valued at fl. 20, his obligations at fl. 1,216 (6 deductions, and fl. 16 in debts to three parties).

11. *Piero di Bartolomeo* (b. 1406), a barber who resided in the Nicchio district of the Santo Spirito quarter, practised his trade in the Piazza della Signoria.[22] As a boy, Piero sang for the Company of San Piero Martire during 1418–19, his only recorded activity as a laudese. Piero rented a house in the parish of San Jacopo, on the Chiasso dei Sapiti, where he lived with his father (65). His assets were negligible, his obligations fl. 474 s. 8 d. 7, and his official fiscal condition 'miserabile'.

12. *Vanni di Martino* (b. 1351) was a professional laudese living in the Red Lion district of the Santa Maria Novella quarter.[23] He served long and regular tenures at the companies of San Piero Martire (1405–24) and Orsanmichele (1403–16).[24] During 1412–17 he sang with his son Martino at both San Piero Martire (1413–17) and Orsanmichele (1412–16), and in 1415 he sang with two of his sons at San Piero Martire. In 1427, however, Vanni (76) lived alone in a rented house with his wife Mona Isabetta (70), the daughter of Pagolo di Francesco Guicciardini. 'Non ha nulla' was the estimation of his assets, and his obligations were fl. 471 s. 8 d. 9. His fiscal condition was described as 'chiaritta miserabile'.

13. *Vettorio d'Agnolo Bordoni* (b. 1382), a resident of the White Lion District of the Santa Maria Novella quarter, described his professional activity as 'atendo a

---

[20] G. Zippel, *I suonatori*, 22–3. The documents published here, including a petition to the city from the Captains of Orsanmichele, again emphasize the official relationship at this time between the two institutions. As for the singer Bernaba di Cristofano (no. 2), employment with the city often entailed, or provided, service in the oratorio of Orsanmichele. Conversely, employment with Orsanmichele might provide access to a civic position, as appears to have been the case for Pagolo. Civic positions must have been desirable, for they paid reasonably well, entailed benefits, and offered a relatively high degree of job security; see G. Brucker, 'Social Welfare in Renaissance Florence', *Journal of Modern History*, 55 (1983), 1–21.

[21] Payments to Pagolo were recorded in 1402: 'e chompagnio di Pagholo che suona cho llui . . . che sonorono a San Giovanni'; 1407–9: 'Vinci piffero e cho[m]pagni' (for the feasts of St Zenobius and St Reparata); 1419: Vinci 'e chompagni sonatore e chantatori perchè sonorono per S. Zanobi a le laude'; 1421: 'perchè suona la ribecha e canta le laude la sera in S. M. del Fiore'; 1428–9: 'Vinci laldese'; and 1433: '. . . vene alle lalde la sera di Sancta Liperata'.

During his tenure at Orsanmichele, Pagolo performed with nos. 2, 4–6, 8, 12, 13, and at San Zanobi he was concurrently employed with nos. 4–6, 8, and 13.

[22] ASF, Catasto 65, fo. 428ᵛ.

[23] Ibid. 76, fo. 396ᵛ.

[24] But he never served at San Zanobi; it was unusual for an active laudese like Vanni not to have served all three major companies if he served regularly at one or two of them. During his term at San Piero Martire, he sang with nos. 4, 8, 11, and 13, at Orsanmichele with nos. 2, 4, and 10.

rivedere (cloth-burling) e chantare le laude'.[25] For at least thirty-four years Vettorio sang regularly for the companies of San Piero Martire (1411–13, 1417–24), San Zanobi (1421–45), and Orsanmichele (1418–36).[26] In 1427, Vettorio (45) rented a small house near the Croce a Trebbio (a cross near the Church of Santa Maria Novella marking the activities of St Peter Martyr), where he lived with his wife Mona Taddea (38) and five children between the ages of 1 and 19. His assets amounted to an 8-fl. debt owed him, his obligations were fl. 1,607 L. 2.

[25] ASF, Catasto 77, fo. 367ᵛ. A *riveditore*, or burler, removed knots and other irregularities from newly woven cloth. He usually worked in the central workshop of an industrial entrepreneur for day wages. F. Edler, *Glossary*, 251.

[26] He was paired with Guasparre (no. 6) for most of his tenure at San Zanobi (esp. 1427–45 as ferial singers) and Orsanmichele. He also sang with nos. 4, 8, and 12 at San Piero Martire, nos. 5, 8, and 10 at San Zanobi, and nos. 2, 5, 8, and 10 at Orsanmichele.

List of Laudesi Company Documents

COMPANY OF ORSANMICHELE

Account Books (OSM)

Ibis–17, 20–42, 58, 464 (CRIA 9566)	*Partiti*, 1361–1403, 1412–1593, 1359–61, 1378–9
17 bis	*Stanziamenti*, 1408–9; *Debitori e Creditori*, 1450
56, 60–2	*Ricordi*, 1366–9, 1409–33
206–15	*Debitori e Creditori*, 1370–1420
262	*Entrata e Uscita*, 1453–4
470	*Testamenti*, 1340–7

Statutes

1294	Castellani, *Nuovi testi fiorentini*, 650–62 (OSM, 476, *Capitoli*, 1291–7; destroyed in 1966 flood)
1297	Ibid. 662–73
1329	Florence, Biblioteca Riccardiana 391 (fragment)
1333	La Sorsa, *La compagnia d'Or San Michele*, 191–205 (OSM, 474, *Capitoli*, 1333; destroyed)
c. 1329–33	Florence, Biblioteca Laurenziana, Antinori 29/66; ed. Biagi, 'I capitoli della Compagnia della Madonna d'Or San Michele', 57–85
1591	OSM 478, *Capitoli*

Other

1329	ASF, Provvisione (30 March 1329) ed. La Sorsa, *La compagnia*, 208–9.
1427	ASF, Catasto 291, fos. 72^r–74^r (tax report)
1438	ASF, Catasto 602, no. 18

COMPANY OF SANTA CROCE

Account Books

ASF, CmRS 1373:
no. 1, fasc. F	*Testi, scritti, 1403–1778*
fo. 2	*Inventario, 1521*
fo. 3	*[Inventario] 1523*
fo. 6	[Letter], 1582
no. 3	*Libro delle dote, 1565–1729*

Statutes

1470	ASF, CmRS, Capitoli 53
1485–1538	ASF, CmRS, Capitoli 874
1589–1634	ASF, CmRS, Capitoli 74

Letters of Indulgence

1290	ASF, Diplomatico Patrimonio Ecclesiastico, 25 May 1290
1296	ASF, Diplomatico Patrimonio Ecclesiastico, 7 Feb. 1296

COMPANY OF SAN ZANOBI

Account Books (SZ)

2170 fasc.4	*Libro dei Testamenti* [1354 ff.]
2170 fasc.5K	*Tratte e Ricordi, 1419–1509*
2171 fasc.6A	*Libri maestri, 1421; Uscita, 1438–94*
2171 fasc.6B–C	*Entrata e Uscita, 1353–1493*
2176 fasc.12–13	*Ricordi e Partiti, 1378–83, 1477–1503*
2177 fasc.16–18	*Partiti, 1440–1512*
2177 fasc.19	*[Uscita], 1493–4*
2178 fasc.23	*Obblighi, 1407–16*
2179 fasc.27–8	*Debitori e Creditori, 1470–1501*
2181 fasc.32–4	*Debitori e Creditori, 1425–1534*
2182 fasc.36–9	*Entrata e Uscita, 1333–1406*
2186 fasc.48	*Partiti, 1427–38*
2195 fasc.70	*Entrata e Uscita, 1470–80*
2196 fasc.74	*Entrata e Uscita, 1529–43*

Statutes

1326	SZ 2170, fasc. 1, *Statuti, 1326–1490; ed. Orioli, Le confraternite medievali, 21–43*

1428	SZ 2170, fasc. 1, *Statuti*, fos. 28^r–55^r (additions through 1490 on fos. 55^v–65^r)
1508	ASF, CmRS, Capitoli 154
1555	ASF, CmRS, Capitoli 155

Other

1427	ASF, Catasto 291, fo. 67^r (tax report)
1427	BNF, Mgl. XXXVII. 298 (*catasto*)

COMPANY OF SAN GILIO

Statutes

1284	BNF, Banco Rari 336 (olim Palatino 1172); ed. Monti, *Le confraternite medievali*, ii. 144–58 (incomplete); Schiaffini, *Testi fiorentini*, 34–54

Account Books

ASF, CmRS 1340, fasc. C	*Interessi diversi*, 1420–1785

Laudario

1374	BNF, Banco Rari 19 (olim Mgl. II. I. 212) [Mgl^2]

Other

1427	ASF, Catasto 291, fo. 72^r (tax report)
1420–1785	ASF, CmRS 1340, fasc. C, *Interessi diversi* [inventory, *c*.1420]

COMPANY OF SAN BASTIANO

Statutes

1263	Morini and Soulier, *Monumenta Ordinis Servorum Sanctae Mariae*, i. 107–8 (on p. 10, the manuscript citation given is BNF, Mgl. 1697. E. 7)
1441	ASF, CmRS, Capitoli 6
1520–34	ASF, CmRS, Capitoli 364

COMPANY OF SAN MARCO

1427   ASF, Catasto 291, fo. 70^r (tax report)

COMPANY OF SAN LORENZO

Letter of Indulgence

1338   Cianfogni, *Memorie istoriche*, 220–1

Other

1313   ASF, Diplomatico Patrimonio Ecclesiastico, 4 Mar. 1313
1427   ASF, Catasto 291, fo. 67^v (tax report)
1427   BNF, Mgl. XXXVII. 298 (*catasto* fragment); ed. in
                             Moreni, *Continuazione*, ii. 380–1

COMPANY OF SAN PIERO MARTIRE

Account Books (SMN)

290   *Giornale*, 1428–36
291–2   *Entrata/Uscita*, 1312–40
294–302   *Entrata e Uscita*, 1389–1503
306   *Debitori e Creditori*, 1445–54
311   *Debitori e Antichi* [1329 ff.]
315–16   *Partiti*, 1509–70
317–18   *Ricordi*, 1419, 1463–73
319   *Ricordanze*, 1470–7
322   *Stanziamenti*, 1420–4
326   *Testamenti*, 1421–3
App. 72   *Libro* [del Cero], 1470–88, 1514–17

Statutes

1447   SMN, 324, *Capitoli*

Letters of Indulgence

1288   ASF, Diplomatico S. Maria Novella, 20 Feb. 1288, ed.
                             Meersseman, *Ordo fraternitatis*, ii. 1042–3
1304   ASF, Diplomatico S. Maria Novella, 9 Apr. 1304, ed.
                             Meersseman, *Ordo fraternitatis*, ii. 1047–8

Other

1285	ASF, Diplomatico S. Maria Novella, 15 Apr. 1285, (Duccio contract), ed. Meersseman, *Ordo fraternitatis*, ii. 1041
1427	ASF, Catasto 291, fos. 74^v–75^r (tax report)
1556	V. Borghigiani, *Cronaca Analistica*, iii. 330–40; ed. Orlandi, *Necrologio di Santa Maria Novella*, ii. 402–3
1617	ASF, Manoscritti 621 (*Sepultuario*, Sermartelli)

COMPANY OF OGNISSANTI

Laudario

14th c.?	BNF, Mgl. XXXVI. 28 (lost, but one lauda transcribed in Burney, *A General History of Music*; see Music Example 5)

COMPANY OF SANT'AGNESE

Account Books (SA)

1	*Ricordanze*, 1515–35
4–5	*Partiti*, 1483–1509, 1548–96
24	*Entrata e Uscita*, 1440–7
29	*Beni*, 1488 [1460 ff.]
98–101	*Entrata e Uscita*, 1424–1553
114	*Debitori e Creditori*, 1447–65
115	*Lasciti e legati*, 1466–1510
125	*Entrata e Uscita*, 1471–1502

Statutes

1280	BNF, Mgl. VIII. 1500, fasc. 9; ed. Piccini, 'Libro degli ordinamenti'; and Schiaffini, *Testi fiorentini*, 55–72
1584–1643	ASF, Acquisti e Doni 44, *Capitoli*

Other

1427	ASF, Catasto 291, fo. 69^r (tax report)

COMPANY OF SAN FREDIANO

Account Books (SF)

4	*Partiti*, 1436–69
5	*Partiti, Entrata e Uscita*, 1468–1510

29–30	*Entrata e Uscita*, 1333–94
31	*Tratta degli Ufficiali*, 1394–1442
32	*Entrata e Uscita*, 1393–1446
39	*Tasse, inventari*, 1344–72
88	*Entrata e Uscita, Lasciti*, 1333–1441
110	*Uscita di fabbrica*, 1443–99
112	*Debitori e Creditori*, 1467–1522

Statutes

1324	BNF, Palatino 154 (additions 1368–1467)
1489	SF 1, *Capitoli* (16th-c. additions)
1565	ASF, Acquisti e Doni 42, *Capitoli*

Other

1427	ASF, Catasto 291, fo. 71^r (tax report)
1488	ASF, Acquisti e Doni 41, *Memoriale*

COMPANY OF SANTO SPIRITO

Account Books (SSP)

1	*Memoriale, ricordanze*, 1419–27
2–3	*Partiti*, 1481–1573, 1575–1628
57–62	*Entrata e Uscita*, 1427–1521
78	*Ricordi contiene i nomi*, 1444–1521
79	*Debitori e Creditori per entratura di Tasse*, 1451–1522

Statutes

1621	ASF, Acquisti e Doni 45, *Capitoli*

Laudario

14th c.	BNF, Banco Rari 18 (olim Mgl. II. I. 122) [Mgl^1]; texts and music ed. Liuzzi, *La lauda*, ii; Grossi, 'The Fourteenth Century Florentine Laudario'

Other

1322	ASF, Provvisione 26, fo. 8bis^r, 20 July 1322
1329	ASF, Spoglio Stroziano 37, 300, fo. 99, 12 May 1329
1333	ASF, Provvisione 26, fo. 40^r, 24 Sept. 1333
1427	ASF, Catasto 291, fo. 71^v (tax report)
1598	ASF, Conventi Soppressi 122 (Santo Spirito), vol. 36, *Memoriale*, 1598

MUSIC EXAMPLES

Ex. 1. 'San Domenico beato', Mgl[1], fos. 116[r]–117[v] (fac. in Liuzzi, *La lauda*, ii, no. LXXVI)

Ex. 2. 'Allegro canto', Mgl[1], fos. 117[v]–119[r] (fac. in Liuzzi, ii, no. LXXVII)

Ex. 3. 'Ave, donna santissma': Cort, fos. 5[v]–6[r] (fac. in Liuzzi, i, no. III; text ed. in Varanini *et al.*, *Laude cortonesi*, i/1, 93–101) and Mgl[1], fos. 48[v]–49[v] (fac. in Liuzzi, ii, no. XXXI)

Ex. 4. 'Ciascun ke fede sente', melodic variants:
(*a*) 'Ciascun ke fede sente', Cort, fos. 96[r]–97[v] (fac. in Liuzzi, i, no. XXXVIII; text ed. in Varanini *et al.*, *Laude cortonesi*, i/1, 263 ff.);
(*b*) 'Ciascun che fede et sente', Mgl[1], fos. 106[r]–107[r] (fac. in Liuzzi, ii, no. LXIX);
(*c*) 'A tutt' or dobbiam laudare', Luc[1], fos. 54[r–v] (text and music in Ziino, 'Frammenti' 308);
(*d*) 'Sancto Agostin doctor', Mgl[1], fos. 98[r]–99[r] (fac. in Liuzzi, ii, no. LXV);
(*e*) 'Gaudiamo tucti quanti', Mgl[1], fos. 96[v]–97[v] (fac. in Liuzzi, ii, no. LXIV)

Ex. 5. 'Alta Trinità beata': Cort, fo. 70[r] (fac. in Liuzzi, i, no. XXXI; text ed. in Varanini *et al.*, *Laude cortonesi*, i/1, 212 ff.); Mgl[1], fos. 5[v]–6[r] (fac. in Liuzzi, ii, no. III); Burney, *General History of Music*, ed. Mercer, i. 631, after Mgl. XXXVI. 28 (now lost)

Ex. 6. 'L'amor a mi venendo': Ven, fo. 144[r], and Pav, fo. 2[v] (text ed. Luisi, *Laudario giustinianeo*, i. 291)

Ex. 7. Serafino Razzi, 'L'amor a me venendo', Razzi[1], fo. 42[v]

Ex. 8. 'O Jesù dolce': Grey, fos. 67[v]–68[r] (fac. in Luisi, *Laudario giustinianeo*, ii, no. XI); Razzi[1], fos. 60[v]–61[r]; and Panc. 27, fo. 50[v] (text ed. Luisi, i. 291)

Ex. 9. Innocentius Dammonis, 'O Iesù dolce', Petrucci[1], fos. 59[v]–60[r]

Ex. 10. 'Con desiderio io vo cerchando', BU, fo. 45[r]

Ex. 11. 'Madre che festi', Ven, fo. 30[v] (text ed. Luisi, *Laudario giustinianeo*, i. 260)

Ex. 1. 'San Domenico beato', Mgl¹, fos. 116ʳ–117ᵛ (fac. in Liuzzi, *La lauda*, ii, no. LXXVI)

Ex. 2. 'Allegro canto', Mgl[1], fos, 117[v]–119[r] (fac. in Liuzzi, ii, no. LXXVII)

Refrain

Al – le – gro can – to, po – pol cri – sti – a – no

del gran – de san Do – me – ni – co,

di tan – ti va – lo – ro – so ca – – pi – ta – no.

Strophe

Ca – pi – ta – no di mol – ti ca – va – lie – ri

fu san – cto pre – ti – o – so,

che do – po Cri – sto l'an – no se – – gui – ta – to;

e fu de li mi – glior gon – fa – lo – nie – ri,

quel fiu – me gra – ti – o – so,

che do – po Cri – sto si – a sta – to tro – va – to;

per lui è su – to sper – to et ri – pro – va – to

og – ni per – ver – so he – re – ti – co

che nel – la fe – de tro – vas – se lon – ta – no.

Ex. 3. 'Ave, donna santissima': Cort, fos. 5ᵛ–6ʳ (fac. in Liuzzi, i, no. III; text ed. in Varanini *et al.*, *Laude cortonesi*, i/l, 93–101) and Mgl¹, fos. 48ᵛ–49ᵛ (fac. in Liuzzi, ii, no. XXXI)

Ex. 4. 'Ciascun ke fedc sente', melodic variants:
(*a*) 'Ciascun ke fede sente Cort, fos. 96ʳ–97ᵛ (fac. in Liuzzi, i, no. XXXVIII; text ed. in Varanini *et al.*, *Laude cortonesi*, i/l, 263 ff.);
(*b*) 'Ciascun che fede et sente', Mgl¹, fos. 106ʳ–107ʳ (fac. in Liuzzi, ii, no. LXIX);
(*c*) 'A tutt' or dobbiam laudare', Luc¹, fos. 54ʳ⁻ᵛ (text and music in Ziino, 'Frammenti', 308);
(*d*) 'Sancto Agostin doctor', Mgl¹, fos. 98ʳ–99ʳ (fac. in Liuzzi, ii, no. LXV);
(*e*) Gaudiamo tucti quanti', Mgl¹, fos, 96ᵛ–97ᵛ (fac. in Liuzzi, ii, no. LXIV)

Music example 4

Ex. 5. 'Alta Trinità beata': Cort, fo. 70ʳ (fac. in Liuzzi, i, no. XXXI; text ed. in Varanini *et al.*, *Laude cortonesi*, i/1, 212 ff.); Mgl¹, fos. 5ᵛ–6ʳ (fac. in Liuzzi, ii, no. III); Burney, *General History of Music*, after Magl. XXXVI. 28 (now lost), ed. in Ziino, 'Laudi e miniature', 83

Ex. 6. 'L'amor a mi venendo': Ven, fo. 144ʳ, and Pav, fo. 2ᵛ (text ed. Luisi, *Laudario giustinianeo*, i. 291)

Ex. 7. Serafino Razzi, 'L'amor a me venendo', Razzi[1], fo. 42[v]

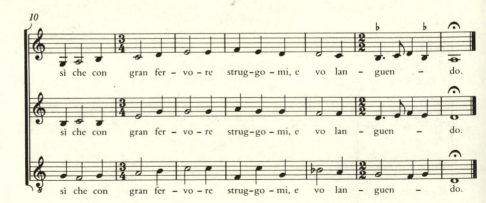

Ex. 8. 'O Jesù dolce': Grey, fos. 67ᵛ–68ʳ (fac. in Luisi, *Laudario giustinianeo*, ii, no. XI); Razzi¹, fos. 60ᵛ–61ʳ; and Panc. 27, fo. 50ᵛ (text ed. Luisi, i. 291)

Music example 8

274   Music example 8

Grey   ti fu – zo e tu me se – gui ogn – ho – ra.

Razzi[1]   gui a tut – te   l'ho – – re.

P. 27   ti fu – zo   e   tu   mi se – gui o – gn'o – ra.

Per qual mio me – ri – to   o
sì lar – ga – men – te nel   mi – –

Per qual mie – i me – r[i] – ti,   O————

Per qual mi – o me – ri – to   o————
sì lar – ga – men – te nel mi – – –

Music example 8

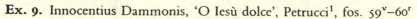

Ex. 9. Innocentius Dammonis, 'O Iesù dolce', Petrucci[1], fos. 59ᵛ–60ʳ

Music example 9

Ex. 10. 'Con desiderio io vo cerchando', BU, fo. 45ʳ

Music example 10

Su – spi – ran – do   per   a –   mor   vo   cer-chan –   do

el   mio   dil – le –   cto;

pos –   sa   non   tro – va   el   mio   co – –

– –   re_____,   tan – to   è

per   a –   mo –   re   con –   –   –

stre –   –   –   –   –   to.

Ex. 11. 'Madre che festi', Ven, fo. 30ᵛ (text ed. Luisi, *Laudario giustinianeo*, i. 260)

BIBLIOGRAPHY

BACCHI, GIUSEPPE, 'La compagnia di S. Maria delle laudi e di Sant'Agnese nel Carmine di Firenze', *Rivista storica carmelitana*, 2 (1930–1), 137–51; 3 (1931–2), 12–39, 97–122.

BARR, CYRILLA, 'Lauda Singing and the Tradition of the Disciplinati Mandato: A Reconstruction of the Two Texts of the Office of Tenebrae', *L'Ars nova italiano del Trecento*, 4 (Certaldo, 1978), 21–44.

—— *The Monophonic Lauda and the Lay Religious Confraternities of Tuscany and Umbria in the Late Middle Ages* (Kalamazoo, Mich., 1988).

—— 'Music and Spectacle in Confraternity Drama of Fifteenth Century Florence: The Reconstruction of a Theatrical Event,' in T. Verdon and J. Henderson (eds.), *Christianity and the Renaissance* (Syracuse, NY, 1990), 377–404.

—— 'A Renaissance Artist in the Service of a Singing Confraternity', in R. Goffen, M. Tetel, and R. Witt (eds.), *Life and Death in Fifteenth-Century Florence* (Durham, NC, 1989), 105–24.

BARTHOLOMAEIS, VINCENZO DE, *Le origini della poesia drammatica* (Bologna, 1924).

BAXANDALL, MICHAEL, *Painting and Experience in Fifteenth-Century Italy* (2nd edn., Oxford, 1988).

BECHERINI, BIANCA, *Catalogo dei manoscritti musicali della Biblioteca Nazionale Centrale di Firenze* (Kassel, 1959).

—— 'Musica italiana a Firenze nel XV secolo', *Revue belge de musicologie*, 8 (1954), 109–21.

—— 'Un canta in panca fiorentino, Antonio di Guido', *Rivista musicale italiana*, 50 (1949), 241–7.

BECKER, MARVIN, 'Aspects of Lay Piety in Early Renaissance Florence', in C. Trinkaus and H. Oberman (eds.), *The Pursuit of Holiness in Late Medieval and Renaissance Religion* (Leiden, 1974), 177–99.

—— 'Church and State on the Eve of the Renaissance', *Speculum*, 37 (1962), 509–27.

—— *Florence in Transition*, 2 vols. (Baltimore, Md., 1967–8).

—— *Medieval Italy: Constraints and Creativity* (Bloomington, Ind., 1981).

BENVENUTI PAPI, ANNA, 'Ordini mendicanti e città: Appunti per un'indagine, il caso di Firenze', in D. Maselli (ed.), *Da Dante a Cosimo I* (Pistoia, 1976), 122–45.

BETTARINI, ROSANNA, 'Notizia di un laudario', *Studi di filologia italiana*, 28 (1970), 55–66.

BIAGI, GUIDO, 'I capitoli della Compagnia della Madonna d'Or San Michele', *Bulletino dell'associazione per la difesa di Firenze antica* (1909), 57–85.

BLACK, ANTONY, *Guilds and Civil Society in European Political Thought from the Twelfth Century to the Present* (Ithaca, NY, 1984).

BLACK, CHRISTOPHER, *Italian Confraternities in the Sixteenth Century* (Cambridge, 1989).

BOCCACCIO, GIOVANNI, *The Decameron*, trans. M. Musa and P. Bondanella (New York, 1982).

BORSOOK, EVE, *The Mural Painters of Tuscany* (2nd edn., Oxford, 1980).

BOSSI, ALESSANDRA, *Ricostruzione grafica delle fasi storiche della chiesa del Carmine* (Florence, 1974).

BRUCKER, GENE, *The Civic World of Early Renaissance Florence* (Princeton, 1977).
—— *Renaissance Florence* (New York, 1969).
—— 'Urban Parishes and their Clergy in Quattrocento Florence: A Preliminary Sondage', in A. Morrogh (ed.), *Renaissance Studies in Honor of Craig Hugh Smyth* (Florence, 1985), 17–28.

BURNEY, CHARLES, *A General History of Music*, 4 vols. (London, 1776–89); ed. F. Mercer, 2 vols. (New York, 1957).

CAMBON, ELISE MURRAY, 'The Italian and Latin Lauda of the Fifteenth Century', Ph.D. thesis (Tulane University, 1975).

CASSIDY, BRENDAN, 'The Financing of the Tabernacle of Orsanmichele', *Source: Notes in the History of Art*, 8 (1988), 2–6.

CASTELLANI, ARRIGO (ed.), *Nuovi testi fiorentini del dugento* (Florence, 1952).

CATTIN, GIULIO, 'I "cantasi come" in una stampa di laude della Biblioteca Riccardiana (Ed. r. 196)', *Quadrivium*, 19 (1978), 5–52.
—— 'Le composizioni musicali del Ms Pavia Aldini 361', *L'Ars nova italiana del Trecento*, 2 (Certaldo, 1968), 1–21.
—— ' "Contrafacta" internazionali: musiche europee per laude italiane', in U. Günther and L. Finscher (eds.), *Musik und Text in der Mehrstimmigkeit des 14. und 15. Jahrhunderts* (Kassel, 1984), 411–42.
—— 'Contributi alla storia della lauda spirituale', *Quadrivium*, 2 (1958), 45–78.
—— (ed.), *Italian Laude and Latin Unica in Ms Capetown, Grey 3. b. 12* (Corpus mensurabilis musicae, 76; Neuhausen-Stuttgart, 1977).
—— 'Musiche per le laude di Castellano Castellani', *Rivista italiana di musicologia*, 12 (1977), 183–230.
—— *Music of the Middle Ages I*, trans S. Botterill (Cambridge, 1986).

CHENU, MARIE-DOMINIQUE, *Nature, Man, and Society in the Twelfth Century: Essays on New Theological Perspectives in the Latin West*, ed. and trans. J. Taylor and L. K. Little (Chicago, 1968).

CIANFOGNI, PIER N., *Memorie istoriche dell' Ambrosiana R. Basilica di S. Lorenzo di Firenze* (Florence, 1804).

CORSI, GIUSEPPE, 'Madrigali inediti del trecento', *Belfagor*, 14 (1959), 72–82, 329–40.

D'ACCONE, FRANK, 'Alcune note sulle compagnie fiorentine dei Laudesi durante il quattrocento', *Rivista italiana di musicologia*, 10 (1975), 86–114.
—— 'Alessandro Coppini and Bartolomeo degli Organi: Two Florentine Composers of the Renaissance', *Analecta musicologica*, 4 (1967), 38–76.
—— 'Le compagnie dei Laudesi in Firenze durante l'Ars nova', *L'Ars nova italiana del Trecento*, 3 (Certaldo, 1970), 253–80.

——— 'Repertory and Performance Practice in Santa Maria Novella at the Turn of the 17th Century', in M. D. Grace (ed.), *A Festschrift for Albert Seay* (Colorado Springs, Colo., 1982), 71–136.

——— 'The Singers of San Giovanni in Florence during the 15th Century', *Journal of the American Musicological Society*, 14 (1961), 307–58.

——— 'Una nuova fonte dell'ars nova italiana: Il codice di San Lorenzo, 2211', *Studi musicali*, 13 (1984), 3–27.

DAMILANO, DON PIERO, 'Fonti musicali della lauda polifonica intorno alle metà del secolo XV', *Collectanea historiae musicae*, 3 (1963), 59–75.

D'ANCONA, ALESSANDRO, *Origini del teatro italiano*, 2 vols. (2nd edn.; Turin, 1891).

DAVIDSOHN, ROBERT, *Forschungen zur Geschichte von Florenz*, 4 vols. (Berlin, 1896–1908).

D'AVRAY, DAVID, *The Preaching of the Friars: Sermons Diffused from Paris before 1300* (Oxford, 1985).

DELCORNO, CARLO, *Giordano da Pisa e l'antica predicazione volgare* (Florence, 1975).

DEL POPOLO, CONCETTO, 'Il laudario della Compagnia di Sant'Egidio', *Studi e problemi di critica testuale*, 16 (1978), 5–26.

DIEDERICHS, ELISABETH, *Die Anfänge der mehrstimmige Lauda vom Ende des 14. bis zur Mitte des 15. Jahrhunderts* (Münchner Veröffentlichungen zur Musikgeschichte, 41; Tützing, 1986).

DOREN, ALFRED, *Le arti fiorentine*, 2 vols. (Florence, 1940).

EDLER, FLORENCE, *Glossary of Mediaeval Terms of Business: Italian Series, 1200–1600* (Cambridge, Mass., 1934).

EMERY, RICHARD, 'The Friars of the Sack', *Speculum*, 18 (1943), 323–34.

FABBRI, MARIO, 'Laude spirituali di travestimento nella Firenze della Rinascenza', in M. Rosito (ed.), *Arte e religione nella Firenze de' Medici* (Florence, 1980), 145–58.

FABBRI, NANCY RASH, and RUTENBURG, NINA, 'The Tabernacle of Orsanmichele in Context', *Art Bulletin*, 63 (1981), 385–405.

FISCHER, KURT VON, 'Quelques remarques sur les relations entre les laudesi et les compositeurs florentins du Trecento', *L'Ars nova italiana del Trecento*, 3 (Certaldo, 1970), 247–52.

——— *Studien zur italienischen Musik des Trecento und frühen Quattrocento* (Bern, 1956).

FLEMING, JOHN, *An Introduction to Franciscan Literature of the Middle Ages* (Chicago, 1977).

FRANCI, RAFFAELLA, and RIGATELLI, LAURA T., *Introduzione all'aritmetica mercantile del medioevo e del rinascimento* (Urbino, 1982).

GALLETTI, GUSTAVO CAMILLO, *Laude spirituali de Feo Belcari, di Lorenzo de' Medici, di Francesco d'Albizzo, di Castellano Castellani e di altri, comprese nelle quattro più antiche raccolte con alcune inedite e con nuovi illustrazioni* (Florence, 1864).

GALLO, F. ALBERTO, 'The Musical and Literary Tradition of Fourteenth-Century Poetry Set to Music', in U. Günther and L. Finscher (eds.), *Musik und Text in der Mehrstimmigkeit des 14. und 15. Jahrhunderts* (Kassel, 1984), 55–76.

GASTON, ROBERT, 'Liturgy and Patronage in San Lorenzo, Florence, 1350–1650', in F. W. Kent and P. Simons (eds.), *Patronage, Art, and Society in Renaissance Italy* (Oxford, 1987), 111–34.

GHISI, FEDERICO, 'Strambotti e laude nel travestimento spirituale della poesia musicale del Quattrocento', *Collectanea historiae musicae*, 1 (1953), 45–78.

GROSSI, JOHN HENRY, 'The Fourteenth Century Florentine Laudario Magliabechiano II, I, 122 (B. R. 18): A Transcription and Study', Ph.D. thesis (Catholic University of America, 1979).

HALL, MARCIA B., *Renovation and Counter-Reformation: Duke Cosimo and Vasari in Santa Maria Novella and Santa Croce 1565–1575* (Oxford, 1979).

HENDERSON, JOHN, 'Confraternities and the Church in Late Medieval Florence', *Studies in Church History*, 23 (1986), 69–83.

—— 'Piety and Charity in Late Medieval Florence: Religious Confraternities from the Middle of the Thirteenth to the Late Fifteenth Century', Ph.D. thesis (University of London, 1983).

HOLMES, GEORGE, 'The Emergence of an Urban Ideology at Florence, c.1250–1450', *Transactions of the Royal Historical Society*, 5th ser., 23 (1973), 111–34.

HORNE, HERBERT P., 'Jacopo del Sellaio', *Burlington Magazine*, 13 (1908), 210–13.

HUECK, IRENE, 'La tavola di Duccio e la Compagnia delle Laudi di Santa Maria Novella', in B. Pacini *et al.* (eds.), *La Maestà di Duccio restaurata* (Gli Uffizi: Studi e Ricerche, 6; Florence, 1990), 33–46.

JEPPESEN, KNUD, *Die mehrstimmige italienische Laude um 1500* (Leipzig, 1935; repr. Bologna, 1971).

KENT, DALE V., and KENT, F. WILLIAM, *Neighbours and Neighbourhood in Renaissance Florence: The District of the Red Lion in the Fifteenth Century* (New York, 1982).

KENT, F. WILLIAM, and SIMONS, PATRICIA (eds.), *Patronage, Art, and Society in Renaissance Italy* (Oxford, 1987).

KIECKHEFER, RICHARD, 'Major Currents in Late Medieval Devotion', in J. Raitt (ed.), *Christian Spirituality II: High Middle Ages and Reformation* (World Spirituality, 17; New York, 1987), 75–108.

LA SORSA, SAVINO, *La compagnia d'Or San Michele* (Trani, 1902).

LESNICK, DANIEL, 'Dominican Preaching and the Creation of a Capitalist Ideology in Late-Medieval Florence', *Memorie domenicane*, NS, 8–9 (1977–8), 199–247.

LIUZZI, FERNANDO, *La lauda e i primordi della melodia italiana*, 2 vols. (Rome, 1935).

LOCKWOOD, LEWIS, *Music in Renaissance Ferrara 1400–1505: The Creation of a Musical Center in the Fifteenth Century* (Cambridge, Mass., 1984).

LUISI, FRANCESCO, *Laudario giustinianeo*, 2 vols. (Venice, 1983).

MACKENNEY, RICHARD, *Tradesmen and Traders: The World of the Guilds in Venice and Europe, c.1250–c.1650* (Totowa, NJ, 1987).

MAZZATINTI, GIUSEPPE, *Inventari dei manoscritti delle biblioteche d'Italia* (Florence, 1890–).

MEERSSEMAN, GILLES-GERARD, 'Nota sull'origine delle Compagnie dei Laudesi (Siena 1267)', *Rivista di storia della chiesa in Italia*, 17 (1963), 395–405.

—— *Ordo fraternitatis: Confraternite e pietà dei laici nel mondo medioevo*, 3 vols.

(Italia Sacra: Studi e Documenti di Storia Ecclesiastica, 24–6; Rome, 1977).

MEISS, MILLARD, *Painting in Florence and Siena after the Black Death* (Princeton, NJ, 1951).

MICALI, OSANNA FANTOZZI, and ROSELLI, PIERO, *Le soppressioni dei conventi a Firenze* (Florence, 1980).

MOLETA, VINCENT, *The Early Poetry of Guittone D'Arezzo* (London, 1976).

—— 'The Illuminated *Laudari* Mgl[1] and Mgl[2]', *Scriptorium*, 32 (1978), 29–50.

MONTI, GENNARO MARIA, *La confraternite medievali dell'alta e media Italia*, 2 vols. (Venice, 1927).

MORENI, DOMENICO, *Continuazione delle memorie istoriche dell Ambrosiana Imperiale Basilica di S. Lorenzo di Firenze*, 2 vols. (Florence, 1816).

MORINI, AUGUSTINO, and SOULIER, PEREGRINO (eds.), *Monumenta Ordinis Servorum Sanctae Mariae* (Brussels, 1897–).

MORPURGO, S., *I manoscritti della R. Biblioteca Riccardiana di Firenze* (Rome, 1900).

MURRAY, ALEXANDER, *Reason and Society in the Middle Ages* (Oxford, 1978).

OFFNER, RICHARD, *A Critical and Historical Corpus of Florentine Painting* (New York, 1930–).

ORIGO, IRIS, *The Merchant of Prato, Francesco di Marco Datini, 1335–1410* (New York, 1957).

ORIOLI, LUCIANO, *Le confraternite medievali e il problema della povertà* (Rome, 1984).

ORLANDI, STEFANO, 'Il VII centenario della predicazione di S. Pietro Martire a Firenze (1245–1945)', *Memorie domenicane*, NS, 21 (1946), 26–41, 59–87; 22 (1947), 31–48, 109–36, 170–211; also published as a book under the same title (Florence, 1946).

—— 'La Madonna di Duccio di Boninsegna e il suo culto in S. Maria Novella', *Memorie domenicane*, 73 (1956), 205–17.

—— *Necrologio di Santa Maria Novella*, 2 vols. (Florence, 1955).

PAATZ, WALTER and ELISABETH, *Die Kirchen von Florenz*, 6 vols. (Frankfurt am Main, 1952–5).

PAPI, MASSIMO D., 'Confraternite ed ordini mendicanti a Firenze, aspetti di una ricerca quantitativa', *Mélanges de l'école française de Rome*, NS, 89 (1977), 723–32.

PICCINI, GIULIO (ed.), 'Libro degli ordinamenti de la Compagnia di Santa Maria del Carmino', in *Scelta di Curiosità letterarie inedite rare dal sec. XIII al XVIII* (Bologna, 1867; repr. Bologna, 1968), 1–47.

PIRROTTA, NINO, *Music and Culture in Italy from the Middle Ages to the Baroque* (Cambridge, Mass., 1984) (contains essays 'Ars Nova and Stil Novo', 'Music for a Text Attributed to Frederick II', 'New Glimpses of an Unwritten Tradition', and 'The Oral and Written Traditions of Music').

POGGI, GIROLAMO, *Il Duomo di Firenze* (Berlin, 1909).

POLIZZOTTO, LORENZO, 'Confraternities, Conventicles and Political Dissent: The Case of the Savonarolan "Capi Rossi"', *Memorie domenicane*, NS, 16 (1985), 235–84.

Polyphonic Music of the Fourteenth Century, Kurt von Fischer, gen. ed. (Monaco, 1956–).

POPE, ISABEL, and KANAZAWA, MASAKATA (eds.), *The Musical Manuscript Monte-cassino 871: A Neapolitan Repertory of Sacred and Secular Music of the Late Fifteenth Century* (Oxford, 1978).

PROCACCI, UGO, 'L'incendio della chiesa del Carmine del 1771', *Rivista d'arte*, 14 (1932), 141–232.

Répertoire international des sources musicales, ser. B. IV/1, *Manuscripts of Polyphonic Music, 11th–early 14th Century*, ed. G. Reaney (Munich, 1969).

RICHA, GIUSEPPE, *Notizie istoriche delle chiese fiorentine, divise ne' suoi quartieri*, 10 vols. (Florence, 1754–62).

RONDEAU, JENNIFER, 'Lay Piety and Spirituality in the Late Middle Ages: The Confraternities of North-Central Italy, *ca.* 1250 to 1348', Ph.D. thesis (Cornell University, 1988).

ROSENWEIN, BARBARA H., and LITTLE, LESTER K., 'Social Meaning in the Monastic and Mendicant Spiritualities', *Past and Present*, 63 (1974), 4–32.

ROUSE, RICHARD and MARY A., *Preachers, Florilegia, and Sermons: Studies on the 'Manipulus florum' of Thomas of Ireland* (Toronto, 1979).

RUBSAMEN, WALTER, 'The Justiniane or Viniziane of the 15th Century', *Acta musicologica*, 29 (1957), 172–84.

SCHIAFFINI, ALFREDO (ed.), *Testi fiorentini del dugento e dei primi del Trecento* (Florence, 1954).

SCRIBNER, R. W., 'Interpreting Religion in Early Modern Europe', *European Studies Review*, 13 (1983), 89–105.

SEAY, ALBERT, 'The 15th-Century Cappella at Santa Maria del Fiore in Florence', *Journal of the American Musicological Society*, 11 (1958), 45–55.

SIMONS, PATRICIA, 'Patronage in the Tornaquinci Chapel, Santa Maria Novella, Florence', in F. W. Kent and P. Simons (eds.), *Patronage, Art, and Society in Renaissance Italy* (Oxford, 1987), 221–50.

SOUTHERN, RICHARD W., *Western Society and the Church in the Middle Ages* (New York, 1970).

STAAFF, ERIC (ed.), 'Le Laudario de Pise du ms. 8521 de la Bibliothèque de l'Arsenal de Paris: Etude linguistique', *Skrifter utgivna av Kungl. Humanistiska Vetenskaps-Samfundet i Uppsala*, 27 (1931–2), 1–295.

STARR, PAMELA, 'The "Ferrara Connection": A Case Study of Musical Recruit-ment in the Renaissance', *Studi Musicali*, 18 (1989), 3–17.

STEPHENS, JOHN N., *The Fall of the Florentine Republic, 1512–1530* (Oxford, 1983).

—— 'Heresy in Medieval and Renaissance Florence', *Past and Present*, 54 (1972), 25–60.

STROCCHIA, SHARON, 'Burials in Renaissance Florence: 1350–1500', Ph.D. thesis (University of California, Berkeley, 1981).

STUBBLEBINE, JAMES H., *Duccio di Buoninsegna and His School*, 2 vols. (Princeton, 1979).

TENNERONI, ANNIBALE, *Inizii di antichi poesie italiane religiose e morali con prospetto dei codici che le contengono e introduzione alle laudi spirituali* (Florence, 1909).

TERRUGGIA, ANGELA MARIA, 'Aggiunta al laudario frammentato dell'Archivio di Stato di Lucca', *Studi e problemi di critica testuale*, 12 (1976), 5–26.

TOSCANI, BERNARD, 'Contributi alla storia musicale delle laude dei Bianchi', *Studi musicali*, 9 (1980), 161–70.

—— *Le laude dei Bianchi* (Florence, 1979).

TREXLER, RICHARD, 'Florentine Religious Experience: The Sacred Image', *Studies in the Renaissance*, 19 (1972), 7–41.

—— *Public Life in Renaissance Florence* (New York, 1980).

—— 'Ritual in Florence: Adolescence and Salvation in the Renaissance', in C. Trinkaus and H. Oberman (eds.), *The Pursuit of Holiness in Late Medieval and Renaissance Religion* (Leiden, 1974), 200–64.

—— *The Spiritual Power: Republican Florence Under Interdict*, ed. H. Oberman (Studies in Medieval and Reformation Thought, 9; Leiden, 1974).

TRINKAUS, CHARLES, and OBERMAN, HEIKO (eds.), *The Pursuit of Holiness in Late Medieval and Renaissance Religion* (Leiden, 1974).

VARANINI, GIORGIO, *Laude dugentesche* (Padua, 1972).

—— BANFI, LUIGI, and BURGIO, ANNA CERUTI (eds.), *Laude cortonesi dal secolo XIII al XV*, 4 vols. (Florence, 1981–5).

VILLANI, GIOVANNI *Cronica di Giovanni Villani a miglior lezione ridotta*, ed. F. Dragomanni, 4 vols. (Florence, 1844–5).

VILLANI, MATTEO, *Cronica di Matteo Villani*, ed. F. Dragomanni, 2 vols. (Florence, 1846).

WADDELL, CHRYSOGONUS, 'The Reform of the Liturgy from a Renaissance Perspective', in R. Benson and G. Constable (eds.), *Renaissance and Renewal in the Twelfth Century* (Cambridge, Mass., 1982), 88–109.

WARREN, CHARLES, 'Punctus Organi and Cantus Coronatus in the Music of Dufay', in A. Atlas (ed.), *Papers Read at the Dufay Quincentenary Conference* (Brooklyn, NY, 1976), 128–43.

WEINSTEIN, DONALD, *Savonarola and Florence: Prophecy and Patriotism in the Renaissance* (Princeton, NJ, 1970).

WEISSMAN, RONALD, *Ritual Brotherhood in Renaissance Florence* (New York, 1982).

WOOD BROWN, J. *The Dominican Church of Santa Maria Novella at Florence* (Edinburgh, 1902).

ZERVAS, DIANE FINIELLO, *The Parte Guelfa, Brunelleschi, and Donatello* (Locust Valley, NY, 1987).

ZIINO, AGOSTINO, 'Adattamenti musicali e tradizione manoscritta nel repertorio laudistico del duecento', in *Scritti in onore di Luigi Ronga* (Milan, 1973), 653–69.

—— *Aspetti della tradizione orale nella musica medioevale*, (Lanciano, 1973); and in D. Carpitella (ed.), *L'Etnomusicologia in Italia* (Palermo, 1975), 169–94.

—— 'Laudi e miniature fiorentine del primo trecento', *Studi musicali*, 7 (1978), 39–83.

ZIPPEL, GIUSEPPE, *I suonatori della Signoria di Firenze* (Trent, 1892).

INDEX

(c = composer, cm = choirmaster, i = instrumentalist, pa = painter, po = poet, s = singer, sm = singing master)